The Developmental Psychology of Planning: Why, How, and When Do We Plan?

The Developmental Psychology of Planning: Why, How, and When Do We Plan?

Edited by

Sarah L. Friedman
National Institute of Child Health and Human Development

Ellin Kofsky Scholnick
University of Maryland, College Park

LAWRENCE ERLBAUM ASSOCIATES, PUBLISHERS

1997   Mahwah, New Jersey   London

Lawrence Erlbaum Associates, Inc., Publishers
10 Industrial Avenue
Mahwah, New Jersey 07430

Library of Congress Cataloging-in-Publication-Data

The developmental psychology of planning : why, how, and when do we plan?
/ edited by Sarah L. Friedman, Ellin Kofsky Scholnick.
        p. cm.
    Includes bibliographic references and index.
    ISBN 0-8058-1515-5 (alk. paper)
    1. Cognition in children. 2. Planning in children. I. Friedman, Sarah L. II.
Scholnick, Ellin Kofsky.
    BF723.C5D498 1997
    153—dc21   97-7420
                                                                      CIP

Books published by Lawrence Erlbaum Associates are printed on acid-free
paper, and their bindings are chosen for strength and durability.

Printed in the United States of America
10 9 8 7 6 5 4 3 2 1

This volume is dedicated to our parents, Esther and Faivel Landau and Irving and Celia Kofsky. We were their apprentices in planning. Our choice of the aspirations and goals that have shaped the plans for our lives reflect their influence. Our plans keep their memory alive.

Contents

III. COGNITION AND PLANNING

IV. MOTIVATIONAL AND PERSONALITY INFLUENCES ON PLANNING

V. SOCIAL INFLUENCES ON PLANNING

Preface

Planning is defined as formulating in advance an organized method for action. As such, planning skill is central to all human behavior. But much of the research on planning has focused on the cognitive processes that enable mature individuals to plan. This book is a continued exploration of the developmental course of planning and an attempt to situate cognitive aspects of planning in the context of other psychological processes and in the context of the social and cultural environment.

People do not plan all the time, and planning does not occur in every situation. There are developmental differences in planning skill and in the motivation to plan. Even among adults, attitudes, beliefs, and goals lead to variations in engagement in the planning process. Moreover, different social groups place different value on planning different events. Planning also has a different meaning at different junctures in the life course. Therefore, this book fills a gap in the literature by exploring how, when, and why we plan. It brings together the contributions of developmental, organizational, and social psychologists to address these issues, tapping planning with tasks that vary from formal problem solving to handling the demands of daily life.

Historically, planning was originally construed as a unitary psychological process, and various writers interpreted it to mean representation, or strategy choice, or strategy execution, and so on. More recently, however, researchers have begun to realize that planning is the orchestration of diverse and interdependent cognitive and motivational processes that are influenced by context and that are brought together in the service of reaching a goal. These processes and their orchestration follow a complex developmental trajectory. This volume is designed to elaborate on and take off from themes found in *Blueprints for Thinking*, a volume we edited with Rodney Cocking in 1987. In the earlier volume the focus was on defining the components of planning and placing planning in a developmental framework. In this volume, greater attention is paid to the reasons for planning and the conditions under which planning occurs.

The origins of our interest in the topic of planning and its development stem from our association with Dr. Susan Chipman when we all worked together at the National Institute of Education in the early 1980s. She was puzzled by the observation that college students often had difficulty organizing their time and their studies even though cognitively they were mature enough to solve complex academic tasks. She convinced us that the solution to the puzzle would be found by bringing together knowledge and ideas from cognitive science and developmental psychology. The support of The National Institute of Mental Health (NIMH) and later the National Institute of Child Health and Human Development (NICHD) have sustained our interest in the area of planning. Moreover, NICHD, under the direction of Dr. Duane Alexander, has actively supported the interest of other investigators in this endeavor.

The more we think about the area of planning, the more we have come to recognize that the freedom to plan, the content of plans, and the opportunity for the execution of plans depend on a supportive social and professional environment. We thank our families and colleagues for their role in bringing this volume to fruition.

—*Sarah L. Friedman*
—*Ellin Kofsky Scholnick*

I

Setting the Stage: An Integrative Framework for Understanding Research on Planning

1

An Evolving "Blueprint" for Planning: Psychological Requirements, Task Characteristics, and Social–Cultural Influences

Sarah L. Friedman
National Institute of Child Health and Human Development
Ellin Kofsky Scholnick[1]
University of Maryland, College Park

When people list the characteristics that make us distinctively human, one characteristic that comes to mind is the ability to plan and thereby to overcome the impulse to respond to the immediate situation. Plans are mental representations of what we want to do and what we are emotionally committed to do (National Advisory Metal Health Council, 1995). Humans are driven by their capacity to create symbolic representations of the past, the present, and the future and to employ these representations to shape things to come. A life without plans has no direction. A problem that is not dealt with planfully may persist forever. Planning involves a very complex set of mental and behavioral operations that bring together cognitive, emotional, and motivational resources in the service of reaching desired goals. This distinctively human ability to plan is not evident at birth or even in early infancy, although the rudiments may be there. Its development unfolds over the life course in ways that are shaped by the environment, which determines why, how, and when we plan.

This question, "Why, how, and when do we plan?" has often been neglected, and the answers turn out to be very complex. This chapter is an historical account of the formulation and elaboration of this question as well as a discussion of the ways the answers influence how we think about

---

[1]The conceptualization and writing of the chapter represents the equal partnership of both authors. The figures were prepared by Daphne R. Friedman, following the authors' specifications.

the development of planning. We describe a progression of five increasingly elaborate and integrated models of planning. The latest of these models serves as a framework for situating the chapters in this volume, and thereby also serves as a road map for this book as a whole.

PLANNING IN HISTORICAL PERSPECTIVE

Paradoxical Data About Planning

Our historical account of conceptualizations of planning is embedded in an attempt to resolve an apparent conflict in the developmental literature about planning. Investigators of adolescents' behavior claim that many of the societal problems associated with this age group stem from a cognitive limitation in the area of planning. For example, the high rate of teenage pregnancy, the high frequency of drunk driving, and the high rate of risk-taking behavior and related injuries are thought to be the products of a failure to plan (Adler, Moore, & Tschann, chapter 13, this volume). At the same time, investigators of early child development report that preschool-age children are capable of planning grocery shopping errands, birthday parties, and even simple versions of the classic laboratory planning task, the Tower of Hanoi (Gauvain & Rogoff, 1989; Hudson & Fivush, 1991; Klahr & Robinson, 1981). Moreover, the same teenagers who do not plan to prevent pregnancy or driving accidents may be very planful when it comes to obtaining illegal liquor or organizing social gatherings. There are two paradoxes. There is an apparent age reversal, because adolescents sometimes seem less planful than preschoolers. Likewise, it is paradoxical that teenagers appear to plan in some situations, but not in others (Chalmers & Lawrence, 1993; Sansone & Berg, 1993).

Model 1: Plans Reflect Individual Cognitive Differences.   The paradox arises because age is used as a marker signaling the achievement of context-free cognitive skills. The underlying assumptions are diagramed in Fig. 1.1. This leads to characterizing planning in terms of a limited set of determinants. A more comprehensive model of the variables that determine engagement and success in planning is needed to resolve the paradox. Let us trace the historical changes in conceptualizations of planning that have led from the simple model in Fig. 1.1 to the present, more complex characterization of the factors influencing planning.

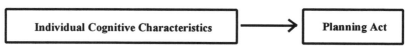

FIG. 1. 1.   Model 1: Plans reflect individual cognitive differences.

In the simplest model of planning, there are two modules: the planner and the act of planning. An example is the approach that some have derived from Piagetian theory (De Lisi, 1987; Inhelder & Piaget, 1958). From this perspective, children are not successful at planning before they arrive at a cognitive stage known as formal operations, in which self-reflection and anticipation guide performance. This view assumes that planning is a generalized cognitive ability and that the ability cannot be demonstrated before the individual reaches a particular cognitive stage. In early adolescence many youngsters have yet to reach formal operations, a fact that researchers used to explain teenagers' deficits in planning. But there is evidence contradicting both assumptions. Even preschoolers generate plans on some tasks although they are clearly not at formal operations. There are other tasks where adults have difficulty in planning, even though presumably they are at formal operations (Chalmers & Lawrence, 1993; Zhang & Norman, 1994). Therefore, adult performance contradicts the view that planning is a general skill that can be applied to any domain or any task within a domain.

Model 2: Cognition and Tasks Affect Planning.　Experimental cognitive psychologists, therefore, modified the two-component scheme depicted in Fig. 1. 1 (Anzai & Simon, 1979; Klahr, 1994; Kotovsky, Hayes, & Simon, 1985; Simon, 1975; Zhang & Norman, 1994). They, like Piaget, equated planning with problem solving. But they broke planning down into a set of activities, and posited a more differentiated and complex model of the planner's cognition. They also added a box to the model to account for task variations (see Fig. 1. 2).

In this revised planning model, as in the previous one, there is a problem that the individual wants to solve, and the person must figure out a way to solve it. A series of activities must be carried out during problem solving. There are various information-processing models of planning (e.g., Miller, Galanter, & Pribram, 1960; Pea & Hawkins, 1987), but they have several

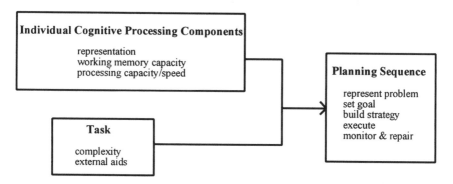

FIG. 1. 2. Model 2: Cognition and tasks affect planning.

components in common. In order to plan, the individual must first construct a *representation* of the problem space and *define a goal*. Once the goal is defined, the problem solver must *anticipate a strategy* that could provide a solution and the problems that might arise in implementing it. They must also *monitor* the strategy as they *execute* it. When problems arise, they must repair the strategy. This refined definition of planning behavior implicates several cognitive processes and skills.[2] The individual must have the capacity to perceive, integrate, and *represent* critical aspects of the environment. Both constructing the representation and strategy draw on *working memory* to assemble and debug a solution. *Processing capacity* is, therefore, a critical determinant of performance. The problems the planner attempted to solve were largely unfamiliar, so even though construction of the representation and the strategy required retrieving material from past problems and solution attempts, the contributions of long-term memory and the knowledge base were largely ignored.

Cognitive psychologists working from this perspective realized that problems differ in the demands that are placed on each of the component processing skills required for planning, and in the demands for orchestrating the component processes into an efficient planning act. They systematically varied the nature of the task to reveal the nature of the component processes and the critical variables that affected those components (Kotovsky, Hayes, & Simon, 1985; Zhang & Norman, 1994). They showed, for example, that the provision of external aids facilitated planning and inferred that planning must rely, therefore, on working memory capacity. Thus, the complexity of the problem, as indexed by the number of rings in the Tower of Hanoi, was another variable receiving attention.

Model 3: Expanding the Components of Cognitive and Task Variables. Meanwhile, investigators in developmental psychology also began to explore the influence of task variations because they contested the claim that formal operations was a prerequisite for planning. One of the ways they did this was to simplify laboratory tasks. The classic planning task was the Tower of Hanoi, which required people to transfer rings from one location to another using certain rules of transfer. Klahr (Klahr & Robinson, 1981) put the task within the capabilities of preschoolers by externalizing the representation of the goal state, reducing the number of elements to be moved, and using a story frame to make the task more intriguing and sensible. In effect, he defined the task properties that influence planning. Others (e.g., Welsh, 1991) continued to simplify the task by varying instructions, material, etc. (Scholnick, Friedman, & Wallner-Allen, chapter 6, this volume).

---

[2]Historically, overlapping constructs within cognitive psychology have been labeled differently. For example, there is some redundancy between "processing capacity" and "size of working memory" or between "executive function" and "self-regulation." Yet, investigators in different periods favored one term over another. In this chapter we used the various labels to reflect the historical perspective.

In addition, cognitive and developmental psychologists expanded the repertoire of planning assignments to include familiar tasks such as errand planning (Hayes-Roth & Hayes-Roth, 1979; Pea & Hawkins, 1987). As cognitive psychologists and cognitive scientists began to account for problem solving and planning in familiar domains, they began to use a broader model of cognition that took into account both processing skills and the individual's knowledge base (Chi, Glaser, & Rees, 1982; Hammond, 1990; Scholnick, 1995). They introduced the notion of expertise that resulted from extensive experience in a domain. In this view, planning was not just a product of processing skills, but reflected the individual's knowledge about the domains in which planning occurred and their prior knowledge of how to plan (Nurmi, 1991). Experts often applied old plans to solve new problems. There are domains where young children are experts. No wonder that they can plan grocery shopping, birthday parties, and trips to the beach. The availability of well-known scripts for these occasions facilitates planning.

As developmental psychologists used these tasks to explore the planning abilities of younger age groups and individuals with mental retardation and learning disabilities, they came to realize that sequencing skill is an important contributor to representation and strategy construction (Spitz, Webster, & Borys, 1982). They also realized how much planning relies on focused attention. In addition, planning tasks began to be conceptualized as tests of executive functions that necessitate foresight, organizational skill, flexibility, and inhibition (Welsh & Pennington, 1988; Welsh, Pennington, & Groisser, 1991).

This led to a view of planning reflected in Fig. 1. 3. It elaborates on both the cognitive module and the task module of the model. Let us see if the model in Fig. 1.3 could resolve the paradoxes with which we began the

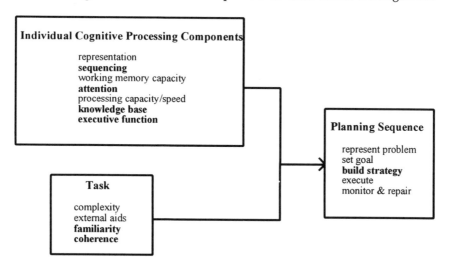

FIG. 1. 3. Model 3: Expanding the components of cognitive and task variables.

chapter. Why do adolescents sometimes fail to plan, yet some young children sometimes look very planful? Understanding the importance of one's knowledge base resolves the paradox. Because some domains are very familiar to young children, they are capable of planning therein, but they are incapable of planning in novel contexts. Likewise, teenagers are able to plan in domains that are familiar to them but not in domains that are unfamiliar. During adolescence, youngsters are on the verge of learning about behaviors such as drinking, driving, and contraceptive use, so they lack the knowledge needed for planning in these domains.

Model 4: Adding Emotions, Social Influences and Environmental Context to the Predictors of Planning. This latter explanation is incomplete, as any educator knows. Often, adolescents dutifully attend courses on sex education, but it does not change their behavior. The model in Fig. 1. 3 leaves out the motivational factors mentioned by several contributors to our 1987 book, *Blueprints for Thinking* (Goodnow, 1987; Kreitler & Kreitler, 1987b). Their writings suggested that planning is not automatic and that the sequence of activities that comprise planning should include a new component, the decision to plan. Additionally, the psychological processes involved in planning should include motivational as well as cognitive components. The box describing tasks needed to be expanded to include interpersonal tasks that incorporate individuals as either pieces of the plan or as planning partners (Goodnow, 1987). In addition, a new box had to be added to account for the influence of culture and the family on

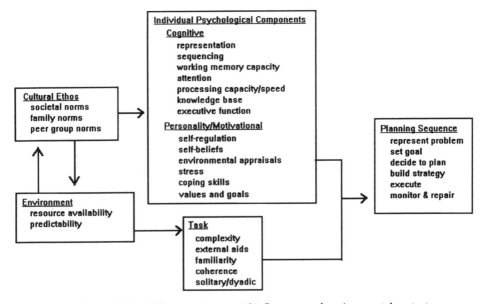

FIG. 1.4. Model 4: Adding emotions, social influences, and environmental context.

the planner(s). Each of these subsequent additions to the model is presented next.

First, a new component was added to the acts that go into planning to reflect the importance of motivational and emotional factors (Kreitler & Kreitler, 1987a; Nurmi, 1991). In a purely cognitive model of planning, people first agree to participate in the planning task, and researchers assume that they are motivated to perform well. The research participants are then given a problem that they are asked to solve. No data are collected about the extent to which these participants are motivated to do their best or to plan in order to solve the problem. Consequently, findings from this type of research cannot illuminate our understanding of planning in the everyday environment. In real life, people have to decide whether they want to plan (Friedman, Scholnick, & Cocking, 1987; Scholnick & Friedman, 1987). Thus, any description of planning behavior has to include the decision to plan.

What influences the decision to plan and the motivation to follow through on planning? This requires elaboration of the box describing individual differences in the psychological variables influencing planning. A basic prerequisite is the impulse control that enables self-regulation (Kopp, Krakow, & Vaughn, 1983). Clearly, the individual also has to believe that planning is important and that the goal toward which planning is directed is important (Nurmi, 1993; Sansone & Berg, 1993). Judgments about what is important are closely linked to the individual's value system (Kreitler & Kreitler, 1987a). The individual must also believe in his or her own capacity as a planner and as an implementer of the particular strategy generated (Nurmi, 1991; Skinner, 1991; Skinner & Connell, 1986).

The preceding analysis explains, at least in part, the adolescent's failure to plan. Assume some teenagers have the requisite information about the long-term danger of smoking and understand the importance of quitting. Before making a decision to quit smoking themselves, they have to weigh the sensual and social pleasures of smoking against this knowledge and become motivated to drop a habit that is hard to kick. Many adolescents do not really want to give up the pleasures associated with smoking for the sake of long-term health benefits. Moreover, their peer group accepts smoking as part of normal behavior. Adolescents value the adult status that smoking confers. They believe that adult demands to stop smoking are needless intrusions on their own authority, and they rebel.

Even if adolescents know that smoking is dangerous, they may not know that they need to plan how to rid themselves of the habit. They may also not trust their ability to plan an effective strategy. Even if they had a strategy, they may not trust their ability to implement it, because they do not think that the success of the strategy is entirely under their control.

Emotional factors play a role in planning and need to be inserted into the box describing individual psychological characteristics. Planning requires some moderate level of emotional arousal (Bandura, 1986). Given an individual with the cognitive capabilities and motivational commitment to planning, a high degree of stress will lead to either the abandonment of planning or to the production of less elaborate or faulty plans.

We now discuss the way Model 4 elaborated on the task variables to be considered in a discussion of planning. In the previous model, consideration was given to individuals' knowledge about particular planning tasks, but tasks vary along other dimensions. Many tasks are done with other people or require other people to implement (Dreher & Oerter, 1987; Goodnow, 1987). Many plans require persuading one or more individuals to provide needed resources or to carry out components of the task. When some developmental and industrial psychologists studied planning, they focused on collaborative planning. Locke, Durham, Poon, and Weldon's chapter discusses what is known and yet to be known about collaborative planning in adults. Developmental psychologists focused primarily on planning done by mother and child or the child in peer groups (Rogoff, 1990). This kind of planning requires a different set of skills than solitary planning. Social skills matter because individuals must negotiate their respective roles. They may bring different knowledge and skills, and the diversity of contributions may lead to a superior product. Alternatively, when there are disparate and clashing perspectives, the enterprise may be doomed. One of the reasons that the Tower of Hanoi may be a poor predictor of contraceptive planning is that the latter is a collaborative act requiring the cooperation of two individuals (see Adler, Moore, & Tschann, chapter 13, this volume). Often, children's plans fail because in their own mind, a part of the plan was to be carried out by someone else (e.g., parent), yet they never communicated their expectation to that other person.

So far we have discussed inherent characteristics of the task itself and ignored the external realities in which the task is embedded. These realities are often neglected in laboratory studies where the task demands are insulated from the context of daily life. The same task (e.g., grocery shopping) will differ in complexity depending on certain variables we include in another box. These are the environmental resources (Scholnick & Friedman, 1993). Some resource conditions are the product of historical events or conditions. Grocery shopping in affluent environments is predictable. Items are known to be available on a regular basis and their location is well known. There are also many choices available. Thus in these conditions, grocery shopping does not require great ingenuity. In time of war, supplies are not as plentiful, and their availability is governed by forces outside the supplier's and shopper's control. Supplies available in one community may not be available in a neighboring one, and the shopper may need to rely on novel means to get the necessities. The cost of the items may change. Societies differ in the resources that they provide their citizens, and within a society, some people have more resources than others. It is one thing to plan when resources are readily available, but limited resources place greater challenges on the planner.

So far we have discussed environments in terms of the resources they provide the planner, but we have not taken into account the beliefs, values, and practices that permeate specific cultures and influence planning (Nurmi, 1991). To do that, we added another box to our model of planning. This box includes the ethos of planning. This ethos can be conceptualized on at least two levels: the proximal and the distal (Bronfenbrenner, 1979). The proximal influences are those coming from the family and peer group. The distal influences reflect the values held by the culture at large as expressed through institutions such as schools and the workplace.

Families provide the knowledge base that is essential for planning in everyday contexts. Family routines that are played out day-in and day-out form the content of anticipated plans (Benson, 1994; Hudson & Fivush, 1991; Kreitler & Kreitler, 1987b). Moreover, the organization of specific routines during the day provides an overarching schedule that is in itself a plan for everyday living. The expertise that is required to carry out these plans is observed by the growing child and internalized. This knowledge base provides the tools that children use when they are faced with situations that require planning. When cognitive psychologists discuss the expertise that planners demonstrate, that expertise originates in family practices to which children are exposed (McGillicuddy-De Lisi, De Lisi, Flaugher, & Sigel, 1987; Nurmi, 1991). Families, like individuals, are not all alike in the extent to which their lives are governed by routines. Families differ in which aspects of their lives are routinized and in the way that they are routinized. Consequently, from the very beginning, children are exposed to different planning experiences. In addition, they are exposed to different levels of reflection about planning. Some families habitually talk about what they are going to do next, thereby socializing their children to reflect about and anticipate the consequences of their actions (McGillicuddy-De Lisi et al., 1987).

These individual differences among families are partly due to the value they place on family routines, and these values are transmitted to children. Parents not only communicate where and when to plan but they also communicate whether and when planning is important. Thus, the set of beliefs that drives the decision to plan is also socialized (Goodnow, chapter 14, this volume). As the social environment of children expands, peers, teachers, and other adults provide examples of routines and planning that the child internalizes.

The family and the child are part of a culture and its institutions, such as schools and the workplace. The culture provides a set of practices that adds to the child's planning vocabulary (Nurmi, 1993). For example, the school day of young children is carefully scripted, enabling the child to anticipate events and plan how to meet assignments. There are also culturally determined age-graded expectations about the roles individuals play and the developmental tasks the individual accomplishes. These may enter into the individual's plans (Nurmi, 1991).

The culture also provides a wider range of practices and ideas about planning. These practices and beliefs may provide another source of learning when families are dysfunctional with respect to planning. The mass media and the social institutions the child encounters send messages about the reasons for planning, planning strategies, appropriate occasions for planning, and even the criteria for judging the worth of plans. For example, in teen culture, seeking thrills has a higher value than planning prevention of automobile accidents and pregnancy. In a recent study, the Insurance Institute for Highway Safety labeled driver error as the cause of 82% of car accidents when teenagers were driving. Only 5% of the drivers had high blood–alcohol levels. The researchers suggested that the risky behaviors manifested by teenage drivers arose because teens had a sense of invulnerability and an attraction to thrill-seeking (Borgman, 1995).

In summary, we have traced historical changes in conceptualizations of planning. Our description began as a simple model of a unitary process that changes with the age of the child. At present, the research literature suggests that planning consists of multiple component skills, evoked by different sets of psychological and environmental circumstances. Therefore, the age at which children demonstrate planning depends on both their skills and the situations in which they are required to plan.

Model 5: Moderators of Planning Competence. The model proposed thus far is a list of variables placed in different boxes, but we prefer a fuller description of the relations among variables in a box, and among the boxes themselves. Figure 1.5 represents a preliminary attempt at this refinement. Some of the psychological components are definitional to planning and, for that matter, any cognitive act. There is no way one can engage in planning if one lacks an adequate representation, working memory, processing capacity, attention, and self-regulation. Moreover, most planning requires sequencing and executive function. Measurement of these capacities is therefore essential to predict planning performance. Thus, someone with impaired memory or poor self-regulation will have more difficulty in planning, no matter what the task or the person's motivation to perform. These are basic competencies, but they might not be utilized (Overton & Newman, 1982). The other variables in the psychological box affect the utilization of competencies. People are less likely to plan in a very novel domain where their knowledge base is insufficient. They may be capable of planning but unwilling to gather the information that would produce an adequate representation or strategy. People with the requisite cognitive competence may not plan because they do not believe they are competent, or they believe the environment is not conducive to planning. Likewise, the values that people have regarding planning in a specific context influence whether or not they will harness their cognitive skills in the service of planning.

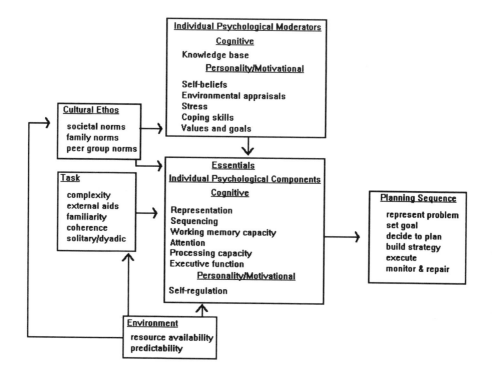

FIG. 1. 5.   Model 5: Moderators of planning competence.

This discussion highlights an important distinction between variables that are essential and those that inhibit or facilitate planning. We think of the latter variables as moderators of planning competence (see Baron & Kenny, 1986; Overton & Newman, 1982). Although some psychological individual difference variables are moderators, usually all external variables function as moderators, too. For example, in our Model 4 of planning, task variables and cultural variables play the role of moderators. In the task box, the complexity of the task influences the demands on representation and working memory. The availability of external aids may decrease the requirements of representation and memory, too. When a task is familiar, the individual can draw on the knowledge base and shortcut other processing demands. When the task is dyadic, processing demands are shared. Societal norms about when and where planning is appropriate moderate an individual's engagement in planning. This is particularly true in matters of the heart and their consequences for sexual activity. Families vary in the extent they save for college education or for retirement, and the extent to which adolescents plan for the future depends on their peer group as well as on their family. Therefore, all the cultural ethos variables affect the decision to plan in specific contexts. But, cultures are more than moderators of planning; they actually influence the formation and exercise of the basic cognitive and self-regulatory skills that are necessary for planning. They provide the knowledge base and routines that are used in much of planning.

Some other refinements are necessary in the model. The components are often interdependent. As an example, it is well-known that experts who have an extensive knowledge base have better short-term memory of material in the domain of their expertise than novices. Presumably experts can chunk material together and thus cram more material into their processing space. One of the key linkages that characterizes more contemporary views of planning is the one between motivation and cognition. There are also linkages between specific components across boxes. For example, when external aids are given, processing capacity may be less important than when no aids are present. In group tasks, individual processing capacity may be less predictive because individuals may share the load.

A box model that lists variables makes it appear that all the variables are of equal weight, even though they may vary in importance. At present there is insufficient empirical work using a comprehensive framework to predict planning performance, but future empirical work may lead to a more detailed model of planning that provides the links between components and their weights.

THE PLAN OF THE BOOK

A succession of models was used to map historical changes in the conceptualizations of planning. The additions to our understanding of planning that found their way into Model 4 are a composite of ideas presented in two volumes: the preceding *Blueprints for Thinking*, and the current volume, *Why, How, and When Do We Plan?* Although our preceding volume discussed motivational issues, the use of the term *blueprint* draws attention to the cognitive structure of planning, whereas the title of the new volume emphasizes the processes underlying planning (*How*), and the motivational (*Why*) and situational (*When*) factors influencing planning.

In this final section of the chapter, we present the structure of the book and situate each contribution in the model we have proposed. The attachment of central ideas by contributors to box locations in our model should serve several purposes. It should demonstrate how this new volume advances our conceptions of planning by adding and elaborating what we know about the field. Also, planning is a complicated and rich process. There are literally over 11,000 abstracts citing planning in PsycLIT. Unless particular chapters are placed within an overarching framework, it would be easy to lose sight of the relevance of each chapter to the central topic, and the place of each chapter in a framework for analyzing planning. The building of connections between the chapters and the model demonstrates a central idea about the process of planning. It is impossible to focus on one aspect of planning without implicitly or explicitly implicating some other aspects.

The Origins of Planning

Each of the models that we presented includes psychological components of planning that are utilized by mature planners. In this chapter we discussed developmental implications, but we did not present a developmental model nor did we address the origins of planning. The issue of origins is the focus of the first section of the volume where several chapters address the precursors of diverse aspects of planning. The second section deals with task factors and cognitive considerations that influence what planning requires and when planning is used. The third section focuses primarily on motivational and situational factors that influence the decision to plan and engagement in planning. In the fourth section, the context broadens to include planning in groups and the ethos of planning.

Several chapters discuss precursors to planning and the emergence of planning. It is interesting to note which aspects of planning are accounted for. Haith considers *anticipation* as the building block for future-oriented processing and examines infants' early representation of sequences of events. He charts a developmental course from the recognition of repeated sequences to the anticipations that lay the groundwork for future-oriented behavior.

Sequencing and temporal knowledge are the subject of Benson's chapter. She begins by examining the development of the concepts of time in 1- to 4-year-olds and claims that planning is dependent on the understanding of the concept of time and the sequences that take place in time. Children do not learn these ideas as abstractions. Often they emerge from their experience with everyday routines. Thus, Benson also examines the emergence of knowledge of routines in 4- to 7-year-olds. In addition, she explores the influence of parental practices on that knowledge.

Like Benson, authors Hudson, Sosa, and Shapiro contend that planning emerges from *knowledge of regularities*. They describe daily routines as well as scripts for recurring events, such as shopping expeditions and birthday parties. They analyze the cognitive processes that contribute to implementing script-based plans during problem solving. Their model is based primarily on memory, and so they explore the effects of internal and external aids on planning, and the impact of task complexity. The developmental model that is proposed to account for planning in 3- to 5-year-olds moves from single-goal, familiar-event planning to coordinated multiple, familiar-event planning, and finally, to planning for novel events.

In Kopp's analysis, planning rests on *understanding environmental regularities* and the capacity to represent those regularities in language. Kopp also implicates the motivational aspects of planning when she claims that awareness of intentions in the self and others is required for generating and understanding plans. She contends that attempts to deal with negative emotions like fear provide a window into children's plans and notes how attempts at emotion regulation become more planful during the preschool period. In Kopp's account, emotions are not just a context for plans because of their centrality to the child's goals. She claims that emotion regulation is an important prerequisite as well as an impetus for planning.

It can be seen that the chapters that deal with the origins of planning implicate every aspect of the box model. Haith's focus on anticipation, Benson's description of sequencing and time, Hudson, Sosa, and Shapiro's reference to knowledge of scripts, and Kopp's discussion of causation and language all implicate the cognitive components in the psychological box. Kopp goes further and talks about impulse regulation. Hudson, Sosa, and Shapiro's experiments manipulate task variables such as complexity, event structure, and external support. Because families differ in the routines they perform, Benson's chapter discusses socialization, which is part of the cultural ethos box of Model 4.

Cognition and Planning

Chapter 4 by Hudson et al. is a bridge to the second section, which focuses on the cognitive components of planning. Scholnick, Friedman, and Wallner-Allen compare some popular planning tasks with respect to the demands they make on representation of the problem, sequencing, processing capacity, and monitoring. The authors demonstrate how the relative importance of these essential components shifts depending on the task.

Scholnick et al. analyze laboratory tasks, whereas Streufert and Nogami attempt to account for planning in the everyday environment. In chapter 7, they propose a theory of cognitive complexity to describe individual differences in planning. In their theory, sequencing and monitoring are prominent elements, but they are not the only elements. In daily life, planning occurs in a dynamic situation that changes as strategies are implemented and the situation is altered. Four levels of complexity are proposed that vary in the breadth of information considered, the range of strategies applied, and the integration of past strategies and future plans into an effective course of action. Streufert and Nogami applied this analysis to studying managers in organizations, and they propose that the same analysis can be used to describe developmental changes in planning skills.

Because planning takes time and effort, and children and adults usually take the easiest route to problem solution, Ellis and Siegler focus on the factors that are used to decide whether to plan. They extend a model of strategy choice that has been applied in the past to academic tasks to account for the cognitive, motivational, and situational considerations that influence the decision to plan. These authors also call our attention to the fact that planning takes place in a cultural context, and they describe the value system that influences Euro-American and Navajo children's decisions to plan.

The same issue, the decision to plan, underlies the chapter written by Berg, Strough, Calderone, Meegan, and Sansone. They focus on planning to remove anticipated obstacles to goal satisfaction. They describe differences across the life span in representations of problems and in degrees of engagement in the anticipation and removal of obstacles. Like the authors of the preceding chapter, they argue that planning has costs that the planner is sometimes unwilling to incur.

Each chapter in the section on Cognition and Planning elaborates on the cognitive components listed in the box of psychological processes found in Model 4. The chapter by Scholnick et al. highlights sequencing and processing constraints. Streufert and Nogami focus on information integration from multiple changing cues and from multiple strategic attempts. Scholnick et al. discuss how knowledge of a domain facilitates organizing a representation of a problem. Ellis and Siegler discuss planning from the perspective of the strategy–choice model.

In addition, some of the chapters in the Cognition and Planning section discuss motivational issues found in Model 4. Ellis and Siegler argue that individuals must decide whether planning is worth the effort. These decisions are based on beliefs about the likelihood of success and personal agency, optimism, and the value of postponing gratification. The chapter by Berg et al. stresses how shifting value systems during the life course influence the decision to anticipate and handle obstacles.

Every chapter in this section deals with the situational and task contexts of planning. Scholnick et al., who note that most laboratory planning tasks require detecting an order and respecting constraints, argue that these two common themes are realized differently in various tasks. They cite some of the same task factors discussed by Hudson et al., such as the familiarity of the domain, the complexity of the task, and the external support for order detection and monitoring. Streufert and Nogami argue that when a problem requires quick and decisive response to an emergency, the planning process the planner will undertake will be simpler than the planning process that the same individual (or group) will engage in when long-term, complex problems arise. Because these task factors influence the process of devising a plan, the same themes appear in the Ellis and Siegler work. Berg et al. describe age-related shifts in domains where problems arise. These shifts reflect different age-related life tasks with which people are confronted.

Two chapters put planning in a broader context. For Ellis and Siegler, the use of different cultural groups provides insight into the cultural factors that influence planning, whereas Berg et al. suggest that there is an age-graded series of tasks and problems that cultures present to individuals.

Finally, each chapter regards planning as a composite of skills. Ellis and Siegler emphasize strategic thinking and the decision to plan; the latter element receives prime emphasis in the chapter by Berg et al. Streufert and Nogami focus on task representation, strategy generation, and monitoring. The task analysis provided by Scholnick, Friedman, and Wallner-Allen is designed to show how different tasks make differential demands on all of the phases of planning.

Motivational and Personality Influences on Planning

Locke, Durham, Poon, and Weldon attempt to explain why people engage in strategic behavior. They focus most of their discussion on goals, where properties of goals, such as specificity and difficulty, are important determinants of planning. Goals stimulate strategy execution, influence engagement in planning, and influence the quality of plans. They provide a taxonomy of the conditions that lead to better performance that includes, in addition to the properties of goals, characteristics of situations and of the planner.

Locke et al. focus on goal-setting. Models that incorporate the decision to plan also include motivational components. In this section, three chapters describe extensively the motivations underlying the decision to plan. Skinner has done extensive research on the set of beliefs that underlie scholastic achievement. She imports that model to account for failure to plan and theorizes that individual differences in control beliefs affect every stage of planning. Her central thesis is that individuals who have the cognitive capacity to plan will not do so if they believe that the desired outcome is not amenable to personal control. Control beliefs are particularly influential in planning tasks that put stress on individual resources. According to Skinner, motivation influences whether or not the individual plans and the effort and persistence exerted in planning; further, she explores the complex relationships between developmental changes in perceived control and planning.

Adler, Moore, and Tschann address motivational issues in a specific applied context, contraceptive planning. Their chapter discusses the illustrative example used in this chapter: Why adolescents fail to plan, even if the capacity for planning exists. But Adler et al. focus on a single issue, the use of contraceptives. They show how teen culture and certain motivations impede planning in sexually active youngsters. More specifically, the pressure for social conformity, the desire to achieve an adult role, and the desire to maintain a relationship are believed to figure in adolescents' decision making about planning. In addition, these authors examine the impact of informational and environmental influences on contraceptive planning and use.

Aspinwall deals with how individual differences in beliefs that may be construed as aspects of personality determine a set of behaviors that overlap with planning. She refers to proactive coping, the set of behaviors that people engage in to forestall potential problems. She describes the stages of proactive coping and compares those stages to the steps in planning. In particular, she claims that people who have optimistic beliefs are more likely to monitor the environment for potential problems that they believe they could offset. Also, optimists are more likely to make accurate assessments of the impact of their proactive coping attempts.

For Adler et al., as well as for Skinner, the motivation lies in the belief system and values of the planner. For Locke et al., the motivation comes from the goals the individual is presented with. The goals that Locke et al. investigate are provided externally through work tasks or experimental manipulations and, as a consequence, the authors, who are industrial/organizational psychologists, tell their readers less about the dispositions of planners that would lead to goals differing in specificity, complexity, or difficulty. Aspinwall focuses on a personality characteristic, optimism, as a determinant of the extent to which problems are recognized and action is taken to deal with their emergence.

Social Influences on Planning

Goodnow begins her chapter with an insightful summary of the planning literature. She contends that the two prevalent perspectives on planning, the cognitive and the motivational, ignore the fact that tasks frequently require other people as collaborators, or pertain to the planning of situations involving individuals as pieces of the plan. Goodnow notes that there are cultural norms that prescribe what can be planned, who can be part of the plan, and when and whether planning is acceptable.

SUMMARY

Planning is based on a set of dispositions, attitudes, and intentions, and a series of cognitive and behavioral acts that are calibrated to adapt to a dynamically changing setting. It has been difficult to pin down the nature of planning because it is such a rich and complicated process, parts of which are hidden because they take place in the mind of the individual. In order to understand planning, researchers have focused on specific aspects. Consequently, the study of planning can be likened to looking through a kaleidoscope, with each view beautiful in itself, but unconnected to the preceding or the following ones. This chapter attempts to organize the multiple views into one cohesive picture and, as its outline emerges, suggests a research agenda. This agenda focuses on the linkages among the components that have already been studied. Following such an agenda will reveal how the components of planning are orchestrated together and why, how, and when planning occurs.

REFERENCES

Anzai, Y., & Simon, H. (1979). The theory of learning by doing. *Psychological Review, 94,* 192–210.

Bandura, A. (1986). *Social foundations of thought and action: A social cognitive theory.* Englewood Cliffs, NJ: Prentice-Hall.

Baron, R. M., & Kenny, D. A. (1986). The moderator–mediator variable distinction in social psychological research: Conceptual, strategic and statistical considerations. *Journal of Personality and Social Psychology, 31,* 1173–1182.

Benson, J. B. (1994). The origins of future orientation in the everyday lives of 9- to 36-month-old infants. In M. M. Haith, J. B. Benson, R. J. Roberts, & B. F. Pennington (Eds.), *The development of future-oriented processes* (pp. 375–408). Chicago: University of Chicago Press.

Borgman, A. (1995, September 16). Studies find most teens who crash aren't drunk, just inexperienced. *The Washington Post,* p. A1.

Bronfenbrenner, U. (1979). *The ecology of human development.* Cambridge, MA: Harvard University Press.

Chalmers, D., & Lawrence, J. (1993). Investigating the effects of planning aids on adults' and adolescents' organization of a complex task. *International Journal of Behavioral Development, 16,* 191–214.

Chi, M. T. H., Glaser, R., & Rees, E. (1982). Expertise in problem solving. In R. J. Sternberg (Ed.), *Advances in the psychology of intelligence* (Vol. 1, pp. 7–76). Hillsdale, NJ: Lawrence Erlbaum Associates.

De Lisi, R. (1987). A cognitive–developmental model of planning. In S. L. Friedman, E. K. Scholnick, & R. R. Cocking (Eds.), *Blueprints for thinking: The role of planning in cognitive development* (pp. 79–109). Cambridge, England; Cambridge University Press.

Dreher, M., & Oerter, R.(1987). Action planning competencies during adolescence and early adulthood. In S. L. Friedman, E. K. Scholnick, & R. R. Cocking (Eds.), *Blueprints for thinking: The role of planning in cognitive development* (pp. 321–355). Cambridge, England; Cambridge University Press.

Friedman, S. L., Scholnick, E. K., & Cocking, R. R. (1987). Reflections on reflection: What planning is and how it develops. In S. L. Friedman, E. K. Scholnick, & R. R. Cocking (Eds.), *Blueprints for thinking: The role of planning in cognitive development* (pp. 515–534). Cambridge, England: Cambridge University Press.

Gauvain, M., & Rogoff, B. (1989). Collaborative problem solving and children's planning skills. *Developmental Psychology, 25,* 139–151.

Goodnow, J. J. (1987). Social aspects of planning. In S. L. Friedman, E. K. Scholnick, & R. R. Cocking (Eds.), *Blueprints for thinking: The role of planning in cognitive development* (pp. 179–201). Cambridge, England: Cambridge University Press.

Hammond, K. J. (1990). Case-based planning: A framework for planning from experience. *Cognitive Science, 14,* 385–444.

Hayes-Roth, B., & Hayes-Roth, F. (1979). A cognitive model of planning. *Cognitive Science, 3,* 275–310.

Hudson, J. A., & Fivush, R. (1991). Planning in the preschool years: The emergence of plans from general event knowledge. *Cognitive Development, 6,* 393–415.

Inhelder B., & Piaget, J. (1958). *The growth of logical thinking from childhood to adolescence.* New York: Basic Books.

Klahr, D. (1994). Discovering the present by predicting the future. In M. M. Haith, J. B. Benson, R. J. Roberts, & B. F. Pennington (Eds.), *The development of future-oriented processes* (pp. 177–218). Chicago: University of Chicago Press.

Klahr, D., & Robinson, M. (1981). Formal assessment of problem-solving and planning processes in preschool children. *Cognitive Psychology, 13,* 113–148.

Kopp, C. B., Krakow, J. B., & Vaughn, B. (1983). Patterns of self-control in young handicapped children. In M. Perlmutter (Ed.), *The Minnesota symposia on child psychology* (Vol. 16, pp. 93–128). Hillsdale, NJ: Lawrence Erlbaum Associates.

Kotovsky, K., Hayes, J. R., & Simon, H. A. (1985). Why are some problems really hard? Evidence from Tower of Hanoi. *Cognitive Psychology, 17,* 248–294.

Kreitler, S., & Kreitler, H. (1987a). Plans and planning: Their motivational and cognitive antecedents. In S. L. Friedman, E. K. Scholnick, & R. R. Cocking (Eds.), *Blueprints for thinking: The role of planning in cognitive development* (pp.110–178). Cambridge, England: Cambridge University Press.

Kreitler, S. & Kreitler, H. (1987b). Conceptions and processes of planning: The developmental perspective. In S. L. Friedman, E. K. Scholnick, & R. R. Cocking (Eds.), *Blueprints for thinking: The role of planning in cognitive development* (pp. 205–272). Cambridge, England: Cambridge University Press.

McGillicuddy-De Lisi, A. V., De Lisi, R., Flaugher, J., & Sigel, I. E. (1987). Familial influences on planning. In S. L. Friedman, E. K. Scholnick, & R. R. Cocking (Eds.), *Blueprints for thinking: The role of planning in cognitive development* (pp. 395–427). Cambridge, England: Cambridge University Press.

Miller G. A., Galanter, E., & Pribram, K. (1960). *Plans and the structure of behavior.* New York: Holt, Rinehart & Winston.

National Advisory Mental Health Council. (1995). *Basic behavioral science research for mental health. A national investment.* U.S. Department of Health and Human Services. NIH Publication No. 95–3682.

Nurmi, J. E. (1991). How do adolescents see their future? A review of the development of future orientation and planning. *Developmental Review, 11,* 1–59.

Nurmi, J. E. (1993). Adolescent development in an age-graded context: The role of personal beliefs, goals, and strategies in the tackling of developmental tasks and standards. *International Journal of Behavioral Development, 16,* 169–189.

Overton, W. F., & Newman, J. L. (1982). Cognitive development: A competence–activation/utilization approach. In T. M. Field, A. Huston, H. C. Quay, L. Troll, & G. E. Finley (Eds.), *Review of human development* (pp. 217–241). New York: Wiley.

Pea, R. D., & Hawkins, J. (1987). Planning in a chore-scheduling task. In S. L. Friedman, E. K. Scholnick, & R. R. Cocking (Eds.), *Blueprints for thinking: The role of planning in cognitive development* (pp. 273–302). Cambridge, England: Cambridge University Press.

Rogoff, B. (1990). *Apprenticeship in thinking: Cognitive development in social context.* New York: Oxford University Press.

Sansone, C., & Berg, C. A. (1993). Adapting to the environment across the life span: Different process or different inputs? *International Journal of Behavioral Development, 16,* 215–241.

Scholnick, E. K. (1995). Knowing and constructing plans. *SRCD Newsletter,* Fall, 1995, 1–2, 17.

Scholnick, E. K., & Friedman, S. L. (1987). The planning construct in the psychological literature. In S. L. Friedman, E. K. Scholnick, & R. R. Cocking (Eds.), *Blueprints for thinking: The role of planning in cognitive development* (pp. 3–38). Cambridge, England: Cambridge University Press.

Scholnick, E. K., & Friedman, S. L. (1993). Planning in context: Developmental and situational considerations. *International Journal of Behavioral Development, 16,* 145–167.

Simon, H. A. (1975). The functional equivalence of problem-solving skills. *Cognitive Psychology, 7,* 268–288.

Skinner, E. A. (1991). Development and perceived control: A dynamic model of action in context. In M. R. Gunnar & L. A. Sroufe (Eds.), *Self-processes and development. The Minnesota symposia on child psychology* (Vol. 23, pp. 167–217). Hillsdale, NJ: Lawrence Erlbaum Associates.

Skinner, E. A., & Connell, J. P. (1986). Control understanding: Suggestions for a developmental framework. In M. M. Baltes & P. B. Baltes (Eds.), *The psychology of control and aging* (pp. 35–69). Hillsdale, NJ: Lawrence Erlbaum Associates.

Spitz, H. H., Webster, N. A., & Borys, S. V. (1982). Further studies of the Tower of Hanoi problem-solving performance of retarded adults and non-retarded children. *Developmental Psychology, 18,* 922–930.

Welsh, M. C. (1991). Rule guided behavior and self-monitoring on the Tower of Hanoi disk transfer task. *Cognitive Development, 6,* 59–76.

Welsh, M. C., & Pennington, B. F. (1988). Assessing frontal lobe functioning in children: Views from developmental psychology. *Developmental Neuropsychology, 4,* 199–230.

Welsh, M. C., Pennington, B. F., & Groisser, D. B. (1991). A normative–developmental study of executive function: A window on prefrontal function in children? *Developmental Neuropsychology, 7,* 131–149.

Zhang, J., & Norman, D. A. (1994). Representations in distributed cognitive tasks. *Cognitive Science, 18,* 87–122.

II

The Origins of Planning

2

The Development of Future Thinking as Essential for the Emergence of Skill in Planning

Marshall M. Haith
University of Denver

As adults, planning is a regular part of our daily lives. We schedule meetings, design presentations, generate our to-do lists, organize our weekend social events, and develop strategies for budgeting our money. Such "think-ahead skills" are not the exclusive province of adults. Children soon learn to save their allowances for video games, remote control cars, compact discs, clothes, and other sundry items. They arrange to meet friends after school, to watch or participate in athletic events, and to attend social gatherings. They set aside time to do homework, watch special TV programs and, in general, adapt to a culture that demands that they organize their lives in a way that requires forethought, priority setting, and scheduling.

These routine planning activities (as opposed to more demanding planning tasks such as creating a blueprint for a house, a federal budget, or a missions and goals statement for a University) seem as natural as life itself. How could anyone get through a day without considering various options for action, and making choices?

Yet, even cursory consideration of the young infant suggests that things may have been different in our earliest months of life. The infant seems embroiled in the "here and now," has little experience to provide a basis for developing sets of options for his activities, is probably unable to simultaneously represent those options, to arrange them according to any priority schemes, or even to do anything about them if he could. Thus, an interesting question arises: Where do planning skills come from?

First, consider the various components of planning that are implied by this discussion. Planning involves selection of a *goal* or a desired end state. The end state involves more than a simple change in the current state of affairs. For planning to be involved, there must be alternatives for reaching or accomplishing the goal. A *decision* or decisions must be made among the alternatives, perhaps even *priority setting* among them. Usually, a *multiple-step sequence* of alternatives is required for goal accomplishment. There may or may not be *subgoals* and requirements for *adjusting* the goals or subgoals. Also, the term *planning* refers to a process by which an individual thinks about the probable consequences of implementing each alternative and whether it will get him closer to the desired end.

A reading of the predecessor to this book, *Blueprints in Thinking: The Role of Planning in Cognitive Development* (Friedman, Scholnick, & Cocking, 1987), suggests reasonable convergence on this perspective among the authors of various chapters. A few quotations convey a flavor of authors' positions:

> Planning relies on representation of the environment, anticipation of solutions to problems, and then monitoring of strategies to see whether they meet the problem and follow the plan ... (p. 3) Plans are the expression of goal-directed behavior, and more specifically, of behavior that is voluntary, self-conscious, and intended (p 5) ... planning takes place in space and time ... the tendency to analyze sequences and notice antecedents and consequences sets the stage for planning. (Scholnick & Friedman, 1987, p. 9)

> ... even a relatively simple planning task such as planning a party requires ... thinking about time, place, causes, functions, consequences, manner of occurrence ... evaluation, integration, and decision making ... (Kreitler & Kreitler, 1987b, p. 209)

> ... Planning is usually thought about as a fully internalized symbolic process that requires mental, symbolic representation and mental operation upon the symbols. (Pea & Hawkins, 1987, p. 277)

> Without the ability to form mental representations, we would be unable to plan. ... (Cocking & Copple, 1987, p. 428)

Moreover, there is reasonable consistency about the underlying processes involved. These authors agree with Piaget (1976, 1978) that representational ability and an understanding of causation are essential and that relevant knowledge, self-control, and monitoring are inherent in the process (e.g., Cocking & Copple, 1987; Kreitler & Kreitler, 1987a; Pea & Hawkins, 1987; Scholnick & Friedman, 1987). Additionally, planning is considered to be a deliberate, conscious, and voluntary process (Covington, 1987; Kreitler & Kreitler, 1987a; Rogoff, Gauvain, & Gardner, 1987; Scholnick & Friedman, 1987).

There are a few points to highlight here for our purposes. First, is the necessity for representational skills in order to plan. Although a goal may or may not be visible, (e.g., the goal is visible when a cookie on the drain board is the issue, but not when one is engaged in an Easter egg hunt), the action alternatives are not; for a person to consider and weigh alternatives and to select among them, representational skill is crucial. Second, is that what is referred to as motor planning would not fit these criteria easily, at least for direct motor acts such as reaching. Reaching activity can change the state of things, a clear aim in planning activity; but it seems unlikely that the actor considers minor variations beforehand and decides among alternatives before executing the act, unless there are obstacles to the reaching goal. In this special case, *planning*, in the sense that we are using that term, might indeed be involved. Third, is that the planner deals with action alternatives; one does not plan for eventualities that lack action implications. Thus, a person may consider various alternatives for a picnic if it rains but does not plan the clouds or the rain, per se. A person plans actions that he or she controls; one can forecast the clouds or the rain but can only control such things as whether shelter will be nearby.

Thus, representational abilities and control over action alternatives seem essential for true planning activity. These are two domains in which the young infant comes up short. Although it is arguable *when* infants possess the ability to represent objects (generally tested by habituation–memory paradigms), there is little evidence that babies can simultaneously represent several alternatives for their own action, at least before they gain some competence in motor control. Nor do they control a great deal in the early months of life. Their crying can energize adults, yet babies do not control the adults' particular actions (e.g., feeding the baby when the baby is hungry), and babies cannot themselves implement a particular alternative among many, even if they were able to represent the alternatives.

Do babies bide their time, then, with regard to planning skill, waiting for the moment when they will have representational capacity and enough motor skill to control events in their worlds? Unlikely. I suggest that an important foundation is being laid in the early months for later planning skills, a foundation that is crucial to later development. This foundation is an emerging understanding of the future—that events will happen. In learning about the future, infants come to understand that events occur at a time, in a place, and in a sequence, aspects that the foregoing quotations indicated are important for planning ability (Kreitler & Kreitler, 1987a, 1987b; Scholnick & Friedman, 1987). There are other parallels between the development of future understanding and planning ability that are addressed later, including the greater importance, early in development, of perceptual supports and external control over relevant elements.

TAKING ACCOUNT OF THE FUTURE

An important feature of planning is that it deals with the future. One does not plan for the past, where there are no alternatives to consider and no decisions to be made. One may wish that things had been different or speculate about what would have happened if they were, but to little avail.

Whatever actions that might have occurred to achieve a goal have already transpired or failed to transpire. Goals, by their very nature, lie in the future, so the alternatives for reaching them must also lie in the future. A person's ability to plan must involve an appreciation of events that have not happened, yet can happen, and that events that have happened before can happen again. In short, to be a planner, one must have some appreciation of the future. Although these claims are not controversial, few careful analyses exist that detail how future thinking plays a role in planning activity or how future thinking develops in its own right. In fact, for psychologists, the future has been so enmeshed in the planning concept that the word "future," more often than not, fails even to appear in papers on planning (exceptions exist; e.g., see Friedman, Scholnick, & Cocking, 1987, p. 523).

Hampering our analysis of future thinking is the lack of an articulated taxonomy for talking about it. Consider past thinking, memory. We have concepts that deal with: the *time domain*—iconic memory, short-term memory, long-term memory, working memory (a misnomer, because it is often future-oriented); *verbal accessibility*—procedural versus declarative memory; *awareness*—implicit versus explicit memory; *physiological structure*—prefrontal areas, the hippocampus, the cerebellum; *neurochemistry*—acetylcholine, dopamine, norepinephrine, glutamate. We have categorized a broad range of *memory* syndromes—Korsikoff's, general amnesia, and Alzheimer's, to name a few. But, with respect to the future, there is no coordinated set of concepts for our kit-bag, no standard way of talking about the time domain, a person's verbal access to what she knows about what may or will happen, her awareness about future events, the physiological structures that support future thinking, or the neurochemistry that might be involved.

Yet, consider the role that future thinking, forecasting, plays in the planning process. To set a goal, one must typically be able to imagine or represent a state of affairs that does not exist now but may exist in the future. (An exception occurs in the Tower of Hanoi task where the goal is perceptually available.) To select among a set of alternatives for action, a person must be able to imagine actions that could occur in the future; ideally, selection among these alternatives involves an understanding of the future consequences of implementing each action. In the typical case, the planner envisions a sequence of future actions and how they build on one another for goal accomplishment. Imagine an individual who has no comprehension of the future, and you have imagined a person who is unable to plan.

Do we, in fact, need to develop a separate vocabulary for conceptualizing future thinking, or is future thinking simply a matter of memory projected forward or replayed? If the latter is true, we can simply adopt the repertoire of concepts that has been developed for memory, make a few adjustments, and we are on our way. The question apparently has not been discussed in the literature. One interesting way to ask if memory and future thinking are essentially the same phenomenon is to explore whether a person who lacks memory has any future perspective. This is not well-furrowed ground, but at least one anecdote exists. Tulving (1985) reported a case study with N. N., an amnesic who had no memory whatever for personal events whether they occurred before or after the amnesia, although he had some knowledge for generalized scripts and other abstract information. A brief transcript relevant to our question about future knowledge follows.

> E. T.: "Let's try the question again about the future. What will you be doing tomorrow?"
>
> (There is a 15-second pause.)
>
> N. N.: smiles faintly, then says, "I don't know."
>
> E. T.: ... "How would you describe your state of mind when you try to think about it?"
>
> (A 5-second pause.)
>
> N. N.: "Blank, I guess ... it's a big blankness sort of thing ... like swimming in the middle of a lake. There's nothing there to hold you up or do anything with." (Tulving 1985, p. 4).

It would be nice to have formal data on this interesting question. Arguing from this one example, however, it appears that memory might be necessary for future thinking. But, is it the same thing?

THE RELATION BETWEEN MEMORY AND FUTURE THINKING

Several of us considered this issue in developing the introduction for a book on the development of future-oriented processes (Haith, Benson, Roberts, & Pennington, 1996). Our general answer was that some types of future thinking seem to be memory replayed, but for other types one can make a clear distinction. Even for those cases for which memory is replayed, however, there are some unique considerations. We distinguished four relations between memory and future thinking with the future as: (a) continuation of a repeating past; (b) projection of past trends; (c) induction from observation; and (d) imagination and invention.

The Future as Continuation of a Repeating Past

Perhaps the most basic future-oriented process is the formation of expectations for repeating events to continue. Such events include the ongoing drumbeat of musical rhythm, the successive rings of a telephone, the diurnal repetition of night and day, and the regularity of the cycle of seasons. The earliest evidence of infants' ability to take future events into consideration is in their formation of expectations for what will happen next in a series of repeating events. When even 6-week-old babies watch a series of pictures that appear and disappear in predictable spatial locations, at predictable times, in what we refer to as the Visual Expectation Paradigm, they quickly form expectations for the place and time of appearance of the next picture (Haith, Hazan, & Goodman, 1988; McCarty, Haith, & Robinson, 1988). They manifest this ability by moving their eyes to the location of the forthcoming picture before it appears (i.e., they anticipate the next picture). Even when 2- and 3-month-olds do not anticipate predictable appearances of pictures, their reaction time to fixate each picture is faster than it is when the picture appearance is unpredictable (i.e., they show response facilitation). Their performance is not easily fit to conditioning models, (Haith, Wentworth, & Canfield, 1993); it is stable over several days, and it is predictive of later performance (Benson et al., 1993; DiLalla et al., 1990; Dougherty & Haith, 1993; Haith & McCarty, 1990). Babies are able to form expectations that are based on increasingly more complex time–space rules as they age, even over the first 2 to 3 months of life (Arehart & Haith, 1992; Canfield & Haith, 1991).

Although performance with predictable picture sequences demonstrates the roots of more elaborate future-oriented processes, it also reflects a limited skill. Essentially, the baby views a repeating pattern, for example, left–right, and begins to forecast that the left picture will go on after the right one disappears, essentially predicting that what has happened before will happen again.

However, this is more than a simple display of memory. The baby could simply detect the repeating pattern and remember it, but do nothing about it. If this were the end of the story, one would have to demonstrate that the baby detected and remembered the pattern, possibly through a typical habituation–recovery paradigm—familiarizing the baby first with the original sequence and then presenting a novel sequence to which the baby might respond differentially. Or, the baby might detect regularity in the sequence, develop memory for it, and even form expectations for forthcoming pictures, but do nothing about those expectations. It is unclear how one might index such expectations without action consequences. Fortunately for us, the babies use their expectations to engage both in forecasting behavior (anticipatory looking) and facilitated responding (reduced reaction times). That is, they not only detect regularity and remember the sequence, they form expectations based on that memory for what will happen next, then use those expectations to control their action. Thus, they display detection, expectation, and future-oriented action in their looking behavior.

It is also interesting to note that, through this accomplishment, babies illustrate an important feature of future-oriented processes—integration of past, present, and future. They utilize past experience (a repeating predictable series of events) and the present circumstances (e.g., disappearance of the left-side picture) to predict a future event (i.e., anticipate what comes next; Haith, Wentworth, and Canfield, 1993). Moreover, they illustrate a point that is often overlooked in memory studies. That is, the key purpose of memory is to adaptively prepare the organism for future events. Seen in this way, it is curious that the field of memory has disproportionately captured the interest of investigators, with so little attention to future thinking.

In any case, even for infants in the first months of life, experience is not simply a series of unknown events to which the baby responds in an ad hoc manner. Rather, the infant picks up on regularities, rapidly maps them and can use those regularities to prepare for what comes next. Interestingly, the baby forms expectations for events over which it has no control whatsoever.

The Future as Projection of Past Trends

As adults, we clearly go beyond simply predicting that what has happened before will happen again, based on repeating cycles. One type of extension of future thinking involves expectations that are based on extrapolations of current trends rather than on simple repetition of the same events. Scientific models, for example, use past history as a guide, but project to future circumstances that may have no precedent. One example is the modeling that takes place to determine if our sources of food will be adequate to supply a growing world population. We develop models of future world population growth based on past birth rates, the age of the current population, and recent historical trends. Included also are recent historical trends for food productivity, the assimilation of new agricultural methods, urbanization in Third World countries, water sources, desertification, and so on. Although we have not actually experienced the state of affairs in the year 2010, we model what it will be like based on trends that we have experienced. Another example of current interest is the modeling of the enormous health and economic impact of the spread of AIDS in various countries of the world (Mann, Tarantola, & Netter, 1992). The ultimate projection model concerns our guesses about whether the universe will expand forever or will reverse current trends and condense for another big bang, based on past and current trends.

Children can also govern their behavior by forecasting situations that have no precedent. Consider the realm of discipline. It is unlikely that two different violations of family rules and the resulting confrontations are ever identical. Rather, a child learns how a parent will react when infringements occur and selects among alternative courses in facing the music for a new violation—truthful reporting, deception, downright lying, or what have you. Based on recollection of what happened when he truthfully reported that he broke a vase in the living room with a ball that he was told not to play with in the house, the child may decide among alternative approaches when he is confronted with the tool he broke when he was specifically told not to use tools without adult supervision. Often, the child even develops his or her strategy depending on the adults' mood or the child's recent status of grace or disgrace. In short, children base expectations on memory and the current context, but they also generalize from old to new situations.

The data are relatively skimpy regarding *when* babies generalize their past experience to form expectations for new situations. In one study, Arehart and Haith (1990) demonstrated that 3-month-olds could use a rule (the rule of alternation) that they acquired in a previous week to form expectations in a new session several days later. So, infants did demonstrate generality across time, but the circumstances were identical. Another, somewhat remotely related example, relates to infants' ability to extrapolate a current event into the future when the future event has not been experienced. Harris (1983) reviewed the literature on infants' tracking of an object that disappeared behind a screen. These studies asked whether the infant would look at the place where the object disappeared as opposed to the other side of the screen or tunnel where the baby might expect the object to reappear if he essentially generalized the "path" of the object's movement through space. Harris concluded that babies did not extrapolate the consequences of the object's path until at least 9 months of age.

However, Baillargeon (1986) found that younger infants are surprised when a moving object does not appear on the opposite side of the screen when there is no obstruction in its path. Baillergeon's studies use "looking time" as the index of surprise rather than the location of fixation, so it is not possible to determine if the baby actually forecasted where the object would appear or whether, instead, the baby noticed that something odd happened, after the fact, when the object failed to appear on the opposite side. When a moving object does not disappear but moves from side-to-side in an up–down, peak and valley trajectory, even 3-month-olds display expectations for the trajectory; for example, if the trajectory toward a peak is foreshortened, the baby continues to track along the "expected" path (Wentworth & Haith, 1987).

Expectations that are projections from past and current trends are probably important in infants' developing appreciation of such routines as bathing, feeding, dressing, and getting set for bed. A given routine, even if similar to past episodes, is rarely an exact match to a prior episode. For example, parents seldom read the same book each night or sequence through routines in as fixed a manner as the picture–expectation study mentioned previously. The development of generalized scripts would, by necessity, depend on reasonable variability in related experiences. An interesting distinction between this and the previous category is that the infant can be an active player in routines and can eventually assume a role in initiating the routine or some of the elements that the infant comes to expect. In fact, parents believe that the learning of steps in routines is central to children's incorporation of the future into their thinking (Benson, 1994).

However, infants do have limitations in their abilities to extrapolate from the flow of past and current events. One key aspect that distinguishes adult and infant extrapolation from past trends is the close tie of the infants' extrapolations to current perceptual support. Routines involve physical actions in a world of objects. The reading of one book may be substituted for another, but reading still follows a change into night clothes, crawling into bed, and the presence and voice of a parent. Adults can extrapolate with or without such support as indicated in the modeling examples previously discussed. A parallel may exist with the development of planning skills. De Lisi (1987) distinguished between four levels of planning skills. In discussing the more basic levels, he noted the distinction that Piaget and Vygotsky made between overt practical action toward goals that involve perceptually available objects and those that require symbolic representation through internal mental operations.

Categorization must play a role in this process. Generalization of experience is essential for predicting the outcome of an action or process that has not occurred before, and such generalization depends on the ability to categorize. An expectation that the steadily increasing loudness of a novel voice will be followed by the appearance of a person in the doorway, or that a falling novel object will continue to fall, or that a smiling novel face will be accompanied by friendly actions, all require categorization—of voice/visual relations, of object properties, and of facial expressions. Although the ability to categorize at some level exists early in infancy, these abilities also improve dramatically throughout the early years (Cohen & Strauss, 1979; Ludemann & Nelson, 1988).

The Future as Construction From Analogy

As adults, we form expectations about the future based not only on our own experience but also on the experience of others. We have never died, yet we know we will. Most of us have never committed a serious crime, yet we form expectations about the consequences if we did, based on the experiences or report of experiences of others. Our work ethic, or lack of it, our involvement in education, and our investments in real estate or the stock market all reflect expectations based on the report of others.

Although research on *how* children form expectations, based on observation, is limited, some guidance exists. Bandura showed through several studies that the behavior of young children is affected when they observe how others are treated when they behave in certain ways (Bandura, 1992). When the behavior of a model yields favorable outcomes, the behavior is copied; when it yields negative outcomes, the behavior is avoided. This research has usually been discussed under the province of imitation and observational learning, but the phenomenon may be equally relevant to the topic of expectation formation. As Bandura noted, the child analogizes from how another's behavior is rewarded to form expectations for how the child will be rewarded if he behaves the same way.

Although a great deal of work has been done on infant imitation, and it is clear that infants do imitate the behavior of others (Meltzoff & Moore, 1992), studies in infancy have not addressed the question of whether infants come to expect that their imitation will have the same consequences as it did for the model. At first, infant imitation has a game-like quality, engaged in for its own sake, and it is based on immediate interpersonal interaction. Emerging during infancy is an ability to display deferred imitation, especially when the context is favorable for reward of an imitated act. Children increasingly use interpersonal and preserved knowledge to guide goal-oriented action, knowledge that is not based on simple memory for personal experiences alone. Of course, social transmission of knowledge and the structure of the educational system manifest this belief—that children form a knowledge base from others and can form expectations from that knowledge base.

The Future as Imagination and Invention

For all of the preceding categories, experience and memory play a central role in future thinking, whether it is the experience of the individual in question, extrapolation from past experience, or induction based on the experience of others. But, we are not limited in our future thinking only to events that have happened before to us or others, or that continue past trends. We are able to imagine and create things and events that have never occurred before. The design of the automobile and the airplane, our trips to the moon, and our visualizing of a space station were all at one time or are even now, unprecedented. Here we are talking about imagination, equally the province of scientists, artists, business people, authors, and almost all people as they go about their everyday lives. Many lists have been constructed about how humans differ from other animals. Surely, the ability to conjure future possibilities and goals that have no precedent must take its rightful place in this list.

Adults enjoy no monopoly in this sphere. Pretend play emerges in late infancy and often involves types of exploration, novel application, and invention that bear resemblance to the adult variety, at least in principle. Bananas become imaginary telephones, shells become pretend cups, and sticks become fantasy horses (Leslie, 1987). In fact, one could validly argue that adult invention bears a closer similarity to the playful pretend activities of the child than is usually appreciated. Infant pretend play first emerges in partnership with older children and adults in which the infant simply imitates a pretend action or fills in a missing piece of a sequence. Gradually, children are able to enact novel pretend sequences on their own, setting the stage for imagining outcomes that have no precedence (Leslie, 1987).

From considering these various examples, it becomes clear that future thinking is related to memory, but it is also clearly distinct. Some of the same concepts that are used in the domain of memory may be applicable, but it is likely that unique concepts also have to be developed as well to deal with future thinking.

It is important to appreciate that these four categories of future thinking— expectation for events in a repeating sequence, extrapolation from past and current trends, forecasting based on induction, and invention and imagination—do *not* constitute a straightforward developmental sequence. The role of sunspots and the El Niño in weather activity on planet Earth are repeating events for which expectations have been formulated only very recently, through advanced scientific analyses. Thus, these are repeating events that were discovered only by sophisticated and mature minds with state-of-the-art instruments. On the other hand, invention and imagination, the category discussed last, are available to the very young as, for example, in pretend play. These are simply four types of future thinking that are separable from the one nonpresent time domain that has preoccupied psychology for so many years, the past, as exemplified by research and thought about memory. Now, we turn to dimensions of expectations that play a role in the development of future thinking.

DIMENSIONS OF FUTURE THINKING

Given the somewhat unique character of future thinking, it may be worthwhile to consider various dimensions of this topic in constructing an understanding of how it develops. It seems likely that development along these dimensions permits increasingly more sophisticated planning activity. Future thinking embraces a range of what we have referred to as "future-oriented processes," processes that are familiar to psychologists: expectation, set, preparation, intention, prediction, and goal formation; in brief, any processes that involve forecasting (Haith, Wentworth, & Canfield, 1993). For the sake of clarity, only one of several future-oriented processes—expectations—will be addressed. Some dimensions that seem important are: the time scale, the representational demand, the source of control, animacy, complexity, familiarity, and specificity.

Time

Expectations vary in how far they project into the future, from the 1-second expectations that are typical of Visual Expectation Paradigm experiments with infants, to the multiyear expectations that people develop for their retirement years. Young infants seem to have fairly limited time frames for their expectations; one of their limitations may reflect limits on working memory. Some preliminary evidence from our laboratories suggests that the time limit for a cycle in a repeating sequence of events (e.g., left, left, right, right) can be no longer than around 5 to 7 seconds in duration at 3 months of age for infants to form expectations for events in that cycle (Bihun, Lanthier & Haith, 1994). As working memory capacity increases, children should be able to pick up regularities over longer intervals of time, enabling them to appreciate familiar routines. Such limitations probably constrain infants in the early months of life to the first two types of memory/future thinking categories discussed earlier.

The Representational Demand

The representational demand for expectations is related to the time dimension; we can agree that the requirement to hold a representation for a forthcoming picture that is only 1 second away places less demand on the system than holding that same representation for 5 minutes. But the two dimensions are separable. For example, expectations differ in the number of events that are involved and their interdependence. The expectation that a traveler will arrive at the local airport may depend on weather reports from both the airport of departure and the airport of arrival. In comparison to an expectation that a picture will appear at the next moment, the arrival expectation demands more of representational skills in terms of the number of issues that must be kept in mind, their causal relation and interdependence, knowledge, and so on.

Source of Control

Babies form expectations for events they do not control, and so do adults. Evidence was presented previously that babies form expectations for the appearance of pictures even when the baby's behavior has no effect on the picture sequence. Similarly, adults form expectations for events that they do not control such as that dark clouds precede rain, lightning means thunder will soon follow, and so on. On the other hand, almost by definition, planning implies control. Noncontrollable and expected events may affect the plan, but controllable action consequences are still involved. Although the earliest expectations for infants are for events that they do not control, it seems reasonable to speculate that these noncontrolled expectations lay the base for the later development of control-based expectations as the baby's motor competencies develop.[1]

---

[1]The term *control* might be interpreted in a number of ways. One might argue that even the youngest infant has at least a crude level of control over visual input because he can choose whether or not to look at it, what we might call "orientational control." At a higher psycholoical level, babies exercise "cognitive control" over their own mental processes by formulating a model or representation of these events, the basis for their expectations. For still a third level of control, what we might call "physical or contingency control," an individual actually affects events of interest rather than serving simply as an observer of those events. It is this third level of control that is at issue here.

If a baby were not aware of the physical rules of its world—that a falling object continues to fall, that a stationary object remains stationary, that animate objects are likely to move and inanimate objects are not—it would be very difficult for the baby to form control-based expectations, that is, control that is based on the baby's own action on such events. A transition from expectations for noncontrolled events to expectations for controlled events involves intermediate stages in which babies participate in ongoing routines that are initiated by others (Leslie, 1987; Nelson, 1993; Rogoff, 1990). The degree to which plans are self-generated constituted a dimension for De Lisi (1987) in designing his "levels" scheme of plans. De Lisi suggested that before children develop their own plans, they participate in plans designed by others. This type of scaffolded transition to internalized self-generated plans is based on Vygotsky's analysis and was echoed by McGillicuddy-DeLisi et al. (1987) and Rogoff, Gauvain, and Gardner (1987). Thus, there is a parallel here in how children learn about the future and how to plan.

The Role of Animacy

Regular events that the infant experiences involve both animate and inanimate objects. In an early observation, K. C. Moore (1896) noted that babies hold out their arms as early as 5 months of age when a parent approaches, in anticipation of being picked up. Lamb & Malkin (1986) discussed the differential expectations that an infant forms for distress relief from the mother, also around 4 to 5 months of age. While expectations form early in infancy as a consequence of interactions with people, expectations are formed also for inanimate events. The pictures in the Visual Expectation Paradigm constitute one example. Another is the game that babies design for themselves in banging a rattle repeatedly against their high-chair table, closing their eyes before each impact in anticipation of the crashing sound.

The role that animacy plays in forming expectations has not been addressed as such. However, Rogoff (1990) has given considerable attention to the uses that babies make of social agents in reaching goals as well as how young children are incorporated into the planning activities of the day. Goodnow (1987) discussed two additional points regarding planning that involves others. The first is that people can be somewhat unpredictable in their actions, in contrast to physical objects. Second, the actions of individuals are typically interdependent, which creates substantial difficulty in predicting any individual's or the group's behavior, as any social scientist is aware. Thus, one's ability to form expectations for animate, social agents could be considerably more difficult than for inanimate objects.

Complexity

Early expectations, such as the ones addressed in the visual expectation experiments, are based on relatively simple perceptual events. But expectations vary in their complexity. Even in the Visual Expectation Paradigm itself, patterns vary in complexity, and we have shown that 2-month-olds can handle the simplest patterns, but that more complex ones are not mastered until 3 months of age. One way in which patterns vary in complexity is the number of items that are incorporated in a repeating episode. At 3 months of age, babies seem to be able to form expectations for patterns that have as many as four events, if they occur quickly enough (Lanthier & Haith, 1993). Although pictures are not alternatives in the same sense that we talk about alternatives in planning, at least babies demonstrate that they can accommodate more than one event at a time, perhaps a basis for the later ability to consider more than one alternative at the same time.

Certainly, as language emerges, children become capable of handling expectations that are engaged by more complex levels of symbolic representation. Consider the sentences: "We are going to grandma's today. What should we take to grandma's?" Based on the child's expectation for how long the ride will be, the child may grab a teddy bear and a blanket for a car nap. If it is summer, and grandma usually picks flowers with the child, the child may also take along her flower book. The upper limit for the complexity of an expectation that a child can develop would also seem to be an upper limit for the complexity of events that a child could include in planning.

Familiarity

Familiarity seems to play a role in the formation of expectations. In an attempt to develop and test a questionnaire to assess the development of future-oriented processes, Janette Benson and I, with others, asked parents of over 200 infants how familiarity affected their children's understanding of future events (Benson , Haith, Bihun, Lanthier, & Thomas, 1992). Parents reported that their children first learn about the future from familiar routines, and they reported that children formed expectations for familiar events several months earlier than for unfamiliar events, whether or not language was the means of communicating the expectations. Given the role that future thinking plays in planning activity, one would suspect that familiarity would play an important role in the development of planning skills also. Indeed, several authors have emphasized the role that developing knowledge plays in the planning process (Friedman, Scholnick, & Cocking, 1987; Piaget, 1978).

Specificity

Expectations, as well as plans, vary in specificity. In the experiments we described on visual expectations in infants, the events were quite specific with regard to location and timing. However, most of these studies did not permit the baby to form an expectation for content—that is, exactly what picture would occur, from one moment to the next. When the content is predictable, infants more readily form expectations for the timing and location of events than when the content is unpredictable (Wentworth & Haith, 1992). Children's expectations may be more or less detailed; for example, a child may know that he is going to the zoo but not know, in many ways, what the experience will entail. Animals will be there of course, but which ones, and what will the layout be like? Whether a child asks to take peanuts on the excursion depends on whether the child expects that she will see monkeys. Haith and Campos (1977) suggested that even in a straightforward search task, such as an A-not-B paradigm, the infant may know it is searching for something but not know what it is searching for. Of course, plans may be more or less specific also, with regard to the goal, the alternative actions, and what the alternative actions may produce.

THE RELATION BETWEEN EXPECTATION FORMATION AND PLANNING

What we have done so far is consider some factors that differentiate various types of expectations and the dimensions on which they may vary. But one can ask, what does all of this have to do with planning? The answer is straightforward. Limitations on an infant's or young child's ability to think about the future place an upper limit on her ability to plan. Inasmuch as the various dimensions we have considered play a role in limiting a child's ability to form expectations or to engage in future thinking, these same dimensions will limit planning activity. Consider the following observation by William Friedman (1990) in discussing the baby's starting point in the evolution of distinguishing between past, present, and future time: "If we could somehow shed all that we had learned about the temporal structure of the world, what would our experience be like? Perhaps we would inhabit a dreamlike region, devoid of causal connections, of a past, present, and future, of a sense of place in time" (p. 85).

As others have suggested, it is hard to imagine that anyone could plan who did not have an appreciation of causal connections, an appreciation that requires a sense of sequence and time. (See Benson, chapter 3, this volume, for a more complete analysis.)

In fact, if one assumes that expectations are the simplest form of future thinking, we can entertain a strong hypothesis. Individual planning ability can never exceed the ability of an infant or child to form expectations for any of the components involved in planning an activity, including the goal, the alternatives, the sequencing of the alternatives, or the forecasting of the outcome of each step in the plan under consideration. We have pointed to several similarities in both the evolution of increasingly more sophisticated expectations and the development of planning—a shift from being able to deal first with the perceptually available before the more abstract, participation in externally controlled situations before self-determination is possible, a need for understanding that events take place in time and space, and the importance of noting the sequence in which events occur.

Perhaps it is worthwhile to emphasize that a child's ability to engage a given level of expectation or any other future-oriented process does not automatically assure planning ability at that same level. There is a lot of difference between knowing (e. g., expecting) and doing. Planning involves selection, execution, monitoring, backtracking, reformulating, and so on, all of which both affect and depend on forecasting processes. But forecasting alone is not enough. In brief, a level of skill in forecasting may be necessary but not sufficient for a comparable level of planning.

This is not to say that all of these elements must fall into place before the child can *participate* in the planning process. Rogoff (1990) made a compelling case for how social agents involve children in plans, from a very early age, that the agents construct and implement. Children can perform some parts of the implementation if other parts are supported by an adult or older child. Still, one can assume a role in a play without understanding the theme, the plot, or the responsibilities of the rest of the cast.

A full appreciation of the big picture requires an understanding of what is, what can be, and how to make it so. This understanding requires forethought and forecasting, essential ingredients for the planning process.

ACKNOWLEDGMENTS

Preparation of this manuscript was supported by a research grant from NICHD (HD20026) to the author and was carried out while M. M. H. was supposed by NIMH Research Scientist Award (MH00367). Helpful comments on earlier draft were made by Janette B. Benson, Joan Bihun, Sarah Friedman, Gary Haith, Ellin Scholnick, and Tara Wass.

REFERENCES

Arehart, D. M., & Haith, M. M. (1992, May). *Infants' use of visual landmarks in forming expectations for complex sequences*. Poster presented at International Conference of Infant Studies, Miami, FL.

Arehart, D. M., & Haith, M. M. (1990, June). *Evidence for space–time rule transfer in 13-week-old infants*. Poster presented at the meetings of the Developmental Psychobiology Research Group, Estes Park, CO.

Baillargeon, R. (1986). Representing the existence and the location of hidden objects: Object permanence in 6- and 8-month-old infants. *Cognition, 23*, 21–41.

Bandura, A. (1992). Social cognitive theory. In R. Vasta (Ed.), *Six theories of child development* (pp. 1–60). Philadelphia: Jessica Kingsley.

Benson, J. (1994). The origins of future orientation in the everyday lives of 9- to 36-month-old infants. In M. M. Haith, J. B. Benson, R. J. Roberts, Jr., & B. F. Pennington (Eds.), *The development of future-oriented processes*. Chicago: University of Chicago Press.

Benson, J. B., Cherny, S. S., Haith, M. M., & Fulker, D. W. (1993). Rapid assessment of infant predictors of adult IQ: Midtwin/Midparent analyses. *Developmental Psychology, 29*, 434–447.

Benson, J. B., Haith, M. M. Bihun, J. T., Lanthier, E., & Thomas, M. (1992). *A questionnaire to assess the development of future-oriented processes in infants and toddlers*. Poster presented at International Conference of Infant Studies, Miami, FL.

Bihun, J. T., Lanthier, E. & Haith, M. M. (1994). *Time limits on infant working memory in the Visual Expectation Paradigm*. Presented at the Biennial Conference on Human Development, Pittsburgh, PA.

Canfield, R. L. & Haith, M. M. (1991). Active expectations in 2- and 3-month-old infants: Complex event sequences. *Developmental Psychology, 27*, 198–208.

Cocking, R. R., & Copple, C. E. (1987). Social influences on representational awareness: Plans for representing and plans as representation. In S. L. Friedman, E. K. Scholnick, & R. R. Cocking (Eds.), *Blueprints for thinking: The role of planning in cognitive development* (pp. 428–465). Cambridge, England: Cambridge University Press.

Cohen, L. B., & Strauss, M. S. (1979). Concept acquisition in the human infant. *Child Development, 50*, 419–424.

Covington, M. (1987). Instruction in problem solving and planning. In S. L. Friedman, E. K. Scholnick, & R. R. Cocking (Eds.) *Blueprints for thinking: The role of planning in cognitive development* (pp. 469–511). Cambridge, England: Cambridge University Press.

Dougherty, T. M., & Haith, M. M. (1993, March). *Relations between manual RT, visual RT, and IQ*. Presented at the meetings of the Society for Research in Child Development, New Orleans, LA.

De Lisi, R. (1987). A cognitive–developmental model of planning. In S. L. Friedman, E. K. Scholnick, & R. R. Cocking (Eds.), *Blueprints for thinking: The role of planning in cognitive development* (pp. 79–109). Cambridge, England: Cambridge University Press.

DiLalla, L. F., Thompson, L. A., Plomin, R., Phillips, K., Fagan, J. F., Haith, M. M., Cyphers, L. H., & Fulker, D. W. (1990). Infant predictors of preschool and adult IQ: A study of infant twins and their parents. *Developmental Psychology, 26*, 759–769.

Friedman, S. L., Scholnick, E. K., & Cocking, R. R. (Eds.). (1987). *Blueprints for thinking: The role of planning in cognitive devlopment*. Cambridge, England: Cambridge University Press.

Friedman, W. (1990). *About time*. Cambridge, MA: MIT Press.

Goodnow, J. (1987). Social aspects of planning. In S. L. Friedman, E. K. Scholnick, and R. R. Cocking (Eds.), *Blueprints for thinking: The role of planning cognitive development* (pp. 179–201). Cambridge, England: Cambridge University Press.

Haith, M. M., Benson, J. B., & Roberts, R. J., Jr., & Pennington, B. F. (1996). *The development of future-oriented processes*. Chicago: University of Chicago Press.

Haith, M. M. & Campos, J. J. (1977). Human infancy. *Annual Review of Psychology, 28*, 251–293.

Haith, M. M., Hazan, C., & Goodman, G. S. (1988). Expectation and anticipation of dynamic visual events by 3.5-month-old babies. *Child Development, 59*, 467–479.

Haith, M. M., & McCarty, M. (1990). Stability of visual expectations at 3.0 months of age. *Developmental Psychology, 26*, 68–74.

Haith, M. M., Wentworth, N., & Canfield, R. L. (1993). The formation of expectations in early infancy. In C. Rovee-Collier & L. P. Lipsitt (Eds.), *Advances in infancy research* (pp. 251–297). Norwood, NJ: Ablex.

Harris, P. (1983). Infant cognition. In M. M. Haith & J. Campos (Eds.), *Handbook of child psychology: Vol. II. Infancy and developmental psychobiology* (pp. 689–782). New York: Wiley.

Kreitler, S., & Kreitler, H. (1987a). Plans and planning: Their motivational and cognitive antecedents. In S. L. Friedman, E. K. Scholnick, & R. R. Cocking (Eds.), *Blueprints for thinking: The role of planning in cognitive development* (pp. 110–178). Cambridge, England: Cambridge University Press.

Kreitler, S., & Kreitler, H. (1987b). Conceptions and processes of planning: The developmental perspective. In S. L. Friedman, E. K. Scholnick, & R. R. Cocking (Eds.), *Blueprints for thinking: The role of planning in cognitive development* (pp. 205–272). Cambridge, England: Cambridge University Press.

Lamb, M. E., & Malkin, C. M. (1986). The development of social expectations in distress-relief sequences: A longitudinal study. *International Journal of Behavioral Development, 9*, 235–249.

Lanthier, E., & Haith, M. M. (1993). *Infants' performance in a double- or triple-alternating sequence in the Visual Expectation Paradigm.* Presented at the meetings of the Society for Research in Child Development, New Orleans, LA.

Leslie, A. M. (1987). Pretense and representation: The origins of "theory of mind." *Psychological Review, 94*, 412–426.

Ludemann, P. M., & Nelson, C. A. (1988). Categorical representation of facial expression by 7-month-old infants. *Developmental Psychology, 24*, 492–501.

Mann, J. M., Tarantola, D. J. M., & Netter, T. W. (1992). *AIDS in the world.* Cambridge, MA: Harvard University Press.

McCarty, M. E., Haith, M. M., & Robinson, N. S. (1988, April). *Stability of visual expectations of 3-month-olds.* Poster presented at the International Conference on Infant Studies, Washington, DC.

McGillicuddy-De Lisi, A.V., De Lisi, R., Flaugher, J., & Sigel, I. E. (1987). Familial influences on planning. In S. L. Friedman, E. K. Scholnick, & R. R. Cocking (Eds.), *Blueprints for thinking: The role of planning in cognitive development* (pp. 395–427). Cambridge, England: Cambridge University Press.

Meltzoff, A. N., & Moore, M. K. (1992). Early imitation within a functional framework: The importance of person identity, movement, and development. *Infant Behavior and Development, 15*, 479–505.

Moore, K. C. (1896). The mental development of a child. *Psychological Review Monograph. Supplement., 1* (3).

Nelson, K. (1993). Events, narratives, memories: What develops? In C. Nelson (Ed.), *Memory and affect in development: Minnesota Symposium on Child Psychology* (Vol. 26, pp. 1–24). Hillsdale, NJ: Lawrence Erlbaum Associates.

Pea, R. D., & Hawkins, J. (1987). Planning in a chore-scheduling task. In S. L. Friedman, E. K. Scholnick, & R. R. Cocking (Eds.), *Blueprints for thinking: The role of planning in cognitive development* (pp. 273–302). Cambridge, England: Cambridge University Press.

Piaget, J. (1976). *The grasp of consciousness: Action and concept in the young child.* Cambridge, MA: Harvard University Press.

Piaget, J. (1978). *Success and understanding.* Cambridge, MA: Harvard University Press.

Rogoff, B. (1990). *Apprenticeship in thinking.* New York: Oxford University Press.

Rogoff, B., Gauvain, M., & Gardner, W. (1987). Children's adjustment of plans to circumstances. In S. L. Friedman, E. K. Scholnick, & R. R. Cocking (Eds.), *Blueprints for thinking: The role of planning cognitive development* (pp. 303–320). Cambridge, England: Cambridge University Press.

Scholnick, E. K., & Friedman, S. L. (1987). The planning construct in the psychological literature. In S. L. Friedman, E. K. Scholnick, & R. R. Cocking (Eds.), *Blueprints for thinking: The role of planning cognitive development* (pp. 33–38). Cambridge, England: Cambridge University Press.

Tulving, E. (1985). Memory and consciousness. *Canadian Psychology, 26*, 1–12.

Wentworth, N., & Haith, M. M. (1987, April). *Reaction and anticipation in infant's tracking of visual movement.* Paper presented at the meetings of the Society for Research in Child Development, Baltimore, MD.

Wentworth, N., & Haith, M. M. (1992). Event-specific expectations of 2- and 3-month-old infants. *Developmental Psychology, 28*, 842–850.

3

The Development of Planning: It's About Time

Janette B. Benson
University of Denver

Much of our daily planning presupposes certain expectations regarding the regularity of the temporal location and the rate of occurrence of events....it would have been almost impossible to plan our lives were we to be totally in the dark as to what might take place when, how often, in what order, and how long.

—Eviatar Zerubavel (1981, p. 13)

The formulation of plans is influenced by past experience, is executed in real present time, and is usually directed toward a future goal. As is true for all behavior, planning occurs in time, is ordered by time, and is experienced over time. Many of our plans are based on knowing when an event will take place (e.g., the plane leaves at 6:15), the likelihood of how often an event occurs (e.g., the 6:15 flight may be late but rarely leaves early), the order of events (e.g., one should be at the boarding gate *before* the flight leaves), and how long an event will take (e.g., the drive to the airport always takes twice as long as it should). Temporal knowledge includes an understanding of the sequence, duration, frequency, and location of events and actions. Although all components of temporal understanding are important, the following discussion focuses primarily on temporal sequence knowledge and its importance for the acquisition of skill in planning.

The concept of time is fundamental to planning behavior. We may plan because we think it will save time (Kreitler & Kreitler, 1987a), or planning may be opportunistic when we realize that there may not be enough time to generate a plan in advance (Rogoff, Gauvain, & Gardner, 1987). However, with few exceptions (e.g., Piaget's (1969) analysis in *The Child's Conception of Time*), the relation between the development of temporal knowledge and the acquisition of skill in planning has enjoyed only passing reference. Why?

One reason is that insufficient attention has been paid to the origins and development of specific cognitive skills that are important for planning. A developmental approach encourages a consideration of how component skills contribute to acquiring planning skill—an approach that would naturally reveal how critical an understanding of time is to planning. Unfortunately, few have adopted this approach in the study of planning. For example, Scholnick and Friedman (1993) criticized the tendency of planning researchers and theorists to conceptualize planning as a monolithic skill, instead of recognizing that different component processes and various motivational and contextual variables influence planning behavior. We (Benson & Haith, 1995; Haith, chapter 2, this volume) also questioned the prevailing tendency in the planning literature to treat planning activity as if it were a singular capacity that emerges in full-blown form. When age-related changes in planning skill are found, they are usually discussed in terms of advances facilitated by general cognitive growth, such as increases in cognitive capacity, efficiency, flexibility, and complexity. Because planning has been viewed as a singular entity, few new insights have been gained about what specific skills contribute to the acquisition of skill in planning, and how planning abilities generally evolve in early development.

In this chapter I argue that temporal abilities are fundamental to learning how to plan because they contribute to how young children come to understand, formulate, and execute a sequence of actions in time that are directed toward obtaining a desired goal. I also argue that the temporal abilities that are key to the acquisition of skill in planning originate early in life from everyday routines that are defined by their temporal sequence and regularity. Family factors contribute to the development of temporal understanding through the child's socialization into the matrix of daily activities and family routines that constitute the patterning of everyday life (Nelson, 1986, 1989, 1991; Norton, 1993; Savage-Rumbaugh, 1990). From this early exposure to everyday routines, young children learn how events are ordered in time, which events lead to particular results, and how to initiate and participate with others in a sequence of actions that leads to a desired outcome.

A discussion of the development of temporal knowledge is important in its own right. However, the review here is selective, as the intent is to support the argument that the development of planning skill is contingent on an understanding of temporal sequence. Although children's temporal knowledge is emphasized as an important component skill for planning, other important skills, such as verbal representational abilities, are discussed as they are certainly involved in the planning process. Also covered is our recent work that examines developmental trends across categories of future orientation that are related to children's development of temporal knowledge, language, and planning skill. Then, different conceptual models are examined to explain how early knowledge of temporal sequence is acquired, especially within the context of social interaction that is part of everyday family routines. These models are helpful for thinking about how children are influenced by the time language they hear, and its impact on the development of planning skill. Evidence is presented from a "timeline" methodology that explores the temporal representations that young children form for the sequence of daily activities in past and future time. Finally, the relations among children's knowledge of temporal sequence, future orientation, exposure to parental time talk during routine activities, and the development of planning skill, especially within the everyday family context are discussed.

WHAT CHILDREN KNOW ABOUT THE TEMPORAL SEQUENCE OF EVENTS IN PAST, PRESENT, AND FUTURE TIME

Time is an abstract entity that can be experienced and conceived in a variety of ways (Levin & Zakay, 1989). Researchers have studied various aspects of the human experience of time, including time perception, time estimation, time orientation, time representation, use of conventional time tools (e.g., clocks and calendars), and so on (e.g., see Macar, Pouthas, & Friedman, 1992). This present discussion is limited to Western, linear conceptions of time and focuses on what children know about those facets of time that are most relevant to planning. These include concepts that pertain to the ability to sequence events that span past (*before*), present (*now*), and future (*after*) time.

The empirical literature on the developmental psychology of time indicates that knowledge about time concepts emerges rather slowly in childhood. There is general agreement that it is typically not until late childhood, and in some instances not until adolescence, that most adult-like concepts of time are acquired by children (Friedman, 1990a, 1992a; 1992b; Lewkowicz, 1989), but there are many disagreements about when and how specific time notions evolve. Part of this controversy stems from the type of evidence that is examined. Evidence for what infants and young children know about time comes primarily from two sources, nonlanguage-based and language-based behavior.

NONLANGUAGE-BASED EVIDENCE OF TEMPORAL SEQUENCE KNOWLEDGE

Philosophers and psychologists have long speculated about what young infants and children know about time. For example, Kant (1965) reasoned that time perception must be innate because it is such a fundamental category for the organization of human experience. The French philosopher Guyau (cited in Droit & Pouthas, 1992), wrote in 1890, "When a child is hungry, it cries and extends it arms towards its nurse: This is the seed of the idea of future." In contrast to Kant, Guyau suggested that it is through subjective experience that young children learn about time. In his example, the infant experiences a sequence of events that are linked in time and result in a future end state—crying and gesturing leads to being fed by a nurse. Because we live in a world that is highly regulated by time, it should not be surprising that early experiences contribute to the acquisition of time knowledge. More recently, developmental psychologists have reported evidence to suggest that even before birth, infants experience regular temporal events that may contribute to the establishment of an early temporal framework from which to organize experience.

Biobehavioral Rhythms

As early as 21 weeks after conception, researchers have observed regular, cyclical movements in the human fetus (Robertson, 1985). After birth, these and other intrinsic biobehavioral rhythms (e.g., sleep–wake cycles, feeding cycles, stereotyped rhythmical movements) may provide infants with an initial temporal framework. At a minimum, this framework permits infants to crudely mark the duration of cycles of activity (Lewkowicz, 1989) because of their regular onsets and offsets, and also to partition time in terms of "now, and not now". These rhythmic cycles may also provide infants with very elementary information about temporal sequence as the offset of one activity marks the onset of another. Eventually these experiences lead to an awareness that certain activities are linked in time in a particular order. For example, infants come to notice that hunger and crying are usually followed by eating.

During the first year of life, there are indications that temporal appreciation grows. By at least 3 months of age, infants can discriminate the relative temporal order of auditory elements when they are presented in rhythmic sequences (Demany, McKenzie, & Vurpillot, 1977), and they can make anticipatory visual fixations to the location of a target before it becomes visible, based on prior experience with a temporal sequence (Haith, Wentworth, & Canfield, 1993). Before the end of the first year, infants make anticipatory hand adjustments in preparation for contact with moving or stationary objects (Hofsten, 1980; Hofsten & Ronnqvist, 1988; Lockman, Ashmead, & Bushnell, 1984; Wentworth, Benson, & Haith, 1996).

These early temporal abilities illustrate that young infants are sensitive to temporal sequence information and that they can and do adapt their behavior to events situated in past, present, and future time. Nevertheless, there are limitations on early temporal abilities. In these various experimental situations, infants are responding to events separated by brief time intervals (e.g., 1,000 ms interstimulus interval [ISI] in Haith et al.'s [1993] Visual Expectation Paradigm) and with relatively rapid behavioral responses (e.g., ballistic reaches or quick visual fixations). These time-sensitive behaviors are likely precursors to later temporal sequence knowledge, but they seem very different from the higher-order conceptual skills that underlie the ability to organize a sequence of events in time such as those that are involved in traditional planning behavior. The type of means–ends behaviors that Piaget studied provide a good example of the sensorimotor skills that are relevant for planning, and that fall between these extremes.

Analyses of Means–Ends Behavior

Piaget's (1952, 1954) analysis of the differentiation of means-to-ends actions provided the basis for his account of how infants create a series of actions that are ordered through time. According to Piaget (1952, 1954), it is not until sensorimotor stage 4, at approximately 8 to 12 months of age, that infants begin to differentiate means from ends, a necessary step for coordinating a series of intentionally ordered actions to achieve a desired goal. During sensorimotor stage 3, infants will repeat actions when they discover, by chance, that the action produces an interesting effect (e.g., the repeated shaking of a rattle to hear the noise it makes). However, these secondary circular reactions did not qualify as planful means or as evidence of intentionally ordered actions for Piaget, because: (a) the relation between action and effect initially occurs by chance; (b) there is little evidence that the infant can distinguish the action from its result—it is a package deal; and (c) there is almost no systematic variation by the infant of the means that are tied to its effect (e.g., the infant does not roll the rattle in addition to shaking it to hear its noise).

During sensorimotor stage 4, infants begin to show early signs of more planful means–ends behavior in which a series of actions is directed toward goals that are coordinated in time. For example, infants will remove a cover to obtain a toy, will pull a cloth upon which an object rests to bring it within reach, and will remove an obstacle to retrieve a toy (Piaget, 1952, 1954; Willatts, 1990). Still, Piaget argued that infants are limited in their appreciation of means–ends relations and temporal sequence in two ways. First, infants only appreciate the temporally ordered behaviors that are tied to their own actions, but not those that they observe. For example, Piaget (1954, obs. 49 and 50) described how Lucienne watched him successively hide an object in three different locations, but confined her search to the first and second hiding locations, and not the third location where the object was last seen. It is not until the beginning of sensorimotor stage 5, at about 1 year of age, that infants will search at the last place an object was seen when it is hidden in successive locations (Piaget, 1954). Second, infants are unable to modify a series of coordinated behaviors used in a specific situation when the situation changes. For example, Piaget (1952, obs. 148) described how Laurent was able to pull a cushion within reach to obtain an object resting on it. However, when Piaget changed the situation by placing the object alongside, but not on the cushion, Laurent still pulled the cushion as he did when the object was resting on it. The modification of old means to adjust to changed circumstances does not usually occur until after sensorimotor stage 5, or until the first birthday.

By the beginning of the second year, infants show flexibility in sequencing their actions, and they are able to create longer chains of actions, ordered in time, to obtain a desired goal. Infants show steady improvements in being able to order their actions to make either reaching or crawling detours when faced with barriers (Bruner, 1970; Lockman, 1984; McKenzie & Bigelow, 1986). Also, 12-month-olds can extend and chain simple means-to-ends skills in a multistep problem-solving task (Willatts, 1990). In one task, 12-month-olds were able to remove an obstacle in order to pull a cloth to bring within reach a string that, when pulled, delivered a desirable toy. Although these findings move us closer to what looks like evidence of early skill in planning, this conclusion is tentative at best. There is no way to determine, in this task situation, how much of the ordered action sequence was planned in advance of action (Willatts, 1990). This raises the issue of what is known about memory and the representation of temporal sequence in infancy and early childhood—the topic addressed next. However, we can conclude that there is evidence that knowledge of temporal sequence expands during the second year as infants appear to be able to order longer series of sequenced actions over time, as demonstrated in a variety of different situations.

The Recall and Representation of Temporally Ordered Events: Evidence from Deferred and Elicited Imitation

Planning necessarily involves the mental representation of images, symbols, and actions that are organized in time (Cocking & Copple, 1987; Kreitler & Kreitler, 1987b; Scholnick & Friedman, 1987). When a person plans, there is a deliberate thinking-through of the consequences of the various steps that lead to a desired goal or end state. Because representational abilities are crucial for planning, we need to consider what is known about young children's abilities to represent and recall a series of temporally sequenced events.

Among other things, the recall of temporal sequences involves the ability to reproduce previously seen acts in the absence of perceptual cues that would reveal, or prompt, their temporal order. In older children and adults, evidence of recall is typically based on language, which, for obvious reasons, is not a useful index for research with very young children. However, researchers have used deferred imitation as evidence of representational abilities in early childhood. Deferred imitation is the ability to recall a previously seen sequence of actions by reproducing the action sequence itself, after some delay period. Some have suggested that deferred imitation occurs very early in infancy (Meltzoff & Moore, 1977; 1989; 1992), often in the form of facial gestures (e.g., tongue protrusion). However, other researchers, most notably Piaget (1962), argued that these early behaviors are only examples of trained pseudo-imitative behavior and that true deferred imitation occurs later in development as a means to represent and recall a sequence of past events. For example, Piaget (1962, obs. 52) reported that his daughter Jacqueline, at 16 months, showed deferred imitation by screaming, trying to move her playpen, and stamping her feet, almost 12 hours after witnessing these behaviors from a playmate who was in a bad temper.

Another index of young children's abilities to represent and recall temporally ordered information is performance on elicited imitation tasks. In a series of programmatic experiments, Bauer and her colleagues (Bauer & Hertsgaard, 1993; Bauer & Mandler, 1989, 1990, 1992) reported that children as young as 11.5 months of age use knowledge of temporal order to recall a sequence of two-act events, and by 20 months, children show relatively high levels of recall for three-act sequences. These claims are based on evidence from an elicited imitation paradigm in which young infants are encouraged to imitate a sequence of actions after they watch an adult use props to model either two- or three-act event sequences. The logic of the paradigm is that if young children can imitate the modelled temporal sequences, they must have encoded the temporal information during its presentation and then retrieved this information from a formed representation (Bauer & Hertsgaard, 1993). Based on analyses that compare the number of reproduced modelled acts and correct pairs of modelled acts that children perform during baseline, immediate imitation, and deferred imitation (e.g., a delay of up to 2 weeks in Bauer & Mandler, 1989), Bauer and colleagues reported that very young children can accurately recall temporally organized actions based on representations of event sequences.

Sequenced events unfold over time, and so by definition they are temporally related, but other relations among events are sometimes possible. Using an elicited-imitation paradigm, researchers have also manipulated temporal sequences as a function of whether the relation among the modelled acts were novel–enabling, novel–arbitrary, or familiar (i.e., based on script-like routine activities). Novel–enabling sequences involved a series of modelled acts that were logically linked to an end state, but were unfamiliar (e.g., putting a button in one cup, covering the first cup with a second one, and then shaking them to make a rattle). Bauer used the term *enabling*, rather than *causal*, because enabling relations specify that "one action in a sequence is both temporally prior to and necessary for a second in the same sequence" to produce an outcome, but the first event does not "cause" the second event (Bauer & Hertsgaard, 1993, p. 1205). The novel–arbitrary sequences included novel acts that were ordered in time, but their sequence was capricious because it did not alter the end state (e.g., putting an animal figure and blocks in a toy truck and putting a sticker on the figure). The familiar sequences involved familiar acts that were based on typical routines (e.g., bathing or feeding a teddy bear).

In general, findings across several studies showed that elicited imitation performance was poorest during imitation for novel–arbitrary sequences and best for the novel–enabling and the familiar sequences. Although performance tended to be poorest for the novel–arbitrary sequences, findings were not always consistent with respect to whether performance was better for the familiar or novel–enabling sequences. The youngest infants (i.e., 11.5 months of age) varied in whether their imitation performance was best for familiar or the novel–enabling sequences as a function of the baseline, immediate, or delayed recall condition (Bauer & Hertsgaard, 1993). Nevertheless, these findings do suggest that early in life infants are sensitive to both temporal and logical information about the relations among events that are presented in sequence. Moreover, because older infants are better at recalling the sequence of familiar events compared with novel–enabling events, we can also conclude that they likely possess procedural knowledge about the temporal sequence of many familiar, everyday routines.

Representation of Temporal Sequence and Planning.   Although Bauer's research focused on factors that influence representation and recall of temporally sequenced information, they also bear on the development of planning skill.

First, the findings provided impressive evidence that young children are sensitive to temporal sequence information that organizes a series of separate acts that they have experienced both in the immediate and longer-term past. Young children apparently use this temporal information to assist their recall as they can imitate both individual acts and temporally paired acts from a longer event sequence. Second, young children are sensitive to the logical relations among sequenced acts as shown by their better recall of enabling or familiar event sequences compared to arbitrary acts that are ordered in time. These data imply that by the second year, children notice information about the relation between sequential acts that lead to an end state. Planning involves the linking of separate actions over time that must be enacted in a logical or causal order to produce a desired end state. The evidence reviewed earlier supports the claim that, by the second year, children have some ability to represent a familiar sequence of events that occur in a logical order—a skill that is centrally involved in planning.

One problem, however, is that young children often do not demonstrate planning skill at a level that is consistent with this conclusion. If young children possess the skills to sequence events in time and they are more likely to do so when the events are logically related to an end state than not, then one might expect that they should be able to plan or generate the necessary steps that are required to reach an end or goal state. The empirical literature does not support this expectation. In a footnote, Bauer and Mandler (1989) described preliminary data that are particularly relevant. They presented 24-month-olds with only the end state of the "button-in-two-cups-to-make-a-rattle" sequence described previously. Then, without having seen either the props dismantled or the modelled sequence of how to put them together, the children were asked to make the rattle. On the basis of having seen only the final goal-state of the rattle, few of the 2-year-olds (25%) were able to generate the sequence of actions required to make the rattle. However, all of the children were able to imitate the sequence of acts to make the rattle after watching an adult model do so. Thus, there is an apparent discrepancy between possessing some of the requisite skills involved in being able to plan (i.e., ordering events in time) and actually doing so (e.g., generating the sequence of events that lead to a goal).

This apparent discrepancy raises several interesting possibilities for how skill in planning might develop. The ability to sequence causally related events in time is necessary but not sufficient for planning. Other factors that influence when children will engage in planning must be considered, such as their motivation to do so. For example, in Bauer and Mandler's study, perhaps the 24-month-olds could indeed generate or plan the sequence of actions to produce the rattle, but they chose not to do so when encouraged by the experimenters. They did produce the sequence, but only after they watched the experimenter model it, perhaps because of the "game-like" nature that often accompanies imitative exchanges. Maybe it was simply more socially motivating for 2-year-olds to imitate the sequence to make a rattle than to produce it when requested.

A second possibility is that it is far easier for young children to reproduce a sequence of events that they have just seen by copying it than it is for them to generate an original sequence of events never before seen. The latter skill more closely resembles what we mean by true planning, where one must invent a novel sequence of actions to reach a desired goal. The ability to "re-produce" a sequence of actions based on seeing those actions modeled by another person clearly involves the representation of the modeled sequence, but resembles planning only with respect to following a sequence of actions that leads to a desired end state. The fact that young children can reproduce a modeled sequence of actions is a key component of planning, and may be an important step in how young children learn about planning from others.

A third possibility is that young children may provide evidence of planning in one situation (e.g., recall of temporal sequence in an elicited imitation task), but not in another (e.g., generating a sequence of acts that result in an end state from information based only on the end state). Little is known about how young children come to generalize complex skills like planning over a variety of contexts. A key question, yet unanswered, is whether young children learn to plan first by noticing that routine sequences of actions lead to desired results, or whether they first have a firmly established goal in mind and then learn to derive the steps required to obtain it.

A fourth possibility is that the apparent discrepancy between children's manifestation of some of the skills involved in planning and their inconsistency in effective planning may reflect more about currently used research procedures than children's actual abilities. For example, children may be more inclined to exhibit planning behavior in some situations than in others, and they may be less inclined to do so in most currently used laboratory situations. We have few established research paradigms in which young children can demonstrate their planning abilities. Yet, there are rich descriptions in the research literature of the behavior of young children that seem planful, but our knowledge is limited because they often come from parental observations based on only a few children. For example, Piaget (1952, obs. 181, p. 339) described evidence of planning when Jacqueline, at 20 months, put down on the ground the blades of grass she was holding in each hand to open a closed door, and then picked up the blades of grass again before passing through the doorway. Or consider the following example given by the parent of a 15-month-old (Benson, 1994),

> She has a videotape of *Bambi* that she loves. She says, "*Bambi, Bambi*" as she beats her hands on the television screen. Then she'll say, "*Bambi, Bambi*. O.K.," to mimic us giving her permission to watch it. Then she tries to put the videotape in [the VCR]. She'll hit the buttons on the remote control and on the TV to try to turn it on. When none of that works, she'll just stand in front of the TV and scream.

There are a few exceptions to anecdotal descriptions of planning in young children (e.g., Wellman, Fabricius, & Sophian, 1985; Willatts, 1990), but almost no accepted experimental paradigms exist that are appropriate for young children in which planning has been operationalized and systematically studied as is the case for older children and adults, such as the Tower of Hanoi (Klahr & Robinson, 1981) or errand-running tasks (Hayes-Roth & Hayes-Roth, 1979). Benson (1994) argued previously that we need laboratory tasks that are based on real-world, everyday situations. We also need rich descriptions of young children's everyday behaviors that are related to planning before we will be able to design meaningful laboratory paradigms from which to systematically study young children's ability to plan.

The evidence examined thus far suggests that young children appear to possess procedural knowledge of the temporal sequence of familiar events that lead to a goal, but do they have explicit knowledge about the sequence that underlies ordered events? Because planning involves both procedural and declarative knowledge (De Lisi, 1987), the explosion in language skills during the second year is likely to affect the development of both temporal sequence knowledge and subsequent skill in planning.

Language is a tool that supports higher-order mental processes that are key for internalizing what children initially learn through their actions (Piaget, 1962) and for imposing order and structure on action (Vygotsky, 1978). Although some of the component skills that are fundamental to the acquisition of skill in planning are likely to be in place long before language, it is important to ask when children are able to generate verbally a sequence of actions that unfolds over time and that leads to a future goal.

LANGUAGE-BASED EVIDENCE OF TEMPORAL SEQUENCE KNOWLEDGE

Receptive and productive language each offer additional avenues for examining young children's abilities understand and represent a temporal sequence of events. At the same time, there is not always a one-to-one relation between what a child knows and what a child says early in development. Young children possess a practical or procedural knowledge of aspects of temporal sequence long before they demonstrate this knowledge with traditional indices of language. In the context of a familiar routine, children can correctly sequence separate acts by the second year—approximately one year prior to when they can correctly use and understand words that indicate temporal sequence knowledge, such as, *before*, and *after* (Carni & French, 1984; French & Nelson, 1985).

Language provides children with the means to talk about events in time, which makes reference to events in time more concrete. Language also permits children to move beyond the "here and now," because language permits reference to events that are displaced in time (e.g., past or future). Instead of depending on images or actions to represent experience, children can use language to reconstruct the past and talk about what might happen in the future. Therefore, advances in language should have an impact on how children conceptualize time, and advances in both language and temporal knowledge should influence skill in planning. Katherine Nelson (1991, p. 280) made this point about the interdependent relation between thought and language in development when she wrote,

> ...language cannot begin to be acquired without a cognitive, that is, conceptual base, but as soon as first language forms appear, the conceptual base becomes transformed. The transformation continues through the course of language development, which does not end in early to middle childhood as commonly supposed, but continues through the life span. Language continuously enters into and changes prior conceptions. Language neither replaces nor becomes identical with cognition, rather, the two continuously interact.

Linguistic Markers of Time

Linguistic evidence of knowledge of temporal sequence involves the expression and comprehension of the ordered relations among events in past, present, and future time. Time is expressed in language by grammatical structures and lexically through word meaning (Nelson, 1991). Grammatical structures, such as tense, modality, and aspect, are the most important ways that time concepts are expressed in language (Bates, Elman, & Li, 1994; Weist, 1989). The grammatical encoding of time has been studied most extensively, but there is surprisingly little work on children's lexical encoding of time terms. The grammatical encoding of time concepts is thought to be acquired before lexical encoding (Nelson, 1991).

Grammatical Markers of Time.   The use of tense, modality, and aspect interact in languages such as English that use tense to mark time (Weist, 1989). In English, inflections are added to verb tenses to indicate the time of an event in the past and present (e.g., the inflection "-ed" indicates the past and "s" indicates present), but there is no inflection for future verb forms. Unlike past events that we are usually certain have occurred, there is often uncertainty about whether future events will actually occur. Modality codes for this feature of necessity and possibility. Modal auxiliaries (e.g., may, will, must) are used to create modal verbs that, in turn, indicate both the future character of the thought and the likelihood that an event will occur (Harner, 1982). Although tense inflections and modality signify the occurrence of an event *in time,* aspect refers to events *over time.* Aspect is also conveyed by inflection and indicates whether an event has begun, is in progress (imperfective aspect) or is completed (perfective aspect; Bates et al., 1994; Pinker, 1994). The following grammatical forms provide an example of how tense and aspect are used to convey information about an event in and over time: *He ate* (past tense); *He eats* (present tense); *He will eat* (future tense); *He is eating* (imperfective aspect); and *He has eaten* (perfective aspect).   There is disagreement about whether aspect is acquired before tense (Bloom, Lahey, Hood, Lifter, & Fiess, 1980) or vice versa (Nelson, 1991), but there is general agreement that children can use both tense and aspect before 2 years of age in their speech (Nelson, 1991).

Lexical Markers of Time.   Other features of language serve as temporal markers, and these features often are used to specify the meaning of temporal relations between and among objects or events. For example, temporal meaning is conveyed through terms that serve as adverbs (e.g., "later," "when," "yesterday"), prepositions (e.g., "at," "after"), and conjunctions (e.g., "and," "or"). The basic grammatical forms of tense and aspect are acquired before children understand and produce lexical terms to specify temporal concepts (Nelson, 1991). However, much less research information exists about children's lexical encoding of temporal concepts.

Language researchers use two basic strategies to uncover what children know about temporal concepts—data from children's spontaneous language production, and children's responses on comprehension tasks. Over 40 years ago, Ames (1946) recorded the spontaneous "time talk" of young children and found that children between the ages of 2.5 and 3 years used temporal adverbs. However, children this young often used these terms incorrectly (e.g., "Yesterday I will go to the zoo"). In a comprehension study, Harner (1981) presented children between 3 and 7 years of age with a sequence of three pictures and sentences that included past and future verbs. Harner reported that while older children performed better than younger ones, yet even children as old as 7 had difficulty correctly selecting the referent for future verbs (i.e., correctly responding 69% of the time) and the referent for past verbs (i.e., correctly responding 84% of the time).

It is important to examine children's language abilities as well as those cognitive skills thought to be associated with temporal understanding. For example, fewer than a dozen studies have examined children's comprehension of "before" and "after," and Weist (1989) claimed that only two studies have examined both language and cognitive achievements related to children's understanding of "before" and "after" (Ferreiro & Sinclair, 1971; Trosberg, 1982). The findings suggest that children's linguistic comprehension is rooted in cognitive achievements that are not mastered until age 6 (e.g., performance on seriation and the understanding of reversibility shown in conservation tasks). Thus, children may use time words that suggest an understanding of temporal relations, such as "before" and "after," but until they can demonstrate an understanding of these concepts through the physical manipulation of objects, their linguistic comprehension of these terms is thought to be limited.

Relations Between Language and Cognition in Time Talk

Based on cross-linguistic evidence from languages as diverse as English and Polish, Weist (1989) proposed a four-stage model that illustrates the interdependencies between advances in language and cognition in children's acquisition of temporal expressions.

Following Weist's (1989) terminology, children come to coordinate tense and aspect through four stages or "time systems" over the first 5 years of life. Weist (1989) described these stages from the framework of three facets of time—event time, speech time, and reference time. *Event time* refers to the time when the event that is being discussed actually occurred. This is the ability to talk about an event by placing it in a temporal framework of the past, present, or future. *Speech time* is the time when the speaker is talking. This is simply the recognition that a speaker's utterances are situated in time, whether the content of speech refers to an event in the past, present, or future. Tense inflections are used to specify event time relative to speech time, such as when a speaker uses the past tense inflection to indicate that event time comes before speech time (Bates et al., 1994). Speakers can also refer to the time of an event at some time other than at the time they are talking (i.e., speech time). This is called *reference time*, and it is the speaker's ability to make references to the time of an event at any point in time, not just at speech time. Reference time permits the recognition that the time when the speaker talks about events can be temporally displaced just as events themselves are displaced in time. The coordination of speech time, event time, and reference time permits speakers to separate events in time, to talk about the relation between the time when events occur, and to talk freely about the forward and backward ordering of sequential events.

Stage 1: Speech Time.   The speech time system, or first stage, occurs from approximately 12 to 18 months. During this stage linguistic constructions are restricted to the "here-and-now." The only functional system is speech time, and the young child codes the event time and reference time as occurring only during speech time. The child's verbalizations appear to be devoid of tense, modality, or aspect (Bates et al., 1994); time talk appears stuck in the present. Children cannot yet verbally express what they know about temporal relations, nor do they have the representational skills to flexibly coordinate events in past, present, and future time.

Stage 2: Event Time.   The event time system emerges between 18 to 30 months of age. Weist (1989) argued that the event time system becomes separated from speech time during this second stage, but reference time is still embedded in speech time. Children recognize the status of an event as completed or ongoing and use aspect in their speech to denote the event's temporal status (e.g., "The milk is gone"). Time talk also goes beyond the "here and now," but is limited only to the coarse separation of "now" and "not now." Children can use past tense to talk about events that occurred in the past (e.g., "I fell"), but in their speech they do not distinguish between the immediate and longer-term past. Until children are able to mark reference time relative to speech time, they are not able to specify the time of an event relative to the time they talk about it (e.g., "I fell yesterday").

According to Weist, during stage 2, children can also refer to future events—speech time prior to event time—especially when expressing their desires (e.g., "I want it"). However, children seem to understand linguistic constructions that refer to the past earlier than those that refer to the future. Weist (1989) reported that children's performance on a comprehension test showed higher levels of correct responses to past tense (92%) than future tense (66%) at 2.5 years of age. Even though children now have the ability to use "displaced reference," that is to talk about and understand events in past or future time (Sachs, 1983), they are not yet able to talk about past and future events relative to each other or to any point in time.

Stage 3: Restricted Reference Time.   From approximately 30 to 36 months of age, reference time emerges in children's time talk, but event time is restricted to either reference time or speech time, but not both. Young children will refer to the timing of an event (e.g., "I fell yesterday"), but they do not yet talk about event time in relation to both speech and reference time (e.g., "I was gonna tell you that I fell yesterday"). Evidence for the understanding of reference time comes primarily from the use of adverbs that denote the time when the event occurs. For example, at this stage children will use time words, such as "yesterday," "today," or "tomorrow," or adverbial phrases, such as "when I grow up." The advantage of the restricted reference time system is that the three conceptual time systems are simultaneously functional in children's speech (Weist, 1989). However, although they can relate events in two time intervals, children cannot talk about a sequence of events that would span all intervals of past, present, and future time.

Whereas the achievements of the previous stages imply that time talk is rooted in children's knowledge of time concepts, at this stage there is a shift in the interdependent relation between language and cognition. Children often demonstrate language skills that, on the surface, suggest that they know more about time than they really do. Nelson (1991) referred to this strategy for acquiring words as "use before meaning" and noted that it is consistent with Vygotsky's (1978) position. This strategy involves children's correct linguistic use of words or phrases in appropriate situations from which they eventually can derive meaning. For example, in the analysis of a child's pre-bed conversations with her parents, Nelson (1991) described how Emily, who is precocious at 26 months, used the phrase "just a minute" after hearing it used by her father (e.g., "I will rock you for just a minute"). Although Emily used this adverbial phrase in a way that implies the coordination of reference time with event time (e.g., "Daddy came in just a minute and rocked me"), there is little evidence that Emily understood that "just a minute" referred to the temporal concept of duration (Nelson, 1991). Children have been observed to use temporal adverbs, such as "yesterday" and "tomorrow" as early as 2 years of age, but they also persist in making errors by confusing these two reference times until 3 years of age (Clark, 1985) and even older (Friedman, 1990a). Thus, Weist argued that it is not until the final stage that children understand and can use relational words to connect two points in time to a third, such as the sequence between two actions that will result in a particular outcome (e.g., "I wash and then dry my hands before I eat").

Stage 4: Free Reference Time.   At the last stage in Weist's framework, children between 36 and 52 months of age achieve the ability to verbally coordinate all three time system concepts without grammatical restriction. Children can establish a reference time that is either antecedent or subsequent to speech time, and they can relate event time to both speech time and reference time. The result is that during this last stage, children first use relational words, such as "before" and "after," to connect events in time, and they can do so when speaking from past, present, or future reference. Weist (1989) presented data to show that as early as 3 years of age, Polish children begin to generate utterances that involve the temporal sequencing of events (e.g., "I will throw [it] then I will pick [it] up" Weist, 1989, pp. 106–107). However, Weist (1989) also concluded that the bulk of the evidence suggests that it is not until 4 to 4.5 years of age that children's speech more generally indicates the free coordination of speech time, event time, and reference time. For example, across several different languages, the use of "before" and "after" does not occur until around 4.5 years (Weist, 1989). Furthermore, Weist (1989, p. 110) suggested that advances in cognitive development constrain children's verbal expressions of temporally ordered events, and, at this stage, children's spontaneous verbalizations "show a strong tendency to match the order of events referred to and the order of events in the world."

In general, there seems to be acceptance of the stage-like, developmental scheme suggested by Weist (e.g., Bates et al., 1994; Pouthas, Droit, & Jacquet, 1993). However, Nelson (1991) remarked that Weist's description of the coordination of speech time, event time, and reference time relations may not be as constrained in development as he suggested. Nelson (1991) cautioned that the evidence cited to support the claims of a close concurrence between cognitive skills and the linguistic expression of temporal relations is only slight. Few studies have directly examined what children actually know about temporal concepts when they use time talk; thus, it is difficult to evaluate the relation between cognition and language that underlies Weist's model of the development of temporal systems in language. It is clear that further research is needed to document the nature of the relation between advances in cognitive skills pertaining to the ordering of events in time, and children's linguistic expression of the temporal relations among ordered events.

Nelson (1991) suggested that there are interdependencies between cognition and language during development in general, and more specifically, with respect to children's temporal knowledge. She argued that temporal concepts are acquired through discourse about everyday events and grow as a function of the child's understanding and representation of events. An important area of study that requires attention from this viewpoint is children's expression of temporal concepts during discourse with others (Nelson, 1991, 1993). In particular, Nelson (1991) claimed that until there are more studies that examine how children actually talk about sequenced events with others, there is "little firm basis at the present time for expecting general cognitive constraints on the expression of temporal relations" (p. 298).

Time Language and Future-Oriented Processes

Few studies have examined parallels between cognition and language with respect to children's temporal development and how parents actually talk to children about sequenced events in the present or future (Nelson, 1993). However, we have some preliminary data, collected for another purpose (i.e., a study of the development of future-oriented processes) that are relevant. These data come from a recent questionnaire study of 286 parents with a child in one of six age groups between 12 and 42 months of age at 6-month intervals (Haith, Benson, Bihun, & Talmi, 1997). This study was primarily concerned with replicating and extending previously reported findings of age-related trends in six different domains of future-oriented processes (Benson, 1994).

Several have recently suggested that future-oriented processes are fundamental to progress in planning skill in early development (Benson & Haith, 1995; Haith, 1994; Haith, chapter 2, this volume; Haith, Benson, Roberts, & Pennington, 1994). By *future-oriented processes*, we mean behaviors and concepts related to "intentionality, goal setting, prediction, set, expectation, preparation, anticipation, planning, and feed forward computation" (Haith, Benson, Roberts, & Pennington, 1994, p. 3). The "Development of Future-Oriented Processes" questionnaire has already been described in detail (Benson, 1994), and so a full description is not included; rather, the focus is on items from this instrument that are relevant to evaluating an extension of Weist's framework to the early development of planning skills.

The "Development of Future-Oriented Processes" questionnaire asked parents to use a 5-point scale to rate how true 54 specific behaviors are in terms of their child's ability to perform them. The anchors of the rating scale range from "not at all true" to "always true" (for my child), and each response alternative was scored from 1 to 5, respectively. Each questionnaire item was stated in the form of a general statement, followed by a specific example (e.g., "My child has expectations for things that will happen. For example, my child expects someone to enter the house when hearing the doorbell"). Parents were encouraged to provide behavioral examples that were specific to their child. The use of a 5-point scale was designed to permit parents to judge the overall degree their child was able to perform particular types of future-oriented behaviors, rather than to force parents to make an absolute categorical judgement that their child displayed a specific behavior. Of 54 future-oriented processes items, a subset of seven items was identified as capturing the types of behaviors and verbalizations about temporally ordered events suggested by each of Weist's four stages. Moreover, these seven items represented four of the six identified domains of future-oriented processes (Benson, 1994), including "Goal Orientation," "Time Tools," "Expectations," and "Order/Sequence." With the exception of only one item that best mapped onto Weist's first stage, two questionnaire items were identified that exemplified each of the remaining three stages. These questionnaire items are shown in Table 3.1 for each of the four stages.

If there is a link between the developmental progression in how young children verbally represent temporal relations among events and the future-oriented processes items, then the mean parental ratings for the items, as categorized in Weist's stages, should show an orderly progression across each age group. That is, items thought to exemplify Weist's first stage should show the highest mean level of reported performance, and items thought to fall under stage 4 should show the lowest. Moreover, the mean level of reported performance for all items should increase systematically with age from 12 to 42 months. As shown in Fig. 3.1, this is exactly what was found when the means for the items for each stage were plotted.

The one questionnaire item that fit into Weist's stage 1 received the highest mean parental rating. Parents of 12-month-olds reported, on average, that it was "sometimes true" that their child could indicate a present want or desire (M = 2.96, SD = 1.43), but it was not until 42 months of age that parents, on average, reported that it was "always true" that their child could do so (M = 4.80, SD = 0.45). As expected, there was a significant main effect for age for this item (F (5,283) = 27.81, p < .0001). Post hoc analyses revealed that the 12-month-olds differed from all other age groups, the 18 month-olds differed from the 30-, 36-, and 42-month-olds; and the 24-month-olds differed from the 36- and 42-month-olds (p < .05).

As expected, the questionnaire items that exemplified Weist's stage 4 received the lowest mean parental rating. These items assessed children's ability to verbally represent a sequence of events. Not surprisingly, parents of 12-month-olds reported, on average, that it was "not at all true" that their

TABLE 3.1
Items from the Development of Future-Oriented Processes Questionnaire that Exemplify Weist's Stages of Time-Language Development.

Weist's Stage 1 (12–18 mo): Focus on the "here and now."

My child knows how to indicate that she or he wants desired things. [item 57a]

Weist's Stage 2 (18–30 mo): Focus on "now and not now," with reference to past and future.

My child asks about things that will happen in the future. [item 49a]

My child can tell me about things he or she wants to do later. [item 49b]

Weist's Stage 3 (30–36 mo): Can relate two points in time, but not their sequence.

My child asks about things that she or he was told would happen in the future but did not. [item 48]

My child can talk about things that will happen if they have happened before. [item 63]

Weist's Stage 4 (36–52 mo): Can coordinate several points in time and the sequence of events across time intervals.

My child says that some things follow other things. [item 49c]

My child can talk about a sequence of things that he or she will do. [item 52a]

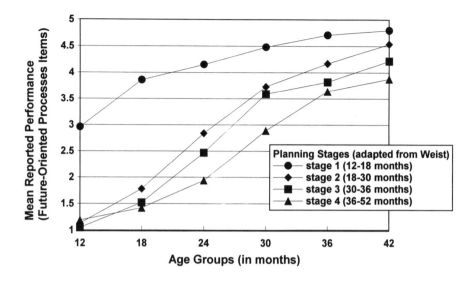

Note: N = 286 (n = 49, 49, 47, 46, 48, and 47 for respective age groups.)

FIG. 3.1.   Age trends for mean future-oriented processes items organized by stages of
planning skill (based on Weist's theory, 1989).

child could talk about the sequence of events (M = 1.18, SD = .51), yet the
parents of 42-month-olds reported, on average, that it was "almost always
true" that their child could (M = 3.88, SD = .94). Again, as expected, there
was a significant main effect of age that closely followed the ages identified
in Weist's stage model (F (5, 282) = 80.08, p < .0001). Also, post hoc analyses
revealed a developmental ordering as the 12-month-olds differed from all
groups between 24- and 42-months, the 18-month- and 24-month-olds
differed from all groups between 30- and 42-months, and the 30-month-
olds differed from both the 36- and 42-month-olds (p < .05).

The remaining questionnaire items that were categorized into Weist's
stages 2 and 3 showed mean parental ratings that fell between ratings for
those questionnaire items that fit within stages 1 and 4. The mean parental
ratings for the items in stages 2 and 3 also showed the same expected effect
of age (F (5, 283) = 120.78, p < .0001; and F (5, 283) = 110.55, p < .0001,
respectively) with post hoc analyses revealing slightly different patterns of
group differences. For the items exemplified by stage 2, there were significant group differences between every age group except between the 36-
and 42-month-olds (p < .05). For the items characterized by stage 3, the
12-month-olds did not differ from the 18-month-olds, but both age groups
differed from all other age groups, the 18-month-olds differed from the
three oldest age groups, and the 36-month-olds differed from the 42-month-
olds (p < .05). Collapsed across age, the mean parental ratings for the items

that fit stages 2 and 3 significantly differed from one another (t (282) = 5.60, p < .0001).

Overall, these items from the "Development of Future-Oriented Processes Questionnaire" fit general stage-like progressions that Weist described with respect to young children's ability to verbalize temporal relations. Thus, these findings provided at least some evidence that children's verbalizations about temporally ordered events emerge systematically and correspond with the developmental appearance of identified domains of future-oriented behavior, many of which also subsume planning skill. Weist provided an exciting framework that offers several possibilities for the conceptualization of how children between the ages of 2 and 5 years might acquire verbal representational skills that suggest evidence of the ability to verbalize a temporal order of events in advance of action, an aspect of planning skill that most closely resembles planning in the traditional sense.

Weist's stages of time system development capture important changes in children's linguistic, cognitive, and temporal sequence ability—component skills related to the acquisition of planning skill—during an age period that has typically been understudied by most planning researchers and theorists. The extent to which Weist's framework will be productive for stimulating planning research remains for further research. At a minimum, his framework provides age-related stages that can guide researchers to the time of transitions in temporal sequence knowledge that are likely to influence how and when children begin to sequence actions directed toward obtaining a desired future goal.

However, as we become increasingly better able to hone in on the developmental timing of children's ability to act on, represent, and talk about the temporal sequencing of events that is involved in the formulation of a plan, questions arise as to how children actually acquire these abilities. Next, I argue that children's acquisition of knowledge about temporal sequence, and the ability to verbally represent and formulate a sequence of actions that lead to an outcome, emerges from discourse with adults, and from their participation in the everyday routines and rituals that make up so much of our daily lives.

LEARNING ABOUT TEMPORAL SEQUENCE: THE INFLUENCE OF EVERYDAY ROUTINES IN THE CONTEXT OF FAMILY LIFE

Much of our daily life is organized by routines and rituals (Szalai, 1972; Zerubavel, 1981). Routines and rituals typically involve a rigid sequence of events that is regularly and frequently repeated. For example, many of us have regular morning routines that might involve showering, dressing, scanning the morning newspaper, and eating breakfast before leaving for work. This routine would be violated if any of the steps were completed out of their usual sequence, such as eating breakfast before taking a shower or leaving for work before dressing. Routines become so automatic that we do them without having to think about each event in the sequence, unless, of course, something happens to disrupt the routine. The repetitive nature of routines and their strict sequence produces a stable temporal structure that allows us to make cognitive predictions about what will happen next. As Zerubavel (1981, p. 12) pointed out,

> The temporal regularity of our social world has some very significant cognitive implications. In allowing us to have certain expectations regarding the temporal structure of our environment, it certainly helps us considerably to develop some sense of orderliness. By providing us with a highly reliable repertoire of what is expected, likely, or unlikely to take place within certain temporal boundaries, it adds a strong touch of predictability to the world around us.

The temporal structure of everyday routines and their significance for cognitive functioning raise some important developmental questions. What role do routines play in the lives of young children, how do children come to participate in routines, and do routines have the same cognitive significance for young children as they do for adults, especially with respect to planning?

Socialization of Routines

Because they provide a stable temporal framework, routines typically evolve for young children from the social context of their families. For most families, daily routines help to temporally and socially synchronize the activities of family members with one another for the smooth running of daily life (Kantor & Lehr, 1975). The role of daily routines in families is especially noteworthy, because parents and children must coordinate their activities to accommodate each other's needs. One of the first tasks to be accomplished soon after a newborn is brought home from the hospital is to establish regular routine patterns for sleeping and feeding—for the obvious benefit of both child and parents.

Children are socialized into everyday family routines and rituals from very early in life through social interaction and discourse with family members, typically their parents. Parents may initially create routines to simplify their everyday lives, and they do so in a way that intuitively recruits the participation of their children, even at ages long before children are able to act as full participants. Parents involve their children by talking to them about what has happened, what is happening, and what will happen next during everyday routines, even before children are able to be conversational partners. For example, parents of infants as young as 9 months report that they frequently talk to their child about things that will happen in the near future, even though they also believe their child understands little about the future (Benson, 1994). It has also been noted that when adults spend time with infants (both human and nonhuman primates) they naturally tend to engage in discourse by talking aloud about things that have happened, are happening now, and are about to happen e.g., Nelson, 1991; Nelson, 1993; Savage-Rumbaugh, 1990). Finally, there is evidence that the level of children's language development, as observed during mother–child discourse during everyday routines, is influenced by the type of interaction. Moerk (1975) reported that children's mean length of utterance (MLU) is positively correlated with interactions during which preschool children described to their mothers a past experience or a plan.

Thus, parents seem to naturally create and involve their infants and young children in everyday routines, especially through social discourse. Although parents may use routines to make their daily lives more manageable, the benefit to young children goes beyond the simplification of family life. By involving their children in everyday routines, parents scaffold several different dimensions of cognitive functioning for their children. Rogoff (1990), in particular, suggested that everyday routines are not only widespread in the daily lives of young children, but they function as natural occasions for promoting cognitive growth.

> In the routine and recurrent interactions between adults and children are many thousands of opportunities for guided participation in solving everyday problems.... It may be through repeated and varied experience in supported routine and challenging situations that children become skilled in specific cognitive processes. For example, Ferrier (1978) and Newson and Newson (1975) argue that the opportunity for language development occurs in routine participation in shared experiences and efforts to communicate as caregivers and infants carry out the thousands of diaperings, feedings, baths, and other recurring activities of daily life. (pp. 151–152)

How might everyday routines influence the ways young children learn about temporal sequence and other cognitive skills related to early planning?

Many of the common routines in which adults and children engage provide a structure for children to learn how to meet specific outcomes or goals. When children are included in routines, they learn about the steps that must be taken to obtain a goal, and they also have an opportunity to form expectations that are shared with others about what will typically happen, when it will happen, and how it will happen. Parents and children together often create elaborate routines in which there is a specific sequence of events that must unfold before the ultimate goal is reached. A good example is the bedtime routine that may first involve the child putting on pajamas, then brushing teeth, followed by saying goodnight to each family member and stuffed animal, and then the reading of a story before the lights are finally turned off.

After many repetitions of the routine, its regular temporal structure should provide a basis for the child to develop expectations about what will happen before it actually does. After sufficient experience with the bedtime routine, a young child should soon understand the physical or verbal actions of the parent that signal the beginning, middle, and end of the routine. Once each signal occurs, the parent assumes that the child has some understanding of the sequence of events that are about to unfold and their eventual outcome. This shared meaning emerges because everyday routines are created from typical parent–child interactions. Although the advantage first goes to the parent to regulate the initiation of the routine, with time the child can capitalize on their shared meaning and the expectations that result to play a role in initiating all or part of the routine.

We might first expect young children to show some aspects of "planning-in-action" by initiating an everyday routine with a particular action, or by anticipating what will happen when a parent initiates a familiar routine. With time, that same child will be able to verbally represent the sequence of events in a familiar routine and even formulate a planned alternative sequence of events, especially when she no longer desires the routine's usual outcome. Parents quickly realize how creative their young child can become in finding ways to delay the inevitable when a familiar bedtime routine is started, (e.g., common strategies children learn for delaying bedtime include, "One more story" or "I need a glass of water"). Thus, everyday routines not only provide a temporal structure for children to participate in planned outcomes, but with time, routines also provide an impetus for improvisational planning by children when they try to avoid an expected, but undesirable, future outcome.

From Everyday Routines to Plans

The developmental picture that is emerging is one in which children, from birth, are exposed to temporal regularities through the everyday routines that simplify daily life. Adults first appear to regulate children's participation in routines by recruiting their involvement and talking to them about what has happened, what is happening, and what will happen next. This other-regulated temporal structure permits children to experience, first-hand, a sequence of events that unfold in real time that typically eventuates in some desired and planned outcome. Routines also contain a regular temporal structure; thus, children are supported in remembering what has happened in the past and, perhaps more importantly, they are also encouraged to form expectations for what will happen next. For example, Lucariello and Nelson (1987) reported that when mothers were asked to speak with their 2-year-old child about a "highly familiar, routine activity," the content was more likely to focus on future talk (77%) rather than past talk (24%). As Lucariello and Nelson (1987) suggested, "it may be that the routine itself suggests topics about routines to come next (for example, napping or going to the park after lunch) or that went before (for example, pre-school morning activities)" (p. 225). Thus, routines appear to provide temporal structure for young children to learn that events are sequenced in time and may also orient them to the recognition that a particular sequence of events leads to a specific future outcome.

Nelson (1986, 1989, 1991) proposed that children first construct scripts, or general event representations, for familiar routine events. In the social discourse process and repetition of everyday routines, children also appear to learn about temporal concepts and how to express them, perhaps by mapping aspects of their parent's time words onto the routine sequence of events as they are experienced. Ultimately, children can begin to use both their cognitive and social expectations of the sequence that leads to a future goal and linguistic means to represent what they want and how to obtain it—all elements that contribute to early skill in planning. In this everyday context of social discourse, children not only experience the consequences of routines for what happens next in their lives, but they can use the structure of routines to exert control over obtaining what they want by either following the sequence to the planned outcome or altering the sequence to avoid it. Moreover, routines place young children in a unique position to acquire the rather arbitrary time language that will permit them to not only remember the sequence of past events, but to verbalize plans for the future.

Empirical Evidence

The consequences that everyday routines have for how children learn about temporal sequence, time language, and the ability to verbally represent a sequence of events seem obvious, make common sense, and have a rich conceptual base that captures the influence of the family context. Yet, it is surprising how the topic of everyday routines has, with a few exceptions, largely escaped the attention of developmental researchers, especially those interested in planning. Although there are some who have written about routines from the perspective of the "sociology of time" (e.g., Weigert, 1981) or family therapy and process (e.g., Fiese & Kline, 1993; Imber-Black, Roberts, & Whiting, 1988; Reiss, 1981), there are only a handful of empirical reports that have explored what children know about everyday routines and their relation to the development of temporal sequence knowledge.

To date, William Friedman has conducted the most systematic empirical research on the development of children's understanding and representation of temporal structure. Some of this work included what children know about the temporal structure of routine daily activities (Friedman, 1977, 1990a, 1990b, 1992b; Friedman & Brudos, 1988). For example, in a series of three experiments, Friedman (1990b) reported evidence that by 4 to 5 years of age, children are able to represent several events that constitute their day by correctly ordering cards that depicted everyday activities, such as waking, eating lunch, eating dinner, and going to bed at night. In this research, children were credited with producing a correct temporal order if their card orders reflected a true sequence, even though the sequence was not restricted to a defined time period, such as a day. For example, children received credit for a correct temporal sequence if they placed the cards in the following order—eating dinner, going to bed, waking, and having lunch—even though that order spans the end of one day and the beginning of another.

Based on temporal order data, Friedman (1992b) theorized that children as young as 3 years have a basic-level knowledge about their daily routine. However, for younger children, card-ordering tasks may be less sensitive in measuring such competence compared with analyses of narratives about the events in their day (e.g., Nelson, 1989).

Consistent with the view presented here, Friedman (1992b) suggested that the richness and regularity of routine events and the social interactions between children and their parents that typically accompany such activities are likely developmental mechanisms for the formation and representation of the temporal sequence of familiar events. Based on his own work, and that of Nelson (1989b), Friedman (1992b) speculated that, in addition to the benefits of the temporal regularities that are inherent in routines, social interactions about everyday routines encourage children to anticipate and review what will happen next, which in turn motivates children to form "temporally organized representations of patterns that are longer than brief series of contiguous actions"(p. 73).

In contrast to Friedman's (1990b) method that examined children's generalized representation of the temporal sequence of four routine activities, we designed a study to examine 4- to 7.5-year-olds' specific representations of the temporal sequence of up to 12 daily activities for the past, present, and future with a "timeline" methodology (Benson, Grossman, & Hanebuth, 1993). In particular, we wanted to know whether children would construct similar temporal representations for the sequence of common, everyday routines for the past (*yesterday*), present (*today*), and future (*tomorrow*).

In one study, 30 4-year-old, 32 5.5-year-old, and 30 7.5-year-old children were presented with 11 daily activity cards that depicted common activities including waking, dressing, eating breakfast, being in school, eating lunch, coming home after school, watching TV, eating dinner, taking a bath, putting on pajamas, and going to sleep. A 12th activity card depicted one unique event that was the activity that the child was engaged in—a child putting cards on the timeline while at the laboratory. The activity cards were presented in a random order, and each child was asked to place the individually presented activity card on an 8-foot timeline that was anchored by a picture of the sun on one end and a picture of the moon on the opposite end of the timeline. Children were asked to show when in the day, between the sun and the moon, they "really and truly" do the activity. Children produced specific temporal sequences of the 12 activity cards for three counterbalanced day conditions that represented "yesterday" (the day before they visited the lab), "today" (the day they visited the lab), and "tomorrow" (the day after their lab visit). In addition, parents of children in this study were also asked to produce a temporal sequence for the same activity cards according to the sequence in which their child typically experiences the different everyday activities depicted in the cards for the three different days. Unlike Friedman's ordering task, our timeline task required that children produce an ordered sequence that matched the order of routine activities as they occur within the constraints of a typical day.

Our primary findings generally support those reported by Friedman that showed that children as young as 4 years of age could temporally sequence routine events, despite the increased number of activity cards in our study (4 versus 12 cards), and the added constraint that they order activities within a typical day. As an index of the accuracy of children's temporal representations, we calculated intraclass correlations between the parent and child sequences for their common daily activity cards. Significant main effects were found across the three day conditions ($F_{(2,91)} = 5.08$, $p < .01$) and across the three age groups ($F_{(2,91)} = 30.18$, $p < .001$), as shown in Fig. 3.2. No significant interaction was found ($F_{(4,91)} = .985$, n.s.). Of the three day conditions, children were most accurate for the temporal sequences they produced for the "yesterday" condition ($M = .83$, $SD = .23$), and they were less accurate for the sequences they produced for the "today" and "tomorrow" conditions ($M = .66$, SD .39; $M = .66$, $SD = .29$, respectively). As expected, their sequencing performance improved with age ($M = .45$, $SD = .37$; $M = .79$, $SD = .21$; $M = .92$, $SD = .11$ for 4.0-, 5.5-, and 7.5-year-olds, respectively). The differences among all age groups were reliable ($p < .05$).

These findings provided additional evidence about the extent to which young children have an understanding about the temporal sequence of the many everyday, routine activities they experience within the context of a day. By 4 years of age, children show a moderate degree of accuracy when sequencing daily activities, especially when they think about the sequence of activities in the recent past (i.e., "yesterday"). However, children's temporal representations for daily activities tended to differ for the past ("yesterday") and future ("tomorrow"). At all ages, children were more accurate when sequencing daily activities for the known past compared to the unknown future, suggesting that they had more difficulty thinking about the sequence of routine activities that would happen in the future. This

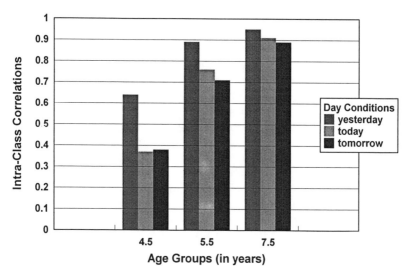

FIG. 3.2. Correlations between parent and child daily activity card sequences.

finding is particularly interesting because children were asked to sequence an identical set of activity cards for each day condition, yet they
did not produce identical sequences across the three-day conditions. The
most notable difference among the sequences they did produce was
usually for the "tomorrow" condition. One possible explanation for this
finding is that at some level, children may recognize that the future
involves a degree of uncertainty about the sequence in which highly
familiar, routine, but "yet-to-be-experienced" events may occur. An
interesting question to ask, relating to how children acquire skill in
planning, is when they recognize that some future events can occur in
any order in a sequence, but some events must occur in a specific order
to eventuate in a desired outcome.

A third empirical approach exists that has found links between temporal
knowledge and the influence of the family context as mediated through
time talk between parents and their children. Norton (1993), drawing from
her 9-year longitudinal research with minority children raised in poverty,
reported a relation between early parental time talk in the context of
everyday life and children's ability to temporally order events at age 3. This
evidence comes from intensive videotaped observations of mother–child
pairs made as frequently as every 6 weeks during the child's first 2 years,
every 3 months until age 3, and every 6 months after age 3. Norton analyzed
the content of family activities, including the structure of daily activities
and the frequency and content of maternal talk. In addition, at ages 3 and
6, standardized tests of cognitive function (e.g., the McCarthy Scales) were
individually administered that included a seriation task in which children
had to produce a temporal sequence for a set of common events.

In analyses of data collected during the first three years of the project, Norton (1993) found an interesting relationship between maternal time talk and child knowledge of temporal sequence as measured by the seriation task. She reported that, at age 3, those children who scored in the top quartile on the seriation task of the McCarthy Scales were those same children whose mothers spoke more about time during daily activities than those children who had lower seriation scores *and* whose mothers talked less to them about time. Furthermore, Norton described those women who spoke more to their children about time as "mothers [who] were more future oriented [because] they voiced plans" (1993, p. 88). Although mothers' verbal statements to their children about time represented less than 2% of the total language statements they made, Norton emphasized that maternal time talk is one index of a more general orientation to time, planfulness, and future orientation that appears to influence individual differences in children's temporal knowledge. Given the unusually rich data set that Norton collected, it will be interesting to see if the initial relations she found between maternal time talk and young children's temporal knowledge persist for measures that were collected from children after age 3.

These different lines of research provide intriguing evidence that suggests that young children understand some aspects of the temporal sequence of common events, and their temporal sequence abilities can be influenced by exposure to parental time talk. Across these different research approaches, there is a consistent finding that even by 3 to 4 years of age, children can demonstrate an understanding of the temporal sequence of common, daily events and activities. For some children, the ability to temporally sequence common events is particularly influenced by the family context by exposure to time talk.

Together, these studies point to the possibility that several component skills and experiences may contribute to the early development of planning skill in young children, including an understanding of temporal sequence, the formation of expectations about future events, and the ability to verbally represent temporal relations. These skills appear to be uniquely supported by children's exposure to everyday routines and parental time talk that naturally accompanies common activities in the lives of most families. Because planning involves the ability to organize and represent a sequence of events that is directed toward achieving a future goal in advance of action, there is at least some preliminary evidence to support the speculation that young children would first need to have some mastery of component skills that are involved in planning before they are capable of formulating a plan in the traditional sense. These skills include being able to sequence events in time, to form expectations about a future goal, and to have some means, probably through their verbalizations, to represent a sequence of steps that lead to a desired goal.

SOME CONCLUSIONS ABOUT THE DEVELOPMENT OF EARLY PLANNING SKILL: TEMPORAL SEQUENCE KNOWLEDGE, FUTURE ORIENTATION, AND EVERYDAY ROUTINES IN SOCIAL CONTEXT

The early acquisition of planning skills continues to be a puzzle yet to be solved by developmental psychologists. Important pieces of the puzzle could likely include the component skills identified here as promising for gaining a better understanding of how young children acquire skill in planning. Although the following scenario of how these skills influence the development of planning seems straightforward, much work remains to document empirically their contribution to how children learn to plan.

Children are exposed to routines very early in everyday life. The temporal structure that defines a routine lays a foundation for children to organize a sequence of events across time. Parental and child time talk is an inherent part of children's experiences with routines and serves to highlight that a particular sequence of events constitutes one routine, whereas a different sequence of events constitutes another routine, with the potential that each sequence will eventuate in a unique outcome. When children can begin to sequence events in time, they can also begin to form, for themselves, expectations about future outcomes. For example, children come to realize that particular sequences lead to some desired outcomes, whereas other sequences lead to different outcomes. The ability to order events and to represent verbally their temporal sequence further influences the course of children's own behavior in time. They can begin to control and direct their own behavior by representing the sequence of events needed to reach a desired future outcome before attempting to enact the sequence. Thus, the ability to formulate a plan that has an expected future outcome is slowly built on skills that emerge from and are supported by experiences with events in time and the ability to represent their temporal sequence.

Weist has presented an interesting developmental framework that carefully describes the interdependent links between cognitive advances in sequencing events in past, present, and future time and children's linguistic representations of these temporal dimensions. I have argued that Weist's stage framework may be useful for conceptualizing how young children acquire skill in planning, because successful planning must be built on an understanding of temporal sequence and the ability to represent the sequence of events in time prior to action. It would seem that the next step to be taken in research on the early development of planning skill is to devise planning tasks that would be suitable for children between the ages of 2 and 5 years, that extend from their everyday experiences, but could be analyzed by the stage-like developmental sequence described by Weist. By pursuing this strategy, researchers and theorists may learn a great deal about the component skills and experiential factors that influence how children acquire skill in planning, particularly at those transition points suggested by Weist's framework.

ACKNOWLEDGMENTS

This work was supported by the MacArthur Foundation Research Network on Transitions in Early Development. I express my gratitude to Robert Emde for his support of this research and his guidance of the MacArthur Research Network, to Marshall M. Haith for many helpful discussions, debates, and his comments on a previous draft of this manuscript, and to Joan Bihun, Lisa Hager, Stacy Grossman, and Elizabeth Hanebuth for their assistance with data collection and analyses.

REFERENCES

Ames, L. B. (1946). The development of the sense of time in the young child. *Journal of Genetic Psychology, 68*, 97–125.

Bates, E., Elman, J., & Li, P. (1994). Language in, on and about time. In M. M. Haith, J. B. Benson, R. R. Roberts, & B. F. Pennington (Eds.), *The development of future-oriented processes* (pp. 293–321). Chicago: University of Chicago Press.

Bauer, P. J., & Hertsgaard, L. A. (1993). Increasing steps in recall of events: Factors facilitating immediate and long-term memory in 13.5- and 16.5-month-old children. *Child Development, 64*, 1204–1223.

Bauer, P. J., & Mandler, J. M. (1989). One thing follows another: Effects of temporal structure on 1- to 2-year-olds' recall of events. *Developmental Psychology, 25*, 197–206.

Bauer, P. J., & Mandler, J. M. (1990). Remembering what happened next: Very young children's recall or event sequences. In R. Fivush & J. Hudson (Eds.), *What young children remember and why—Emory Symposium in Cognition* (pp. 9–29). New York: Cambridge University Press.

Bauer, P. J., & Mandler, J. M. (1992). Putting the horse before the cart: The use of temporal order in recall of events by 1-year-old children. *Developmental Psychology, 28*, 441–452.

Benson, J. B. (1994). The origins of future-orientation in the everyday lives of 9- to 36-mo-old infants. In M. M. Haith, J. B. Benson, R. R. Roberts, & B. F. Pennington (Eds.), *The development of future-oriented processes* (pp. 375–407). Chicago: University of Chicago Press.

Benson, J. B., Grossman, S. E., & Hanebuth, E. (March, 1993). *Young children's temporal representations: Past, present, and future daily activities.* Poster presented at the meetings of the Society for Research in Child Development, New Orleans, LA.

Benson, J. B., & Haith, M. M. (1995). Future-oriented processes: A foundation for planning behavior in infants and toddlers. *Infancia y Aprendizaje, 69–70*, 127–140.

Bloom, L., Lahey, M., Hood, L., Lifter, K., & Fiess, K. (1980). Complex sentences: Acquisition of syntactic connectives and the semantic relation they encode. *Journal of Child Language, 7*, 235–262.

Bruner, J. S. (1970). The growth and structure of skill. In K. Connolly (Ed.), *Mechanisims of motor skill development* (pp. 63–94). London: Academic Press.

Carni, E., & French, L. A. (1984). The acquisition of before and after reconsidered: What develops? *Journal of Experimental Child Psychology, 37*, 394–403.

Clark, E. V. (1985). Acquisition of romance, with special reference to French. In D. I. Slobin (Ed.), *The crosslinguistic study of language acquisition* (pp. 687–782). Hillsdale, NJ: Lawrence Erlbaum Associates.

Cocking, R. R., & Copple, C. E., (1987). Social influences on representational awareness: Plans for representing and plans as representation. In S. L. Friedman, E. K. Scholnick, & R. R. Cocking (Eds.), *Blueprints for thinking: The role of planning in cognitive development* (pp. 428–465). Cambridge, England: Cambridge University Press.

Demany, L., McKenzie, B., & Vurpillot, E. (1977). Rhythm perception in early infancy. *Nature, 266,* 718–719.

De Lisi, R. (1987). A cognitive-developmental model of planning. In S. L. Friedman, E. K. Scholnick, & R. C. Cocking (Eds.), *Blueprints for thinking: The role of planning in cognitive development* (pp. 79–109). Cambridge, England: Cambridge University Press.

Droit, S., & Pouthas, V. (1992). Changes in temporal regulation of behavior in young children: From action to representation. In F. Macar, V. Pouthas, & W. J. Friedman (Eds.), *Time, action, and cognition* (pp. 45–53). Dordrecht, Netherlands: Kluwer.

Ferreiro, E., & Sinclair, H. (1971). Temporal relations in language. *International Journal of Psychology, 6,* 39–47.

Ferrier, L. (1978). Word, context and imitation. In A. Lock (Ed.), *Action, gesture and symbol: The emergence of language.* New York: Academic Press.

Fiese, B. H., & Kline, C. A. (1993). Development of the Family Ritual Questionnaire: Initial reliability and validation studies. *Journal of Family Psychology, 6,* 290–299.

French, L. A., & Nelson, K. (1985). *Young children's knowledge of relational terms: Some ifs, ors, and buts.* New York: Springer.

Friedman, W. J. (1977). The development of children's knowledge of cyclic aspects of time. *Child Development, 48,* 1593–1599.

Friedman, W. J. (1990a). *About time.* Cambridge, MA: MIT Press.

Friedman, W. J. (1990b). Children's representations of the pattern of daily activities. *Child Development, 61,* 1399–1412.

Friedman, W. J. (1992a). Time concepts and adaptation: Developmental approaches. In F. Macar, V. Pouthas, & W. J. Friedman (Eds.), *Time, action, and cognition: Towards bridging the gap* (pp. 9–12). Dordrecht, Netherlands: Kluwer.

Friedman, W. J. (1992b). The development of children's representations of temporal structure. In F. Macar, V. Pouthas, & W. J. Friedman (Eds.), *Time, action, and cognition: Towards bridging the gap* (pp. 67–75). Dordrecht, Netherlands: Kluwer.

Friedman, W. J., & Brudos, S. L. (1988). On routines and routines: The early development of spatial and temporal representations. *Cognitive Development, 3,* 167–182.

Haith, M. M. (1994). Visual expectations as the first step toward the development of future-oriented processes. In M. M. Haith, J. B. Benson, R. J. Roberts, & B. F. Pennington, (Eds.), *The development of future-oriented processes.* Chicago, IL: University of Chicago Press.

Haith, M. M, Benson, J. B., Bihun, J. T., & Talmi, A. (1997). *The development of future-oriented processes in early infancy.* Manuscript in preparation.

Haith, M. M., Benson, J. B., Roberts, R. J., & Pennington, B. F. (1994), Introduction. In M. M. Heath, J. B. Benson, R. J. Roberts, & B. F. Pennington (Eds.), *The development of future-oriented processes* (pp. 1–7). Chicago: University of Chicago Press.

Haith, M. M, Wentworth, N., & Canfield, R. L. (1993). The formation of expectations in early infancy. In C. Rovee-Collier & L. P. Lipsitt (Eds.), *Advances in infancy research* (pp. 251–297). Norwood, NJ: Ablex.

Harner, L. (1981). Children talk about time and aspect of actions. *Child Development, 52,* 498–506.

Harner, L. (1982). Thinking about the past and the future. In W. J. Friedman (Ed.), *The developmental psychology of time* (pp. 141–169). New York: Academic Press.

Hayes-Roth, B., & Hayes-Roth, F. (1979). A cognitive model of planning. *Cognitive Science, 3,* 25–310.

Hofsten, von, C. (1980). Predictive reaching for moving objects by human infants. *Journal of Experimental Child Psychology, 30,* 369–383.

Hofsten, von, C., & Ronnqvist, L. (1988). Preparation for grasping an object: A developmental study. *Journal of Experimental Psychology: Human Perception and Performance, 14,* 610–621.

Imber-Black, E., Roberts, J., & Whiting, R.A. (1988). *Rituals in families and family therapy.* New York: Norton.

Kant, I. (1965). Critique of pure reason. (N. Smith, Trans.) New York: St. Martin's Press.

Kantor, D., & Lehr, W. (1975). *Inside the family.* San Francisco: Jossey-Bass.

Klahr, D., & Robinson, M. (1981). Formal assessment of problem-solving and planning processes in preschool children. *Cognitive Psychology, 13*, 113–148.

Kreitler, S., & Kreitler, H. (1987a). Conceptions and processes of planning: The developmental perspective. In S.L. Friedman, E. K. Scholnick, & R. R. Cocking (Eds.), *Blueprints for thinking: The role of planning in cognitive development.* (pp. 110–178). Cambridge, England: Cambridge University Press.

Kreitler, S., & Kreitler, H. (1987b). Plans and planning: Their motivational and cognitive antecedents. In S. L. Friedman, E. K. Scholnick, & R. R. Cocking (Eds.), *Blueprints for thinking: The role of planning in cognitive development* (pp. 205–272). Cambridge, England: Cambridge University Press.

Levin, I., & Zakay, D. (1989). Introduction. *Time and human cognition.* Amsterdam: North-Holland.

Lewkowicz, D. J. (1989). The role of temporal factors in infant behavior and development. In I. Levin & D. Zakay (Eds.), *Time and human cognition* (pp. 9–62). Amsterdam: North-Holland.

Lockman, J. J. (1984). The development of detour ability in infancy. *Child Development, 55*, 482–491.

Lockman, J. J., Ashmead, D. H., & Bushnell, E. W. (1984). The development of anticipatory hand orientation during infancy. *Journal of Experimental Child Psychology, 37*, 176–186.

Lucariello, J., & Nelson, K. (1987). Remembering and planning talk. *Discourse Processes, 10*, 219–235.

Macar, F., Pouthas, V., & Friedman, W.J. (1992). *Time, action, and cognition.* Dordrecht, Netherlands: Kluwer.

McKenzie, B. E., & Bigelow, E. (1986). Detour behavior in young human infants. *British Journal of Developmental Psychology, 4*, 217–225.

Meltzoff, A. N ., & Moore, M. K. (1977). Imitation of facial and manual gestures by human neonates. *Science, 198*, 75–78.

Meltzoff, A. N., & Moore, M. K. (1989). Imitation in newborn infants: Exploring the range of gestures imitated and the underlying mechanisms. *Developmental Psychology, 25*, 954–962.

Meltzoff, A. N., & Moore, M. K. (1992). Early imitation within a functional framework: The importance of person identity, movement, and development. *Infant Behavior and Development, 15*, 479–505.

Moerk, E. L. (1975). Verbal interactions between children and their mothers during the preschool years. *Developmental Psychology, 11*, 788–794.

Nelson, K. (1993). Events, narratives, memory: What develops? In C. A. Nelson (Ed.), *Memory and affect in development: The Minnesota symposium on child psychology* (Vol. 26, pp. 1–24). Hillsdale, NJ: Lawrence Erlbaum Associates.

Nelson, K. (1986). *Event knowledge: Structure and function in development.* Hillsdale, NJ: Lawrence Erlbaum Associates.

Nelson, K. (1989). Monologues as construction of self in time. In K. Nelson (Ed.), *Narratives from the crib* (pp. 27–72). Cambridge, MA: Harvard University Press.

Nelson, K. (1991). The matter of time: Interdependencies between language and thought in development. In S. A. Gelman & J. P. Byrnes (Eds.), *Perspectives on language and thought* (pp. 278–318). Cambridge, England: Cambridge University Press.

Newson, J., & Newson, E. (1974). Intersubjectivity and the transmission of culture: On the social origins of symbolic functioning. *Bulletin of the British Psychological Society, 28*, 437–446.

Norton, D. G. (1993). Diversity, early socialization, and temporal development: The dual perspective revisited. *Social Work, 38*, 82–90.

Piaget, J. (1952).*The origins of intelligence in children.* New York: Norton Library.

Piaget, J. (1954). *The construction of reality in the child.* New York: Basic Books.

Piaget, J. (1962). *Play, dreams and imitation in childhood.* New York: Norton.

Piaget, J. (1969). *The child's conception of time.* New York: Basic Books.

Pinker, S. (1994). *The language instinct.* New York: Morrow.

Pouthas, V., Droit, S., & Jacquet, A. (1993). Temporal experiences and time knowledge in infancy and early childhood. *Time and Society, 2*, 199–218.

Reiss, D. (1981). *The family's construction of reality.* Cambridge, MA: Harvard University Press.

Robertson, S. S. (1985). Cyclic motor activity in the human fetus after midgestation. *Developmental Psychobiology, 18*, 411–419.

Rogoff, B. (1990). *Apprenticeship in thinking.* New York: Oxford University Press.

Rogoff, B., Gauvain, M., & Gardner, W. (1987). Children's adjustment of plans to circumstances. In S.L. Friedman, E. K. Scholnick, & R. R. Cocking (Eds.), *Blueprints for thinking: The role of planning in cognitive development* (pp. 303–320). Cambridge, England: Cambridge University Press.

Sachs, J. (1983). Talking about the there and then: The emergence of displaced reference in parent–child discourse. In K. E. Nelson (Ed.), *Children's language* (Vol. 4, pp. 3–28). Hillsdale, NJ: Lawrence Erlbaum Associates.

Savage-Rumbaugh, E. S. (1990). Language as a cause–effect communication system. *Philosophical Psychology 3*, 55–76.

Scholnick, E. K., & Friedman, S. L. (1987). The planning construct in the psychological literature. In S. L. Friedman, E. K. Scholnick, & R. R. Cocking (Eds.), *Blueprints for thinking: The role of planning in cognitive development* (pp. 3–38). Cambridge, England: Cambridge University Press.

Scholnick, E. K., & Friedman, S. L. (1993). Planning in context: Developmental and situational considerations. *International Journal of Behavioral Development, 16*, 145–167.

Szalai, A. (1972). *The uses of time: Daily activities of urban and suburban populations in twelve countries.* The Hague: Mouton.

Trosborg, A. (1982). Childrens's comprehension of before and after reinvestigated. *Journal of Child Language, 9*, 381–402.

Vygotsky, L. S. (1978). *Mind in society: The development of higher psychological processes.* Cambridge, MA: Harvard University Press.

Weist, R. M. (1989). Time concepts in language and thought: Filling the Piagetian void from 2 to 5 years. In I. Levin & D. Zakay (Eds.), *Time and human cognition: A life-span perspective.* North-Holland: Elsevier.

Wellman, H. M., Fabricius, W. V., & Sophian, C. (1985). The early development of planning. In H. M. Wellman (Ed.), *Children's searching* (pp. 123–149). Hillsdale, NJ: Lawrence Erlbaum Associates.

Wentworth, N., Benson, J. B., & Haith, M. M. (1996). *The development of infants' reaches for stationary and moving targets.* Manuscript submitted for publication.

Willatts, P. (1990). Development of problem-solving strategies in infancy. In D. F. Bjorklund (Ed.), *Children's strategies* (pp. 23–66). Hillsdale, NJ: Lawrence Erlbaum Associates.

Zerubavel, E. (1981). *Hidden rhythms.* Chicago: University of Chicago Press.

4

Scripts and Plans: The Development of Preschool Children's Event Knowledge and Event Planning

Judith A. Hudson
Brandi B. Sosa
Rutgers University

Lauren R. Shapiro
University of North Carolina at Chapel Hill

Research by Nelson and her colleagues (Nelson, 1986) showed that preschool children possess well-organized general knowledge about many familiar events organized in the form of generalized event representations (GERs). GERs are spatially and temporally organized schematic representations constructed from experience in real-world events that define the expected sequence of actions, actors, and props for familiar events (Nelson & Gruendel, 1983; Slackman, Hudson, & Fivush, 1986). Children rely on GERs when providing script reports for "what happens" in familiar events (Nelson & Gruendel, 1981, 1986), and they can also draw on general event knowledge to support cognitive activities such as story production (Hudson & Shapiro, 1990), inferential reasoning (Hudson & Slackman, 1991), discourse (Nelson & Gruendel, 1979), memory (Hudson, 1986), and categorization (Lucariello & Nelson, 1985). This chapter examines how children draw on GERs in planning.

There are several characteristics of GERs that make them particularly useful for planning. Consider the following script reports from preschool children who were asked to report "what happens" when you go to the grocery store:

3-year-old: I just buy things to eat. We get a cart or a box to hold it. When we're done, we just get in the car and go home.

5-year-old: You check around the house before you go and make a list. You drive there. You look on the list and go find things. Everything on the list. And when you're done buying it, you cross it out. After you check, you go home.

These scripts include a list of the expected sequence of actions in the correct temporal order. They are general accounts, not specific memories and are derived from knowledge of what usually happens across many instances, rather than being a memory of what happened on one occasion (Hudson & Shapiro, 1991; Nelson & Gruendel, 1986; Slackman, Hudson, & Fivush, 1986).

Children also mention open slots for "things" to get at the store. GERs include open slots or categories of information about the event that are instantiated according to the requirements of the specific event. Information about the possible range of appropriate slot-fillers is also represented in the GER. For example, the things you could get at the grocery store would be different from the things you would buy at a hardware store. Some children also mention alternative actions in their scripts: You can get a cart or a box; you can use the food right away or put it in the refrigerator.

GERs, then, represent the organization and variability of familiar events. To construct an event plan, a child simply has to access a general event representation and mentally fill in the open slots and alternative actions in the sequence. Yet, the task of constructing an event plan using general event knowledge may be more difficult to a young child than one might think. Some actions are more salient than others when planning for an event instead of just anticipating what is most likely to occur. A child must select the information that is most relevant for the future goal and make decisions regarding alternative actions and slot fillers. This requires some degree of reflection and decision-making ability. Our research has focused on how children make the transition from knowing about events to planning for events, from having coherent generalized event representations to being able to use that knowledge in the service of planning.

THE RELATIONSHIP BETWEEN EVENT KNOWLEDGE AND EVENT PLANNING

The studies we conducted are based on a model of the relationship between event knowledge and planning first proposed by Hudson and Fivush (1991). In that model, it was proposed that general event knowledge is a critical component in children's ability to construct and execute event plans. However, there are other variables that may contribute to the development of children's event planning. Both *internal supports* and *external supports* play a role in children's planning performance.

Event knowledge can be considered one very crucial type of internal support that an individual can bring to the task of planning (Barsalou, 1991; DeLisi, 1987; Hammond, 1990; Hayes-Roth & Hayes-Roth, 1979; Kreitler & Kreitler, 1987; Pea & Hawkins, 1987; Schank & Abelson; 1977; Scholnick & Friedman, 1987, 1993). In planning predictable event sequences, the steps to obtain a familiar goal are already represented in memory (Scholnick & Friedman, 1993). In fact, young children report that their planning activities consist primarily of anticipating familiar routines (Kreitler & Kreitler, 1987).

However, sometimes events do not transpire as predicted or as planned. Mishaps can and do occur. Hammond (1990) and Schank (1982) proposed that a crucial part of planning is being able to learn from past mistakes and to use our knowledge of script failures to predict when failures are likely to occur again. In Schank's (1982) dynamic memory model, strategies for solving problems encountered in familiar events are represented in memory as thematic organizing packets (TOPs). TOPs include information about how to repair and modify event sequences in response to script violations (e.g., the grocery store is all out of an item you wish to purchase). In Hammond's (1990) case-based planning model, memories of successful episodes can be retrieved to generate viable plans for future events, and memories of failed plans are used to anticipate and avoid problems in the future. Similarly, Abelson (1981) argued that after repeated experience with various script violations, one acquires knowledge of corrective prescriptions to remedy common mishaps. Thus, event knowledge can include not only knowledge of what typically happens, but also knowledge of what can go wrong and how to repair it. This latter type of knowledge may be essential for correcting problems encountered in enacting event plans. However, research based on children's script reports does not indicate the degree to which children possess knowledge of mishaps and repairs.

Other types of knowledge can provide internal supports for planning such as an explicit understanding of causality or knowledge about time constraints. The ability to construct more complex and more efficient plans may depend on the development of various kinds of planning-relevant knowledge beyond knowledge of predictable routines, common mishaps, and corrective prescriptions.

Equally important is the contribution of *external support* to planning. This component includes various supports in the physical and social environment. For example, one might plan a route through a city to get to a particular location based on information provided on a map; however, if the street names are not marked by signs, then one's plan may go awry due to characteristics of the physical environment. Similarly, a child may plan to construct a pretend edifice using various construction materials; but if the blocks cannot be found in their usual location, the plan can go awry. Thus, predictable and well-organized environments may contribute to better planning.

Social interactions with other planners, especially more competent planners, is another type of external support that has been shown to affect young children's planning abilities. Parents use a variety of techniques to guide children's planning efforts in collaborative planning tasks (Gauvain & Rogoff, 1989). They may suggest appropriate actions or provide children with feedback regarding their success. In discussing future events, they may elicit their children's preferences and predictions ("What do you want to do?" "Who do you think we'll see there?"; Hudson & Sosa, 1995). These techniques make the planning process more transparent to young children and relieve children of some of the responsibility for carrying out the planning enterprise. In everyday contexts, parents may provide naturalistic models for how to plan for events as children observe their parents making shopping lists or talking aloud as they pack for a vacation. In the Hudson and Fivush (1991) model, children's event planning efforts draw on both internal and external supports. The amount of external support required for successful planning may depend on the availability of internal supports. In familiar planning contexts where children can draw on well-organized event knowledge, they may require only minimal support from the external environment to construct and execute event plans. In unfamiliar planning contexts where children have very little background knowledge of the situation to draw on, they may rely more on support from others in constructing and executing plans.

Hudson and Fivush (1991) also proposed that there are at least four levels in the development of event-based planning. Children's first planning efforts may involve accessing GERs and using them to anticipate future actions and activities. For example, a child can anticipate what will happen when she gets up in the morning based on her general event knowledge for routine morning activities. At this level, *Level 0: Plans equal GER*, children's plans are not differentiated from the general event knowledge, and there is no evidence of any advance planning activities beyond simply anticipating a sequence of actions for a familiar event.

At the first level of actual planning, *Level 1: Single goal event planning*, children can access a GER and mentally instantiate the open and alternative slots in the action sequence with a specific future goal in mind. For example, children's GERs for what happens in the morning include the action of getting dressed, which includes a slot for the particular items of clothing that are put on. In constructing a plan, a child may instantiate the clothing slot with different items depending on whether it is a warm or cold day or whether or not it is a school day.

At *Level 2: Multiple event goal planning*, children can mentally instantiate slots in a GER based on multiple event goals, for example, planning to buy both food items and cleaning supplies at the grocery store. At *Level 3: Coordinated event planning*, children can mentally decompose event sequences into different subgoals and can hierarchically organize subgoals from different events. Finally, at *Level 4: Novel event planning*, event sequences can be decomposed into component actions and subgoals, and components can be modified and joined with components from different events to construct novel action sequences. Thus, at higher planning levels, children become more aware of the relationship between actions and goals so that goals, rather than predictable action sequences, can be used to organize plans.

The following investigations examine different aspects of the relationship between children's general event knowledge and their planning ability. For the most part, we have concentrated on planning at Levels 0 through 2. The first investigation compared characteristics of preschool children's scripts and verbal plans to examine the degree to which planning for an event differed from simply reporting what usually happens. In this study, we also examined whether preschool children could construct plans to remedy and prevent common mishaps that occur in routine events. The second study investigated how external supports affect preschool children's ability to construct and execute single versus multiple event plans in a pretend planning situation. The third study examined how differences in the availability of internal and external supports and variations in causal structure affected 4-year-olds' abilities to construct and then execute plans for actual events (as opposed to pretend or hypothetical events). Our final investigation extends our previous work in two ways. First, we replicated the effects of causal structure on children's planning found in Study 3. Second, we examined the effects of providing children with examples of event planning while they were learning new events on their ability to plan for the new events.

STUDY 1: PRESCHOOL CHILDREN'S SCRIPTS AND PLANS FOR FAMILIAR EVENTS

Although a vast number of studies have shown that children as young as 3 years can easily report general scripts for "what happens" in familiar events (see Hudson, 1993; Nelson, 1986), can they use that knowledge when planning for familiar events? In this investigation (Hudson, Shapiro, & Sosa, 1995) we compared children's verbal plans for familiar events to same-aged children's verbal scripts for the same events. Of course, we expected both types of accounts to be very similar because both accounts draw on children's GERs for the events. However, the degree to which children mention different activities or focus on different parts of the event sequence when providing a verbal plan, than when recounting a script, is an indication of the degree to which they perceive the task of planning aloud to be different from merely reporting what typically happens. This is a crucial difference between Level 0 and Level 1 planning. At Level 0, children are able to use event knowledge to predict future actions, but are not aware of the need to plan for the future. At Level 1, children can use their event knowledge to plan; they can draw on general event knowledge to construct an event plan that includes elements of a GER, but is not isomorphic to the GER.

Constructing Event Plans From Event Knowledge

Planning an event can involve several kinds of planning activities. First, one must be able to construct *advance plans*, that is, a representation of an expected sequence of actions planned in advance of action. Planning can also involve *remedy planning*—constructing contingency plans to remedy unexpected mishaps that may occur in the process of carrying out advance plans. Finally, expert planners are able to construct *prevention plans*,which are advance plans that include actions intended to prevent mishaps from occurring. Although GERs provide a foundation for constructing advance plans for familiar events, they may not be adequate for constructing remedy and prevention plans. Children's event knowledge must include knowledge about potential mishaps and how to repair them in order to construct remedy and prevention plans (Hammond, 1990; Schank, 1982).

To examine preschool children's abilities to construct advance plans, we asked 3-, 4-, and 5-year-old children either to recount a script or to construct an event plan for two familiar events, going grocery shopping and going to the beach. To examine their ability to construct remedy plans, we also asked children in both conditions to plan remedies for common mishaps, for example, "What could you do if you did not have enough money to pay for your groceries?" and "What could you do if you forgot to bring your lunch to the beach?" Finally, all children were asked to construct prevention plans to prevent the mishaps from occurring, "What could you do to make sure that didn't happen the next time you went grocery shopping (or to the beach)?"

Children's Advance Plans for Familiar Events

Examples of children's scripts and verbal plans are shown in Table 4.1. Notice that they are very similar in structure. Children reported both scripts and plans in the timeless present tense using the general pronoun, "you," and tended to report general level actions. However, there were important differences in the two types of reports that indicated children were emphasizing different types of information in their plans than in their scripts.

First, the amount of information that children reported varied by age and condition. As shown in Fig. 4.1, 3-year-olds mentioned more propositions in their scripts than in their plans, there was no difference in number of propositions mentioned in scripts and plans by 4-year-olds, and 5-year-olds mentioned more propositions in their plans than in their scripts. Moreover, the number of propositions mentioned in children's scripts did not vary significantly by age, but with increasing age, children mentioned more propositions in their plans.

A second measure used to examine the degree of planfulness in children's verbal plans was the proportion of actions that children mentioned concerning the onset or preparatory portions of the event sequence. For going to the grocery store, the onset phase included the actions involved in getting ready to go, going to the store, going into the store, and selecting a grocery cart or basket. For going to the beach, this included the actions involved in packing, getting to the beach, and setting up at the beach, such as changing one's clothes, and putting on sunscreen lotion. We reasoned that if children were cognizant that the planning involves advance preparation, their plan reports would include a higher proportion of onset activities than their script reports.

Five-year-olds reported proportionally more onset activities in their scripts and plans ($M = .24$) than either 3- and 4-year-olds ($M = .13$ and $M = .15$, respectively). However, children at all ages reported more onset activities in the plan condition ($M = .21$) than in the script condition ($M = .14$). This indicates that children at all ages understood the preparatory nature of planning, and were able to provide more preparation information than

TABLE 4.1

Examples of Children's Scripts and Plans, Study I

Scripts, Grocery Store

I just buy things to eat. We get a cart or box to hold it. When we're done, we just get in the car and go home. (3-year old)

You drive and then you go in and get a cart. You go and buy food. And then you leave. (4-year-old)

You buy some food. You pay. You look around. You buy stuff. You walk down the aisles. (5-year-old)

Plans, Grocery Store

Get food. Get a carriage to put the food in. Pay for it. Go back home. (3-year- old)

You have to make a list. And if you don't have no food, you have cans, cans of corn if you want some; and Diet Pepsi if you don't have anymore; and Sprite. And you can bring steak ribs; I love ribs. And if you don't have no more milk, you can buy some. (4-year-old)

You have to buy food. You gotta pay for it. If you gotta buy something it will cost a lot of money. Gotta get a cart. And put your food in your cart. Gotta remember to put it back once you're finished. Make sure you have a list and coupons for everything. (5-year-old)

Scripts, Beach

You can play. You can play in the sand. We can make sailboats and pirate ships. When you're done playing in the beach, you go back home and take your suit off and change into your clothes. (3-year-old)

You go in the water. And you play in the sand. And you can bring a beach towel. And eat lunch. And then to cool yourself off, you can go in the water. (4-year-old)

You go and swim. And you go fishing. And you make a sand castle. And sometimes it has a boardwalk. And sometimes you can pick up animals, dead things that get washed out of the ocean. (5-year-old)

Plans, Beach

Put on a bathing suit. I think you could bring lunch. It's very hot at the beach. Go swimming. You could go play in the waves. (3-year-old)

You get your bathing suits. You bring some towels. You have to change. If you are at the beach with your bathing suit it's easier because you don't have to change outside. You have to be careful so you won't drown. You have to make sure that you have water rings to make sure you don't drown. You can stay in front so you don't drown. You have to make sure everything is packed up in the bag. (4-year-old)

You have to bring a beach umbrella so the sun stays out of your face. And after that you put down nice warm blanket. And after that you will put down a nice warm pillow. And after that you will go in the ocean. And after that take a nap on the sand. And after that you will go back home and take your other nap. (5 year-old)

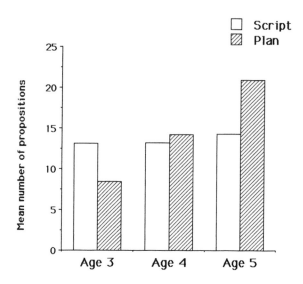

FIG. 4.1. Mean number of propositions mentioned in childrens' scripts and plans by age, Study 1.

they would typically give in a script report for the same event. Children also mentioned proportionally more onset activities for going to the beach (M = .20) than for going grocery shopping (M = .14).

Finally, we coded the content of children's reports to analyze the number of specific planning activities mentioned by children in each condition. These included both *advance preparations*, such as getting money for going to the grocery store and putting on sun screen at the beach, and *decision-making activities* such as deciding when to go to the store and whether or not to go to the beach depending on the weather. As shown in Table 4.2, 5-year-olds mentioned more planning activities than the younger age groups, but only in the planning condition. Thus, 5-year-olds were the only age group that mentioned more planning activities in the planning condition than in the script condition. Moreover, 3- and 4-year-olds mentioned more planning activities for going to the beach than for grocery shopping, but there was no significant event difference for 5-year-olds.

These results indicate that with increasing age, children's plans were more differentiated from children's script reports and included more planning-related activities in addition to common script actions. Although 3-year-olds tended to mention the same kinds of activities in both the script and planning conditions, they did focus more on script actions occurring at the onset of the events when reporting plans than when reporting scripts. In contrast, 5-year olds not only focused on preparation actions when reporting event plans, but children in the planning condition also men-

TABLE 4.2

Mean Number of Planning Activities Mentioned by A&E Condition, An Event, Study 1

		Grocery	Beach	Mean
			Scripts	
Age:	3	1.17	2.0	1.59
	4	1.33	2.58	1.96
	5	2.92	2.92	2.92
			Plans	
Age:	3	.33	1.83	1.08
	4	1.00	2.50	1.65
	5	5.25	4.38	4.92

tioned more planning and decision-making activities than children in the script condition. Finally, event differences indicated that children tended to mention a higher proportion of preparation actions and more planning activities in their scripts and plans for going to the beach than for going grocery shopping.

Remedy and Prevention Planning

Examples of adequate remedy and prevention plan responses are shown in Table 4.3. The mean number of remedy and prevention plans produced by children at each age for each event (out of 2 possible) are shown in Fig. 4.2. Children's performance generally improved with age and children produced more adequate remedy plans than adequate prevention plans. However, 3- and 4-year olds were better at providing remedy plans than providing prevention plans, but there was no difference between performance on the two types of questions for 5-year-olds. Children at all ages produced more remedy and prevention plan responses for going to the beach.

TABLE 4.3

Examples of Remedy and Prevention Plan Responses, Study I

Remedy Plans

You could just have a sign on your front door or your side door, whichever one you go out, This sign remembers you to take your list. (3-year-old)

First go to the bank, to have money, and then you come back to the grocery shopping, get in line, and you have more money to pay with for the food. (4-year-old)

You could eat lunch inside, in a restaurant. (5-year-old)

Prevention Plans

You have to build another one [sand castle]. You have to move it over to where no water comes. (3-year-old)

Build another one [sand castle]. You have to watch over it. Or put something over it, big. (4-year-old)

Check around the house and make that list and put it on the dresser because Daddy always has to get money from his dresser. (5-year-old)

You count your money and if you don't have enough you go to the bank. (5-year-old)

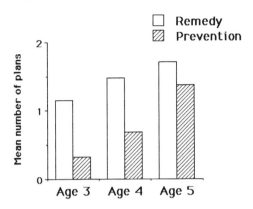

FIG. 4.2. Mean number of remedy and prevention plan responses produced by age,

Conclusions

Children from 3 to 5 years were able to use general event knowledge in constructing several types of verbal plans; advance plans for familiar events, plans to remedy potential mishaps, and plans to prevent mishaps from occurring. There were also developmental differences in children's abilities to distinguish verbal plans from verbal scripts and in their ability to construct remedy and prevention plans. The 3- and 4-year olds' plans most closely resembled planning at Level 1, single-goal event planning. They were able to use their knowledge of what happens in familiar events to anticipate event sequences, focus on preparation activities, and even remedy common mishaps, but they showed little ability to coordinate plans and goals in order to prevent mishaps from occurring. The 5-year-olds' abilities to construct prevention plans suggests that they are able to flexibly adapt their plans to meet new goals, skills that may be similar to those used in Level 2, multiple-goal planning, and Level 3, coordinated event planning.

Children mentioned proportionally more preparation actions, reported more specific planning activities, and provided more remedy and prevention plans for going to the beach than for going grocery store. There are many differences between the two events that could have contributed to these effects. Perhaps children were better able to plan for going to the beach because this is an event that they found more interesting than going grocery shopping. Or perhaps the temporal–causal structure of the events could have influenced children's planning ability (see Studies 3 and 4). Finally, the events may have varied in terms of familiarity to the children. In any case, these event differences indicated that children's planning abilities are affected by the activity for which they are planning.

STUDY 2: COORDINATING MULTIPLE EVENT GOALS
IN PLAN CONSTRUCTION AND EXECUTION

Once they have formed an event plan, are preschool children able to *remember* that plan and carry it out effectively? In one study (Hudson & Fivush, 1991), we asked 3-, 4-, and 5-year-old children to plan a trip to the grocery store and carry out their plans in a play grocery store.

Because we were interested in whether young children could coordinate knowledge of two or more event goals in planning, that is, whether they were capable of Level 1 and Level 2 event planning, we asked them to shop with two event goals in mind, having breakfast and having a birthday party. Half of the children were asked to shop for each event one at a time (the *successive* condition). They were asked to plan in advance what they would need to buy at the store when shopping for a birthday party or for breakfast. Then they went to the play grocery store and selected the items they needed. When they were done, they were asked to shop for the second event the same way. This task only required that children be able to plan at Level 1, single event goal planning. The other half of the children were asked to plan for both events at the same time (the *simultaneous* planning condition). They planned only once for all the items they would need for both events, then they went shopping and were asked to select all the items they needed for both events at the same time. This condition required Level 2, multiple event goal planning. We also manipulated the degree of external support available during plan execution by varying the arrangement of items on the shelves. Half of the children viewed a *clustered* display in which five breakfast items were clustered together on one shelf and five birthday party items were clustered together on another shelf; the other half of the children viewed an *interleaved* display in which items for each event were interleaved with each other and with 10 distractor items on the shelves. The clustered display should have provided children with more support for locating appropriate items than the interleaved display.

Relationship Between Plan Construction
and Plan Execution

In general, children's plans improved with age; that is, older children mentioned more appropriate items in their advance plans for shopping than did the younger children. But were they able to carry out the plans that they had constructed? To measure the degree to which children actually selected the items that they had mentioned in their plans, shopping scores were computed for each child. First, the proportion of appropriate items that children actually selected was calculated, followed by the proportion of inappropriate items that children selected. We then subtracted the proportion of inappropriate items from the proportion of appropriate items selected. Figure 4.3 shows the mean shopping scores for each condition and age.

Five-year-olds' shopping scores did not differ significantly in the successive and simultaneous conditions, but 3- and 4-year-olds performed better in the successive condition than in the simultaneous condition. Five-year-olds were also less affected by the item display than the younger age groups who performed better with the clustered, than with the interleaved, display. Three-year-olds, in particular, had great difficulty in selecting the items for which they had planned. They often abandoned their original plans entirely and simply selected everything in the store.

Providing Additional External Support

We introduced another type of external support to see if we could improve children's abilities to carry out their plans. In a second experiment with 3- and 4-year-olds, we reminded children of the shopping goal while they were in the store. After they had selected their second item, an experimenter said, "Remember, you're shopping for breakfast things." Children were provided with reminders in both the standard version of the task and in the clustered version. Mean shopping scores are shown in Fig. 4.4 broken down by age, condition, and type of display. Results indicated that the addition of a reminder, along with the clustered item display boosted 4-year-olds' performance-to almost ceiling levels across all shopping conditions; 3-year-olds' performances reached ceiling levels for one event at a

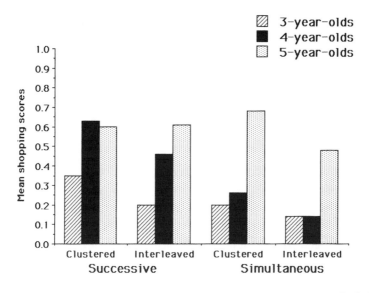

FIG. 4.3. Mean shopping scores by age, condition, and display, Experiment 1, Study 2.

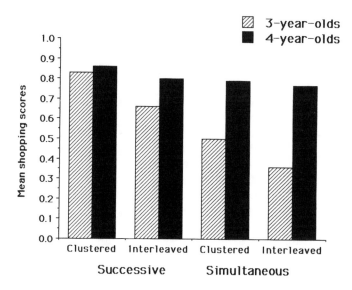

FIG. 4.4. Mean shopping scores by age, condition, and display, Experiment 2, Study 2.

time and were much improved when shopping for two events at the same time.

Conclusions

This study found evidence for developmental differences in children's abilities to construct event plans and in children's abilities to keep a plan in mind and use it to guide behavior. However, the availability of external support from the environment was important in determining children's abilities to execute their plans. Many age differences in children's plan execution that we observed when children were not given any support disappeared when we provided reminders and support in the physical environment.

Three-year-olds were capable of Level 1, single goal planning when given some external support (as with the clustered display in the first experiment). In the second experiment, with additional social support during plan execution, some 3-year-olds showed evidence of Level 2, multiple goal planning. Four-year-olds' performances fell between Levels 1 and 2. They did not depend on external support to plan for a single event goal and, when provided with adult assistance (Experiment 2), they were capable of executing multiple goal event plans. However, 5-year-olds were capable of independent Level 2 planning and did not require external support in constructing and executing multiple goal event plans.

STUDY 3: EFFECTS OF CAUSAL STRUCTURE
ON CHILDREN'S EVENT PLANNING

In Study 2, children were asked only to construct and execute plans for item selection, not the entire sequence of actions involved in grocery shopping. In contrast, Study 1 focused on children's abilities to construct advance plans for entire events, but they were not required to execute those plans. In Study 3, we investigated preschool children's abilities to both construct and execute plans for entire event sequences (Shapiro & Hudson, 1992). In addition, we examined the effects of causal structure of events on children's abilities to construct and execute event plans. Children learned two novel event sequences that varied in terms of their causal structure and then they were asked to construct and execute event plans for both events. Thus, in this study, we examined whether preschool children are capable of Level 1 planning after learning novel event sequences and whether the causal structure of the event influenced Level 1 planning.

Causal Structure of Events

Several script interview and story recall studies of preschool children have shown that causally connected events are more often recalled in their canonical order than arbitrarily connected events (Hudson & Nelson, 1983; Nelson & Gruendel, 1981, 1986; Slackman, Hudson, & Fivush, 1986). In addition, studies using behavioral enactment as a recall measure have shown, in general, that children's recall and sequencing of causally structured events was better than for events with arbitrary temporal connections (Bauer, 1992; Bauer & Mandler, 1990; Bauer & Shore, 1987; Fivush, Kuebli, & Clubb, 1992; Ratner, Smith, & Dion, 1986). However, it is unclear whether causal relations provide an organizational advantage in constructing and executing plans for complex events. With the exception of Ratner et al. (1986), most of the research on effects of event structure on children's memory examined recall of simple sequences without embedded sub-sequences of actions. In contrast, the art projects used in this study required that children learn how to complete a complex series of activities including embedded subacts that were either arbitrarily or causally connected.

Four-year-olds were asked to construct and execute plans for two novel art projects that varied in terms of their causal structure. As shown in Table 4.4, the suncatcher project involved more causal (enabling) links between actions than the more arbitrarily sequenced project of making hats. Children participated in two training sessions in the art room of their day care center in groups of two children with an experimenter. After the last training session, children were interviewed and asked to provide verbal scripts for "what happens" in making the projects. One week later, children returned individually to the art room for a final planning session. They

TABLE 4.4
Sequence of Activities for Art Projects, Study 2

Suncatchers:	Causally Constrained
1. Preparation:	Turn on iron. Place towel on table
2. Wax paper:	Tear off two sheets of wax paper.
3. Crayons:	Select two crayons. Shave crayon onto wax paper using pencil sharpener.
4. Ironing:	Cover first piece of wax paper with second. Cover way Paper with towel. Iron.
5. Shape:	Select a cardboard shape. Trace shape on paper. Cut out shape.
6. String:	Punch hole at top. Cut string. Insert and tie string.
7. Finishing:	Put on name tag. Hang up.
Hats: Arbitrary sequence	
1. Prepare plate:	Cut paper plate in half.
2. Glue:	Pour glue into cup. Put glue on plate using paint brush.
3. Glitter:	Sprinkle glitter on plate. Shake off excess.
4. Feathers:	Select 4 feathers. Dip feathers in glue Place feathers on plate.
5. Stickers:	Select 4 stickers. Place stickers on plate.
6. String:	Measure elastic string to head. Cut needed length. Staple string to plate.
7. Finishing:	Put on name tag. Hang up.

Note. Arrows indicate causal enabling links.

were asked to verbally plan the actions they needed to perform and what supplies they needed to get. Then, they selected the supplies they needed, and children were asked to direct the project on their own. The experimenter did not intervene in children's plan construction or execution, even if children made errors in enacting their plans.

Comparison of Scripts, Plans, and Execution

When asked to list the supplies they would need to complete the projects and select the appropriate items from the shelves, children's mean selection scores (computed the same way as the shopping scores in Study 2) were .80 for both projects. As compared to 4-year-olds' shopping scores when shopping for a single event without assistance in Study 2, children were more successful in selecting supplies in this study. There are many differences between the two studies, but it is possible that children were more successful in this study because they were actually going to use the supplies in a real event.

Figure 4.5 shows the mean number of acts (out of a total of 7) that children mentioned in their scripts and verbal plans and that they performed in plan execution. There were no significant differences across the two projects, but children performed more acts in execution than they mentioned in their scripts and plans.

Effects of Causal Structure on Sequencing

The mean proportions of actions either mentioned or performed in the correct sequence are shown in Fig. 4.6. There were no effects of type of art project for children's scripts and plans, but during plan execution, children sequenced the arbitrarily connected project more accurately than the causally connected project. This finding was somewhat surprising in light of past research that showed an organizational advantage of causal structure on children's event recall and enactment.

Examination of children's performances during plan execution showed that when children made mistakes in making hats, this did not disrupt the overall completion of the project. Yet, when they made mistakes in constructing the suncatchers, they often had to repeat actions out of sequence to successfully complete the project. For example, one child forgot to iron the pieces of wax paper together before tracing a shape on the paper. When she tried to cut the shape, the crayon shavings fell out. She then had to iron the paper together and repeat the action of tracing and cutting.

Providing Additional Support: Extra Training and Cued Execution

In an two additional experiments, we introduced manipulations to examine whether increasing internal and external support for planning would improve children's performance, particularly their plan enactments. First,

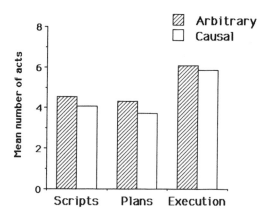

FIG. 4.5. Mean number of actions included in children's scripts, verbal plans, and execution, Study 3.

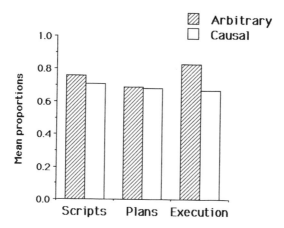

FIG. 4.6. Mean proportion of actions mentioned or performed in correct sequence, Study 3.

we provided children with four training sessions instead of two. Perhaps the two sessions did not give them enough training with the novel events to recall all of the component actions and subactions in the correct sequence. Results indicated that children's performances were virtually identical to the performance in the first experiment. Children mentioned the same number of actions in their scripts and plans, performed the same number of actions during execution, and produced the same number of errors.

In a third experiment, we displayed finished art projects for children to examine while they were planning aloud and while they were executing their plans. The finished projects could provide memory cues for the actions required to complete the projects. Although children mentioned more subactions in their verbal plans, they produced the same number of errors during plan execution. Thus, the external cues were helpful in reminding children to verbally describe the specific subactions involved, but they did not help children avoid errors in sequencing the actions during execution.

Conclusions

Although the causal structure of the event did not affect children's scripts and verbal plans, it did affect children's plan executions. The causally connected sequence included more critical links that had to be completed in the correct sequence in order to complete the goal. Children therefore had more difficulty maintaining and repairing the correct sequence of actions in executing plans for the causally connected project. Extra training and the presence of visual cues did not improve children's sequencing performance.

These results suggest that plan construction and plan execution are separate phases in planning that draw on different types of knowledge and skill. Whereas development in plan construction may depend on the development of increasingly complex event knowledge, development in plan execution may depend on the acquisition of strategies for monitoring and repairing plans. In addition, children may need to learn how to use external supports to aid execution, particularly in enacting complex event sequences. Merely providing information that could be used as a memory aid may not be enough to ensure that children use that information to monitor their plans during execution.

STUDY 4: PROVIDING INDIRECT INSTRUCTION IN EVENT PLANNING

Children's difficulty in constructing and executing effective plans in Study 3, even under reduced task demands, may be a by-product of their inexperience with this assignment. Results from our previous research clearly showed that children can and do anticipate familiar actions (Study 1) and objects (Study 2) needed to carry out hypothetical or pretend events. Moreover, children were able to learn novel events and devise advance plans (Study 3). However, children in Study 3, unlike those in Studies 1 and 2, were allowed to suffer the consequences of poor planning. Although even young preschool children can explain how to repair common mishaps in familiar events, children in Study 3 showed a diminished capacity for repairing faulty *plans* during execution, particularly for the causally constrained event. Just as children in Study 1 were unable to produce adequate prevention plans before the age of 5, children in Study 3 could not effectively consider potential execution problems in advance.

In everyday contexts, preschool children may not be given many opportunities to plan for events or to carry out their plans and may not recognize the need to anticipate actions in advance. However, if they were more involved in planning an event from the beginning of their experience with a novel event, they might incorporate planning and preparation into their GER and hence, be better prepared to plan on their own. In Study 4 (Sosa, 1994), we examined whether providing children with increased exposure to event planning during their process of learning new event sequences could increase their awareness of the importance of planning and could improve their subsequent planning performance. We were also interested in replicating the effects of event structure on planning found in Study 3 by using new activities that varied the number of causal links between acts.

Children at 3, 4, and 5 years were taught two novel event sequences, an arbitrarily structured snack and a causally structured art project. The action sequences are described in Table 4.5. Children learned how to make the two

TABLE 4.5

Sequence of Activities for Snack and Art Project: Study 4

Snack: Causally Constrained

1. Make crust:	Pick two *tortillas/crepes* Place side by side	
2. Make filling:	Cut *cheese/break chocolate* Grate *cheese/chocolate* Spread on tortilla crepe Cover with other tortilla crepe	
3. Cook:	Put tortilla crepe on oven tray Put in oven and cook	
4. Cut shapes:	Select cookie cutter Punch shape in snack	

Puppet: Arbitrary Sequence

1. Put on handle:	Place stick on body Tear off piece of tape Secure stick with tape
2. Put on eye:	Select eye sticker Put on head
3. Draw mouth:	Pick one marker Draw on mouth
4. Put on tail:	Pick two *feathers/cotton balls* Dip in *glue/glue on paper* Put *feathers/cotton balls* on paper

Note: Object and action variations are in italics. Arrows indicate causal enabling links.

projects in a separate room in their day-care center during two training sessions. They were asked to provide a script report for each event after each training experience. During the third and final session (the plan session), children were asked to construct verbal plans for completing the events and for selecting objects prior to enacting their plans.

Half of the children in each age group listened to the experimenter verbally plan for the events prior to enacting them in each of the two training sessions (the preparation condition). They were told, "This project is difficult, so it is very important for us to have a plan." Then the experimenter told them the sequence of actions for completing the project. Children in the preparation condition also participated in item selection during the training sessions. The experimenter read off the list of needed items and children retrieved them from shelves where all the items were displayed along with distractor cooking and art supplies. The other half of the children did not receive this extra planning support during training (the standard condition). They simply observed the experimenter as she selected the necessary items and then followed the experimenter's instructions for completing the projects (as was done in Study 3). However, the experimenter provided verbal instruction to the children in both groups when they created the projects (e.g., "The first thing we do is the crust. We have to pick two tortillas. Can you do that?").

Number of Actions Mentioned and Enacted

The mean number of actions (out of 10 per event) mentioned in children's scripts and plans and enacted during plan execution are shown in Table 4.6. Three-year-olds in the preparation condition reported and enacted more actions than in the standard condition; however, there was no significant effect of condition for 4- and 5-year-olds. This finding suggests that the youngest children, who tended to report and enact fewer actions, benefitted more from the enriched preparation condition. Younger children may need more structure to guide them in reporting a complete script or plan and in carrying out an advance plan. As in Study 3, children at all ages enacted more actions than they mentioned in their scripts and plans.

Number of Objects Reported and Selected

In the planning session, children were asked to tell the experimenter all the items that would be needed to complete the projects, and then they selected the required objects from an array of appropriate and distractor cooking and art supplies displayed on shelves. As shown in Table 4.7, the 4- and 5-year-olds reported more necessary objects (out of 5 possible for each event) than did the 3-year-olds. However, there were no age differences in the number of necessary items actually selected. This finding suggests that older children were better able to plan for the necessary items during the interview phase when no external cues were available. However, when shown a set of objects consisting of the necessary supplies, even 3-year-olds were able to recognize and choose the appropriate items.

More importantly, 3- and 5-year-old children in the preparation condition reported more of the necessary items than children in the standard condition. Thus, the youngest (and least experienced) and the oldest (and

TABLE 4.6

Mean Number of Actions Reported/Performed in Scripts, Plans, and Plan Enactments, Study 4

	Script 1	Script 2	Plan	Enactment
		Preparation Condition		
3-year-olds	3.92	4.83	4.00	8.92
4-year-olds	4.63	4.79	4.75	9.25
5-year-olds	6.04	6.04	7.13	9.75
		Standard Condition		
3-year-olds	3.03	2.29	2.67	8.25
4-year-olds	4.79	4.62	5.25	9.50
5-year-olds	5.25	4.96	5.46	9.38

TABLE 4.7

Mean Number of Objects Reported in Plans and Selected During Plan Enactment by
Age, Event, and Condition, Study 4

	Snack		Puppet	
	Plan	Enactment	Plan	Enactment
	Preparation Condition			
3-year-olds	2.75	4.83	2.33	4.75
4-year-olds	3.67	5.00	2.83	4.92
5-year-olds	4.42	5.00	4.33	5.00
	Standard Condition			
3-year-olds	1.67	4.50	1.33	4.75
4-year-olds	3.67	5.00	3.25	4.92
5-year-olds	3.67	4.92	3.25	4.92

most experienced) children who had listened to an adult plan aloud in advance were better able to select appropriate items when placed in the role of planner.

Sequencing Errors and Repetitions in Plans

As in Study 3, the number of sequence errors and repetitions in children's plan enactment was analyzed. In general, children made proportionally more sequencing errors for the causally constrained snack project ($M = .22$) than the arbitrarily connected puppet project ($M = .11$). In addition, 3-year-olds produced more errors than did 4- and 5-year-olds, but only in the snack project.

Proportion of Preparatory Actions

In addition to mentioning the original actions in their scripts and plans, children also included important preparation information about the events such as going to get supplies and taking the basket of supplies to the table. These actions were performed during each training session, but were not mentioned by the experimenter when she told the children the plan for how to complete the projects. The proportion of preparation information reported by each child for each event was calculated by dividing the number of preparation actions mentioned by the total number of actions mentioned in a script or plan. Children in the preparation condition reported significantly more preparation information ($M = .21$) than did children in the standard condition ($M = .12$). Hearing an adult prepare for an event and emphasize the importance of planning may have encouraged children in the preparation condition to be more aware of the advance preparations required to carry out the events.

Conclusions

Providing indirect instruction in planning an event was effective in improving children's advance planning under certain conditions. The youngest children showed the most improvement when they were given extra support in planning during the training sessions. They mentioned more actions and objects in their scripts and advance plans compared with same-age children in the standard condition. Similar gains were demonstrated by the oldest children in the preparation condition when listing the items necessary for carrying out the events. In addition, children at all ages mentioned more preparation information in their plans than did children in the standard condition.

Listening to a skilled adult stress the importance of advance planning and provide a complete verbal plan may have helped children understand the relevance of planning to a goal-directed activity and also provided children with a model of an event plan. However, this support did not affect children's plan execution. Because the planning support during training concentrated on plan construction, this support may only have made the advance planning phase more explicit to children. The preparation condition did not provide children with strategies for monitoring or repairing plans. More direct modeling of these processes may be needed to help children develop plan execution strategies.

As found in the previous study, causal constraints made sequencing a more complex event more difficult than sequencing a more arbitrarily ordered event. That is, one sequencing error often led to mis-sequencing and repetition of several of the subsequent steps as the child tried to correct the mistake. In contrast, mistakes made when enacting plans for the arbitrary event usually went unnoticed because rectifying them did not require backtracking in the action sequence and did not affect the ultimate outcome. Not surprisingly, the youngest subjects had the greatest difficulty in maintaining the correct order of actions in the causally constrained event.

EVENT KNOWLEDGE AND EVENT PLANNING: WHAT DEVELOPS?

Preschool children possess a great deal of knowledge about the sequence of routine events that is extremely useful in planning event sequences in advance. Reliance on GERs provides children with a framework for anticipating complete event sequences and for selecting slot-fillers and options when planning for future occurrences of familiar events. However, from 3 to 5 years of age, there is considerable development in a child's ability to reflect on specific event knowledge and focus on the planning-related components. Children are better able to construct plans to remedy and to prevent hypothetical mishaps (Study 1), to consider multiple event goals in planning (Study 2), and to enact plans for causally constrained event sequences (Study 4).

Our research also indicates that preschool children's abilities to construct advance plans develop earlier than their abilities to execute their plans (Studies 2, 3, and 4). The ability to execute an advance plan involves additional cognitive skills for remembering and monitoring plans during enactment. Moreover, the temporal–causal structure of the event that is being enacted strongly influences children's plan execution (Studies 3 and 4). Event sequences that are more causally constrained are sometimes more difficult to enact because errors are more difficult to repair than in more loosely organized sequences.

Despite consistent age differences in planning performance, it is important to note that most of the developmental trends found in our research were mediated by the degree of external support provided for children during planning. Preschool children can take advantage of some kinds of external support such as reminders of the event goal during plan enactment (Study 2), cues in the physical environment (Studies 2 and 3), and observation of adult planning (Study 4). Thus, children's event planning abilities must be viewed as a potential that may or may not be realized in any particular situation depending on the availability of both internal and external supports.

Developmental Mechanisms

What causes these developments in children's abilities to use event knowledge effectively in planning? Several factors may play a role. First, with increasing age and experience with events, children acquire more complex event knowledge that includes more knowledge about options and alternatives, as well as greater knowledge about planning components of events. Study 1 showed that 5-year-old children included more information about planning when providing both scripts and plans for familiar events than did 3- and 4-year-olds. This indicates that their knowledge about what happens in familiar events included more knowledge of how to plan for events. In the same study, 5-year-olds' superior abilities to construct remedy plans for mishaps may also be a result of increased experience with events and greater familiarity with event variations. Increased knowledge about variations allows for more complete advance planning and for better remedy and prevention planning (Hammond, 1990; Schank, 1982).

Second, with increasing age, children may become more flexible in their use of event knowledge in performing various cognitive tasks. This increased flexibility allows children to reflect on one's script knowledge, decompose the sequence into separate actions, analyze the component parts, understand relationships between actions and goals, and finally, rearrange the parts into novel sequences. These skills are necessary for planning at Levels 2 through 4 in Hudson and Fivush's (1991) model. In Study 1, the 5-year-old children's abilities to form remedy plans required that they could mentally repair a mishap by reordering action sequences or inserting alternative action paths into the sequence. In Study 2, the 4- and 5-year-olds demonstrated at least Level 2 planning as evidenced by their abilities to consider two event goals simultaneously in plan construction and execution. To do so, they had to decompose and integrate components from two familiar events. These integration and repair skills depend on the ability to use event knowledge flexibly rather than simply "running off" an event schema stored in memory.

Similar developments in children's abilities to reflect on general event knowledge were reported in studies of children's uses of scripts as retrieval guides in memory tasks (Hudson, 1988, 1993; Hudson & Fivush, 1983; Hudson & Nelson, 1983). Older children seem better able to reflect on their event knowledge and use it strategically to guide recall and to plan, rather than simply allowing schematic structures to guide these processes in an automatic fashion (see also Hudson & Fivush, 1991; Hudson & Slackman, 1990).

Finally, as children mature, they may be given more responsibility for planning and may be given more explicit instruction in how to plan for future events. One reason that young children's planning skills have not been fully developed may be because they have not been provided with opportunities to use and refine their event planning skills. Simply having general event knowledge does not ensure that young children will be able to translate that knowledge into advance plans, nor ensure that they will be able to carry out their advance plans. Three-year-olds' difficulties in carrying out shopping plans in Study 1 and in generating verbal plans in Study 2 indicates that knowing what happens is not enough to plan. The 4-year-olds in Study 3 also had difficulty enacting a plan despite the fact that they could provide scripts and verbal plans for the art projects. However, preschool children in Study 4 showed they benefitted from even very minimal instruction in planning. Thus, preschool children's early planning skills may be facilitated by providing them with more experience in planning and by providing them with support in plan construction and execution.

REFERENCES

Abelson, R. P. (1981). Psychological status of the script concept. *American Psychologist, 36,* 715–729.

Barsalou, L. W. (1991). Deriving categories to achieve goals. In G. H. Bower (Ed.), *The psychology of learning and motivation: Advances in research and theory* (Vol. 27, pp. 1–64) New York: Academic Press.

Bauer, P. J. (1992). Holding it all together: How enabling relations facilitate young children's event recall. *Cognitive Development, 7*, 1–28.

Bauer, P. J., & Mandler, J. M. (1990). Remembering what happened next: Very young children's recall of event sequences. In R. Fivush & J. A. Hudson (Eds.), *Knowing and remembering in young children* (pp. 9–29). New York: Cambridge University Press.

Bauer, P., & Shore, C. (1987). Toddlers' recall of arbitrary, causal, and conventional action sequences. *Cognitive Development, 2*, 327–338.

DeLisi, R. (1987). A cognitive-developmental model of planning. In S. L. Friedman, E. K. Scholnick, & R. R. Cocking (Eds.). *Blueprints for thinking: The role of planning in cognitive development* (pp. 79–109). Cambridge, England: Cambridge University Press.

Fivush, R., Kuebli, J. & Clubb, P. A. (1992). The structure of events and event representations: A developmental analysis. *Child Development, 63*, 188–201.

Fivush, R., & Slackman, E. A. (1986). The acquisition and development of scripts. In K. Nelson (Ed.), *Event knowledge: Structure and function in development* (pp. 71–98). Hillsdale, NJ: Lawrence Erlbaum Associates.

Friedman, S. L., Scholnick, E. K., & Cocking, R. R. (1987). Reflections on reflections: What planning is and how it develops. In S. L. Friedman, E. K. Scholnick, & R. R. Cocking (Eds.), *Blueprints for thinking: The role of planning in cognitive development* (pp. 515–534). Cambridge, England: Cambridge University Press.

Gauvain, M., & Rogoff, B. (1989). Collaborative problem solving and children's planning skills. *Developmental Psychology, 25*, 139–151.

Hammond, K. J. (1990). Case-based planning: A framework for planning from experience. *Cognitive Science, 14*, 385–443.

Hayes-Roth, B., & Hayes-Roth, F. (1979). A cognitive model of planning. *Cognitive Science, 3*, 275–310.

Hudson, J. A. (1986). Memories are made of this: General event knowledge and the development of autobiographic memory. In K. Nelson (Ed.), *Event knowledge: Structure and function in development* (pp. 97–118). Hillsdale, NJ: Lawrence Erlbaum Associates.

Hudson, J. A. (1988). Children's memory for atypical actions in script based stories: Evidence for a disruption effect. *Journal of Experimental Child Psychology, 46*, 159–173. Hudson, J. A. (1993). Understanding events: The development of script knowledge. In M. Bennett (Ed.), *The child as psychologist* (pp. 142–167). London: Wiley.

Hudson, J., & Fivush, R. (1983). Categorical and schematic organization and the development of retrieval strategies. *Journal of Experimental Child Psychology, 36*, 32–42.

Hudson, J. A., & Fivush, R. (1991). Planning in the preschool years: The emergence of plans from general event knowledge. *Cognitive Development, 6*, 393–415.

Hudson, J., & Nelson, K. (1983). Effects of script structure on children's story recall. *Developmental Psychology, 19*, 625–635.

Hudson, J. A., & Shapiro, L. R. (1991). From knowing to telling: Children's scripts, stories, and personal narratives. In A. McCabe & C. Peterson (Eds.), *Developing narrative structure.* (pp. 89–36). Hillsdale, NJ: Lawrence Erlbaum Associates.

Hudson, J. A., Shapiro, L. R., & Sosa, B. B. (1995). Planning in the real world: Preschool children's scripts and plans for familiar events. *Child Development, 4*(3), 984–998.

Hudson, J. A., & Slackman, E. A. (1990). Children's use of scripts in inferential text processing. *Discourse Processes, 13*, 375–385.

Hudson, J. A., & Sosa, B. B. (1995). *Scripts and plans in mother–child conversations about future events.* Paper presented at the meetings of the Society for Research in Child Development, Indianapolis, IN.

Kreitler, S., & Kreitler, H. (1987). Conceptions and processes of planning: The developmental perspective. In S. L. Friedman, E. K. Scholnick, & R. R. Cocking (Eds.), *Blueprints for thinking: The role of planning in cognitive development* (pp. 205–272). Cambridge, England: Cambridge University Press.

Lucariello, J., & Nelson, K. (1985). Slot-filler categories as memory organizers for young children. *Developmental Psychology, 21*, 272–282.

Nelson, K. (Ed.). (1986). *Event knowledge: Structure and function in development.* Hillsdale, NJ: Lawrence Erlbaum Associates.

Nelson, K., & Gruendel, J. (1979). At morning it's lunchtime: A scriptal view of children's dialogues. *Discourse Processes, 2*, 73–94.

Nelson, K., & Gruendel, J. (1981). Generalized event representations: Basic building blocks of cognitive development. In M. E. Lamb & A. L. Brown (Eds.), *Advances in developmental psychology* (Vol. 1, pp. 21–46). Hillsdale, NJ: Lawrence Erlbaum Associates.

Nelson, K., & Gruendel, J. (1986). Children's scripts. In K. Nelson (Ed.), *Event knowledge: Structure and function in development* (pp. 231–247). Hillsdale, NJ: Lawrence Erlbaum Associates.

Nelson, K., & Hudson, J. (1988). Scripts and memory: Functional relationships in development. In F. E. Weinert & M. Perlmutter (Eds.), *Memory development: Universal changes and individual differences* (pp. 147–167). Hillsdale, NJ: Lawrence Erlbaum Associates.

Oppenheimer, L. (1987). Cognitive and social variables in the plan of action. In S. L. Friedman, E. K. Scholnick, & R. R. Cocking (Eds.), *Blueprints for thinking: The role of planning in cognitive development* (pp. 356–392). Cambridge, England: Cambridge University Press.

Pea, R. D., & Hawkins, J. (1987). Planning in a chore–scheduling task. In S. L. Friedman, E. K. Scholnick, & R. R. Cocking (Eds.), *Blueprints for thinking: The role of planning in cognitive development* (pp. 273–302). Cambridge, England: Cambridge University Press.

Ratner, H. H., Smith, B. A., & Dion, S. E. (1986). Development of memory for events. *Journal of Experimental Child Psychology, 41,* 1–24.

Rogoff, B., Gauvain, M., & Gardner, W. (1987). The development of children's skills in adjusting plans to circumstances. In S. L. Friedman, E. K. Scholnick, & R. R. Cocking (Eds.), *Blueprints for thinking: The role of planning in cognitive development* (pp. 303–320). Cambridge, England: Cambridge University Press.

Schank, R. (1982). *Dynamic memory: A theory of learning in computers and people.* New York: Cambridge University Press.

Schank, R., & Abelson, R. P. (1977). *Scripts, plans, goals. and understanding.* Hillsdale, NJ: Lawrence Erlbaum Associates.

Scholnick, E. K., & Friedman, S. L. (1987). The planning construct in the psychological literature. In S. L. Friedman, E. K. Scholnick, & R. R. Cocking (Eds.), *Blueprints for thinking: The role of planning in cognitive development* (pp. 2–29). Cambridge, England: Cambridge University Press.

Scholnick, E. K., & Friedman, S. L. (1993). Planning in context: Developmental and situational considerations. *International Journal of Behavioral Development, 16,* 145–167.

Shapiro, L. R., & Hudson, J. A. (1992, April). *From start to finish: What does it take for preschoolers to construct plans from novel scripts?* Presented at the Conference on Human Development, Atlanta, GA.

Slackman, E. A., Hudson, J. A., & Fivush, R. (1986). Actions, actors, links, and goals: The structure of children's event representations. In K. Nelson (Ed.), *Event knowledge: Structure and function in development* (pp. 47–69). Hillsdale, NJ: Lawrence Erlbaum Associates.

Sosa, B. B. (1994). *From knowledge to planning.* Unpublished master's thesis, Rutgers University.

5

Young Children: Emotion Management, Instrumental Control, and Plans

---

Claire B. Kopp
Claremont Graduate School

Negotiation with peers over the legality of a soccer goal; working out a chess move with a classmate; figuring out how to get an older sister to be less bossy—these are examples of everyday challenges that confront children. Effective solutions often involve planning: thinking about a goal, laying out strategies, anticipating options, and evaluating courses of action—all of this in the service of meeting self-needs.

That school-age children frequently engage in planful behavior is well documented (see, e.g., Friedman, Scholnick, & Cocking, 1987; Gauvain, 1989). Whether children of younger ages engage in planning is less clear. Although some researchers have mentioned planful behaviors in infants, toddlers, and young preschoolers, the evidence is not fully convincing. The reason is, in part, related to the constituents of planning that are not sufficiently developed in young children. For example, self-related motivations are essential for mature forms of planning as is some form of monitoring as a plan proceeds (e.g., Newell & Simon, 1972). However, self-reflection, self-monitoring, and evaluation are difficult for preschoolers (e.g., Wellman, Fabricius, & Sophian, 1985), much less for infants and toddler-aged children.

Disagreements about the equivalency of immature and mature forms of behaviors are not unique in the developmental literature (e.g., Fischer & Bidel, 1991). One way to inform the issue entails using an agreed-upon definition of the mature behavior and identifying attributes found in the immature form. This is the strategy adopted in this chapter. Relevant aspects of infant, toddler, and early preschool development are described and associated with constituents of mature planful behavior—defining a problem space, considering options, goal setting, organizing steps to reach a goal, calculating potential obstacles to a plan, revising a plan as war-

103

ranted, and evaluating strategies that have been used (e.g., Friedman, Scholnick, & Cocking, 1987; Gauvain, 1989, 1992; Scholnick, 1994, 1995).

It is now acknowledged that development and context are inseparable. Thus, in proposing a developmental picture of nascent plans there must be a role for context.[1] The focus here is on contexts that provide compelling incentives to avoid or to control unpleasant emotion situations. Recognize, though, that developmental-contextual links emerge over time. Early skills are fragmented, unpredictable in appearance, and inconsistently functional in contexts. In time these skills become integrated and contextually appropriate. Then, given compelling events, young children have the potential to draw on their behavioral repertoire to produce deliberate, organized, and potent courses of action. Some of the repertoire also can be effectively directed to contexts that involve distressful events such as frustrations and fears. In time, some behaviors begin to resemble planful actions, coping, and *psychological control* (Skinner & Wellborn, 1994).

In summary, this chapter has three goals. The first is to suggest *when* elements of behavior that are intrinsic to planning appear in the developmental repertoire and *how* these behaviors can be functionally used by the young child. The second is to emphasize the saliency of distressful events and emotions in the lives of young children and to suggest this saliency is a catalyst for facilitating young children's planful-like behaviors in the service of emotion control. The third is to highlight the differential role of negative emotion events in promoting planning.

This chapter provides a selective view of relevant literature. Its content does not cover the extensive number of studies on planful behaviors in older children and adults nor does it address the vast amount of theory and research on early emotion development. The former is represented in this book and the latter can be found in Denham's comprehensive review (in press).

CHAPTER ORGANIZATION

The chapter has four parts. The first part of the chapter orients the reader to a summary of developmental assumptions that guide my thinking about growth in the earliest years of life. The second part provides a window into the young child's increasing control of the object and physical world. This control, singularly important for adaptive behaviors, is often reflected in the growth of instrumental acts. Thus, an underlying theme calls attention to the growth of instrumental behaviors and their application to distressful

---

[1]Context has long been an integral part of planning research albeit the definition of context and its role has varied. Studies have incorporated context-specific strategies (e.g., memory; Scholnick & Friedman, 1992), contexts that provide cues (e.g., De Lisi, 1987; Kreiter & Kreiter, 1987), and contexts that provide teaching for mothers (Gauvain, 1995).

events and also notes the foundational role that instrumental behaviors play in to the growth of planning. Several developmental questions guide the specific content of this section: (a) what negative events are common to the lives of young children, (b) what resources does the young child have to control these negative events, and (c) when does the functional use of these resources approximate the beginnings of a plan, or, actually represent a plan? The age periods discussed are the first year of life, then the toddler and young preschool periods. These ages probably represent foundation periods for planning. The crucial role of caregivers in modeling, teaching, and guiding children toward control of their behavior is mentioned as well.

The third section focuses on the nature of events that cause children distress. Here, events that cause fear are contrasted with those that provoke anger, and reasons why controllability is more likely to occur with the former rather than the latter are offered. Nascent planning actions should emerge in distressful events that do not involve anger. Lastly, the chapter then shifts from a developmental theme to highlight questions about possible origins of individual differences in young children's options for control and to generate planful acts. There are implications for emotion management.

DEVELOPMENTAL ORIENTATION

Conceptualizing Early Development

Premises.   In considering the development of a particular behavioral system, reasonable questions include: (a) what behaviors are available to the young infant (or young child) at Time $_{1, 2, n ...}$, (b) what can the child do with the behaviors that are available, (c) how do the available behaviors impact other aspects of the developing system, and (d) what new behaviors will/should come online and thereby modify the behaviors currently in the repertoire?

Relatedly, the human developmental repertoire consists of general, normative properties albeit variabilities exists in developmental trajectories and paths. Stated another way, there are general features of sensorimotor development that are observable in all normal infants reared in relatively supportive environments. These general features make it possible to describe the major configuration of social interactions, object play, the nature of speech, or the constituents of planful behavior at any age. The point is that it is possible to specify how the emergent behaviors of infancy, the toddler period, and the preschool years can additively connect with one another, become integrated into a functional system, and increasingly become mature. This is the picture to be developed with reference to the constituents of planning.

New Behaviors and Their Functional Application.   How are behaviors that come online initially used by the young child, how are the behaviors/skills mastered so they can be used in instrumental ways? These questions could refer to the *how* of the big developmental picture (e.g., see Fischer, 1980; Karmiloff-Smith, 1992; Thelen & Smith, 1994) or merely to descriptions of a behavior emerging, becoming ontogenetically mature (however that happens), and then becoming a *tool* for the child. The latter, more simple view is the focus here.

The translation of a new behavior into an instrumental function is partly due to infant efforts and partly due to supports given by caregivers. Ultimately however, it is the infant and young child who is the self-organizing unit, and it is the infant/young child who must effectively integrate new behaviors into the repertoire so there will be greater flexibility in dealing with an increasing range of situations. During this cohering process, behavioral integration is often fragmented, and the functional use of behaviors in the repertoire is frequently limited or so singularly context-dependent that it is severely constrained (e.g., Fischer & Bidell, 1991; Thelen & Ulrich, 1991). Considerable time may elapse between the time a behavior emerges and its developmental transformation into a decontextualized, instrumental tool. There are implications for planning such that behaviors that will eventually feed into planful activities are likely to be inefficient some of the time.

A Motivating Force for Developmental Growth.   Long before there is a measurable, definable self, young infants seem to possess an amorphous, unstable, preconscious, implicit sense of *being* that underlies a motive to explore, to discriminate their surroundings, to seek pleasure, and to avoid distress (e.g., see Brownell & Kopp, 1991; Neisser, 1988; Stern, 1985; Wenar, 1982). It is possible that this preconscious knowledge is the source of young infants' attempts to alleviate negative emotional states. Indeed, self-soothing is common among infants (Stifter, 1993). At a somewhat later period, with a conscious, albeit nascent awareness of self, and the emergence of new competencies, the young toddler has conscious intentionality, motives, and some resources to fashion instrumental behavior that have some of the hallmarks of plans. Then given the right conditions, emergent planful like behaviors can be utilized to control some distressing events.

THE ONTOGENESIS OF BEHAVIORS:
MOVING TOWARD PLANNING

Starting at the Beginning: The First Year of Life

The Nature of Distressful Events.   Distress during the first year can be classified as a function of physiological upsets and psychologically imbued events. The former are most common and prominent in the first months of life and include digestive difficulties, irritability, and fatigue due to immaturity of the central nervous system, respiratory upsets leading to hiccups, coughing, and the like. Psychological distress is more common after 3 months and includes internal states of boredom, a desire for social closeness, dislikes (e.g., food), and external events that cause anxiousness about highly novel situations, a sense of fear or loss due to separation from attachment figures, pain, and exposure to unanticipated events such as looming objects or loud voices (see summaries in Kopp, 1994).

Resources Available to Control Distress Events.   There is growing consensus that much of very early development consists of biologically primed *special purpose responses* (Fischer & Bidell, 1991) that are restricted to specific stimuli in a special group of situations. The label *procedural knowledge* is frequently applied to these responses, albeit procedural knowledge is not restricted to infancy.

Procedural knowledge in infancy is preconscious, nonsymbolic, goal-driven in a context-dependent setting, spur-of-the-moment, and frequently constrained by the need for interpersonal supports (Clyman, 1991; Emde, Biringen, Clyman, & Oppenheim, 1991). Procedural knowledge lays an important foundation for later development. Examples of early procedural knowledge (Emde, Biringen, Clyman, & Oppenheim, 1991; Flavell, Miller, & Miller, 1993; Kopp, 1982, 1989; Nelson, 1996) include the ability of infants to:

- show behavioral synchrony with parents and other familiar individuals,
- recognize social signals and cues of specific individuals and anticipate accordingly,
- reveal emotion expressiveness to familiar individuals,
- monitor the actions and locations of some individuals and physical objects,
- activate mechanisms to modulate emotion distress in certain circumstances,
- control visual responsivity to certain stimuli,
- communicate with familiar others,
- acquire basic and particular information about specific objects, movements, and simple cause-and-effect relations,
- understand near and far space in familiar surroundings; distinguish depth, hardness, and softness.

Procedural knowledge provides a limited form of control for distressful events. Oral actions such as voluntary thumb-or pacifier-sucking, visual distraction in the form of seeking out interesting objects and patterns to look at, communicating mild distress signals to others with frets, or distraction with play and body exploration are examples (e.g., Cohn & Tronick, 1983; Kaye & Fogel, 1980; Kopp, 1989; Rothbart & Derryberry, 1981). With increasing ability to manipulate playthings and to move about independently, and with growing affiliation and affection to specific others, infants widen their opportunities for instrumental acts in the service of control. Many 9-month-olds, for example, exposed to intrusive strangers turn away and nuzzle a caregiver's shoulder to shut out the unwanted stimulus.

By age 1, infants apparently recognize (and anticipate) those events that cause them distress and they understand their own role in controlling some distressful events. One strategy involves using hands in instrumental ways. Year-old infants who were given the opportunity to manage the actions of a mechanical monkey showed more willingness to activate the monkey and cried less than infants who were denied control (Gunnar-vonGnechten, 1978). In subsequent research, Gunnar and colleagues (e.g., Gunnar, 1980; Gunnar-vonGnechten, 1978; Parritz, Mangelsdorf, & Gunnar, 1992) replicated the effect of control on infant distress management. Parritz et al. (1992) suggested that taking command of an event changes the meaning of the event for the infant.

Thus, in the first year of life a transition occurs from merely engaging in a simple act such as thumb sucking oriented to soothing to more complex acts such as maneuvering an object's operating mechanism to control events that might cause distress. The latter is clearly anticipatory and preventive. The impressive growth in distress management comes out of the development of other systems. A particularly powerful advance involves the ability to use hands as instrumental tools. To reach this developmental milestone, an infant had to have gained voluntary control of reach and grasp, detected the role of grasp in object play, and discovered how and when hands and fingers can be used in social communication. This latter skill is exemplified in Rogoff, Mistry, Radziszewska, and Germond's (1992) study of emergent instrumental communication among young infants. Note that instrumental competencies are brought into focus by caregivers when they provide prompts and learning opportunities for social and object play. Prompts are likely to include specifics about how to use hands in games such as pat-a-cake and in applying different soothing strategies (Bowlby, 1988; Calkins, 1994; Cassidy, 1994). By the end of the first year, infants display increasingly diversified forms of hand proficiency for both pleasurable and distress contexts.

Overall then, the infant's skill in instrumental action has come out of a biological *given*, a great deal of practice, considerable amounts of caregiver support, play, soothing, and many opportunities to try out one's hands in a variety of exploratory situations. Increasingly, hands become instrumental tools for distress management.

Do Infant Behavioral Skills and Resources Bear Resemblance to the Beginnings of a Plan? Discrete goal-directed actions (e.g., a pick-me-up gesture) do not represent plans; these behaviors are too skeletal to approximate the richness of mature plans. However, the fact that *planning* is inchoate at this age does not negate the important substructure that is being laid: the *acquisition of knowledge,* the *instrumental use of knowledge,* and the nascent *awareness of how one's own actions* influence how one feels. Table 5.1 suggests how each of these elements could have a role in a functionally mature plan. The next section, highlighting toddlers, continues the focus on emergent behaviors and their role in plans.

The Toddler and Early Preschool Years

A number of theorists believe the end of the first year marks a turning point in children's cognitive, social, and emotional skills (e.g., Campos & Barrett, 1984; Fischer, 1980; Kopp, 1982; Piaget, 1952; Sroufe, 1979; Shora, 1994). Intentions, goal-seeking, signs of intelligent behavior, behavioral inhibition, engagement of adults around physical objects, behavioral organization, and elementary problem solving are terms used to describe these behaviors (see, e.g., Diamond, 1990; Kopp, 1982; Piaget, 1952), albeit some

TABLE 5.1

Elements of Mature Planning and Their Links to Earlier Developmental Acquisitions

Elements	Developmental Timetable
Acquiring a *knowledge* base that helps define a 'problem'	Basic forms of procedural knowledge start to be acquired during early infancy; declarative knowledge begins to emerge during the 2nd/3rd years.
Recognizing *obstacles* to the goal	Infants recognize physical obstacles by the end of the 1st year; the recognition of obstacles to mentally represented goals (e.g., beliefs) emerges around the 3rd year.
Being able to represent a *goal* that will *solve* the problem	Year-old infants overcome some physical obstacles (e.g., a ball rolling behind a couch); the mental representation of obstacles seems to emerge around 2 years (e.g., deception geared to bypass behavioral prohibitions).
Recognizing that one can act *intentionally* to reach the goal	Intentionality, particularly in terms of specific communications (e.g., pointing) directed toward a specific person, is observed around the end of the 1st year.
Recognizing that solving a problem aids one's *self*	Self-recognition, self-consciousness, and awareness of self-possessions emerge around 18-to 24-months; recognition and labeling self-feelings (e.g., mad, bad) occurs around 2 years; self-evaluative emotions appear about 2 to 3 years.
Laying out one or more *options* to reach the goal	School years.
Organizing a specific *series of steps* to reach the goal	Use of scripts is a forerunner of this behavior, and scripted play is observed in the 2nd year; preschool aged children devise *steps* for certain kinds of play (e.g., first we'll...., then we'll....); mentally representing a series of steps emerges during the school years.
Evaluating the strategy or strategies that one uses	School years.

disagreement exists about specific definitions, origins, and constituents of intention (Gopnik, 1993; Lewis, 1991; Piaget, 1952). The emergent behavioral qualities of this age seem to be partly indicative of increasing activation and interaction of the prefrontal cortex (Diamond, 1990). Whatever the causal factors, there is consensus that by 1 year of age, infant behavior is often deliberate, motivated, and goal-directed. A child picks up a toy, explores it, takes it to a caregiver to see, and then resumes her play.

There will be additional dramatic changes that surface between the first and third years. These include the growth of script knowledge, the conscious recognition of different states of arousal, concern for the self, the ability to show dynamic responsivity to rapidly changing situations, comprehension and speech, and awareness that actions used in one situation can be generalized to another. As these new competencies come on board and become integrated into the developmental repertoire, the stage is set for increasing diversity of instrumental acts and the beginning construction of plans. The mature planning process is in the process of becoming.

Emergent forms of planning are labeled *protoplans* to call attention to their incompleteness and to differentiate clearly the immature and mature act. Before moving to a discussion of emerging skills, protoplans, and emotion management, distressful events common to this age are reviewed.

The Nature of Distressful Events.   Many developmental changes in child skill at this age lead to new demands from caregivers. Independent locomotion, along with a desire to explore, often means that caregivers initiate everyday "do's and don'ts" (Gralinski & Kopp, 1993). In turn, "do's and don'ts" lead to an increase in conflicts between parent and child (Dunn et al., 1987; Eisenberg et al., 1988). Upsets also occur because of the young child's limited ability to make wants known and the need for autonomous action. It is not surprising that crying increases appreciably between 18 and 21 months or so (Kopp, 1992).

Resources Available to Control Distress.   The second and third years are witness to important developmental changes in cognitive, social, linguistic, and emotional competencies that will have ramifications for the growth of protoplans. The following paragraphs highlight three competencies: script production, the role of selfhood, and the instrumental use of language. Each has a role in maturing planful behavior. The section ends with an example of a protoplan used for emotion control.

Behavioral Links, Bundles, and Scripts.   It is developmentally less mature to engage in a single intentional act with another person (e.g., raise one's arms in a pick-me-up gesture) than to bundle several behaviors into a package (e.g., a pick-me-up gesture combined with eye-to-eye contact and a spoken word *bah* for bottle). The developmental transition from one act to two or more combined acts is important in its own right but also has implications for the development of planful behavior. A plan, by definition, includes multiple behaviors.

Behavioral linkages and bundling are increasingly observed early in the second year (Fischer, 1980; Piaget, 1952; Sinclair, Stambak, Lezine, Rayna, & Verba, 1989), and are observed most clearly in play with objects. Most important, behavioral linkages open the way for dramatic expansion in the child's overall behavioral reserves and prepares for *scripts*. These involve a combination of a sequence of multiple acts with a defined end point, typically first observed in the second year. Multiple acts are often script-like and appear relatively regularly in the pretend play of toddlers and young preschool aged children (e.g., Bretherton, 1984; Nelson, 1986, 1990; Nelson & Gruendal, 1981).

Several features of pretend play have implications for the structure of more fully integrated plans that older children devise. First, in creating a situation that resembles a real life script, the young child who plays on his own *exercises control* over props, participants, and roles (Sinclair et al., 1989). Second, in situations that involve peers, pretend play involves planning the script or structure of the play sequence, negotiation over roles and context, and coordination of roles (e.g., see discussion in Bretherton, 1984). Third, shared play contexts impose some constraints on a script sequence, albeit not everything in the sequence is fully worked out (Nelson & Gruendel, 1981). A plan must have some constraints in its organization. Fourth, a play sequence set up by young peers permits one or another partner to evaluate whether the sequence is moving along as designed. A fully developed plan incorporates some form of evaluation.

As potent as scripts are, script production is not effortless. Young children engage in considerable trial and error learning to figure out how things work and how one makes things happen. Even the simplest of routines are not necessarily understood by the young child, and there is potential for frustration. Scripts also have limitations because distractions and interruptions can lead to disintegration of even a well-practiced script (e.g., Fivush & Hudson, 1990). Distractions may be one of the reasons that young children find it difficult to sustain sufficient memories for online planning (Bidell & Fischer, in press).

The fragility of script knowledge relates to the fragility control in distressful events. Although sometimes young toddlers utilize a self-generated script to alleviate distress,[2] often they rely on others (e.g., Shatz, 1994). Indeed between 18 and 24 months, many young children come to recognize their limitations with respect to solving puzzles and

---

[2]Lieberman (1993) recounted how one day, a 2-year-old whose mother had died took socks from the family laundry basket and spread them around the house. The child was enacting a script in that her mother had used socks to dust furniture. The script format changed when the child was pressed by her new caregiver to put the socks back in the basket. At that point, the child kept one and pressed it to her chest.

executingcomplexphysicalacts(e.g.,dressingone'sself).Insteadofcrying, they prevent frustration by defining the situation and their abilities, and when warranted, seek assistance from others (e.g., Bridges & Grolnick, 1995).

The Emergence of Selfhood, and Implications for Control of Events. The ability to control an event takes on greater urgency when there is *a commitment to and a sense of allegiance to self-generated goals.* In order for this to happen, the child must consciously perceive: a self and some of its elements and be aware that the self is permanent and differentiated from others (Butterworth, 1990; Lewis, 1993), the self's actions and psychological boundaries (Brownell & Kopp, 1991; Kagan, 1981), those experiences that can be organized to respond to self-defined needs (see e.g., Brownell & Kopp, 1991; Emde et al., 1991; Lewis, 1991), a self related memory that embodies one's existence "outside the present moment," and the *privacy* of one's own experiences (Neisser, 1988). It is self-awareness, Emde et al., (1991) argued, that brings motives into consciousness. Representation (i.e., declarative knowledge) defends the self and monitors affect (Emde et al., 1991). In all, this level of selfhood, which clearly implicates representational thinking and a memory that is capable of retrieval, is typically in nascent form at about 2 years.

As young children become more knowledgeable about their own selves, the more emotional gratification becomes an issue for them. Indeed, Harris (1989) suggested that young children often view their emotional lives in hedonic terms, working to achieve what they want when they want it. Not surprising, attempts at duplicity and peer aggression over possessions increase at this age (e.g., Jones & Burks, 1936). In effect, these kinds of behavior are attempts to control events.

Language as an Instrumental Tool. Functional speech allows young children to tell others what they like and dislike, what bothers them, and their desires for upcoming events (e.g., Nelson, 1996). It is language (as representative of symbolic thought) that allows children to think and compare current happenings with those of the past and the future. Functional language is intrinsic to overall competence (Hart & Risley, 1995). Although language is a formidable instrumental tool there is a dearth of information about linkages between language use and planning.

However, a considerable amount of research exists about language and emotions. State words (e.g., mad, bad), statements about emotion causes, and nascent ideas about emotion control are commonly emitted by young children (Bretherton, Fritz, Zahn-Waxler, & Ridgeway, 1986; Dunn, Bretherton, & Munn, 1987; Wolf, Rygh, Altshuler, 1984). And as Denham (in press) and Shatz (1994) comment, young children use language to organize (i.e., control) others, to manipulate others' feelings, and to increase their understanding of cultural scripts for emotion. Language takes on a role in self-generated control even for a toddler with only two word sentences (Lieberman, 1993). A child close to 2 years generated the following: "no, myself," "be careful," and "mommy help." The first was a signal to others that he could do things on his own, the second served as an instruction to himself as he engaged in a "bold" new activity involving a playground swing, and the third secured help when needed.

That language has an increasing role in emotion management has been discussed previously (Kopp, 1989). The way in which preschoolers use fantasy play to work out happenings that are unsettling to them and school-aged children turn to their peers to talk about distressing events was noted. Given the direct role of language in emotion regulation, it is difficult to fathom how planning (whatever the goal) could occur without words. An actual plan could be wordless in execution, but the strategies that are enlisted for the process of planning would likely involve ideation (using words).

A Summary.   Seemingly, the second and third years are singularly important for adding to the foundations of planful behavior. Sequential acts, recognition of the self and self-needs, and the ability to engage in symbolic thought combined with the use of words are essential and necessary components of planning. These new competencies together with those developed earlier (e.g., acquisition of knowledge and how to use it) allow the child to pull together a string of behaviors for intentional, conscious, self-motivated functional management of events and emotions. Nonetheless, important features (e.g., evaluation and monitoring) of planning are missing or a planful-like act may be dependent on others. For this reason, the term *protoplan* is used to signify an incomplete plan. An example follows.

A Protoplan.   A recognized need for self-protection and a desire to overcome a negative emotion state is exemplified in the following vignette. The child's actions illustrate a goal and a series of steps that lead to the goal of taking control of an event that caused fear. Many of the emergent skills described previously contribute to this complex and rich behavioral scenario. Note though, the child's intent rests on his mother's willing and sensitive assistance. The challenge is too great for him to handle on his own.

The setting: Peter is 30 months of age. It is my first visit to the family home to collect data. Peter, his mother, and I sit on the uncarpeted living room floor while Peter plays with toys I have brought. Peter finds a yellow toy plastic football, perhaps 3 in. long. The football has six spider-like legs protruding from its bottom and a wind-up key to activate the legs. Peter hands the football to his mother who winds the key and puts the football on the floor. The football moves fairly quickly along the floor making a slightly tinny noise. Peter gasps, "I scared!, I scared!", as he scoots under a nearby table. He shivers. His mother comforts him. I grab the football, run outside to my car and place it on the hood of the car. I hastily return to find that Peter is now calm.

The protoplan: It is an hour later, and I am ready to leave. Peter's mother asks him if he would like to walk me to the car. He says, "yes", and the three of us head down the driveway to the car. I have forgotten the football, but Peter quickly spies it on the hood. He pulls his mother to the car hood, gestures for her to retrieve it and to wind the football key. She does, and then puts the football on the sidewalk. As his mother crouches on the ground with the football, Peter runs behind her and grasps her back. He peers from her side and looks at the football as it makes its way down the sidewalk. He does not say a word. After some time, Peter's mother tells him it is time for me to go. She picks up the football and hands it to me. I leave.

Peter, obviously fascinated by the football although fearing it, reveals classic examples of psychologically opposing forces of approach and avoidance. On rediscovering the football, Peter seized the opportunity for *approach* by asking his mother to operate the football while using her as a *fear shield*. Could he have also realized that the sidewalk's surface would slow the football's spidery legs to a crawl? In any event, consider that few other everyday experiences save emotional distress have the driving force to wrest new forms of mature cognitive functioning from young children (e.g., protoplans).

Moving from Protoplans to Mature Planfulness.   The documented growth of young children's cognitive skills facilitates the transition to planful behavior (see summary of cognitive changes in Flavell, Miller, & Miller, 1993, and developmental growth in planning in Gauvain, 1995). Even with burgeoning competencies, the transition to mature planning is unlikely to move forward with lockstep precision and timing. Despite the documented overall linear trend in developmental competencies, ontogenesis is often intersected with plateaus and instabilities (e.g., see Thelen & Ulrich, 1991). This is surely true of maturing *planful* behaviors. The very complexity of plans and the skills that go into plans necessitate a long period of integration and consolidation. And, it is important to recognize that even though the elements of plans are in place, there is no guarantee they will be used.

Several factors are likely to facilitate the growth of planning. For example, school-aged children have internally generated motivations related to organizing and controlling their lives and material wants. Children of this age are also the recipients of increasing pressure from teachers and parents to be more grown-up. Some demands pertain to acting in planful ways in order to balance homework assignments, family chore responsibilities, and recreational desires.

Another View of Plans and Emotions.   Although plans were high-lighted, as were the control of distressful events and emotion management, situations surely arise when emotion control is effective although strategies are skeletal, preconscious, and minimally organized. In these instances, resourcefulness may rely on a vast storehouse of knowledge and the memory of past successes and failures in handling one's own emotions. In other words, one does not always need to engage in complex reasoning to produce a plan for emotion regulation. An example that comes to mind involves behavior reported as an aftermath of recent earthquakes in Los Angeles. Of course these events are terrifying, but several individuals reported they just knew they had to control their fear all the while they engaged in automatic-like acts to check for gas leaks, water supplies, structural dangers, and neighbors' well-being.

Lastly, there is the sense that planful emotion management represents only a fraction of the plans that individuals devise to meet the challenges of their daily lives. The business of living, including job and family respon-sibilities, in and of themselves, demands considerable psychic and physical energy. Intuitively it would seem that planful emotion management is reserved for selected situations, and depends on an individual's anticipa-tion, appraisal, and knowledge of what will be upsetting.

FACTORS THAT MITIGATE USE OF PLANS:
THE EMOTIONAL STATE OF YOUNG CHILDREN

This chapter becomes more speculative at this point. Specifically, it is proposed that a greater number of opportunities arise for planful-like emotion management in fearful situations than in anger episodes (particu-larly those directed to caregivers). In general, planful-like emotion manage-ment is likely to come out of a child's strong motivation to protect the self in a negative emotion experience; the child somehow recognizes it is possible to modify his or her own state or the cause of the emotion; he or she can act unilaterally without reproach from others. Fearful episodes often meet these requirements.

In contrast, the resolution of anger turns on the issue of controllability (Lazarus, 1991). Young children face limitations in their control of others. They have even less control when experiencing anger,[3] have less skill in

---

[3]A caveat to bear in mind when discussing differentiated emotions concerns ascribing an emotion state to young children in the absence of their own verbal descriptions. What is an emotional experience? Lewis (1993) suggests that two processes are essential: (a) "the knowl-edge that the bodily changes are uniquely different from other changes," and (b) "the evaluation of these changes" (p. 228). In the absence of these, very young children can be in an emotional state and yet not experience it (Lewis, 1993). Thus, ascriptions of anger, for example, to young children may not be fully accurate. Lazarus (1984), in agreement with Lewis, suggests that children's abilities to experience particular emotions depend on the development of an understanding of the social context and its significance.

anticipating the sequence and outcome of conflicts, and fewer opportunities to manage the time frame for resolution of an emotion episode. These constraints are likely to propel the young child to manage anger with direct and expedient strategies that are socially acceptable. Thus overall, planful behaviors in the service of anger management will be uncommon because of constraints on interpersonal and temporal controls, and self and cognitive resources.

The following paragraphs expand these ideas further, and also contain brief descriptions of fear and anger in young children.[4]

Fear.   Fear is a basic human response that plays an important role in survival. Fear has high adaptive value, and even very young infants respond with distress to looming objects. At what point can we identify an *appraised* (i.e., cognitively derived) fear experience in the very young. Probably toward the end of the first year when many infants respond with strong protests to the appearance of a stranger or when familiar caregivers depart (i.e., separation distress) . In either condition the infants' responses appear to indicate they sense *danger* and want the reassurance of comfort (Izard, 1977; Lewis, 1993).

Fear is often experienced as a function of *event* but it can also arise due to the *actions of others*. Potent fear factors include stimuli that are sudden, unexpected, intense, and prolonged. Specific fear inducers reflect diversity, and include a doctor's visit, loud sounds, close proximity to a stranger, and being left alone (Lewis & Brooks, 1974; Marks, 1987; Sroufe, 1996). Waters, Matas, and Sroufe (1975) provided support for a potency factor, noting that the intensity of a stimulus determines whether an infant will respond with laughter or fear. Child state is also a relevant factor: Consider the effects of a sudden approach of a stranger upon the child who is fully awake and alert in contrast to one who is drowsy.

The onset of the preschool years brings new fears to children's lives (see summary, Marks, 1987). Children not only encounter a variety of new experiences but they also have the ability to imagine the personal implications of scary events. Preschoolers report that they have fears related to animals, darkness, strange noises, monsters, storms, abandonment, large machines, and physician visits. The fears of a particular child are a function of temperament, family factors such as parental manifestations of emotions and emotion control strategies, and actual everyday experiences. The child's cognitive development is also a contributing factor. Cognitive growth (e.g., attention, knowledge, reasoning skills) surely influences the

---

[4]Discussion focuses on inferred meaning of emotion events for young children, and not on their verbal reports. Using reports, findings reveal that young children indicate anger and sadness are more changeable than happiness (Carlson, Felleman, & Masters, 1983), and that children learn to differentiate the kinds of techniques more useful for one kind of emotion than another (e.g., Fabes & Eisenberg, 1992). Whether reports have counterparts in actual behavior has rarely been explored.

emergence of preschoolers' fears as well as the decline in fears over time. Indeed, for many children, most fears disappear by the early school years (MacFarlane, Allen, & Honzik, 1954; Marks, 1987). Although there is a scant research on why fears diminish, in all probability children become more adept at reasoning about real versus imaginary events and they become more skilled at fear avoidance and prevention.

Although empirical research is sparse with respect to young children managing fears with planful-like behaviors, anecdotal reports confirm that young children can generate instrumental acts to control worrisome events. In the following examples, note the elaborate sequence of behaviors ostensibly aimed at relieving anxiousness provoked by a sense of lost or of physical danger. There is a goal to protect the self.

A 20-month-old boy, having just discovered that little girls do not have penises, goes alone to his room where he undresses himself from the waist down. There he sits quietly, covering and uncovering his penis with a plastic cup as if to reassure himself that his penis will not disappear (Lieberman, 1993). Fear management was also described by Shatz (1994) in relation to her 30-month-old grandson. The most intriguing one concerns the boy and his beloved toy cars. He was rarely without one, even when going to bed. Shatz stated, "there was something comforting, almost talismanic, in his devotion to the cars. He would put one in his pocket before going out. Just having it in his pocket seemed to provide comfort" One day, she continued, the child came to her laboratory. When she suggested they retrieve mail from the mailroom, which was a place unfamiliar to him, the boy insisted that he and his grandmother each hold a toy car in their hands.

Obsessive-like behaviors and ritual-like acts become increasingly common in the late toddler and early preschool years. Seemingly, these are developmental phenomena that provide both security and control in a world which may often seem uncertain and unpredictable. The behaviors themselves are varied and idiosyncratic (e.g., use of *security objects*, the insistence that objects be positioned in a certain way, the seemingly endless repetition of certain words and phrases as if speech offers protection). With regard to rituals, Marks (1987) speculated about their important role in fear reduction and the promotion of self-confidence. It is also intriguing that self-protection is a common theme in young children's stories (Ames & Ilg, 1976). It is even more intriguing that preschoolers seem to provoke their own fear by including violent acts in their stories (e.g., people get hurt, shot, die), but then the children invariably repair the consequences of violence (e.g., people who were hurt get better). This kind of creative rehearsal may influence the young child's planful-like emotion management.

Although there are many unanswered questions about young children's handling of fears there are impressive accounts of their ability to generate self-directed, intentional, goal-directed coping sequences that have plan-like qualities. Of course, it is important to emphasize that parental input and support also facilitate this growth.

Frustration.   Frustration, similar to fear, is typically event related. A person plans to make breakfast and because of ineptitude or inattention, burns the toast, overcooks the eggs, puts the coffee on too late, and so on (Ortony, Clore, Collins, 1988). Responses to one's ensuing frustration may include being curt or ornery to others (e.g., spouse, children, pets). However, the other person is not responsible for frustrating events.[5]

Barrier studies are fine examples of frustrating eliciting situations—a child sees a desirable toy but a barrier prevents contact with the toy. The toddler age child may cry with frustration, but she is just as likely to seek help from another to change the situation. Frustration can be ideal situations for problem solving about how to control distress. An exemplar was provided above: the boy who devised a plan to prevent frustration when his dog interfered with his block building.

Anger.   "Anger refers not only to a disturbed physiological, subjective and behavioral state, but to cognitions about a hostile environmental agent" (Lazarus, Coyne, & Folkman, 1984, p 225). Anger stems from our belief that another person is to blame for an event, and, that person was in control and could have acted differently (Lazarus, 1991). The anger that adults and older children feel is built out of a background of positive and negative experiences that individuals have encountered, their interpretation of these experiences, a set of expectations people develop about the interactions we have with others, and an underlying awareness of self vulnerability. Anger occurs with violation of our expectations and the potential compromise of our self integrity. The first feelings of anger, the intense arousal, may occur before we think. Accordingly, angry behavior invariably has potential influences on others (Lazarus, 1991). This is probably due to the fact that individuals often have "a primitive experience of anger" even before they engage in cognitive processing (Berkowitz, 1989).

Anger in young children, along with its elicitors, mediating factors such as gender and temperament, and anger's effects, have received considerable attention in recent empirical studies (e.g., Eisenberg & Fabes, 1994: Fabes, Eisenberg, Smith, & Murphy, 1996; Lemerise & Dodge, 1993). Anger directed to parents often relates to thwarted goals whereas anger to peers often relates to possessions (Lemerise & Dodge, 1993). Research emphasizes how parents socialize their children to anger control (e.g., use words rather than fists), and how children respond to anger among peers.

Anger contexts do not provide good candidates for young children's implementation of planful acts for emotion management. Children's feelings of anger are often intense, and high arousal frequently interferes with thinking. Equally as important, because anger occurs *in relation to another person*, emotion control means handling one's own feelings and simultane-

---

[5]Researchers do not agree about frustration as an emotion.

ously trying to control the other's aversive actions. As noted earlier, planful management of anger may be most difficult when there is little control over another (e.g., a child losing a battle with parents, a child angered by an older, aggressive peer). This lack of interpersonal control is captured in Shatz's (1994) account of her toddler grandson who had a dispute with his grandparents. The child was clearly angry; he handled his anger by standing in a corner facing a wall. (This was a strategy he often used when he was angered by his parents.) Later, while still angry with his grandparents' intransigence he left the scene and went upstairs. The boy coped by withdrawing, an approach that many older individuals also use to control their anger. Perhaps intentional, albeit non-planful, acts are more common in anger management.

In contrast to fear, anger does not appear to diminish during early childhood; rather, anger control strategies become more socially acceptable (Goodenough, 1931; Jones & Burks, 1936). How this happens is not as yet fully understood. Clearly, caregivers exert a great deal of socialization pressure (see Denham, in press). Indeed, parental reports (Kopp & Bean, 1992) on annoying child behaviors reveal the highest levels of annoyance with children's disobedience and with arguing and talking back. Because of parent pressure, children probably devote considerable psychic effort toward a meeting parental demands about anger measurement. They may find it most expedient to ignore or hide one's anger with an adult caregiver, and then work through the anger in other contexts (e.g., fantasy play, stories).

In summary, this section has called attention to contextual factors that may inhibit or facilitate the implementation of plans particularly as they could be used in management of emotions. Intense emotion states, power struggles, and challenges to authority are likely to act against the initiation and implementation of plans by young children. This premise can be tested in empirical studies. Equally as important, empirical studies could provide information about the situations that are most likely to elicit planful-like behaviors in young children and those that are the most inhibiting.

Lastly, it is worth speculating about a feedback loop involving emotion, planful emotion management, and subsequent cognitive growth. Harris (1994) suggested that children's own emotional experiences play a central role in promoting cognitive development. It would seem that young children's use of planful-like behaviors for emotion control would have implications for increasing use of plans in other everyday activities.

CONCLUDING COMMENTS:
ORIGINS OF INDIVIDUAL DIFFERENCES

This chapter has highlighted developmental factors in the growth of plans. Procedural knowledge, protoplans, and fully developed plans have been described as a sequential developmental process. Does this mean that a competency such as planning, which is inherently developmental, will reveal itself in the repertoires of most children? Stated another way, are all youngsters potential planners? If not, what internal and external influences individual variation are the growth and implementation of planning skills?

Three factors are important influences. One factor has to do with caregivers and their support and enhancement of infants' procedural knowledge, and their availability to toddlers' need for interpersonal supports. Some research has been directed to identifying caregiver inputs to young children's planning (see Rogoff, 1990) but many questions remain. Does lack of caregiver support for procedural acts of infants compromise the eventual elaboration of the behavioral repertoire? Are some caregiver behaviors more essential for the development of planful behaviors than others? Notably, the sparse research literature on caregiver supports for nascent planning stands in marked contrast to the burgeoning literature on caregiver roles in emotion regulation.

A second factor turns on within-child qualities such as temperament proneness. There is already clear evidence that emotions and emotion management is a function of sociability, activity, and mood (e.g., Rubin, Coplan, Fox, & Calkins, 1995). Because planful behaviors demand inhibition, rehearsal, and analytic reasoning, it seems likely there is a complex relation between temperament style and the ability to plan. How much and in what situations do impulsive individuals plan in contrast to those who are more restrained?

A third factor relates to variation in cognitive functioning. It would seem that even marginal difficulties in any number of cognitive processes—attention, processing information, analytic reasoning, perspective taking—could interfere with the development of planning and its implementation within and across settings. A study of the ontogeny of planning among children who are developmentally delayed might be particularly informative about necessary precursors.

In summary, individual differences in processes that form the corpus of planning probably influence whether, how often, and how much young children can move toward planful-like behaviors. Deterrents to the growth of planning surely have ramifications for the growth of emotion management strategies. As noted earlier in this chapter and elsewhere (e.g., Kopp 1989, 1995), developmental competence requires that children begin to take increasing responsibility for their social behavior and emotion responses. The ability to plan has implications for both.

REFERENCES

Ames, L. B., & Ilg, F. L. (1976). *Your three year old*. New York: Delacorte Press.
Berkowitz, L. (1989). Frustration-aggression hypothesis: Examination and reformulation. *Psychological Bulletin, 106*, 59–73.

Bidell, T., & Fischer, K. W. (in press). Developmental transitions in children's early on-line planning. In M. M. Haith (Ed.), *Development and future-oriented processes*. Chicago: University of Chicago Press.

Bowlby, J. (1969). *Attachment and loss: Vol. 1. Attachment*. New York: Basic Books.

Bretherton, I. (1984). *Symbolic play*. Orlando: Academic Press.

Bretherton, I., Fritz, J., Zahn-Waxler, C., & Ridgeway, D. (1986). Learning to talk about emotions: A functionalist perspective. *Child Development, 57*, 529–548.

Bridges, L., & Grolnick, W. (1995). The development of emotional self-regulation in infancy and early childhood. In N. Eisenberg (Ed.), *Social development: Review of personality and social psychology. 15*. Thousand Oaks, CA: Sage Publications.

Brownell, C. A., & Kopp, C. B. (1991). Common threads, diverse solutions: Concluding commentary. *Developmental Review, 11*, 288–303.

Butterworth, G. (1990). Self perception in infancy. In D. Cicchetti & M. Beeghly (Eds.), *The self in transition: Infancy to childhood*. Chicago: University of Chicago Press.

Calkins, S. (1994). Origins and outcomes of individual differences in emotion regulation. In N. Fox (Ed.), The development of emotion regulation: Biological and behavioral considerations. *Monographs of the Society for Research in Child Development. 59*. (2–3, Serial No. 240).

Carlson, C., Felleman, E. S., & Masters, J. C. (1983). Influence of children's emotional states on the recognition of emotion in peers and social motives to change another's emotional state. *Motivation and Emotion, 7*, 61–79.

Campos, J. J., & Barrett, K. C. (1984). Toward a new understanding of their emotions and their development. In C. E. Izard, J. Kagan, & R. B. Zajonc (Eds.), *Emotions, cognition, and behavior*. Cambridge, England: Cambridge University Press.

Cassidy, J. (1994). Emotion regulation: Influence of attachment relationships. In N. Fox (1994), The development of emotion regulation: Biological and behavioral considerations. *Monographs of the Society for Research in Child Development, 59*, (2–3, Serial No. 240).

Clyman, R. (1991). The procedural organization of emotions: A contribution from cognitive science to the psychoanalytic theory of therapeutic action. *Journal of American Psychiatric Association, 39*, 349–382.

Cohn, J., & Tronick, E. (1983). Three-month-old infants' reaction to simulated maternal depression. *Child Development, 54*, 185–193

De Lisi, R. (1987). A cognitive-developmental analysis of planning. In S. L. Friedman, E. K. Scholnick, & R. R. Cocking (Eds.), *Blueprints for thinking: The role of planning in cognitive development* (pp. 79–109). Cambridge, England: Cambridge University Press.

Denham, S. (in press). *Emotional development*. New York: Guilford.

Diamond, A. (1990). Developmental time course in human infants and infant monkeys, and the neural bases of inhibitory control in reaching. In A. Diamond (Ed.), The development of and neural bases of high cognitive functions. *Annals of the New York Academy of Sciences, 608*, 637–676.

Dunn, J., Bretherton, I., & Munn, P. (1987). Conversations about feeling states between mothers and their young children. *Developmental Psychology, 23*, 132–139.

Eisenberg, N., & Fabes, R. A. (1994). Mothers' reactions to children"s negative emotions: Relations to children's temperament and anger behavior. *Merrill-Palmer Quarterly, 40*, 138–150.

Eisenberg, N., Fabes, R. A., Bustamante, D., Mathy, R. M., Miller, P., & Lindholm, E. (1988). Differentiation of vicariously-induced emotional reactions in children. *Developmental Psychology, 24*, 237–246.

Emde, R. N., Biringen, Z., Clyman, R. B., & Oppenheim, D. (1991). The moral self of infancy: Affective core and procedural knowledge. *Developmental Review, 11*, 251–270.

Fabes, R. A., & Eisenberg, N. (1992). Young children's coping with interpersonal anger. *Child Development, 63*, 116–128.

Fabes, R. A., Eisenberg, N., Smith, M. C., & Murphy, B. C. (1996). Getting angry with peers: Associations with liking of the provocateur. *Child Development, 67*, 942–956.

Fischer, K. W. (1980). A theory of cognitive development: The construal and construction of hierarchies of skills. *Psychological Review, 87*, 477–531.

Fischer, K. W., & Bidell, T. R. (1991). Constraining nativist inferences about cognitive capacities. In S. Carey & R. Gelman (Eds.), *The epigenesis of mind: Essays on biology and knowledge*. Hillsdale, NJ: Lawrence Erlbaum Associates.

Flavell, J., Miller, P. H., & Miller, S. (1993). *Cognitive development* (3rd ed.). Englewood Cliffs, NJ: Prentice-Hall.

Fivush, R., & Hudson, J. A. (1990). *Knowing and remembering in young children*. Cambridge, England: Cambridge University Press.

Friedman, S. L., Scholnick, E. K., & Cocking, R. R. (1987). *Blueprints for thinking: The role of planning in cognitive development*. Cambridge, England: Cambridge University Press.

Gauvain, M. (1989). Children's planning in a social context: An observational study of kindergartners' planning in the classroom. In L. T. Winegar (Ed.), *Social interaction and the development of children's understanding*. Norwood, NJ: Ablex.

Gauvain, M. (1992). Social influences on the development of skill at planning during action. *International Journal of Behavioral Development, 15*, 377–398.

Gauvain, M. (1995). *Proposal: Socio-cultural influences on the development of planning*. Unpublished manuscript.

Goodenough, F. (1931). *Anger in young children*. Minneapolis: University of Minnesota Press.

Gopnik, A. (1993). How we know our minds: The illusion of first-person knowledge of intentionality. *Behavioral and Brain Sciences, 16*, 1–14.

Gralinski, J. H., & Kopp, C. B. (1993). Everyday rules for behavior: Mothers' requests to young children. *Developmental Psychology, 29*, 573–584.

Gunnar, M. R. (1980). Control, warning signals and distress in infancy. *Developmental Psychology, 16*, 281–289.

Gunnar-vonGnechten, M. R. (1978). Changing a frightening toy into a pleasant toy by allowing the infant to control its actions. *Developmental Psychology, 14*, 157–162.

Harris, P. (1989). *Children and emotion: The development of psychological understanding*. Oxford: Basil Blackwell.

Harris, P. (1994). The child's understanding of emotion: Developmental change and the family environment. *Journal of Child Psychology and Psychiatry, 35*, 3–28.

Hart, B., & Risley, T. (1995). *Meaningful differences*. Baltimore: Paul Brookes.

Izard, C. E. (1977). *Human emotions*. New York: Plenum Press.

Jones, M.C., & Burks, B.S. (1936). Personality development in childhood: A survey of problems, methods and experimental findings. *Monographs of the Society for Research in Child Development, 1*, (4).

Kagan, J. (1981). *The second year: The emergence of self-awareness*. Cambridge, MA: Harvard University Press.

Karmiloff-Smith, A. (1992). *Beyond modularity: A developmental perspective on cognitive science*. Cambridge, MA: MIT Press.

Kaye, K., & Fogel, A. (1980). The temporal structure of face-to-face communication between mothers and infants. *Developmental Psychology, 16*, 454–464.

Kopp, C. B. (1982). The antecedents of self-regulation: A developmental perspective. *Developmental Psychology, 18*, 199–214.

Kopp, C. B. (1989). Regulation of distress and negative emotions: A developmental view. *Developmental Psychology, 25*, 343–354.

Kopp, C. B. (1992). Emotion distress and control in young children. In N. Eisenberg & R. Fabes (Eds.), *Emotion and its regulation in early development. New directions for child development* (No. 55, pp. 41–56). New York: Freeman.

Kopp, C. B. (1994). *Baby steps: The "whys" of your child's behavior in the first two years*. New York: Freeman.

Kopp, C. B. (1995, Fall). Presidential address. *Division 7 Newsletter*.

Kopp, C. B., & Bean, D. (1992). *Mothers' annoyances about preschoolers' behaviors*. Unpublished manuscript.

Kreitler, S., & Kreitler, H. (1987). Conceptions and processes of planning: The developmental perspective. In S. L. Friedman, E. K. Scholnick, & R. R. Cocking (Eds.), *Blueprints for thinking: The role of planning in cognitive development* (pp. 79–109). Cambridge, England: Cambridge University Press.

Lazarus, R. A., Coyne, J. C., & Folkman, S. (1982). Cognition, emotion, and motivation: The doctoring of Humpty-Dumpty. In R. W. J. Neufeld (Ed.), *Psychological stress and psychopathology* (pp. 218–239). New York: McGraw-Hill.

Lazarus, R. S. (1984). On the primacy of cognition. *American Psychologist, 39*, 124–129.

Lazarus, R. S. (1991). *Emotion and adaptation*. New York: Oxford University Press.

Lazarus, R. S., & Folkman, S. (1984) *Stress, appraisal, and coping.* New York: Springer.
Lemerise, E. A., & Dodge, K. A. (1993). The development of anger and hostile interactions. In M. Lewis & J. M. Haviland (Eds.), *Handbook of emotions* (pp. 537–546). New York: Guilford.
Lewis, M. (1991). Ways of knowing the self. *Developmental Review, 11,* 231–242.
Lewis, M. (1993). The emergence of human emotions. In M. Lewis & J. M. Haviland (Eds.), *Handbook of emotions.* (pp. 223–236). New York: Guilford.
Lewis, M., & Brooks, J. (1974). Self, others, and fear: Infants' reactions to people. In M. Lewis & L. Rosenblum (Eds.), *The origins of fear: The origins of behavior* (pp. 195–228). New York: Wiley.
Lieberman, A.F. (1993). *The emotional life of the toddler.* New York: Free Press.
MacFarlane, J. W., Allen, L., & Honzik, M. P. (1954). *Behavioral problems of normal children between 21 months and 14 years.* Berkeley: University of California Press.
Marks, I. (1987). The development of normal fear: A review. *Journal of Child Psychology and Psychiatry, 28,* 667–697.
Neisser, U. (1988). Five kinds of self knowledge. *Philosophical Psychology, 1,* 35–59.
Nelson, K. (1986). *Event knowledge: Structure and function in development.* Hillsdale, N.J.: Lawrence Erlbaum Associates.
Nelson, K. (1990). Remembering, forgetting, and childhood amnesia. In R. Fivush & J. A. Hudson (Eds.), *Knowing and remembering in young children* (pp. 301–316). Cambridge, England: Cambridge University Press.
Nelson, K. (1996). *Language in cognitive development.* New York: Cambridge University Press.
Nelson, K., & Gruendel, J. (1981). General event representations: Basic building blocks of cognitive development. In A. Brown & M. Lamb (Eds.), *Advances in developmental psychology* (Vol. 1). Hillsdale, NJ: Lawrence Erlbaum Associates.
Newell, A., & Simon, H. (1972). *Human problem solving.* Englewood Cliffs, NJ: Prentice-Hall.
Ortony, A., Clore, G. L., & Collins, A. (1988). *The cognitive structure of emotions.* New York: Cambridge.
Parritz, R. H., Mangelsdorf, S., & Gunnar, M. R. (1992). Control, social referencing, and the infant's appraisal of threat. In S. Feinman (Ed.), *Social referencing and the social construction of reality in infancy* (pp. 209–228). New York: Plenum.
Piaget, J. (1952). *The origins of intelligence in children* (M. Cook, Trans.). New York: International Universities Press. (Original work published 1936)
Rogoff, B. (1990). *Apprenticeship in thinking.* New York: Oxford University Press.
Rogoff, B., Mistry, J., Radziszewska, B., & Germond, J. (1992). Infants' instrumental social interaction with adults. In S. Feinman (Ed.), *Social referencing and the social construction of reality in infancy* (pp. 323–348). New York: Plenum.
Rothbart, M. K., & Derryberry, D. (1981). Development of individual differences in temperament. In M. E. Lamb & A. L. Brown (Eds.), *Advances in developmental psychology* (Vol. 1). Hillsdale, NJ: Lawrence Erlbaum Associates.
Rubin, K. H., Coplan, R. J., Fox, N. A., Calkins, S. D. (1995). Emotionality, emotion regulation, and preschoolers' social adaptation. *Development and Psychopathology, 7,* 49–62.
Scholnick, E. K. (1994). Planning. In *Encyclopedia of human behavior* (Vol. 3, pp. 525–534). New York: Academic Press.
Scholnick, E. K. (1995, Fall). Knowing and constructing plans. *SRCD Newsletter.*
Scholnick, E. K., & Friedman, S. L. (1992, April). *Planning in context: Developmental and situational considerations.* Paper presented at the biennial meeting of the Society for Research in Child Development, Seattle.
Shatz, M. (1994). *A toddler's life: Becoming a person.* New York: Oxford University Press.
Shore, A. N. (1994). *Affect regulation and the origins of the self: The neurobiology of emotion development.* Hillsdale, NJ: Lawrence Erlbaum Associates.
Sinclair, H., Stambak, M., Lezine, I., Rayna, S., & Verba, M. (1989). *Infants and objects: The creativity of cognitive development.* San Diego: Academic Press.
Skinner, E., & Wellborn, J. G. (1994). Coping during childhood and adolescence: A motivational perspective. In D. Featherman, R. Lerner, & M. Perlmutter (Eds.), *Life-span development and behavior.* Hillsdale: Lawrence Erlbaum Associates.
Sroufe, L. A. (1979). Socioemotional development. In J. Osofsky (Ed.), *Handbook of infant development.* New York: Wiley.

Sroufe, L. A. (1984). *Your baby*. Englewood Cliffs, NJ: Prentice-Hall.

Sroufe, L. A. (1996). *Emotional development: The organization of emotional life in the early years*. New York: Cambridge University Press.

Stern, D. (1985). *The interpersonal world of the infant*. New York: Basic Books.

Stifter, C. (1993, April). *Infant emotion regulation*. Paper presented at the Biennial Meeting of the Society for Research in Child Development, New Orleans.

Thelen, E., & Smith, L. B. (1994). *A dynamic systems approach to the development of cognition and action*. Cambridge, MA: MIT Press.

Thelen, E., & Ulrich, B. D. (1991). Hidden skills. *Monograph of the Society for Research in Child Development, 56*(223), 1.

Waters, E., Matas, H., & Sroufe, L. A. (1975). Infants' reactions to an approaching stranger: Description, validation, and functional significance of wariness. *Child Development, 46*, 348–356.

Wellman, H., Fabricius, W., & Sophian, C. (1985). The early development of planning. In H. Wellman (Ed.), *Children's searching: The development of search skills and spatial representation*. Hillsdale, NJ: Lawrence Erlbaum Associates.

Wenar, C. (1982). On negativism. *Human Development, 25*, 1–23.

Wolf, D., Rygh, J., & Altshuler, J. (1984). Agency and experience: Actions and states in play narratives. In I. Bretherton (Ed.), *Symbolic play: The development of social understanding* (pp. 195–213). Orlando, FL: Academic Press.

III

Cognition and Planning

6

What Do They Really Measure? A Comparative Analysis of Planning Tasks

Ellin Kofsky Scholnick
University of Maryland, College Park

Sarah L. Friedman
National Institute of Child Health and Human Development

Kathleen E. Wallner-Allen
University of Maryland, College Park

Doing a homework assignment, taking a trip, writing a mystery, going shopping, hunting for a job, launching a political campaign—it is not hard to generate a list of common activities that require planning. The human information-processing system is beset by resource and temporal limitations, so cognitive models often include a set of principles or an executive function that allocates attentional resources and schedules operations during problem solving. The executive function acts as a master planner. Thus planning pervades our daily life and cognitive models of problem solving. Even the stock of knowledge about goal attainment and the strategic activities used in problem solving have been called plans (Miller, Galanter, & Pribram, 1960; Schank & Abelson, 1977; Scholnick, 1994).

The pervasiveness and centrality of planning in daily life have been problematical for understanding planning. What are the commonalities between writing an essay and running a set of errands during lunchtime? Is planning an activity or the invocation of a stored library of knowledge (Hammond, 1989, 1990)? Is planfulness a general trait or a domain-specific ability? Is planning a single ability or an assembly of skills welded together to achieve specific goals? These are unresolved questions.

Often, researchers have sought to encapsulate the diverse activities called planning into a set of instruments. A piece of the entire conceptual field of planning is used to represent the entire field. The instruments focus on planning as an activity, rather than as the accumulation of knowledge about successful strategies and their revision, and the planning skills sampled are comparatively narrow. Just as concrete operational thought in Piagetian theory has been reified as solution of conservation tasks, short-term memory has been operationalized as Digit Span, and meta-memory has been indexed by the accuracy of estimates of recall, the Tower of Hanoi and errand planning have become the standard approaches to measuring planning. These two tasks were originally designed to explore the nature of problem solving, not to characterize individual differences in planning.

The path from a broad concept to a constrained task invites careful exploration. What aspects of the larger domain of planning do particular measures of planning represent? In this chapter, we argue that many laboratory tasks of planning have a common element—sequencing under constraints. However, the various measures of planning differ in the kinds of sequences and constraints they embody, and consequently, how ordering and constraint management are orchestrated into a plan.

In the first section of the chapter, we situate two laboratory measures, the Tower of Hanoi (TOH) and grocery shopping, within the broad arena of planning, and we analyze the common abilities these tasks require. In the second section, we compare the two tasks and suggest how different variations tap the same component processes in different ways. The third section of the chapter returns to the broader issues. Is planning a trait to be indexed by specific measures with known psychometric properties or a set of activities highly dependent on task context and the individual's knowledge base? If planning is a construct embodied in particular tasks, what aspects of planning are omitted from current measures? These issues are not unique to the planning literature but pervade the entire domain of the study of human thinking that has been variously characterized as intelligence or cognitive psychology.

DIVIDING THE DOMAIN

Planning as Generating and Sequencing

In earlier work, we suggested that planning involves representing a problem, setting a goal, deciding to plan, creating a plan, implementing and monitoring the plan, and then reviewing the outcome (Friedman, Scholnick, & Cocking, 1987; Scholnick & Friedman, 1987, 1993). This description equates any purposeful behavior, particularly problem solving, with planning. Often, researchers narrow the field further to refer to a strategy constructed in advance of action as a response to temporal and resource limitations (Scholnick, 1994).

Two paradigms have been used to investigate plan construction. Researchers in artificial intelligence describe plan creation as a process by which remembered strategies for achieving a goal are adapted to fit new circumstances, tested, repaired if necessary, and then stored for future usage (Hammond, 1989, 1990; Kolodner, 1994; Schank, 1982). Planning occurs through remembering old experiences and learning from the application of old strategies to new events. In contrast, in the information-processing approach, planning refers to the creation of new plans during the course of problem solving. The nature of planning exemplifies the paradigm of a solitary serial processor with limited capacities and resources (Klahr, 1994; Simon, 1975). In this chapter we adopt initially the information-processing approach because it suggests a taxonomy for planning tasks and allows closer examination of problem representation, creation of plans, and monitoring during planning.

When resources are limited, the planner's task is to generate elements, prioritize them, and sequence them efficiently. For example, packing for a trip involves planning. Travelers are limited by the kind of luggage and wardrobe they possess and the purpose of the trip. The individual must generate a list of items to be packed and set priorities because not everything may fit in the suitcase or be appropriate for the purpose of the trip. The sequence of items in the suitcase will be determined by a set of criteria, such as the weight and desired accessibility of the clothes. Writing an essay also involves generating ideas, eliminating irrelevancies, and organizing the ideas into a coherent sequence (Bereiter & Scardamalia, 1982; Flower & Hayes, 1981). Wedding planners generate a list of tasks and guests and wean both lists based on resources. The scheduling of these tasks is determined by the time they require for completion, and by their links to other tasks. For example, the wedding site must be chosen before invitations are ordered.

Planning as Generating

Although many daily planning tasks involve generating, prioritizing, and sequencing elements, some laboratory planning tasks focus on just generation and selection. For example, social planning tasks require a child to generate and then evaluate alternative ways of solving an interpersonal problem, such as gaining access to a coveted toy or breaking into a new social group (Dodge, Pettit, McClaskey, & Brown, 1986; Rubin & Krasnor, 1986; Spivack & Shure, 1974; Wallner, 1996). Strategy choice in memory and academic tasks (Borkowski & Burke, 1996; Siegler & Shrager, 1984) has been likened to planning because the child must generate the means for solving a problem and then prune the choices based on self-knowledge and content-specific information. Performance on these tasks may be very domain-specific because plans are based on knowledge of the material and of the task. Although these tasks may involve planning, they are generally classified by their domain of application (e.g., strategy choice, social skill).

Planning as Sequencing

However, a subset of strategic behaviors has often been designated as exemplars of planning in general or executive functioning. In these planning tasks, the elements and moves are supplied, but the planner must figure out how to sequence them according to explicit or implicit constraints. In one variant of the Tower of Hanoi, rings stacked in size order on one peg must be transferred to another peg without violating the size order. The individual must devise the minimal sequence of moves to complete the transfer (Anzai & Simon, 1979). Hayes-Roth and Hayes-Roth (1979) designed a planning task in which a series of errands must be accomplished in a limited time period. The list must be prioritized and sequenced to meet geographic and temporal constraints. Child versions of the task include completing chores in a schoolroom (Pea & Hawkins, 1987) and shopping at a grocery store (Gauvain & Rogoff, 1989; Hudson & Fivush, 1991). Another popular planning task involves traveling through a maze by ordering segments of the path to avoid blind alleys (Ellis & Siegler, chapter 8, this volume; Rogoff, 1990). Gauvain and Rogoff (1989) created a task where the child must stack items in a truck for efficient delivery at dropoff points along a route. In each example, planning is based on an appreciation of the inherent order of events and construction of a temporal or spatial sequence that reflects this order.

TASK ANALYSIS

Components of Planning

What skills and knowledge are required to construct an order? Do different kinds of order tap these components differently? There are four interdependent aspects of constructing an order: (a) detecting an order, (b) noticing constraints, (c) using memory, and (d) monitoring the mapping of the constructed order onto the domain.

Detecting an Order. The planner must organize the problem representation in a way that permits construction of an ordered sequence of actions. Not all ordering devices are equally salient and usable. Planning tasks typically draw on some combination of three ordering devices—efficiency, subgoaling, and alignment with a quantitative dimension.

Efficiency is the vaguest criterion for organizing action. The definition set by the investigator may not be the one the planner adopts, particularly when the task is attractive and the cost of errors is low. Sansone and Berg (1993) noted that people often anticipate obstacles to carrying out a plan that they ignore because dealing with the obstacles may prove entertaining. Efficiency may also not be a high priority. When teenagers shop, they may care less about rapidly accomplishing a set of tasks than having the opportunity to cruise a mall. Frequently, the goal of efficiency needs to be translated into detection of the subgoal structure of the task that allows effective action or use of a conventional ordering system to weigh different alternatives.

Often, planning is required because the necessary conditions for goal attainment are absent, and the individual must first produce these conditions before reaching the goal. Sometimes obstacles must be removed before producing the condition that allows goal attainment. Producing the precondition is called subgoaling. Packing clothes first requires luggage that may be in storage. Planning tasks that require subgoaling draw on anticipation of sequential dependencies. Planning tasks vary in difficulty depending on the number of subgoals and the obviousness of the dependencies (Kotovsky, Hayes, & Simon, 1985; Zhang & Norman, 1994).

Other sequences are based on ordered, quantitative continua such as size, number, and spatial proximity. For adults, when the dimension is salient and the order of constituents on the dimension is easily retrievable, planning is easy (Kotovsky, Hayes, & Simon, 1985; Zhang & Norman, 1994). But when errand planning occurs in an unfamiliar terrain, the constant need to refer to a map when choosing an efficient route may detract from constructing a plan. Young children may be handicapped in planning several moves ahead because they are less knowledgeable about numerical and temporal markers. Lacking familiarity with temporal or spatial sequences, they may be unable to plan a sequence of moves in time or space. Thus, one of the issues in planning is finding an order and representing it in the plan.

Noticing Constraints. Planning tasks vary in the ease with which they allow alignment of moves in sequence. In errand planning, all the stores may be open at the same time, but if the stores are accessible at different hours, planning is harder. Tasks differ in the constraints they impose on mapping a perceived or constructed order onto a plan.

Using Memory. Both the demands on ordering and constraint management have implications for memory usage. Planning uses internal resources to conserve external ones. Planners map out a problem and a solution in their heads, test it, and then implement it in the environment. The internal planning process is designed to prevent costly errors and inefficiencies. When representing the initial, current, or final state of a problem is demanding, either the planner uses external aids, such as lists, or planning is impeded because there is little room for allocating resources to forging an anticipatory schema. In laboratory tasks, access to external aids is limited or nonexistent. So, the number of possible problem states and their interconnections will influence how many steps ahead the planner can anticipate and thus the ease of constructing an order (Klahr & Robinson, 1981; Kotovsky et al., 1985). An additional memory demand arises from the constraints on movement. The planner has to keep these constraints in mind while searching among alternatives for the appropriate, best, and legal move. When subgoaling (e.g., obstacle removal) is necessary to produce the ideal order, the memory load may be extensive.

Monitoring.   Once the plan has been produced, individuals must keep track of their own progress in a dynamically shifting environment. Often, unanticipated consequences of actions necessitate revision of plans. Hence, ordering tasks requires appreciating the sequence, obeying constraints, using working memory, and monitoring. These are interrelated facets of planning. An integrated representation frees up memory space enabling allocation of more resources to monitoring.

Researchers who use sequential planning tasks must ask: (a) what kind of order is required, (b) what constraints must be obeyed in producing the order, (c) what are the demands on working memory, and (d) what are the monitoring requirements of the task? Failures on any sequential planning task may not reflect a generic incapacity to plan, but difficulties in detecting the basis for order, appreciating and applying the ordering constraints, or limitations in working memory or in monitoring (Kotovsky, Hayes, & Simon, 1985). Moreover, different planning tasks, different versions of the same task, and different strategies for task solution may produce different patterns of performance because the pieces that comprise planning must be assembled in distinctive ways, and the role of one component may be magnified while the contribution of another component may be shrunk (Simon, 1975). Rather than concluding that planning is, therefore, a kaleidoscope that presents a beautiful but shifting image, systematic manipulation and comparison of the key dimensions of planning might enable teasing out the processes and variables that influence planning.

Whereas there are several systematic comparisons of problem isomorphs of the Tower of Hanoi aimed at examining the factors that contribute to task difficulty for adults (Kotovsky, Hayes, & Simon, 1985; Zhang & Norman, 1994), few systematic task comparisons of either problem isomorphs or diverse planning tasks exist in the developmental literature (for exceptions see Gnys & Willis, 1991; Klahr, 1994; Klahr & Robinson, 1981). The following sections compare two types of "sequential" planning tasks, the Tower of Hanoi (TOH) and grocery shopping, with respect to the nature of the sequence and constraints that govern plan construction as well as the memory and monitoring requirements. We argue that the grocery task emphasizes the search for an externalized conventional order whereas TOH tasks emphasize constraint management during subgoaling. Then, we analyze two versions of the Tower of Hanoi in greater detail and show how changes in the task affect detecting an order, managing constraints, memory processing, and monitoring.

Task Description

The Tower of Hanoi.   The typical Tower of Hanoi apparatus (Anzai & Simon, 1979; Bidell & Fischer, 1994; Borys, Spitz, & Dorans, 1982; Piaget, 1976) shown in Fig. 6.1 is a board containing a line of three identical pegs. The pegs house an arrangement of rings or disks differing in size. The task requires rearranging the rings. For example, the leftmost peg might contain three rings stacked in size order from the largest on the bottom to the smallest ring on the top. The goal might be to reproduce the same pyramid on the rightmost peg. The task requires serial processing because only one ring can be moved at a time and only transfers between pegs are permitted. So the player cannot store a ring in one hand or on the table while moving another. There are also order constraints; transfers must not violate the size order. Therefore, a ring can only be transferred to a peg on which it will be the smallest. The player must construct a plan to accomplish the transfer in a minimal number of moves.

In the TOH task, a particular size order is the explicit starting point and goal. Executing the plan, though, requires ordering subgoals to remove the impediments that smaller rings pose for free movement of larger rings. Superficially, this task appears to require ordering rings, but it really requires ordering subgoals (see Fig. 6.2). The subgoal sequence is recursive, not linear. The sequence begins with steps to free the largest ring and move

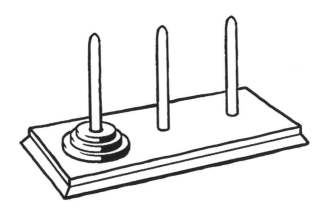

FIG. 6.1. The Tower of Hanoi.

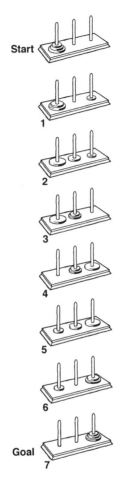

FIG. 6.2.   Optimal moves in the Tower of Hanoi task.

it to a cleared goal post, and then steps to move the next largest ring to a freed goal post, etc.

The TOH has been used to study the effects of memory and representational processes on means–end problem solving (Kotovsky, et al., 1985; Simon, 1975; Zhang & Norman, 1994). Individual differences in intelligence, neurological status, and cognitive functioning have also been measured using the TOH (Borys, Spitz, & Dorans, 1982; Klahr & Robinson, 1981; Welsh, 1991).

Grocery Shopping.   There are many variants of the errand planning/grocery shopping task, differing widely in their constituents and the size and nature of the problem space. We chose one that has been used frequently with young children (Gauvain & Rogoff, 1989; Wallner, 1996). The task is presented using a miniature model grocery store with a checkout counter near its entrance and aisles of shelving (see Fig. 6.3). The size of the model permits a bird's eye view of the layout of the entire store. Pictures of items are distributed on the shelves to represent diverse grocery items. Items in a given category, such as vegetables, are shelved together, as they are in most supermarkets. The shopper receives a list comprised of cards with duplicate pictures of items to be found in the store. The child is asked to travel through the grocery store and pick up all the items in the shortest route. To do so requires the child to search through the dozens of items in the store to find just those on the list. The representational requirements are detecting item locations and constructing a path.

There are two constraints. As in daily life, the child cannot "fly" over aisles to shorten the path. The path must also be efficient. The shortest route is dictated implicitly by the spatial layout of the store that also encodes the category structure of grocery items.

Most investigations of the grocery task have not focused on memory and monitoring during planning by varying systematically the number of items on the list or the number of items and categories in the store (but see Dreher & Oerter, 1987; Hudson & Fivush, 1991). Instead, verbal comments during the task, movement paths, and items collected have been analyzed to determine the extent to which individuals generate whole or partial opportunistic plans. Additionally, the grocery planning task has been used to examine the advantages of collaborative, as opposed to solitary, planning (Gauvain & Rogoff, 1989).

FIG. 6.3. The layout of the grocery store.

Task Comparisons of the TOH and Grocery Shopping

In the TOH task, the size order underlying both the initial and final state is known. But the real planning task is subgoaling under constraints. The subgoaling sequence, not just size order, dictates the order of steps in the plan. In grocery shopping, the list appears to be a set of disparate, unconnected items. Their final order is unknown. The real planning task involves locating the items in the store and using an integrated spatial configuration to chart the best route. The few constraints on movement pose no major impediment for travel. In the following sections, we spell out the implications for planning of these and other structural differences.

Detecting the Order

Table 6.1 compares the Tower of Hanoi and the grocery shopping tasks in terms of the demands involved in detecting an order.

TOH.   There are two orders in the TOH task, a stimulus order and a subgoal order. Zhang and Norman (1994) characterized the stimuli in the "standard" TOH as varying on an ordinal dimension (size) and a nominal dimension (peg location). The pegs serve as landmarks for representing and tracking problem states. Size organizes the goal state and constrains movement. The planner must preserve the size order of the rings while sequencing their transfers across various pegs.

Therefore, the planner must attend to size, discriminate sizes, and order them. Increasing the number of rings makes size discrimination and ordering harder. Adults may find ordering several elements very easy, but young children do not. Consequently, for the young child, the demands of constructing a size order will add to the task of encoding the current state of the problem, the desired goal, and legal moves to approach the goal.

TABLE 6.1

Detecting an Order

TOH	Grocery Shopping
Nature of the Order	
1. Efficiency (fewest moves)	Efficiency (shortest path)
2. Size	Spatial location on a route
3. Subgoals	
Sources of Difficulty	
1. Conceptualizing the size order when rings distributed across many pegs	Searching for items based on category membership
2. Detecting the subgoal structure	Detecting the role of spatial organization
3. Integrating the moves into subgoal satisfaction sequences	Integrating items into a route

Similarly, when the goal configuration is formed by rings distributed across various pegs (as opposed to having them all on one peg), the size order may be less salient and representation of the goal state harder (Klahr & Robinson, 1981).

Once the size order is grasped, the planner must understand why the smallest ring is always on top of each pile. An adequate rationale for the size order would enable the person to relate movement constraints to the goal state. It would enable the planner to grasp the underlying order in the task, which is subgoaling. No such rationale is provided.

Grocery Shopping. In contrast, grocery shopping is a familiar task with familiar goals, rationales for action, and constraints. The nominal dimension (item category) and the ordinal dimension (location) are correlated. If the individual is aware of the category membership of the item and the organization of items in the store by category, then planning becomes easier because category membership narrows the search to the region of the store where the item resides, and serves as an external marker for that location. However, young children's category structure and search procedures, such as scanning from left to right, may not be well-developed. Moreover, the presence of distractor items in the store may hamper the child from focusing on just those items that need to be collected and ordered.

The underlying task is not merely to find items but to order them on an efficient path. The need for order may be less clear in the grocery task than in the TOH because the TOH presents an ordered stack and travel rules that stress an ordered relation among rings (see Table 6.1). There is also a definite starting and end point. In contrast, the shopper receives a disorganized stack of items and a license to travel at will. Any order of item collection is legal though not efficient. The presented list structure of the shopping task and the freedom of movement do not alert shoppers to the inherent sequential and spatial dependencies. If, for example, there are four items to be collected, the efficient shopper needs to order them by distance from near to far (or far to near). The efficient route follows that distance order beginning with, for example, the nearest and then the next nearest, etc. The centrality of constructing a linear path as a means of achieving efficient travel is never stated explicitly in task instructions.

The development of spatial representations has been characterized as moving from recognition of separate landmarks, to construction of separate routes, to integration of those routes (Siegel & White, 1975). Shopping requires minimally the ability to link item locations to a route through a store. Moreover, the representation must be flexible enough to be edited by deleting parts where no items are located.

The planner must have sufficient understanding of distance to evaluate the efficiency of alternative routes. The temptation to explore may interfere with the instructions to travel the shortest route. Young children may be more susceptible to distractions that may sidetrack them (Hudson & Fivush, 1991).

Constraint Management

Table 6.2 compares the tasks in terms of their demands on constraint management.

TOH. The rings in the TOH form a stack; the grocery items are an unstructured list. The TOH task is an exercise in constrained object transfer, whereas the shopping expedition involves free collection of objects. These differences create different challenges for recognizing and dealing with constraints during plan construction.

The external physical stack that comprises the Tower of Hanoi epitomizes a goal stack (Anzai & Simon, 1979; Bidell & Fischer, 1994; Klahr & Robinson, 1981). Movement of each ring to its final resting place constitutes a goal; transfers of the smaller rings are subgoals allowing freedom of movement for the larger ones. The planner must remove obstacles to reach the initial member of the sequence, the largest ring. However, until the transferred smaller rings reach their final positions in the goal stack, they may obstruct other rings. The planner must figure out how to get to an obstructed ring in order to move it and where to put the obstructing ring so it will provide minimal impediment to future movements. To complicate matters, the movement of the rings may never violate the size order. Thus, the task contains many sequential dependencies because ring transfers are interdependent and constrained, creating many impediments for straightforward mapping of moves towards a goal. Failure to appreciate these dependencies and constraints impedes TOH planning (Bidell & Fischer, 1994; Klahr, 1978; Kotovsky et al., 1985).

Plan construction can be facilitated if the planner understands that these dependencies are nested. A recursive strategy of obstacle removal can be

TABLE 6.2
Constraint Management

TOH	Grocery Shopping
Nature of Constraints	
1. The rings and goals form a stack that creates obstacles to accessibility	Items are independent and directly accessible
2. Each decision requires considering whether a ring is free to move and has a free legal destination	Once order is created, no barriers exist to following it
Sources of Difficulty	
1. Managing each precondition	Relatively easy mapping of imagined order onto travel path
2. Recognizing the implication of satisfaction of one subgoal for satisfaction of other related subgoals	

built that enables the planner to go progressively down to the bottom of the stack using the same routine. For example, the three-ring TOH problem contains three subproblems, placing each of the rings correctly on the goal peg. The first subproblem involves first freeing the bottom ring by moving all the obstructors, then clearing the goal post, and finally moving the bottom ring to the goal post (Simon, 1975). The second subproblem has the same structure, freeing the medium ring and clearing the goal post to receive it. The final step moves the smallest ring to the goal post. This constrained and nested subgoaling makes TOH planning distinctive.

Grocery Shopping.   Constraint management in grocery shopping is much easier than in the TOH task because the sequence of points along the shopping path is not arranged in a subgoal stack like the rings in the TOH (see Table 6.2.). Once the shopper recognizes the efficient route, executing the plan poses few problems. There are no obstacles to overcome. Moreover, the first item in the sequence is directly accessible. In contrast, on the TOH task, reaching the first goal in the sequence—transferring the largest ring—requires satisfying multiple subgoals, each of which is a problem in itself.

Demands on Working Memory

Table 6.3 compares the demands on working memory posed by the two tasks.

TOH.   The TOH gauges memory span and memory strategies. The addition of rings requires encoding more items, greater forward search, and

TABLE 6.3
Working Memory

TOH	Grocery Shopping
Nature of Demands	
1. Depending on strategy, must remember moves, subgoals, or configurations of rings	Depending on strategy must remember items or route configurations
2. To evaluate best move must evaluate different possibilities and their consequences	Unless plans opportunistically, evaluating different routes on line unnecessary
3. The only external aid is the current configuration of rings	External aids for recall of accomplishments, goals
4. Subgoals eliminated slowly	Fast reduction of list
Sources of Difficulty	
1. Depth of search required	Minimal depth of search if route constructed in advance
2. Recall of constraints	Minimal constraints
3. Length of move sequences	Few moves
4. Number of subgoals	External aids to recall goals

greater division of multistep problems into smaller subproblems (Bidell & Fischer, 1994; Karat, 1982). Like memorizing a list, TOH planning is influenced by the way items are coded and chunked. The items in memory are not single rings or moves, they are changing configurations of rings on three pegs. The planner must integrate information across all the pegs at a particular problem state, and distinguish among different problem states that contain the same elements distributed in new ways across the same locations. As in tasks of mental rotation (Cooper, 1982), different strategies of mental representation may place different memory demands on the processor. Planners capable of forming integrated spatial representations may be at an advantage on the task, whereas those who code the rings and problem states piecemeal may be at a disadvantage.

The second demand on memory arises from the number of steps that must be performed to complete the task. Individuals can reduce the extent to which they must think ahead by breaking down the task into subproblems, using a recursive strategy or using some movement pattern (Simon, 1975).

Another demand on memory arises from the rules provided to planners. The arbitrary nature of the TOH task and the invocation of constraints on movement require the problem solver to devote memory resources to defining the problem space. Certain TOH rules are hard to remember, and students often embark on the problem before they learn the rules and understand their application (Kotovsky et al., 1985). Performance can be markedly improved by training people to recognize rule violations easily and accurately prior to planning.

Grocery Shopping.   The grocery shopping task is not usually thought of as a memory task because so many of the memory demands are externalized. The items to be collected are represented by cards. The order of the cards can be arranged to reflect the order of the route. The locations of items can be encoded by distinctive landmarks. The rules constraining shopping are trivial to remember.

Monitoring

Table 6.4 compares monitoring in the two tasks.

TOH.   Monitoring requires pinpointing past, present, and desired future locations in the problem space. Additionally, crucial decisions need to be made about whether an intended step will narrow the gap between the current state and the goal state. Monitoring TOH progress is difficult because there are few distinctive ways to mark problem states. Pegs differ only in position. Because the rings at any point may be spread across three locations, the individual has to integrate them to form a single image.

Gauging how much of the task was already accomplished and what remains to be completed is hard because: (a) judgment of the effectiveness

TABLE 6.4

Monitoring

TOH	Grocery Shopping
Nature of Monitoring Demands	
1. Encoding rings already placed in proper order on goal peg	1. Encoding items already collected
2. Keeping track of the alternative next steps, which may resemble one another because the displays are so similar	2. Weighing next choices
3. Deciding which is the most efficient next move	3. Deciding where to go
4. Keeping one's place in problem, despite constantly changing landscape	4. Staying on chosen path
Sources of Difficulty	
1. The goal peg signals completion of each subproblem making goal tracking easy	Collected items signal goal achievement
2. Keeping track of subgoals hard because the problem states and moves are easily confused; information on each state is distributed across problem locations	Locations are distinctly marked and the entire problem is visible
3. Evaluating alternatives must be done in the head, but process can be simplified by using recursive structure	Evaluating alternative may be done in the head, but process can be simplified by using route schema
4. The landscape changes with each ring transfer and the subgoals may increase or decrease	The external landscape is constant and goals dwindle with each item collection

of each move must often be based on anticipating several moves ahead; (b) the recombining of elements at each move makes recalling the changes producing the present move and anticipating future moves confusing; and (c) the landscape is changing dynamically. One has to rely on memory to hold in mind past moves and the configuration of past, present, and future moves in an overlapping, similar, and continuously changing problem.

Grocery Shopping.   Both the TOH task and the shopping task involve a dynamically changing configuration of problem states. But the sources of constancy and change differ. Shopping requires efficient and exhaustive collection of items. Monitoring progress in item collection is easy. The location of the items on the store shelves remains constant and the only source of item change is the shrinkage of the list as items are collected. The list, shopping basket, or empty shelves are external reminders of progress.

Monitoring achievement of the second goal of shopping, efficiency, is more difficult because the shopper is constantly changing locations. Therefore, the relative distance between the shopper and the items to be collected shifts. However, the supermarket layout provides a variegated terrain to mark one's progress. The grocery store landscape is constant and well-differentiated with clues to mark item location. Consequently, the planner can easily monitor progress toward the final goal. This contrasts with the dynamically changing and overlapping configurations of rings in the TOH.

The ease of monitoring depends on the planner's strategy and goals. If the shopper only considers exhaustive collection of disparate items as the goal, monitoring is easy. At the other extreme, when the shopper understands that the list contains a set of items connected to each other by their location in the store along a minimal distance path, monitoring is also easy. The strategy of moving left to right or right to left in the store is easy to conceptualize and to monitor. The shopper can simply imagine the entire path and follow it. The imagined path guides the actual route and marks progress on it. The items, the path, and the memory load shrink in a predictable fashion. The planner has two cues—the layout of the store and the cards constituting the shopping list—to guide construction and execution of the plan.

However, if the planner acts opportunistically with only sporadic concern for efficiency, then the number and arrangements of elements in memory must shift dynamically to reflect the changing position of the shopper in the store. Keeping track of progress becomes more difficult because the planner's position in space and resulting distance calculations change dramatically.

Summary

Each of these two planning tasks measures construction of a sequence of actions to accomplish a goal. Each requires rearranging a set of elements. In each there are sequential dependencies in that accomplishment of one goal has implications for the accomplishment of other goals, and each move has implications for other moves in the sequence. But the tasks emphasize different aspects of planning. The grocery shopping task requires searching for the relevant items, guided by categorical knowledge and geographical knowledge. Categorical knowledge narrows the choice of search locations. Once the items are located, geographical knowledge needs to be used to create an integrated representation and to plot a route. Lacking route knowledge and the means to compute distances, planning will be inefficient. The construction of the route constitutes the goal. Once constructed, execution and monitoring are relatively easy. Arrangement of the cards containing the items to reflect the planned route will help the planner in executing and monitoring the plan. Thus once the plan is formed, it can be externalized.

The goal for the TOH is explicit. There are no irrelevant items to be ignored. But the representation of the problem is difficult because the rules for movement are constrained and superficially arbitrary, and the representations of the intermediate states in goal attainment are distributed across three peg locations and involve recombinations of items distinguishable only by size. Unlike the grocery task, there are obstacles to obtaining the rings and constraints on their removal. As the number of rings increases, the number of legal problem states and the number of moves required to achieve a goal increases exponentially, increasing the memory demands. Moreover, the sequential dependencies in the task require the planner to anticipate several moves ahead. Efficient use of memory requires a strategy of chunking moves. Each problem must be conceptualized, not as a series of independent moves, but as subproblems that have as their goal freeing the largest ring that is not on its goal post and moving it to its goal post. Monitoring progress toward goal achievement is difficult due to the paucity of external reminders to help the individual gauge distance from the goal, and to the shifting configuration of similar rings across similar pegs.

Therefore, when a person fails to construct an efficient TOH plan, there is no reason to conclude that the person will fail on the shopping task, because the two tasks differ in the demands they place on the component skills of planning and on the knowledge base. However, comparison of performance on the two tasks provides a means of diagnosing the aspects of planning that pose difficulties for a given individual. Grocery shopping requires focusing of attention, spatial understanding, and search. The TOH requires constraint management, careful monitoring, and efficient use of memory resources.

TOH Variants

Experimental investigations of the TOH pursued the agenda of studying the components that contribute to differences in performance by shifting task parameters such as the stimulus dimensions, the number of rules stated, and the cover story. Studies of the TOH produced convincing evidence of the effect of problem and constraint representation on planning in adults. Providing rules that are consistent with real-world knowledge and that are externalized in a physical representation that makes sense of the rules alleviates some of the processing problems that plague planners. Adult problem solvers need to go through a familiarization phase in which they discover how the task works before they can produce efficient plans (Karat, 1982; Kotovsky et al., 1985; Zhang & Norman, 1994). Obviously, increasing the number of rings challenges the capacity of working memory. Moves that require greater forward search take longer to execute and produce more errors (Bidell & Fischer, 1994; Klahr & Robinson, 1981; Kotovsky et al., 1985). Early in the problem, when the greatest forward search is required, the most monitoring errors occur (Klahr & Robinson, 1981).

Adaptations of the task to young children are very revealing because they indicate the investigator's assumptions about the essential components of planning. Presumably there are certain prerequisites to planning without which planning cannot occur. For example, without a solid understanding of the task, children would be unable to use working memory to form and monitor the anticipatory plans the TOH task requires. So adapters of the TOH task attempted to provide a more distinctive representation, externalize the movement constraints of the task, incorporate real world knowledge, and include extensive familiarization. They wanted to shift the demands of the TOH from problem representation to anticipation and monitoring. Some of the modifications also changed the role of other aspects of TOH planning. A comparison of the "standard" TOH task and the revisions enables diagnosing the shifting configurations of sources of difficulty in TOH planning. Empirical investigations would validate the impact of task differences and possibly reveal developmental changes in the importance of different processes and remediation devices. We now discuss two popular revisions of the task with these aims in mind (see Table 6.5).

Welsh's Task.   Welsh's procedure includes some modification of the testing apparatus and major changes in testing procedures (Welsh, 1991; Welsh & Pennington, 1988; Welsh, Pennington, & Groisser, 1991; Welsh, Pennington, Ozonoff, Rouse, & McCabe, 1990; see Fig. 6.4). The rings differ in color as well as size and the three pegs are tapered in order to hinder placement of the smallest ring on the bottom of a stack. Whereas the standard TOH task is presented on a single apparatus for ring transfer,

TABLE 6.5
Three TOH Variants

Standard	Welsh	Klahr
Task Apparatus		
1 apparatus	1 working apparatus	1 initial state apparatus
	1 goal apparatus	1 goal apparatus
Rings differ in size	Rings differ in size, color	Cans differ in size, color, identity
3 pegs	3 tapered pegs	3 pegs(trees)
Rules		
Single ring, one-handed transfer	Single ring, one-handed transfer	Single can, one-handed transfer
Smallest ring on top	Smallest ring on top	Largest can on top
Instructions		
No cover story	No cover story	Copycat monkey family
Efficient solution	Efficient solution	Efficient solution
Procedures		
Minimal familiarization	Extensive testing of rule understanding, practice tasks	Extensive testing of rule understanding, practice tasks
Ascending order of difficulty	Ascending order of difficulty	Ascending order of difficulty
1 try per problem	6 tries on same problem	1 try per problem
	Problems overlap	Varied problems
May talk aloud while moving	Move	Tell plan

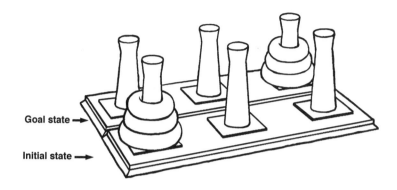

FIG. 6.4. Welsh's Tower of Hanoi.

Welsh provided a second apparatus as a reminder of the goal to be achieved.

The rules of the game resemble the standard rules. But Welsh provided a cover story borrowed from Klahr for children younger than 7 years, and she tested at every age to make sure the children could discriminate illegal from legal moves. Children had to show attentiveness and compliance by satisfactory performance on rudimentary 1- or 2- move problems. Thus, children were thoroughly familiarized with the task before proceeding.

Welsh drew on the work of Borys, Spitz, and Dorans (1982) and Byrnes and Spitz (1977) to alter radically the procedure for testing. She constructed a set of problems with the same final state, but the initial states varied in whether the goal tower could be produced in 2 to 7 moves for the 3-ring problems, or 7, 11, or 15 moves for the 4-ring problem. The harder problems were inclusive of the earlier ones. Thus, the 3-ring, 6-move problem was identical to the 7-move problem except that the initial optimal move had been taken so that the individual had only 6 moves to the goal; the 5-move problem had a configuration where the first 2 moves had been made, leaving only the next 5 moves to plan. Analogous to the Stanford–Binet, the child began at a fixed point and if the child failed to enact two errorless, optimal sequences of moves, the child dropped back to an easier problem. Once the baseline problem was located, the child received problems in ascending order of difficulty. The child had to solve the same problem optimally twice in a row in a maximum of six attempts in order to progress to the next level of difficulty. Scoring was based on the number of attempts to achieve two optimal solutions at a given move length, and on analyses of moves.

Klahr's Task.   Klahr (1978, 1985, 1994, Klahr & Robinson, 1981) used a strikingly different set of objects, cover story, instructions, and performance requirements (see Fig. 6.5). Cans differing in size, color, and identity were substituted for rings. The cans represented a family of monkeys whose size reflected their roles: father, mother, and baby. The pegs were trees on which the monkeys (cans) rested. The cans were stacked on the pegs in inverted order because only a larger can could slip over a smaller one. To reverse the order would cause a smaller container to slip off the top of other cans. Klahr also used two physical models, one representing the initial state and the other, the goal state.

The rules of the game and its rationale were embodied in a cover story about a monkey family who jumps from tree to tree according to monkey customs. These customs dictated which jumps were legal—those maintaining the size order—and which were illegal. One set of monkeys, those in the initial state, were copycat monkeys desirous of looking like the goal monkeys. The child was asked to help the copycat monkeys accomplish the task by *telling* the experimenter how to move the cans. The child was then given four familiarization problems, each requiring one move, and the experimenter carried out the plan and corrected inefficient moves.

After this familiarization process, a set of problems was presented. Children had to describe their plan without enactment. The problems occurred in ascending order with progressively more moves (1–7) required for completion. But the problems in each path length were different. Half

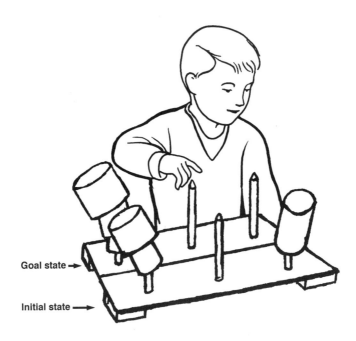

FIG. 6.5. Klahr's version of the Tower of Hanoi task.

ended in a tower in which all cans were concentrated on one peg, and half ended with cans distributed across more than one peg (flat-ending). The successive problems were not usually embedded. A problem at an earlier level did not appear at the next level with one step added. Moreover, the child had only one trial on a given problem. Children tackled every problem at each level of difficulty unless they refused to continue, or produced multiple rule violations and nonoptimal moves.

Comparison of Task Representation. How might these different versions affect constructing an order, understanding constraints, remembering, and monitoring (see Table 6.6.)? Both may facilitate perceptual discrimination and understanding of movement constraints. However, the

TABLE 6.6
Consequences of Task Variations

Standard	Welsh	Klahr
Representation		
Fewer cues differentiate rings so order less obvious	A nominal & ordinal cue differentiate rings so rings more discriminable	2 ordinal and 1 nominal attribute so order more obvious and cans more discriminable
Movement constraint not externalized	Pegs reinforce movement constraint	Cans reinforce movement constraint
No cover story	No cover story	Cover story for can transfer, can movement, making task elements sensible
No reminder of goal	Reminder of goal allowing current and present state to be related	Reminder of goal and initial state, framing the problem
Goal states vary	Tower-ending goal states so goal constant	Goal states vary
Constraints		
Obstacle removal	Obstacle removal	Obstacle removal
No reminders	Peg reminds and rationalize rules	Cans remind and rationalize rules
Memory Demands		
Varies	Reduced by repetitive and overlapping tasks	Same as standard task
Can see recent move only	Can see recent move and goal, so less demanding	Sees goals, initial state, but not moves, increasing memory load
Monitoring Demands		
Result of move visible, aiding goal tracking	Result of move visible aiding monitoring	Cannot see move outcome, so monitoring difficult
Trials were not repeated	Repeating trials helps repair strategies	Like standard task
Trials do not overlap	Overlapping trials aid monitoring, debugging	Like standard task

Klahr task may promote a more differentiated and integrated representation than the Welsh task.

In the Welsh task, the redundant dimensions of size and color differentiate the rings, and the tapering of the pegs externalizes and subtly reinforces the injunction to keep the smallest ring on top. The added physical presence of the goal configuration may enable children to encompass in one representation both the current state of the problem and the desired goal.

The Klahr task differentiates the stimuli even further because the cans differ in size, color, and identity. The constraints on moves are dramatically externalized because it is physically impossible to violate the size order and attempts that violate the rule are doomed to failure. When one can is physically contained in another, it is clear the container is an obstacle for the contained and that the size of the container is relevant to the relation among cans as well as to the sequence of object transfers. In the Welsh task, the pegs constrain movement, but in Klahr's task, the cans, which are the movables, dictate their course of movement.

Klahr also provided a cover story that enables the child to draw on real-world knowledge to integrate and enrich the problem representation. The story motivates the game and may also motivate the child. Monkeys move from tree to tree and like many animals, they are hierarchical with bigger, powerful, parents providing obstacles for the achievement of child goals. The linked family roles may help the child integrate the cans into one representation. The goal makes sense because it is in the nature of copycats to be like their models.

Despite all of these advantages to the Klahr task, it contains one element that may inhibit representation, the nature of the goal. Klahr (1985) noted that flat-ending problems are problematical because they require the child to integrate information across pegs. The order of the goal objects across the pegs may not be detected or encoded easily.

Comparison of Constraints.   Neither task eliminates the subgoaling and movement constraints inherent in the TOH, although a clear representation of the problem facilitates ordering the sequence of moves.

Comparison of Memory Demands.   If the Klahr task provides a better task representation, the Welsh administration of the task reduces memory load because the child acts rather than talks about action. So, the child has an external embodiment of the current state to enhance the internal processing that anticipation of future moves requires. In the action sequence, the child can concentrate on moving one ring, while relying on accessible perceptual data to encode the status of the remaining rings. In contrast, in the Klahr problem, the child may describe just the movement of a focal monkey but has to keep in mind the unverbalized status of the other monkeys.

The repetition of steps within the same problem until an optimal set of moves is made helps the child in the Welsh task construct and remember the planning routine, and may actually teach the child to plan. The Welsh task resembles cumulative rehearsal of a list where the individual repeats one word, then that word and the next, and so on. The Klahr task lacks this quality; it is more memory-intensive.

Bidell and Fischer (1994) claimed that the TOH taps qualitative as well as quantitative differences in processing. Planning some moves requires simply transferring a ring to a new location, whereas other more complex moves require obstacle removal with careful attention to implications for later transfers. More of the shortest Welsh problems contain simpler moves than the Klahr problems.

Comparison of Monitoring Demands.   The differences in verbal versus action planning and in cumulative and noncumulative sequences have consequences for monitoring. Progress in the Klahr task is harder to monitor than in the Welsh task. Although verbalization can lead to more reflection, it is harder to keep track of the past, present, and future because the verbal message fades as it is uttered. The Klahr task sequence also involves more variety. Children start and end at different points in each problem. Even though tower-ending and flat-ending problems are presented in separate blocks, the child may need to switch strategies when switching types of goal. Because the child has to traverse more of the problem space and approach goals through different paths, the problem of keeping track of present location and distance from the goal is formidable.

Welsh's task simplifies monitoring because the child encounters multiple repetitions of the same problem. Imperfect plans can be repaired in the six attempts allowed. Strategies can be solidified because new problems are simply extensions of old ones.

BROADER ISSUES

We have traced the path from a broad construct—planning— to particular measures. We are now ready to elaborate on the question, "What do planning tasks measure?" We will suggest there are three different ways of answering this question that have different implications for the way planning measures are used in developmental research. In the succeeding sections, we ask whether the TOH and errand tasks represent the entire domain of planning. Finally, we address whether current analyses of performance on these tasks, which are from a cognitive perspective, capture all of the ingredients in planning. We discuss each of these issues in turn.

What Do Planning Tasks Measure?

There are three different research traditions in the study of planning. In the individual difference literature, planning is regarded as a general ability. On a broad conceptual level, there is commonality across planning tasks. Without such commonalities, the construct of planning would be useless. We have argued that one feature possessed by the tasks conventionally used to tap this ability is generating in advance a sequence of actions that meet certain constraints. Each planning task requires monitoring execution of the plan and repair of faulty anticipations. But more empirical work is needed to determine the amount of shared variance across specific popular measures of planning (e.g., Gnys & Willis, 1991; Naglieri & Das, 1990; Parila, Aysto, & Das, 1994). Do people who tend to organize diverse chores into an efficiently scheduled route also think through the series of moves in the TOH task, and plan in advance their order of priorities for the day? Are these tasks equally sensitive to specific neurological deficits that lead to the impairment of inhibition, sequencing, and resource allocation (Llamas & Diamond, 1991)? Do groups labeled by some external criterion as excellent planners or as deficient planners differ on tasks we think of as assessing planning? Because so many cognitive abilities change and are reorganized during the life span, a close examination of the impact of developmental changes will produce a richer data base to answer these questions.

The individual difference tradition seeks to determine how planning skill influences other daily activities like running an organization or writing an essay. It also examines how neurological status influences planning. Planning is a means to examining other activities. In the cognitive tradition, planning is a subject in its own right, and the investigator tries to analyze the mechanisms by which planning is realized. Planning is considered a central part of problem solving. It is assumed that the same components that govern problem solving govern planning, but specific planning tasks tap these processes to different extents.

We analyzed several measures of planning and suggest four components: (a) detection of order, (b) constraint management, (c) working memory load, and (d) monitoring. We showed how different tasks and even different versions of the same task draw on these components to varying degrees. Presenting the TOH as a series of nested cans makes obeying the constraints easier than presenting a stack of rings. Comparison of the two tasks enables assessment of the impact of constraint management on planning. Task analyses and comparisons enable specification of the underlying component processes that affect all planning tasks and diagnosis of the extent to which each planning task draws on these processes.

Some planning tasks will be more useful for diagnosing the impact of certain processes than others. This kind of task analysis motivated our chapter. Because each component skill may change during the course of development, task comparisons provide an important tool for examining the nature of development of these components and the impact of their development on planning tasks. Perhaps demands on working memory or monitoring may be more onerous at one age. Hence, at a particular point in development, tasks that facilitate monitoring or externalize rules may have a different impact on performance than later.

The third perspective is an extension of the preceding one. It takes a more dynamic view of the components and their relations. Planning involves a coalition of skills such as the ability to form an anticipatory representation, to order goals, and to monitor and repair anticipatory plans. But the influence of these skills in a coalition varies with the task and the abilities and strategies of the planner (Thelen & Smith, 1994). Thus, comparative studies of planning tasks across diverse populations varying in level of skills provide the opportunity to examine how planning is orchestrated.

Bidell and Fischer (1994) noted that there are qualitative changes in development reflecting different ways the moves are integrated in the Tower of Hanoi. Simon (1975) described different strategies for planning ranging from recursive subgoaling, to perceptual analyses, to memorization of sequence patterns. Each strategy changes the demands on working memory, and each strategy deals with different ordering devices. Hence, developmental investigations combined with task analyses can be used to chart the emergence, integration, and refinement of planning.

Do TOH and Errand Planning Represent the Field of Planning?

Earlier we argued that the two measures of planning—errand tasks and the TOH—represent an important piece of a larger field. These two tasks measure the online generation of plans during problem solving. They rely on short-term memory processing, and construction and detection of an order. Not all planning tasks require the same processes and even the errand planning task might be solved in an entirely different way. By expanding the repertoire of tasks and ways of thinking about planning, we might learn more about planning.

In the artificial intelligence literature, planning is conceptualized as a dynamic remembering process. The individual pulls up past plans used in the identical, or a similar, situation and then adapts the retrieved plan to fit the task at hand. In order to do so, the individual must first analyze the situation to know what stored plans are relevant, and plans must be stored in a way that fits the analysis. The plan library in memory must be organized by the problems a plan addresses and the pitfalls those plans handle. Once a candidate plan is retrieved, further knowledge is required to know how to adapt the old plan to the new circumstance. And should the plan be inadequate, further causal analysis will suggest the cause of failure and the means to repair it. (Hammond, 1989, 1990). In this view, planning is a by-product of goal-directed activities and learning from experience. It is not surprising that experts in a domain tend to engage in more planning (Chi, Glaser, & Rees, 1982).

This kind of planning that draws heavily on the knowledge base is not measured by the TOH and may not tap memory and problem representation in the same way. Instead, planning is based on long-term memory organization and analogical thinking. Nor do our current analyses of performance on errand tasks begin with an evaluation of how much prior knowledge the children have of shopping, food taxonomies, and spatial arrangements of supermarkets.

Yet, when developmentalists describe the origin of planning, they invoke scripts and routines (e.g., Hudson & Fivush, 1991). Perhaps we would learn something about planning by tracing how knowledge of scripts is transformed into plans and by using tasks that draw more heavily on daily life. We might have a different picture of development than the one provided by conventional laboratory measures. For example, one of the reasons that adolescents may seem less planful is that they are encountering arenas such as drinking and sexual behavior where they have little experience. Moreover, there is often little opportunity to learn from observing others, and little direct instruction. Thus, they lack the rich knowledge base to produce effective plans and to repair ineffective ones. Note that both process-based plans and knowledge-based plans require adaptation and monitoring. It would be interesting to ascertain if the modifications are similar for both kinds of planning.

Moreover, tasks of planning to meet sequential constraints have been situated in environments where the events are predictable and the plans satisfy short-term goals. The plan's outcome depends on the foresight of a solitary problem solver. But in real life, people, businesses, and government organizations frequently make long-range plans. The outcome of their plans may not be dependent on short-term memory, much less the ability to solve the TOH (Streufert & Nogami, chapter 7, this volume). More needs to be known about the relation of the piece of planning we have analyzed to other measures and ways of examining planning. This will be especially challenging because the artificial intelligence tradition is based on computer simulations of behavior, not assessment of people's minds.

Is There Anything Missing in Cognitive Analyses of Planning?

The preceding section suggested that planning covers a larger territory than mentally constructing ordered sequences prior to action. Here we argue that even within this framework, there are subprocesses that conventional cognitive views of planning omit, such as the decision to plan or commitment to the planning process. Simon (1995) noted the neglect of the motivational aspects of planning from analyses. We often use a paradigm that deemphasizes motivational elements, and we fail to assess the participants' attitudes about the task.

There are hidden assumptions in the TOH procedure. We only study people who consent to be in the experiment, and we assume that their consent means that they are deeply engaged in the task and committed to devoting effort to planning. We do not ask them about their motives and beliefs about themselves as planners and about the task environment as an appropriate planning milieu. Tasks like the Tower of Hanoi are intellectual challenges. So, performance rests on individuals' beliefs about their intellectual abilities, their interest in the task, the goals they set for themselves, and the value they place on strategy planning (see Skinner, chapter 11, this volume; Locke, Durham, Poon, & Weldon, chapter 10, this volume).

When we use the TOH and errand planning tasks, we may minimize the effects of belief systems and attitudes on planning. Performance on these laboratory tasks may not predict whether people will choose to plan in other circumstances. Both the tasks take place in predictable environments. Vocational and retirement planning do not. When the environment is more uncertain, people's beliefs about the control they can exert may influence planning. That is, the person who values intellectual challenges and strategic planning might do well in plotting minimal grocery routes but may not do well in career planning. Some other components need to be added to the cognitive analyses of planning. These components, like the cognitive ones, will exert different influences on different tasks and may have a distinct developmental course. Moreover, they should be added to the list of factors that influence individual differences in planning. We need to develop comprehensive models that address questions such as "Why, how, and when do we plan?"

ACKNOWLEDGMENT

Matthew Scholnick drafted the artwork based on sources provided by the authors.

REFERENCES

Anzai, Y., & Simon, H. (1979). The theory of learning by doing. *Psychological Review, 94*, 192–210.
Bereiter, C., & Scardamalia, M. (1982). From conversation to composition: The role of instruction in a developmental process. In R. Glaser (Ed.), *Advances in instructional psychology* (Vol. 2, pp. 1–64). Hillsdale, NJ: Lawrence Erlbaum Associates.

Bidell, T. R., & Fischer, K. W. (1994). Developmental transitions in children's online planning. In M. M. Haith, J. B. Benson, R. J. Roberts, & B. F. Pennington (Eds.), *The development of future-oriented processes* (pp. 141–176). Chicago: University of Chicago Press.

Borkowski, W., & Burke, J. E. (1996). Theories, models and measurements of executive functioning: An information processing perspective. In G. R. Lyon (Ed.), *Attention, memory and executive function* (pp. 235–261). Baltimore, MD: Brookes Publishing.

Borys, S. V., Spitz, H. H., & Dorans, B. A. (1982). Tower of Hanoi performance of retarded young adults and nonretarded children as a function of solution length and goal state. *Journal of Experimental Child Psychology, 33,* 87–110.

Byrnes, M. A., & Spitz, H. H.(1977). Performance of retarded adolescents and nonretarded children on the Tower of Hanoi problem. *American Journal of Mental Deficiency, 81,* 561–569.

Chi, M. T. H., Glaser, R., & Rees, E. (1982). Expertise in problem solving. In R. J. Sternberg (Ed.), *Advances in the psychology of intelligence* (Vol. 1, pp. 7–75). Hillsdale, NJ: Lawrence Erlbaum Associates.

Cooper, L. A. (1982). Strategies for visual comparison and representation: Individual differences. In R. J. Sternberg (Ed.), *Advances in the psychology of intelligence* (Vol. 1, pp. 77–124). Hillsdale, NJ: Lawrence Erlbaum Associates.

Dodge, K. A., Pettit, G. S., McClaskey, C. L., & Brown, M. (1986). *Social competence in children., Monographs of the Society for Research in Child Development, 51*(2, Serial No. 213).

Dreher, M., & Oerter, R. (1987). Action planning competencies during adolescence and early adulthood. In S. L. Friedman, E. K. Scholnick, & R. R. Cocking (Eds.), *Blueprints for thinking: The role of planning in cognitive development* (pp. 515–534). Cambridge, England: Cambridge University Press.

Flower, L., & Hayes, J. R. (1981). Plans that guide the composing process. In C. H. Fredericksen & J. F. Dominic (Eds.), *Writing: The nature, development and teaching of written communication* (Vol. 2, pp. 39–58). Hillsdale, NJ: Lawrence Erlbaum Associates.

Friedman, S. L., Scholnick, E. K., & Cocking, R. R. (1987). Reflections on reflection: What planning is and how it develops. In S. L. Friedman, E. K. Scholnick, & R. R. Cocking (Eds.), *Blueprints for thinking: The role of planning in cognitive development* (pp. 515–534). Cambridge, England: Cambridge University Press.

Gauvain, M., & Rogoff, B. (1989). Collaborative problem-solving and children's planning skills. *Developmental Psychology, 25,* 139–151.

Gnys, J. A., & Willis, W. G. (1991). Validation of executive function tasks with young children. *Developmental Neuropsychology, 7,* 487–501.

Hammond, K. J. (1989). CHEF. In C. K. Riesbeck & R. C. Schank (Eds.), *Inside case-based reasoning* (pp. 165–212). Hillsdale, NJ: Lawrence Erlbaum Associates.

Hammond, K. J. (1990). Case-based planning: A framework for planning from experience. *Cognitive Science, 14,* 385–444.

Hayes-Roth, B., & Hayes-Roth, F. (1979). A cognitive model of planning. *Cognitive Science, 3,* 275–310.

Hudson, J. A., & Fivush, R. (1991). Planning in the preschool years: The emergence of plans from general event knowledge. *Cognitive Development, 6,* 393–415.

Karat, J. (1982). A model of problem-solving with incomplete constraint knowledge. *Cognitive Psychology, 14,* 538–559.

Klahr, D. (1978). Goal formation, planning and learning by preschool problem solvers or "my socks are in the dryer." In R. S. Siegler (Ed.), *Children's thinking: What develops?* (pp. 181–212). Hillsdale, NJ: Lawrence Erlbaum Associates.

Klahr, D. (1985). Solving problems with ambiguous subgoal ordering: Preschoolers' performance. *Child Development, 56,* 940–952.

Klahr, D. (1994). Discovering the present by predicting the future. In M. M. Haith, J. B. Benson, R. J. Roberts, & B. F. Pennington (Eds.), *The development of future-oriented processes* (pp. 177–218). Chicago: University of Chicago Press.

Klahr, D., & Robinson, M. (1981). Formal assessment of problem solving and planning processes in preschool children. *Cognitive Psychology, 13,* 113–148.

Kolodner, J. L. (1994). From natural language understanding to case-based reasoning and beyond: A perspective on the cognitive model that ties it all together. In R. C. Schank & E. Langer (Eds.), *Beliefs, reasoning, and decision making: Psycho-logic in honor of Bob Abelson* (pp. 55–110). Hillsdale, NJ: Lawrence Erlbaum Associates.

Kotovsky, K., Hayes, J. R., & Simon, H. A. (1985). Why are some problems really hard? Evidence from Tower of Hanoi. *Cognitive Psychology, 17*, 248–294.

Llamas, C., & Diamond, A. (1991). *Development of frontal cortex abilities in children between 3 and 8 years of age.* Paper presented at the Biennial meeting of SRCD, Seattle, Washington.

Miller, G. A., Galanter, E., & Pribram, K. (1960). *Plans and the structure of behavior.* New York: Holt, Rinehart & Winston.

Naglieri, J. A., & Das, J. P. (1990). Planning, attention, simultaneous and successive (PASS) cognitive processes as a model for intelligence. *Journal of Psychoeducational Assessment, 8,* 303–337.

Parila, R. K., Aysto, S., & Das, J. P. (1994) Development of planning in relation to age, attention, simultaneous, and successive processing. *Journal of Psychoeducational Assessment, 12,* 212–227.

Pea, R. D., & Hawkins, J. (1987). Planning in a chore-scheduling task. In S. L. Friedman, E. K. Scholnick, & R. R. Cocking (Eds.), *Blueprints for thinking: The role of planning in cognitive development* (pp. 303–320). Cambridge, England: Cambridge University Press.

Piaget, J. (1976). *The grasp of consciousness: Action and concept in the young child.* Cambridge, MA: Harvard University Press.

Rogoff, B. (1990). *Apprenticeship in thinking: Cognitive development in social context.* New York: Oxford University Press.

Rubin, K. H., & Krasnor, L. R. (1986). Social-cognitive and social behavioral perspectives on problem solving. In M. Perlmutter (Ed.), *Cognitive perspectives on children's social and behavioral development. The Minnesota symposia on child psychology* (Vol. 18, pp. 1–68). Hillsdale, NJ: Lawrence Erlbaum Associates.

Sansone, C., & Berg, C. A. (1993). Adapting to the environment across the life span: Different process or different inputs? *International Journal of Behavioral Development, 16,* 215–241.

Schank, R. C. (1982). *Dynamic memory: A theory of reminding and learning in computers and people.* New York: Cambridge University Press.

Schank, R. C., & Abelson, R. P. (1977). *Scripts, plans, goals and understanding: An inquiry into human knowledge structures.* Hillsdale, NJ: Lawrence Erlbaum Associates.

Scholnick, E. K. (1994). Planning. *Encyclopedia of human behavior* (Vol. 3, pp. 525–535). Orlando, FL: Academic Press.

Scholnick, E. K., & Friedman, S. L. (1987). The planning construct in the psychological literature. In S. L. Friedman, E. K. Scholnick, & R. R. Cocking (Eds.), *Blueprints for thinking: The role of planning in cognitive development* (pp. 3–38). Cambridge, England: Cambridge University Press.

Scholnick, E. K., & Friedman, S. L. (1993). Planning in context: Developmental and situational considerations. *International Journal of Behavioral Development, 16,* 145–167.

Siegel, A. W., & White, S. H. (1975). The development of spatial representations of large-scale environments. In H. W. Reese (Ed.), *Advances in child development and behavior* (Vol. 10, pp. 9–55). New York: Academic Press.

Siegler, R. S., & Shrager, J. C. (1984). A model of strategy choice. In C. Sophian (Ed.), *Origin of cognitive skills* (pp.229–293). Hillsdale, NJ: Lawrence Erlbaum Associates.

Simon, H. A. (1975). The functional equivalence of problem-solving skills. *Cognitive Psychology, 7,* 268–288.

Simon, H. A. (1995). The information-processing theory of mind. *American Psychologist, 50,* 507–508.

Spivack, G., & Shure, M. B. (1974). *Social adjustment of young children: A cognitive approach to solving real-life problems.* San Francisco: Jossey-Bass.

Thelen, E., & Smith, L. B. (1994). *A dynamic systems approach to the development of cognition and action.* Cambridge, MA: MIT Press.

Wallner, K. (1996). *Executive functioning and its relation to planning skill in seven-year-old children.* Unpublished doctoral dissertation, University of Maryland, College Park.

Welsh, M. C. (1991). Rule guided behavior and self-monitoring on the Tower of Hanoi disk transfer task. *Cognitive Development, 6,* 59–76.

Welsh, M. C., Pennington, B. F. (1988). Assessing frontal lobe functioning in children: View from developmental psychology. *Developmental Neuropsychology, 4,* 199–230.

Welsh, M. C., Pennington, B. F., & Groisser, D. B. (1991). A normative developmental study of executive function: A window on prefrontal function in children. *Developmental Neuropsychology, 7,* 131–149.

Welsh, M. C., Pennington, B. F., Ozonoff, S., Rouse, B., & McCabe, E. R. B. (1990). Neuropsy-
    chology of early-treated phenylketonuria: Specific executive function deficits. *Child Devel-
    opment, 61*, 1697–1713.
Zhang, J., & Norman, D. A. (1994). Representations in distributed cognitive tasks. *Cognitive
    Science, 18*, 87–122.

7

Analysis and Assessment of Planning: The View From Complexity Theory

Siegfried Streufert
Pennsylvania State University College of Medicine

Glenda Y. Nogami
U.S. Army War College

Planning can vary from simple considerations of "what to do next" to exceedingly complex thought and action sequences that might require months or even years to complete. Yet, all planning activities have something in common. They are based on conceptualizations of the current environment. They are teleological. They anticipate a reality that does not yet (or does not yet quite) exist. They control cognitions and behaviors that are oriented toward goal attainment, involving both thought and action (cf. Scholnick & Friedman, 1987). In addition, planning requires the utilization of the time dimension by interconnecting the present with the future: Planning involves present cognitions and actions that are designed to attain a future outcome or, at least, planning requires "waiting" for an anticipated outcome that may occur in and of itself.

How do people plan? How do they interrelate their present with an anticipated future? How can we measure aspects of planning? Which components of the planning process lend themselves to assessment and which do not?

Before we consider how the planning process might be captured in numerical and graphic formats, we briefly review a theoretical orientation that underlies the assessment procedures we will present. Our conceptualizations of planning and strategic action, as well as the associated measurement techniques, are based on complexity theory. For present purposes, we consider the tenets of complexity theory only where they are needed to communicate our basis for measurement. Readers who are interested in greater detail about the theory are referred to several original sources (Streufert & Nogami, 1989; Streufert & Streufert, 1978; Streufert & Swezey, 1986; Suedfeld, 1988, 1992).

THEORY BASE FOR MEASURING PLANNING
AND STRATEGIC ACTION

Cognitive complexity (sometimes called conceptual complexity) theory emerged some four decades ago, built on earlier developmental views of Lewin (1936), Mead (1934), Schachtel (1959), and Werner (1957). Early trait-based complexity theories focused on cognitive "differentiation" (Bieri, 1955; Kelly, 1955)—the use of multiple dimensions in interpersonal perception. Harvey, Hunt, and Schroder (1961) added the concept of *integration*, the flexible and adaptive assembly of multidimensional thought processes into unique approaches to the environment.

Schroder, Driver, and Streufert (1967) developed a state–trait theory by including the effects of concurrent environmental conditions as predictors of differentiated and integrated functioning. Streufert and Streufert (1978), as well as Streufert and Swezey (1986), broadened complexity theory to cover a wide range of human cognitions and behaviors. Finally, Streufert and Nogami (1989) and Suedfeld (1992) added a meta-component. All of these views, however, have a common core: a joint focus on information *processing*—on the *structure* of human thought and action. All of the complexity theorists have been more concerned with *how* people think than with *what* they think. Cognitive complexity theories consider how people view (and relate to) their concurrent environment and how they view and approach the future. The more recent development of yet another (science-wide) complexity theory that is based on the interplay of order and chaos (Gleick, 1987) provides considerable parallels (Streufert, in press; cf. Lewin, 1992, and Waldrop, 1992, for popular summaries).

Complexity theory breaks with the Newtonian–Leibnitzian philosophy of science. It argues that *unique* behavior emerges at the level of each system or level of functioning, that this behavior cannot be anticipated on the basis of understanding the component elements that produce the system. Systems function in terms of nonlinear dynamics. That nonlinearity makes predictions of *specific* system-based behaviors difficult or impossible. In other words, it is often difficult to anticipate the specific *content* of behavior as developmental growth generates more advanced cognitive systems (processes). However, it is possible to observe and record particular events or actions and to analyze the probability of various outcomes (e.g., sets of behaviors) that emerge on the basis of systemic characteristics. Such probabilities are based on an analysis of the cognitive processes that underlie functioning, (i.e., the *structure* of thought that underlies behavior). Behavior is based on different unique processes at the various stages of development, representing unique skills that are available only after any particular stage has been attained (cf. the somewhat parallel notions of developmental psychologists such as Case, 1992; Fischer, 1980; Hunt, 1966; Hunt & Sullivan, 1974).

Despite its emphasis on growth through development, complexity theory would not necessarily equate a "higher" level of development with greater adaptation to *all* environmental conditions that might be experienced. Rather, the theory considers optimal functioning to occur when the concurrent complexity of any present environment and the cognitive complexity level of an individual are matched. Such a view, among others, fulfills Fischer's demand that developmental theories must focus on the organism's control of skills that are relevant to specific environments.

COMPLEXITY THEORY AND DEVELOPMENT

Before we discuss the developmental concepts advanced by complexity theory, it may be necessary to define three terms that will recur repeatedly: The terms are *goal*, *planning*, and *strategy*.

A *goal* is a desired end state. In most cases, the person pursuing a goal believes that its attainment will produce a cognitive, affective, and/or material reward.

A *plan* is a cognitive representation of the means (e.g., action [s]) needed to achieve a specific goal end state.

A *strategy* represents the association of at least two different sequential actions, based on one or more plans, intended to generate conditions that either attain a subgoal, a goal end state, or at least outcomes that should modify conditions to make an end state more attainable via the application of subsequent plans, strategies, and/or actions. Strategies, in other words are planned teleological action *sequences* which interconnect diverse activities that occur at different points in time. How do these teleological planning/strategy processes develop?

Behavioral complexity theory suggests that development of a person's cognitive structure, that is, his or her characteristic information processing, may proceed through a number of levels. A concept of *levels* or *stages* of development is, of course, not new. Early psychological theorists such as Freud (1938) spoke about stages, about development, and about potential arrestation of development. Piaget's (1952) work on childhood development provided the basis for much of developmental psychology. Many other theorists and researchers followed in Piaget's footsteps. Yet, there are considerable differences between those approaches and the views and techniques of complexity theorists.

In contrast, complexity theorists were concerned with the development of conceptual (i.e., verbal) *dimensionality*. As a result, they paid less attention to the very early stages of development (e.g., in infancy) and elaborated more (additional) later stages (levels) of functioning that cannot occur until verbal and potentially dimensional skills become established in the child. Likely, the developmental levels considered by complexity theorists do not come into their own until a child has reached the *representational* tier proposed by Fischer (1980). Harvey et al. (1961), in their early work on cognitive complexity, for example, distinguished between *concrete* and three more *abstract* levels of cognitive functioning with concrete thought, nonetheless requiring verbal (conceptual) representation of objects or events. Similarly, the developmental views of Breuer (1983) were founded on verbal representation of attained knowledge.

Complexity theory argues that verbal *unidimensional* representations of understanding emerge, first in a global sense, later in a dimensional sense. During global thought, principles of inclusion versus exclusion tend to exist: Perceived objects or persons either *do* or *do not* belong to a *category* (e.g., a person either is or is not *Mother*). As dimension(s) with verbal end points emerge (most often the evaluative dimension), objects or persons may initially be classified on contrasting end points, (e.g., as either [absolutely] "good" or "bad"). Later, the good–bad dimension may begin to be subdivided into intermediate points (i.e., "shades of grey"). As comprehension increases, other verbal labels may be placed on end points of *apparently* different dimensional judgments. In effect, however, these on-the-surface *different* dimensions, where employed by unidimensional persons, tend to be highly intercorrelated.[1]

Unidimensional cognitive processes typically show relatively little teleological sophistication and are generally of limited value for more than rudimentary planning activities. Of course, the unidimensional person might "want" certain events to occur in his or her environment, but will hardly approach the desired event in a "strategic" fashion, certainly not by employing (inventing) a novel strategy. Often, a single action is seen as the appropriate antecedent of a hoped for subsequent outcome.

Beyond the unidimensional "system" or "level," development may result in broader interactions with the external environment. Thought and consequent behavior may now extend beyond the use of a single dimension. Suppose a person is contemplating whether to engage in a particular behavior. That potential action may be considered on two dimensions: For example, it may be considered on the basis of: (a) is the action good or bad? (evaluation) and (b) will this action get the result I want? (utility). A person who has the capacity to employ different dimensions, frequently selected on the basis of current "salience," has attained the most basic (initial) level of *multidimensionality*. Behavioral complexity theory describes the process underlying this most basic form of multidimensional functioning as dimensional *differentiation*. In more applied terms, individuals who apply differentiation employ a greater "breadth of approach."

---

[1]Let us take the game of football as an example. We could certainly place the concept "football player" on a good–bad dimension (we would want good ones for our team). We could also locate the football player on a fast–slow dimension. On the surface, the two appear different. For most persons, however, they are intercorrelated and do not differ. They cannot conceive of a football player who would be both good and slow. A coach, however, might. Not all kickers need to be good and fast. They need to be accurate.

For a person who functions unidimensionally, evaluation and utility mean the same thing. For example, the unidimensional egocentric individual might have evaluated an activity that produces a desired outcome as "good." The unidimensional moral person, on the other hand, might have argued that only "good" things are "useful." But, with the emergence of differentiation, the two concepts can exist quite independently of each other as separate "dimensions of judgment."[2] The decision to take particular action may sometimes be based on the evaluative, at other times on the utility, and at yet other times on still other dimensions that have become part of the differentiator's cognitive system.

If we know about a unidimensional person's attitudes and intentions, we can probably predict his or her behavior with some accuracy. With the advent of multidimensional functioning, however, prediction becomes much more difficult. Earlier principles that can be used to predict unidimensional behavior no longer apply: Unique behaviors emerge. Often, we cannot know in advance which dimension may be selected (may be salient) at any one time. However, with differentiation as the initial level of multidimensionality, we enter a realm that allows a different kind of prediction. We can now focus on a person's specific *systemic* level. We can, if we have studied the relevant individual adequately, (a) indicate which dimensions are available and (b) predict the *likelihood of success* for that person's interaction with the present task environment, based on the "match" of his or her dimensional information processing characteristics with the degree of complexity of that concurrent environment (ideographic analysis).

Planning, at the differentiation level of information processing, may become more varied, but its strategic adequacy is still limited. Alternate limited goals may be established; multiple actions, often directed toward a specific goal, may emerge. Generally, any one action would still focus on one specific goal. If such an action does not obtain the desired goal end state, another action may be tried or another goal might be approached. Utilization of the time dimension in planning activities should, as was the case for unidimensional functioning, be generally limited to a single step that connects an action directly with an anticipated outcome. Such single steps might be short (flip the switch and the light will come on) or very long (starting to save early to have a good life during retirement 40 years from now). The decisive issue is not the length of the time span, but rather the lack of *sequential subgoals* and the *absence of intermediate steps* in planning and strategy processes.

At the next level of multidimensional development, more extended teleological planning and strategic activities emerge. The person is now

---

[2] Individuals do not progress from unidimensional to differentiative functioning all at once. Complexity theory suggests that development is often domain specific. For example, a person may function in unidimensional fashion in his or her interaction with a spouse, may differentiate with regard to an aspect of his work, and may even use a more highly developed integrative process in yet another domain.

able to "integrate" dimensions. Time to goal attainment takes on a new meaning: It is not used passively but actively (acting sequentially to make things happen). The unidimensional person and even, in general, the differentiator had employed "time" to repeat prior actions or to engage in alternate actions toward a goal when the initial action did not "work." The integrator, in contrast, may not even assume that an (initial) action will generate the goal end state. Rather, if required by the task, he or she might develop subgoals that will bring the final (end state) goal more into reach. Actions may now be designed to generate the basis for subsequent actions. Only later actions, planned tentatively for some more distant point in the future, may be intended to attain goals. In other words, the approach to a desired end state can become a two-step or multistep process. Two diverse actions, often representing the *integrated* coordination of several separate (differentiated) judgmental dimensions may be combined sequentially over time toward a joint intended outcome. Where environments are complex and where outcomes depend on more than one antecedent, such integrative processes can be considerably more adaptive.

Another step in development takes the individual into still another system of multidimensional functioning. Planning becomes much more involved. Several alternate plans toward a single goal may emerge. If one plan turns out not to be successful, others are actively available and are potentially actively pursued. Even plans may be organized in sequential fashion. ("To get the job, I need to know higher mathematics. So, I will take extra math in high school; I will work hard to do well; that will allow me to get into a good college and major in math and science. Then, maybe, I can go to graduate school at a place like MIT. After that, some company that I would enjoy working for will want to hire me.")

As a result of step-wise planning, strategies tend to become sequential as needed (not only actions are interconnected, but strategic action–action relationships become interconnected with other strategic action–action relationships). In addition, several goals as well as many individual strategic actions designed to attain those goals, can become interconnected with each other. Strategies may serve more than one goal. A highly interconnected *network* of actions may emerge over time. The multiple interconnections in an individual's information-processing network reflect the multiple purposeful use of planning and that person's efforts to realize those plans through complex interactive strategic sequences. The teleological effort not only involves individual plans, but planning itself becomes subject to teleological sequencing. Complexity theorists call this level (system) of functioning *complex integration*. In a more applied sense, it has been designated as *advanced strategy*.

Finally, yet another *kind* (level) of information processing is described by the term *meta-complexity* (Streufert & Nogami, 1989) or as a *cognitive manager* (Suedfeld, 1992). Meta-complexity cannot emerge prior to the existence of an integrative system. It may (in the optimal sense) or may not include the capacity to employ complex integration. An individual who is capable of meta-complexity can actively (intentionally) apply different information-processing *systems* to diverse environments. In other words, he or she is able to adapt (i.e., to optimize) his or her actions by *matching* the cognitive processing system to *concurrent characteristics of settings* with which that individual interacts.

What Is Optimal Functioning?

When we speak of development, we often assume that a higher level of development is necessarily better. Such an assumption may not always be correct. Rather than asking how high a level of development a person may have attained, we might ask whether a person is adapted to or is functioning optimally in his or her specific concurrent environment. In fact, all the levels of development toward greater cognitive complexity that we have discussed can be adaptive and all of those levels can be maladaptive. A very simple environment may be best handled by a unidimensional process that recognizes which actions are considered right (and rewarded) and which actions are considered wrong (and may be severely punished). Alternative thinking (differentiation, breadth of approach) could get someone dealing with very simple environments into deep trouble. The differentiator may, at least occasionally, select unacceptable alternate behaviors. Someone applying strategic activities might fare even worse: The strategist may be seen as a deviant manipulator who cannot be trusted, or whose wishy-washy thinking indicates that he or she does not understand or appreciate societal norms.

On the opposite side, a fluid, uncertain, and highly complex environment that provides only delayed and partial feedback cannot be successfully handled by unidimensional persons or by differentiators. Integrators will do better; but it takes persons capable of complex integration to be truly successful.

Finally, environmental demands may suddenly shift. At one point, a person may have ample time to plan and to develop complex strategies, to evaluate feedback, to modify tentative follow-on plans made earlier, to clarify goals once initial actions have been successful, and so forth. However, as a sudden emergency occurs, such highly complex forms of functioning may no longer be appropriate. Often an emergency must be handled decisively. If there is one single correct way to resolve the emergency (e.g., on the basis of training or experience), that action must be chosen immediately. If there are alternate actions that may (or may not) resolve the problem, several may have to be tried quickly. During an emergency or in response to a "simple" stable environment, a unidimensional or, at best, a differentiated approach would be appropriate. At such times, highly complex integrative functioning can be counterproductive.

Ideally, individuals should be able to shift the cognitive complexity of their approach and, as long as needed, adopt the currently most appropriate system of functioning. Where meta-complexity exists, such a shift toward adaptive functioning is possible. Without meta-complexity, sudden changes in the environment may not generate adaptive modifications of systemic functioning, often resulting in inappropriate and maladaptive behavior. To summarize, optimal development does not necessarily lead ever upwards toward the highest possible and therefore always best "level" or "system." Unless meta-complexity is available, development would ideally stabilize to a point where optimal adaptation to the person's typical day-to-day environment is obtained.

Measurement

We have defined goals, planning, and strategy. We have discussed how complexity theory views development and optimal adaptation to the environment and to changes in that environment. Now we translate those concepts into the measurement of planning.

How do we assess planning skills? How do we determine whether a particular set of plans is optimal under given environmental or task conditions? How can we even know when and what people are planning? Unfortunately, we cannot read people's minds. Of course, we could ask them about their plans. But, in most settings such questions interrupt behavior that is continuing across time. Unless carefully designed and matched to the task (as we do in our simulation settings), such questions interfere with and might even modify the underlying cognitive processes. In contrast, if we were to ask about plans, strategies, and goals on a post hoc basis, omissions and biases (e.g., social desirability) might distort our data. Purely observational techniques may be yet more seriously flawed. In other words, obtaining accurate information about human planning in normal or controlled research environments can be quite difficult.

Even if we obtain an accurate and complete list of all relevant plans, how do we generate hard data from such a list? How, for example, do we know whether some specific action is associated with any one plan or set of plans? How do we know when and whether a plan is translated into a strategy?

Over a period of three decades we have developed a number of reliable and valid (e.g., Breuer & Streufert, in press; Streufert, Pogash, & Piasecki, 1988) measures that provide information about planning activities. To overcome the fact that we cannot accurately read people's minds, we chose a focus on actions, on prior environmental information that has led to those actions, on plans that exist at the time an action is taken[3] (i.e., plans that interconnect present with future actions), and finally on opportunistic behaviors that make use of prior actions. In other words, we developed

---

[3] Rather than asking about plans in general, we ask about plans associated with any action taken at the time the action is taken. Such questions are easier to answer, generate less, if any, bias, and provide information about the process that interconnects strategic planning sequences.

techniques that utilize the evident outcome of the cognitive goal–plan-ning–strategy networks that people employ as they interact with their ongoing and anticipated environments. We built queries about planned future actions into a simulated task setting where such questions appear eminently reasonable and helpful as part of the task environment, without biasing obtained responses. To illustrate the characteristic outcomes of such procedures, we consider Streufert's Time–Event Matrix (1990), a graphic representation that includes information about planning behavior and its consequences across a given period of time.

The Time–Event Matrix

Time–Event Matrices, as used in our laboratory, are most often constructed by a computer system. Matrices reflect the thoughts and activities of an individual or group that participated in one of our complex simulations for an entire day. However, computer assistance and lengthy participation are not vital: Time–Event Matrices can be constructed by hand and can be based on more time-limited cognition–action sequences of research participants. Information that must be available to construct such a matrix (and to calculate scores on a number of measures discussed later in this chapter) requires collecting data that represent five elements of the cognition–action process. We need to obtain information about:

1. The content and timing of any action taken.
2. Any information that was considered by the person (or group) as the action was taken.
3. The time when that information was received.
4. Any and all relevant plan(s) for future action(s) that existed at the time the individual or group engaged in an action.
5. Any past action(s) of this individual or group that, in the view of that individual or group, aided, or contributed to, the present action, or made that action possible.

By obtaining the information listed in items 1 through 5, we can recon-struct a participant's relevant "network" of plans, strategies, and actions across time. For easier visual comprehension, we represent this information in a two- (or, in some cases, three-) dimensional Time–Event Matrix. For present purposes, let us consider a two-dimensional matrix. Vertically, we list the different kinds of actions a participant has taken. Let us place this list on the left side of the page. The number and diversity of actions in this list reflects the breadth of approach to the problem, or, in terms of cognitive complexity theory, "differentiation." Note that similar or repetitive actions would be listed as the same kind of action (i.e., would not add to breadth and would not represent "differentiation").

We can now plot the progress of time on the bottom of our matrix (i.e., on the horizontal axis). Each action by a participant can now be represented as a point, placed horizontally next to the kind of action it represents and vertically above the time when that action was taken. If an action responded to prior information, then the time when that information arrived can be indicated by a star, placed horizontally in front of the subsequent action and directly above the time when it was received. For convenience, we might want to circle the resulting action, indicating that it responded to prior information.

Let us now consider planning activities. Whenever a person makes a decision or takes an action (e.g., as part of one of our simulations), we inquire whether this action provides the basis for some future action, that is, whether he or she is planning future action(s) that will (or may) be made possible or easier by the present action.[4] If the answer is affirmative, we obtain details about the planned actions. If such a planned future action is subsequently realized and if, at that later time, the participant(s) still remembered that they are now following up on the prior action, then a line is drawn to connect the two actions in the matrix. Whenever those two actions differ in their characteristics (i.e., reflect different kinds of actions that we had listed on the vertical), the connecting line will be a diagonal. We draw that diagonal with an arrowhead pointing forward in time (toward the right), and ending in the second of the two actions. Such a forward diagonal indicates that a single strategy was employed. In terms of complexity theory, a forward diagonal reflects an "integration."

At times, participants may conclude that a present action can be made more effective by utilizing some consequence(s) of a prior action, even though the present action had not been planned at the time of the previous action. Again, where the two actions differ in kind, they can be connected with a diagonal line. In this case, the diagonal would be drawn with an arrowhead pointing backward (ending at the earlier action), indicating an opportunistic activity. In terms of cognitive complexity theory, such a backward diagonal is defined as a "backward integration." (For easier comprehension of computer-generated matrices, diagonals representing forward integrative strategies are often drawn in green; opportunistic backward integrations are drawn in red).

Finally, let us consider one more entry into the matrix. Participants may develop a plan and engage in an initial action, always with the intent to continue the strategic sequence by carrying out the planned second action later, as appropriate. However, that second action may never materialize. It may be forgotten, it may become unnecessary, or changes in the task environment may render it inappropriate. Alternate plans and strategies toward the same goal(s) may already have been effective. Whenever prior

---

[4] In our simulations, such questions are made part of the simulated setting to assure that participants do not perceive queries as interruptions.

plans are not carried through, we can draw a vertical line. It begins at the initial action with the arrowhead pointing toward the kind of action that had been planned. Typically, the presence of a moderate number of vertical lines in the matrix is expected and reflects "normal" (quality) functioning. However, an inordinate number of vertical lines, especially in the absence of multiple diagonal interconnections among various actions, suggests that the participant engages in planning activities, but is typically failing to carry out those plans.

Examples of Time–Event Matrices

Time–Event Matrices differ from person to person. The matrices provide a unique ideographic description of each individual's cognitive–behavior process. But they differ even more widely across the diverse processing systems described by complexity theory. To demonstrate those differences, five computer-generated matrices from the simulation participation of adult managers are provided in Figs. 7.1–7.5. These matrices were selected because they reflect relatively pure forms of unidimensional, differentiative, integrative, complex integrative and meta-complex functioning. Of course, not all matrices that represent the unique behavior of research participants will display the same purity. Some matrices reflect characteristics of more than one processing system providing, for example, evidence for intermediate stages of development.

The computer-generated matrices in Figs. 7.1–7.5 list action (decision) categories as three-digit numbers on the vertical. Time is plotted on the horizontal. Each time unit represents 2 minutes–the total time of simulation participation was 360 minutes or 6 hours.

Figure 7.1 presents the behavior of a unidimensional manager. The number of decision (action) categories reflecting breadth and differentiation is rather limited. Diagonals (strategies, integrations) are absent. Actions are typically taken in quick response to incoming information.

Figure 7.2 reflects the functioning of a differentiator. In this case, the number of decision categories is considerably greater: Breadth is now present. Often, somewhat more time is taken prior to action. Diagonal connections (strategies, integrations) are still absent.

In Fig. 7.3 the presence of strategic action is evident. The integrator who generated this matrix interconnects actions with each other, but does not engage in considerable sequential strategy: In most cases, the various diagonals remain fairly isolated from each other. Actions are sometimes taken rapidly on arrival of information; at other times, the integrator waited until additional information was obtained.

The complex integrator who produced Fig. 7.4 generated a quite different matrix. Multiple overall strategies are interconnected with each other, culminating in complex planning activities toward multiple goals that are approached sequentially via subgoals. Plans are not precisely formulated

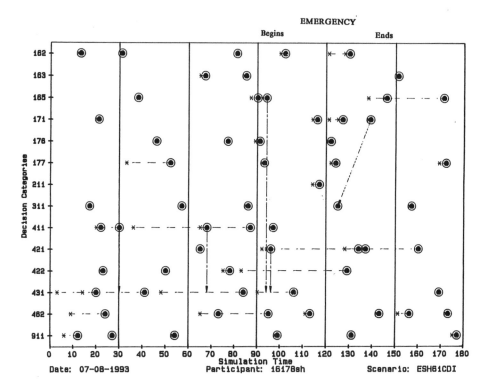

FIG. 7.1.   A Time–Event Matrix reflecting unidimensional functioning.

until the time for their implementation has arrived. Goals that cannot be achieved rapidly, or strategies that will be carried out some time later, are left relatively vague, allowing for modification as more information becomes available across time. In some cases, multiple information, collected over considerable periods of time, is used to decide on actions. At other times, responses to information, where needed, come quickly and decisively.

Each participant in the simulation, including those depicted in Figs. 7.1–7.4, was presented with an emergency that required decisive, quick, and simple responding. During that emergency, differentiated and integrated functioning was not useful or even counterproductive. An examination of Figs. 7.1 through 7.4, however, shows little change in the functioning of simulation participants over time. In contrast, the person who produced Fig. 7.5 demonstrated meta-complexity.[5] He was able to shift from a strategic mode to a decisive mode and back to a strategic mode, as required by concurrent environmental conditions. Although his behavior

[5] Figure 7.5 is reproduced from several previous publications with permission (e.g., Streufert, 1992).

was generally similar to that of the person described by Fig. 7.4, he shifted toward simpler (unidimensional) functioning upon advent of the emergency—near the beginning of the fourth task period. He returned to complex strategic functioning as the emergency resolved itself at the end of the fifth task period (see Fig. 7.5).

The various Time–Event Matrices provide a good visual impression of specific system (developmental-level) based information processing. Yet, if we want to compare individuals to each other, or if we wish to compare them with a criterion, we prefer hard data. Streufert's Time–Event Matrices, after all, are merely reorganizations of raw data into a graphic format. However, hard data can be calculated on the basis of the obtained raw data. First, however, let us apply the Time–Event Matrix technology as it pertains to earlier levels of development. Relevant scoring procedures are discussed later in this chapter. Rather than dealing with managers, we focus on the experiences, goals, plans, and strategies of an imaginary child. To do that, we tell the story of "Johnny" and explore how a child might think and plan at different levels of cognitive complexity.

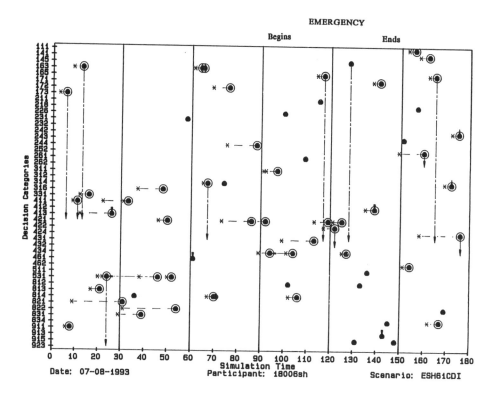

FIG. 7.2. A Time–Event Matrix reflecting multidimensional differentiation (breadth of approach).

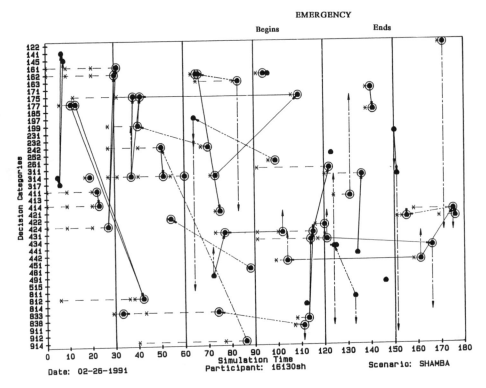

FIG. 7.3. A Time–Event Matrix reflecting multidimensional integration
(use of strategy).

JOHNNY'S PLANS AND STRATEGIES

Johnny wants a new cartridge for his Game-Boy™. He has saved his
allowance for a few weeks, but, at present, has been able to save only about
two-thirds of what the cartridge will cost. Nonetheless, he wants the
cartridge today.

Let us assume, for the moment, that Johnny thinks and plans in a
unidimensional fashion. He approaches one of his parents and asks:
"Would you advance me the money for the cartridge?" The response is very
straightforward: "No." Johnny cries: "Please, I would like it so much!"
Johnny may try several more times, but still approach the same goal in a
very straightforward way. Maybe his parents will give in; maybe they will
not. If they do give in, he will be rewarded for unidimensionality: It is an
effective process and produces the desired goal! If we were to draw a
Time–Event Matrix for this child's actions, it would look very much like
Fig. 7.1, possibly with even fewer categories on the left vertical and fewer
action points within the matrix.

If Johnny were a differentiator, he may have used a broader approach. He may have approached his parents separately. If not successful, he might have offered to cut the grass or to help with washing the dishes. He would have been tempted to use a number of different approaches or techniques that he thought his parents might respond to. He might even have turned his attention to a different goal. Again, if resorting to various alternate ways of attaining the Game-Boy™ cartridge had worked, differentiation might have been reinforced. If we were to draw a Time–Event Matrix for Johnny as a differentiator, it would look similar to Fig. 7.2. If his environment (in this case his parents) had favored and expected unidimensional behavior, he would probably have gotten in trouble for his diverse attempts to get his way. "Don't bug us. You should know better than asking over and over again. I said 'no' and I mean no!"

If Johnny were an integrator, he might have employed a strategy. He may have approached subgoals on the way to the final goal. For example, he might have done something that would put him into the good graces of his parents before he asked. To save space, we do not expand on basic integration but proceed immediately to functioning at the next level, to complex

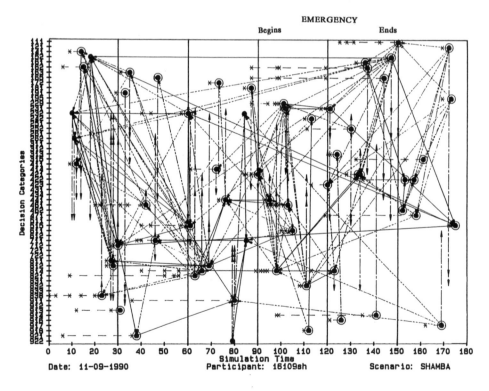

FIG. 7.4. A Time–Event Matrix reflecting complex integration.

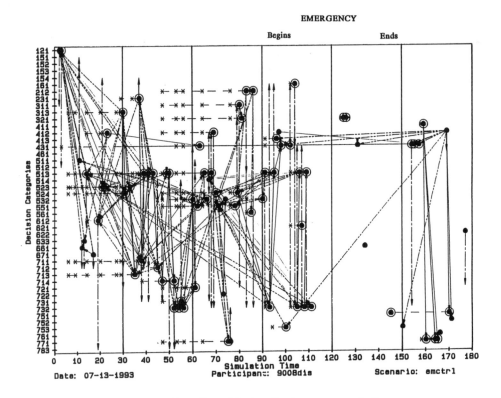

FIG. 7.5. A Time–Event Matrix reflecting meta-complexity.

integration. Complex integrative processes can be extremely involved. To communicate to readers who are unfamiliar with measurement via complexity theory, we will use a relatively simple example of complex integration. How might Johnny approach his parents if he were capable of complex integration and, of course, if his parental environment would potentially reward such behavior? In other words, what would an adaptive series of actions look like? There are, of course, many uses that can be made of the capacity to employ complex integration. We select one that is often seen in certain children: an attempt to "manipulate" the parents.[6]

Johnny knows that his mother sometimes gives him additional money, but she is not in a good mood today. His father probably will not help; he feels that kids should play ball with other kids outside, not sit alone in the house "fiddling with their electronic gadgets." What kind of plan can Johnny develop if he wants to attain his goal of getting the cartridge today?

---

[6] Note that "manipulation" and "complex integration" are far from identical. One describes the content of thinking, the other is concerned with the process that is being used. Integrative (and other) processes may be employed to utilize a wide range of action contents. Manipulation, as in this case, represents only one of those contents.

Of course, he could simply ask both parents separately and hope that one of them might cooperate. He knows, however, that he would most likely be turned down in each case.

Johnny has considerable experience with the reactions of his parents. Perhaps, he has even developed some level of cognitive meta-complexity, especially in the domain that regulates interactions with his parents. Initially, he might consider the current thinking of his mother. He knows that his parents had a fight last night. Whenever that happens, she feels rejected and wants someone to care about her. She likes love and attention. This one is easy; he can give her lots of affection. After all, he does love her very much.

His father, on the other hand, has very strong opinions on what kids should do with their lives. He wants Johnny to have close friends. He thinks that Johnny should be involved in sports. He would be pleased if Johnny would spend some time outside, playing with a kid next door. He would like it even better if the two played ball.

Johnny now considers his options. He knows that he can have an impact on the thought processes of his parents if he approaches them in the most appropriate way. If he is not successful with one of them, it might work with the other. Johnny now thinks about how he is going to approach his parents. Initially that means establishing subgoals. First his mother: He must put her into a better mood. He has to show her that he cares (after all, he does), and if she turns out not to be certain whether she should pay for part of the cartridge, he can always offer to "help out with whatever she is doing" in payment.

As far as his father is concerned, Johnny believes that he should let dad have his way. For good reason. His father will be more pliable if he feels that he is not pushed—and especially whenever his father feels that any action is in his own interest. (Johnny may not use exactly those words to describe his parents' characteristics but, nonetheless, he understands the situation).

Before providing a detailed description of Johnny's actions, we must briefly interrupt the story. To aid the reader later on, when we discuss a graphic representation and measurement, we will have to label Johnny's thoughts and actions sequentially. Four different labels will be used at the beginning of sentences that describe Johnny's behavior: His actions will be labeled sequentially (A 1), (A 2), and so forth. Plans will be listed as (P 1), (P 2), and so forth. Information that Johnny has received earlier, if it has a potential influence on his actions and is utilized in subsequent decisions will be identified as (I 1), (I 2), and, finally, if Johnny makes opportunistic use of prior actions, but had not planned the current action at the time of that prior action, the label (O 1), and so on, will be added. Now let us get back to Johnny and his attempts to obtain that cartridge.

Johnny engages in a bit of information search. (A 1) He decides to check out what is going on with both parents. (I 1) His mother is just slamming a door. This would be a bad time to approach her. (P 1) He decides that he will wait a while before he approaches his mother. He will try later when she is in a better mood. Maybe then he can say something that will get her to feel even better and be more pliable. (I 2) His father is watching a sports program on television. Dad probably feels ok—"his" team is winning. This would probably be a good time to speak to him, but not while the game is on. As far as his father is concerned, (P 2) Johnny plans to talk nicely to him during the next commercial. That will, among other things, give him a chance to make sure about Dad's mood. (P 3) If Dad sounds positive then, Johnny already plans to do whatever he thinks his father wants; he will even play ball for a while if he has to. In other words, he will make sure that his father is happy, so he can get a more favorable response when he asks Dad for the cartridge. To get that response, Johnny plans to call his friend Paul and invite him to play ball (P 4), but, of course, only if his father seems positive. Otherwise it would be a waste: Johnny does not really want to play ball. And then, after he has satisfied Dad by offering to play ball, Johnny intends to ask Dad for the cartridge (P 5).

As the next commercial starts, he casually mentions: (A 2) "Dad, I thought I might call up Paul and ask him to play ball outside." (I 3) His father smiles: "Good idea!" "Great," Johnny thinks, "I have already won him half over. So this is the time to bring up the cartridge. Maybe he will go for it. Or, at least, he will become aware of the issue and I can bring up the issue with Dad again later on" (P 6, a plan that was not completed, as Johnny modified his approach later).

(A 3) "And Dad," Johnny continues, "you know I would like that sports cartridge for my Game-Boy™. But I don't have all the money together yet. I've got most of it. Can you help out? You liked that cartridge, too, when Paul brought his over, didn't you?"

Father thinks for a moment. (I 4) "Yeah, that was a good one. (I 5) But you can save up a bit longer, can't you?"

The commercial was over and the televised game was on again. Johnny has brought up the issue and knows that he should let the seed grow. Most of all, he should not interrupt his father again while the game is on the TV. Johnny has accomplished four things: (a) he has monitored his Dad's reactions—they were moderately positive; (b) father now knows that Johnny only needs some of the money; (c) his father remembers the quality of the cartridge; and, (d) his father feels good that Johnny is going to play ball outside with Paul. (P 7) At this point Johnny will call Paul and (P 8) will carry through with the plan to play ball to soften up his Dad. After all, Dad's somewhat favorable reaction to the cartridge will make success more probable.

(A 4) Consequently, Johnny calls his friend Paul: "Can you come over and play ball with me?" (I 6) Paul is willing. It occurs to Johnny that it might be better if Paul brings his Game Boy™ and his sports cartridge. That might help. He might be able to utilize Paul's ownership of the cartridge to advantage. That is it: With the link system, they could play that game against each other, but only if both had the cartridge. So Johnny continues: (A 5) "Would you bring your Game-Boy™ and the link system so we can play together after we are done playing ball? And would you bring that sports cartridge?" (P 9) Johnny is thinking about demonstrating to his father that they could have played that sports game together if he too would have had the same cartridge. That is what he must get across to Dad, of course after they have finished their ball game. For that matter, it would be a good idea to coach Paul on what to say to Dad.

(I 7) But Paul does not think that bringing the Game-Boy™ is such a great idea. He would rather play ball for a longer period of time. But Johnny knows how to deal with Paul: (A 6) He plays angry and upset. If he can control Paul right now, then Paul will do whatever Johnny wants for the rest of the day. He probably would even be able to get Paul to talk to Dad about that sports cartridge (P 10). What a good idea! Paul will be here anyway; he should be able to make use of that fact (O 1). That has to work. So Johnny acts very angry. (I 8) Paul, who never wants his friends to reject him, gives in quickly. (I 9) "OK, I'll come and I will bring the stuff. But we can play ball outside first, right?" (P 11) Johnny makes sure that Paul feels good after that little conflict. After all, he wants Paul's help later on. (A 7) "Sure," answers Johnny, "it will be fun to play ball."

Before Paul arrives, Johnny finds his mother. She seems to feel a bit better. This is the time he has been waiting for. (A 8) "Mom, I love you!" he says. "You are the best mommy ever." That should put her into a better mood and it should make her more willing to help with the cartridge! (P 12) His approach has provided the opportunity to ask her in a minute or two. Mom smiles and even laughs just a little. "Johnny, would you like some lunch?" (I 10) He notices that he has already improved her mood. He will approach her while she is making lunch.

(A 9) "Sure, Mom, but I have to eat it fast. Paul is coming over to play ball."

The apparent fact that his mother feels better means that a subgoal on the way to the goal has been achieved. He takes the next step while his mother is making a sandwich. (A 10) He asks her for the rest of the money he needs to buy the cartridge. But his mother recognizes the attempted manipulation and becomes furious. (I 11) "You just acted nice to get me to buy that stupid thing for you. Forget it and make your own sandwich." She walks out.

It did not work. Perhaps the strategy was too simple. Or maybe it was not simple enough. His mother was under stress and that stress might have made her respond in a quite unidimensional fashion. As a result, she resented and rejected Johnny's multidimensional approach. Although she might not have liked the manipulativeness of his approach, at another time she may have been somewhat amused by it, and might have taken the opportunity to discourage that (content) aspect of his multidimensionality, but not today. As a result, Johnny will continue on his course.

Johnny lost the opportunity to persuade his mother. But there is still the other strategy with Dad. It is a bit more complex. (A 11) Johnny checks where his mother is going. If she talks to Dad about what just happened, that will be the end! (I 12) Thank God, she is going upstairs. It is good that his parents still do not talk to each other. That could have ruined everything.

(A 12) Johnny finishes his sandwich and eats it, (A 13) then greets Paul at the door. (A 14) They will have to play ball outside for a while. Johnny makes sure that they play long and loud enough for his father to notice and to assure his father's "goodwill." As they begin their game, Johnny thinks: "I bet Dad feels good about things. His team is winning and we are about to play ball outside. (P 13) All I need to do is to get Paul to ask him after we have played ball for a while, then he might just agree!" After they have thrown the ball around for a few minutes, Johnny mentions to Paul: (A 15) "It would be nice if we could play that sports game against each other." (P 14) Johnny is trying to interest Paul in cooperating on getting the cartridge. He wants Paul to approach his father. But, Paul must first realize how much fun a joint game would be.

(I 13) 'But we need two cartridges for that!" Paul answers. That is exactly Johnny's point.

(A 16) "I am going to get one; I am saving up for it. But I don't have it yet. I asked my father if he would let me have the rest of the money, but he has not quite agreed (P 15). But it would be fun if we could do that, wouldn't it?" (I 14) Paul nods his head. He thinks it would be fun too. (P 16, 17) Here is the great opportunity to join the various plans and the opportunity to attain the next subgoal. Johnny continues: (A 17) "Maybe if you asked him and would tell him we could play better together, he will come around. After all, it is a sports cartridge."

(I 15) Paul agrees to try. Subgoal accomplished. All Johnny needs to do now is to provide a bit of a script for Paul. He thinks about how to best do that. Johnny knows his father. (P 18) The script must include the playing together part. He understands what his father responds to. (A 18) So, he gives Paul exact instructions on how to approach his dad and what he should and should not say to get Dad to buy the cartridge today. Paul carries it out as instructed. (I 16) It works. The game on TV is over and Johnny's father has nothing to do. (A 19) So he takes the two boys to a store to buy the cartridge. Johnny has attained his goal.

Johnny is a manipulator. From a strictly unidimensional point of view, this is a "bad" characteristic, but it has had the effect that Johnny wanted to achieve. In this chapter, we do not intend to judge the morality of Johnny's actions. It was our purpose to provide one of many possible examples of goal-directed, planning–strategy–action sequences. In some cases, complex integrative strategies are used for purposes we may not appreciate; in other cases such processes may be used for purposes that we heartily applaud. Rather than judge the "worthiness" of Johnny's actions, let us look at them from the standpoint of adaptation: Johnny was well-adapted to his concurrent environment as far as his father was concerned, but not as well-adapted to the current environment represented by his mother.

A Time–Event Matrix for Johnny

The example of Johnny and his attempts to obtain that Game-Boy™ cartridge listed a number of specific actions. No matter how well we would have known Johnny, we might not have been able to predict exactly *what* he would do *when*. After all, Johnny uses a rudimentary form of complex integration. As complexity theory has argued: behaviors at each system level are unique to that system, making prediction of specific events very difficult at best. However, our example shows that there is something we can predict at least in terms of probability; we can anticipate the *process* of thought and action that Johnny employs. In addition, if we understand the concurrent characteristics and demands of Johnny's environment, we should be able to estimate his probability of success. To put it differently, we should be able to anticipate how "adaptive" Johnny's planning behavior would be.

Based on our story of Johnny's exploits, and on the discussion of matrix construction above, a Time–Event Matrix was drawn and is seen as Fig. 7.6. For convenience, actions, plans (strategies shown as diagonals), information received, and opportunistic behavior are labeled in the matrix exactly as they had been indicated in the story itself.

SCORING THE PROCESS EVIDENT IN THE TIME–EVENT MATRIX

Over the years, we have developed more than 60 measures that assess the process (i.e., the structure) of human functioning in complex settings. It would take a book-length manuscript to discuss all of these measures. Moreover, only some of them are related to planning activity—to the teleological sequence that leads from cognition to initial action, to potential future strategic action(s) or to action sequences that are intended to progress, via subgoals, to the attainment of final goal states. We will consider a few among those measures next.

Many of the measures are simple counts. We can count the *number of actions* that are intended to attain any particular goal. The formula for this measure may be written as

$$\sum_{i=1}^{p} A$$

where 1 through p indicates the time periods of interest and A represents the action(s) taken during that time.

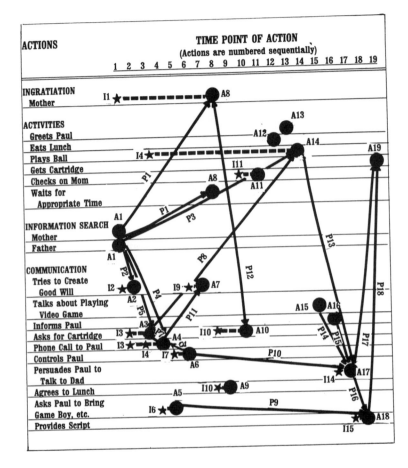

We can distinguish two kinds of actions: those that are taken in response to information (respondent actions) and those that develop independent of environmental stimulation (actions that reflect initiative). *Respondent actions* are calculated according to

$$\sum_{i=1}^{p} R_i$$

where R_i is an action in response to information, regardless of whether that action responds to one or more items of information.

Actions indicating *initiative* (nonrespondent actions) may be calculated as

$$\sum_{i=1}^{p} A - R_i$$

We may count the number of different kinds of actions listed on the vertical axis of the Time–Event Matrix (i.e., the *breadth of functioning*). The resulting value is a good indicator of *differentiation* as defined by complexity theory. The relevant formula can be written as

$$\sum_{i=1}^{p} C$$

where C indicates meaningfully different actions that were taken.

We can measure the number of forward diagonals in the matrix (*integrations, strategies*) and the number of backward diagonals (*backward integrations, opportunistic actions*).

The formula for the two values are

$$\sum_{i=1}^{p} I_f \text{ or } \sum_{i=1}^{p} I_b \text{ or } \sum_{i=1}^{p} I_b + I_f = \sum_{i=1}^{p} I$$

where I_f are forward integrations (strategies), I_b are backward integrations (opportunistic activities) and I are (diagonal) relationships among actions whenever the direction of association cannot be established.

Further, we can count the number of vertical arrows (plans that were not carried out). By comparing the number of vertical arrows with the number of forward diagonals, we can calculate the *proportion of plans realized* as:

$$\sum_{i=1}^{p} \frac{I_f}{I_p}$$

where I_p are the planned forward integrations (plans to carry out a strategy).

We can further calculate scores for the *time delay* between receipt of information and action.

$$\frac{\sum_{i=1}^{p} T_r}{R_p}$$

where T_r is the elapsed time between information receipt and any subsequent respondent action and R_p indicates respondent actions taken between 1 and p. Two procedures are possible; either the average elapsed time between the arrival of all relevant information items and the time of action may be counted. Alternately, only the time elapsed since the arrival of the last relevant item of information may be considered. In both cases, scores on this measure are only meaningful as long as the action of interest was indeed taken in response to information. Actions reflecting initiative should be excluded from this count (i.e., are not entered as 0 values into the formula).

Another measure provides scores for the *number of information items considered* as actions are taken.

Finally, we can determine whether strategies remain isolated or are sequentially interrelated, whether they reflect a series of plans toward subgoals on the way to one or more overall goals. The measure indicates whether *complex strategy* is employed.

$$\sum_{i=1}^{p} I_f + N_p + N_f$$

where N_p is the number of future forward integrations (strategies) connecting to the decision point at the beginning of any I_f diagonal and N_f is the number of forward integrations connecting to the decision point at the end of any I_f diagonal.

Note, that these measures can be calculated for diverse p values, i. e., for different specified time periods during data collection. The specification of separate component time periods is especially valuable where the environmental impact intentionally or unintentionally changes over time, allowing (within) comparisons of functioning under diverse experience or treatments.

Where considerable differences between individuals or groups are expected, i.e., where some individuals are likely to produce very high scores on some measures, whereas others are expected to generate much lower values, linear log transformations of raw scores can be useful.

As already suggested, many more measures are computer-calculated at our labs. These calculations, typically of quite complex functioning, are necessary to assess the decision-making behavior of highly experienced managers. It is less likely that such measures would be needed to assess the characteristics of planning behavior during childhood and adolescence.

THE CONTEXT OF MEASUREMENT

How useful the obtained data will be depends, of course, on the context of measurement, on the experience that researchers have gained with that context, the extent to which confounds are absent, and the extent to which reliability has been demonstrated and validity is given. Let us briefly consider some of these issues.

In our simulation research, we obtain scores in task settings that are highly standardized, yet provide complex and fluid environments. The obtained data are highly reliable (R = .80 to .94). Validity has been demonstrated in several cultures (validity coefficients in excess of .6). Without such standardization, without identical or equivalent treatment across individuals, planning behavior could not be compared across different persons. Without standardization of task settings, behavioral data cannot be evaluated in terms of a "criterion." In other words, it is important to provide equivalent task experience across individuals.

Where an individual's functioning may be assessed repeatedly (e.g., to measure growth over time or the impact of treatment versus placebo), equivalent tasks that generate the same demands, yet involve quite different task content, should be employed. Repeated exposure to the same task may result in learning confounds. Equivalent tasks employing the same measures must, of course, be evaluated in terms of test–retest reliability. Our research utilizes three different simulation scenarios (designed for use with intelligent adults, such as managers). These scenarios were designed to generate highly equivalent task demands over time (with some effort, similar simulation scenarios could be developed for use with children or teens). Finally, task setting(s) must be extensively validated to assure that measures do not unintentionally assess content related competence which would, of course, vary as task content changes. In other words, the measures should be sensitive to *process* variables—they must tell us how and whether a research participant functions adequately in response to the particular demands generated by a given task environment. Is the participant able to match the demands of the environment with a structural system that optimizes responding? Or, to ask that question in another way, is the participant increasing his or her chances for success by functioning appropriately?

Finally, researchers might consider designing task environments that differ in terms of their processing demands at different time points during data collection. Such methodologies permit us to evaluate which kind of environment a particular individual can optimally handle, and whether a participant is able to adapt to diverse demands (meta-complexity).

We are not suggesting that Time–Event Matrices, or the scoring procedures we have discussed, can only be utilized in carefully controlled environments. They can be based on observations in natural (non-recurring) settings. Such analyses will tell us how an individual dealt with a particular environment at a particular time. It may provide one, in some cases even a representative, sample of functioning and should tell us whether the sampled behavior is adaptive to the concurrent environment. However, such a procedure cannot tell us how this person compares to others, to a particular criterion, and it cannot provide adequate information on how this person might function in different task settings.

REFERENCES

Bieri, J. (1955). Cognitive complexity–simplicity and predictive behavior. *Journal of Abnormal and Social Psychology 51*, 263–268.

Breuer, K. (1983). Personen und Medien in Interaktion [Interaction between persons and media]. *Schulpraxis, 3–4*, 22–25.

Breuer, K., & Streufert, S. (in press). The strategic management simulations (SMS): A case-comparison analysis of the German SMS versions. In M. Mulder, W. J. Nijhoff, & R. O. Brinkerhoff (Eds.) *Corporate training for effective performance*. Boston: Kluwer.

Case, R. (1992). Neo-Piagetian theories of child development. In R. J. Sternberg & C. A. Berg (Eds.), *Intellectual development* (pp. 161–196). New York: Cambridge University Press.

Fischer, K. W. (1980). A theory of cognitive development: The control and construction of hierarchies of skills. *Psychological Review, 87*, 477–531.

Freud, S. (1938) *Basic writings*. (A. A. Brill, Trans.) New York: Modern Library.

Gleick, J. (1987). *Chaos: Making of a new science*. New York: Penguin Books.

Harvey, O. J., Hunt, D., & Schroder, H. M. (1961). *Conceptual systems and personality organization*. New York: Wiley.

Hunt, D. E. (1966). A conceptual systems change model. In O. J. Harvey (Ed.), *Experience, structure and adaptability*. New York: Springer.

Hunt, D. E., & Sullivan, E. V. (1974). *Between psychology and education*. Hinsdale, IL: Dryden.

Kelly, G. A. (1955). *The psychology of personal constructs: Vol. 1. A theory of personality*. New York: Norton.

Lewin, K. (1936). *Principles of topological psychology*. New York: McGraw-Hill.

Lewin, R. (1992). *Complexity: Life at the edge of chaos*. New York: MacMillan.

Mead, G. H. (1934). *Self, mind and society*. Chicago: University of Chicago Press.

Piaget, J. (1952). *The origins of intelligence in children*. New York: International Universities Press.

Schachtel, E. G. (1959). *Metamorphosis*. New York: Basic Books.

Scholnick, E. K., & Friedman, S. L. (1987). The planning construct in the psychological literature. In S. L. Friedman, E. K. Scholnick, & R. R. Cocking (Eds.), *Blueprints for thinking: The role of planning in cognitive development*. Cambridge, England: Cambridge University Press.

Schroder, H. M., Driver, M. J., & Streufert, S. (1967). *Human information processing*. New York: Holt, Rinehart & Winston.

Streufert, S. (1990). Zur Simulation komplexer Entscheidungen. In R. Fisch & M. Boos (Eds.), *Vom Umgang mit Komplexität in Organisationen* [Dealing with complexity in organizations]. Konstanz, Germany: Universitätsverlag.

Streufert, S. (1992). *Assessing and training senior personnel with the strategic management simulation* [Transcript of a paper presented at the 1992 American Psychological Association Convention].

Streufert, S., & Nogami, G. Y. (1989). Cognitive style and complexity: Implications for I–O psychology. *International Review of Industrial and Organizational Psychology* (pp. 93–143). London: Wiley.

Streufert, S., Pogash, R., & Piasecki, M. (1988). Simulation based assessment of managerial competence: Reliability and validity. *Personnel Psychology, 41*, 537–557.

Streufert, S., & Streufert, S. C. (1978). *Behavior in the complex environment*. New York: Wiley.

Streufert, S., & Swezey, R. W. (1986). *Complexity, managers and organizations*. London: Academic Press.

Suedfeld, P. (1988). Are simple decisions always worse? *Transaction/Society, 25/5*, 25–27.

Suedfeld, P. (1992). Cognitive managers and their critics. *Political Psychology, 13*, 435–453.

Waldrop, M. M. (1992). *Complexity: The emerging science at the edge of order and chaos*. New York: Simon & Schuster.

Werner, H. (1957). *Comparative psychology of mental development*. New York: International Universities Press.

8

Planning as a Strategy Choice, or Why Don't Children Plan When They Should?

Shari Ellis
Robert S. Siegler
Carnegie Mellon University

Planning often helps children solve problems. Despite this benefit, children often jump directly into problem solving without prior planning, even when planning would help them find the solution. In this chapter, we first discuss evidence regarding children's frequent failure to plan, then present a theory of why they fail to do so, and finally describe evidence relevant to the theory's predictions.

Before discussing the research and theory, it may be worthwhile to consider the relation between problem solving and planning. Clearly, the two are closely related. Both occur in the context of goal-directed activity, both are triggered by encountering an obstacle to goal attainment, and in both, the task is to surmount the obstacle and attain the goal. However, they are not identical. Planning is a frequent, but not invariant, process within problem solving. What distinguishes planning is that it is inherently an indirect attempt to reach a solution. If problem solving is interrupted immediately after the completion of planning, the problem solution will not have been attained. Plans are constructed in anticipation of future action. Sometimes that action will occur far in the future, perhaps so far that planning is at times less a precise description of future behavior than a working model of one's dreams and aspirations (Friedman, Scholnick, & Cocking, 1987). Thus, the name of this volume's predecessor, *Blueprints for Thinking*, was aptly chosen.

The distinction between planning and problem solving can be illustrated by considering tasks that demand problem solving but not planning. Mednick's (1962) remote associates task provides one such example. On this task, subjects need to identify items that are highly associated with two items that are themselves unrelated. For example, subjects might need to think of a term that is highly associated with both "rat" and "blue" (the answer is "cheese"). This task clearly demands problem solving. However, it does not demand planning; saying "cheese" completes the problem-solving process. In summary, our emphasis in this chapter is on planning as an indirect method of problem solving, aimed at choosing actions that, when executed in the future, will solve the problem.

EVIDENCE FOR PLANNING AS AN AVAILABLE AND EFFECTIVE STRATEGY

Perhaps the single most common theme in discussions of planning (e.g., Friedman, Scholnick, & Cocking, 1987) is that children (and adults) plan less than they should. This theme reflects two assumptions: that the relevant population is capable of planning, and that their problem solving would benefit if they did so more often. Later, we discuss evidence relevant to these assumptions.

Availability of Planning Across Tasks and Populations

One reason for planning being a process of such great interest is that it can be used across an extremely wide range of tasks. We can plan both whether to do and how to do almost any future activity. Another reason for the interest in planning is that it is an activity that can be undertaken by a very broad range of populations. Even infants are capable of some types of planning. Studies by Willats (1989, 1990) with 9- and 12-month-olds, Case (1985) with 12- to 18-month-olds, and DeLoache (1984) with 18- to 24-month-olds all provide evidence that such capabilities are present very early. Willats' (1990) study with 12-month-olds is especially compelling. The babies encountered one of two almost identical arrangements. In each, they sat in front of a foam rubber barrier, behind which was a cloth; attached to the back of the cloth was a string, and near the cloth was a toy. There was only one difference between the arrangements. In the planning condition, the string was attached to the toy; in the control condition, the string and toy were visibly separate. Thus, infants in the planning condition could obtain the toy by pushing the barrier out of the way, reeling in the cloth, and then pulling on the string, whereas infants in the control condition could not.

The 12-month-olds reacted to these conditions quite differently. Those in the planning condition were quicker to remove the barrier and to touch the cloth. They also reeled in the string more often. The only straightforward reason they would remove the barrier and touch the cloth more quickly would be as a means to the end of obtaining the toy. Thus, the 12-month-olds in this condition showed they were capable of executing a three-step plan: Remove the barrier, reel in the cloth, and pull the string to obtain the toy.

Effects of Planning

Although even infants can plan problem-solving strategies, adolescents and adults frequently do not. One possibility is that these failures to plan on problem-solving tasks are due to plans not facilitating problem solving. Although most researchers assume planning to be helpful, few studies actually assess whether planning is causally related to (as opposed to correlated with) effective problem solving. However, a few studies have tested the causal efficacy of encouraging people to plan, and they have tended to obtain positive results (Mischel & Patterson, 1978; Patterson, Massad, & Cosgrove, 1978; Siegler, 1977).

Consider the study by Siegler (1977) in which seventh and eighth graders were presented a task resembling the familiar game "20 Questions." Subjects encountered 4 X 6 matrices either containing the numbers 1 to 24 or the letters A to X. Sometimes the numbers or letters were presented in ascending order in the matrices; other times they were not (Fig. 8.1). The goal was to identify the particular number or letter the experimenter had in mind by asking a series of questions that could be answered "yes" or "no." Unlike

7	12	21	5
16	2	8	23
24	6	13	3
15	18	10	22
11	19	4	1
17	9	20	14

FIG. 8.1. One kind of number matrix used in Siegler (1977). There were four types of matrices: Numbers from 1 to 24 in ascending order, the same numbers in random order, letters from A to X in ascending order, and the same letters in random order.

standard "20-Questions" games, the experimenter's response to each question did not reflect a preset answer. Instead, the experimenter always gave the answer that would reduce the alternatives by the smaller amount. Thus, if a child's first question was "Is it 18 or less," the experimenter would answer "yes," because that answer would eliminate 6, rather than 18, possibilities.

One purpose of the study was to examine how the problem-solving "set" influenced the adolescents' question-asking strategies. Each subject received one of each type of matrix; some were presented the letter matrix first, and others were presented the number matrix first. The basic expectation was that subjects who received the number matrix first would perform better on both matrices than those who received the letter version first. It is both easier and more familiar to divide sets of numbers in half than to divide letters in the same way. More people know, for example, that asking "Is it greater than 12" divides in half the numbers 1–24 than know that asking "Is it after L" does the same for the letters A–X.

As predicted, those who encountered number matrices before letter matrices were able to identify the correct answer in significantly fewer questions on both types of matrices. A more direct measure of the informativeness of the questions yielded parallel results. Each question reduced the number of remaining alternatives by a certain percentage. The greatest uncertainty reduction possible was .50, which meant that the question eliminated half the alternatives. The smallest reduction in uncertainty was 0, which meant that no alternatives had been eliminated. Thus, the uncertainty reduction measure ranged from 0 (maximally uninformative) to .50 (maximally informative). This measure could be applied only to the first five questions, because a maximally efficient questioning sequence would identify the answer by then.

Results on this measure closely paralleled those on the measure of number of questions to solution. Again, encountering the number matrices first led to more informative questions on both number and letter matrices. Also as on the previous measure, the absolute values for number and letter matrices were very similar within a questioning order. Apparently, initial experience with the number matrices led the adolescents to apply the same type of relatively informative questions to the letter matrices (e.g., Is it before L?), whereas initial experience with the letter matrices led them to ask the same type of relatively uninformative question on the number matrices (e.g., Is it 2, 4, or 6?).

Although the relative efficiency of questioning in this experiment followed the expected pattern, the absolute efficiency in all conditions was far less than optimal. Informal observation indicated one potential reason—the children seemed to spend almost no time planning their questions; they began to ask questions almost as soon as the experimenter stopped reciting the instructions. This suggested that creating conditions under which they would plan questions in advance of asking them might lead to more efficient questioning.

To test this hypothesis, children from the same classrooms in the same school were presented a second experiment. The seventh and eighth graders in Experiment 2 were provided with pencil and paper (hereafter referred to as the planning sheets) and then told:

> I want you to plan ahead the sequence of questions you will ask. The idea is to ask questions that rule out as many answers as possible, no matter what my answer to the question is. In other words, you want to ask questions so that you will be able to find the correct answer quickly, no matter what answer I give you. If you think of the best questions possible, you will be able to solve the problem in 5 questions. So try to get as close to 5 questions as possible. Do you understand? You have 3 minutes to plan your questions. Write down the questions you think of so you don't forget them.

Aside from these instructions, and the addition of the 3-minute planning period during which children could plan but could not ask the experimenter any questions, the procedure in this second experiment was identical to that in the first.

The instructions to plan improved the efficiency of the adolescents' questions and helped overcome the difficulty induced by encountering the letter matrices first. The latter benefit was largely due to reduction in the number of questions that were needed when children encountered the letter matrices before the ones with numbers. The adolescents in Experiment 2 who encountered letter before number matrices required on average 2.9 fewer questions to identify the answer than their classmates in Experiment 1, whereas those who encountered the matrices in the opposite order required only 1 fewer question on average than their peers in the first experiment. Mean number of questions required to identify the solution fell from 11 to 9. Results from the uncertainty reduction measure showed the same pattern. Thus, the instructions to plan led adolescents in all conditions to solve the problem in fewer questions and were especially beneficial for those who encountered the matrices in the less favorable order.

Examination of the planning sheets linked planning directly to the improvement. All 40 adolescents wrote at least one question; the mean was 5.5. More than 90% of the adolescents asked at least one of the planned questions; the mean was 2.4. Interestingly, adolescents tended to ask these planned questions at the beginning of their questioning. Once they diverged from their planned queries, they rarely returned to them. Of the 96 planned questions that they asked, 90 were asked before any nonplanned questions had been inserted.

Most important, planning facilitated problem solving at the level of the individual questions. The planned questions yielded significantly greater reduction of uncertainty than did the unplanned ones. The greater informativeness of the planned questions was present on both letter and number matrices, and for both presentation orders.

These results suggested that the encouragement to plan in the Experiment 2 instructions was what led to the more informative questions.

Another possibility, however, was that the effect was not due to the encouragement to plan and the planning that followed, but rather to other differences in the instructions. The Experiment 2 instructions not only encouraged children to plan, they also provided more information about the task than did the instructions in Experiment 1. Therefore, in Experiment 3, children at another school were provided instructions that were identical to those in Experiment 2 except for deletion of the three sentences specifically about planning: The first sentence ("I want you to plan ahead the sequence of questions you will ask") and the last two sentences ("You have 3 minutes to plan your questions. Write down the questions you think of so that you don't forget them"). The logic was that if planning was critical to eliminating the effects of presentation order, and the instructions to plan were no longer present, then the effects of presentation order seen in Experiment 1 should return.

Consistent with the view that the instructions to plan were critical, deleting them resulted in the order effects returning. Once again, children solved both types of matrices in significantly fewer questions when they encountered the number matrices before the ones with letters. Encountering the number matrices first led to fewer questions being needed to solve the letter matrices, and encountering the letter matrices first resulted in more questions being needed to solve the number matrices. These findings strengthened the evidence that telling children to plan, and providing them the means, opportunity, and time to do so, was critical to their asking more informative questions regardless of whether the order of matrices was facilitative or not.

A THEORETICAL FRAMEWORK FOR THINKING ABOUT PLANNING

Given that planning is a broadly available process across tasks and populations, and given that it can enhance problem solving and other activities, it seems worthwhile to try to place it within a broader theoretical framework. The strategy choice model (Siegler, 1996; Siegler & Shipley, 1995) provides such a theoretical framework.

The Strategy Choice Perspective

Traditionally, theories of cognitive development have depicted a great many types of cognition as a sequence of monolithic states. At early ages, children are described as thinking in one way; at somewhat later ages, they are described as thinking in another way; at even later stages, they are described as thinking in a third way. This view is often associated with stage theories such as Piaget's, but it fits equally well a variety of alternative approaches that take as their basic unit more domain-specific entities such as rules, strategies, and theories.

Closer examination often reveals considerably more complexity than these monolithic accounts suggest. Children and adults often know and use a variety of approaches for solving problems. For example, rather than 5-year-olds consistently not rehearsing and 8-year-olds consistently rehearsing on serial recall tasks, closer examination reveals that at each age, children sometimes do not rehearse, sometimes use one type of rehearsal strategy, and sometimes use a different type of rehearsal strategy (McGilly & Siegler, 1989, 1990). This variability in thinking is evident within as well as between individuals (Siegler & Robinson, 1982), on the same problem given to the same child on two successive days (Siegler & Shrager, 1984), and even within a single trial as indicated by separate measures of speech and gesture (Goldin-Meadow, Alibali, & Church, 1993).

The fact that children use diverse strategies is not a mere idiosyncracy of human cognition. There are good reasons for people to know and use multiple strategies. Strategies differ in their accuracy, in the amount of time needed to execute them, in their processing demands, in concomitant costs, and in the range of problems to which they apply. Strategy choices involve tradeoffs among these different properties. The broader the range of strategies children know, the more precisely they can shape their approaches to the demands of particular circumstances and particular goals. Even young children often capitalize on the strengths of different strategies and use each most often on problems where its advantages are greatest.

Siegler and his colleagues have documented children's use of diverse strategies in many domains. To spell words, 7- and 8-year-olds sometimes sound them out, sometimes look the words up in dictionaries, sometimes write out alternative forms and try to recognize which is correct, and sometimes recall the spelling from memory (Siegler, 1986). To tell time, 7- to 9-year-olds sometimes count forward from the hour by ones and/or fives, sometimes count backward from the hour by ones and/or fives, sometimes count from reference points such as the half hour, and sometimes retrieve the time that corresponds to the clock hands' configuration (Siegler & McGilly, 1989). To multiply, 8- to 10-year-olds sometimes repeatedly add one of the multiplicands, sometimes write the problem and then recognize the answer, sometimes write and then count groups of hatch marks that represent the problem, and sometimes retrieve the answer from memory (Siegler, 1988).

These diverse strategies are not artifacts of one child using one strategy and a different child using another one. Most individuals at all ages in all of these domains have been found to use at least two strategies; in most of the domains, the norm has been to use three or more. These experiments have called into serious question the belief that children of a given age consistently use a particular strategy in a given domain.

Children's choices among strategies are adaptive in several ways. In most domains where strategy choice has been studied, children have a choice between retrieving an answer from memory or using any of a

number of backup strategies (defined as any strategy not involving retrieval). Children are most likely to choose backup strategies on problems
determined to be difficult by either percentage of errors or by length of
solution times. These are also the problems on which the advantage of
backup strategies over retrieval for producing correct answers is greatest.

Choices among alternative backup strategies also are generally adaptive.
For example, first graders sometimes add by counting from 1 and sometimes by counting from the larger addend (Siegler, 1987). They most frequently count from the larger addend on problems with large differences
between addends, where that strategy produces its greatest advantage over
counting from one.

Finally, trial-to-trial changes in strategy use tend to be adaptive. Children
shift strategies most often when two conditions are met: their previous answer
was wrong, and they generated it by one of their easier-to-use but less effective
strategies (McGilly & Siegler, 1989). Again this makes sense: if the strategy
produced the right answer, there is no reason to shift, and if you do not know
any more accurate strategies, shifting would not be likely to help.

What emerges from these findings is the view that higher and lower level
cognition usually involves a variety of competing entities, whose use
depends on their relative advantages and disadvantages in particular
situations. At both early and later ages, in domains as diverse as arithmetic,
reading, spelling, time-telling, serial recall, and physics problem solving,
children, adolescents, and adults tend to choose adaptively among alternative strategies. Their choices reflect both the advantages of the approaches
they most often choose to solve a given type of problem and the disadvantages of alternatives for the demands of that type of problem and situation.

Planning and Strategy Choice

The strategy choice perspective provides a potentially useful way of thinking about planning. Planning can be viewed as one among a number of
competing strategies that might be employed to solve a problem. Whether
a child plans or not is a function of both the value of planning for the child
in that situation and the value of alternative courses other than planning.

Most research on the development of planning skills characterizes planning in the same monolithic way as researchers in the past characterized
the memory or arithmetic strategies of children of a given age. Tasks used
to study planning are rarely analyzed in terms of the range of strategies
children can and do apply in that context. Even more rare is a rationale for
why planning would be the best of all strategies to employ in that problem-
solving context. Traditionally, research on planning has emphasized elegant, error-free solutions to problems without assessing fully the true costs
and benefits of planning as opposed to other strategies.

It is easy to find examples of planning as strategy choice in children's
everyday lives. To have someone to play with on a Saturday afternoon, a

child may sometimes walk around the neighborhood in search of an age mate, play in their own yard hoping for someone to come by, phone a friend on Friday night with a Saturday activity in mind, join a sports team that competes on Saturdays, or wait for someone to call. To have dessert after dinner, a child may sometimes suggest eating at a restaurant where the family routinely orders dessert, sometimes negotiate before dinner how many bites of each dish they have to consume in order to be allowed dessert, sometimes request dessert after dinner, and sometimes sneak ice cream from the refrigerator once the adults retreat from the room.

As these examples illustrate, planning competes with a range of other problem-solving strategies such as responding to obstacles as the need arises, passively waiting for desirable outcomes, and using rules or routines. Different forms of planning also compete with each other; for example, asking a friend on Friday to come over on Saturday may compete with deciding to play in a prominent place on Saturday where other children can see you and decide for themselves to come over.

Given the range of strategies available to children, what would it mean to plan adaptively? A general principle underlying strategy choice is that children and adults use the fastest and easiest strategy on simplest problems and save the more effortful strategies for problems that cannot be solved consistently with the easier approaches. Because planning takes time and effort, it would not ordinarily be the first strategy chosen when solving easy problems. Instead, planning would be reserved for difficult tasks, where it is essential for success. The likelihood that children will plan on a given task should also change over time. As children acquire greater understanding of tasks, they may become more planful until the task becomes sufficiently well-learned that planning no longer is needed.

WHEN WILL PLANNING BE CHOSEN OVER OTHER STRATEGIES?

The Paradox of Planning

An assumption of the strategy choice framework is that a variety of strategies coexist and that problem solvers select adaptively among them. This framework provides a basis for addressing the central mystery of planning: Children can plan, and when they do, they solve problems more effectively, yet they often choose not to plan. The question is: Why does planning lose out?

Why Planning Loses the Competition

As we think about planning in the framework of strategy choice, it is clear that the decision whether to plan is influenced by a variety of factors not easily interpreted in terms of either efficiency or accuracy, the concerns demonstrated to influence strategy choice in most domains studied to date (Siegler & Shipley, 1995). Decisions whether to plan are tied to a host of personal and contextual influences (Baker-Sennett, Matusov, & Rogoff, 1993; Scholnick & Friedman, 1993). A child might know that phoning a friend is both quicker and more likely to yield a playmate the next day than waiting around the house for someone to call, but may feel embarrassed to be the one to call. The same child may well show sophisticated planning abilities when she and a friend organize a neighborhood yard sale together as a way to earn some spending money. Similarly, a child who wants to climb a tree with a main branch fairly high above the ground might know that standing on a chair would be both faster and more likely to lead to success, but might still repeatedly try to reach the branch by jumping so that they could reach the goal "like the big kids do." The same child may be encouraged to plan a more strategic approach to the problem when his repeated attempts to reach the branch prove too frustrating for the adult nearby. Findings from studies of children's planning reveal at least 10 factors—some cognitive, others social and motivational—that lead children not to plan even when planning would be useful (Table 8.1). The importance of these factors changes over the course of childhood, resulting in changes in the frequency of planning at different ages.

Immediate Attainment of Goals Is Often Assigned a Higher Value Than Delayed Attainment.   Children may be able to abstractly identify when and why they should plan during problem solving, but view the time spent waiting as too high a cost. The ability to delay gratification develops gradually over the course of childhood. In laboratory studies, the ability to defer gratification often is examined by having children choose between a smaller, immediate reward (e.g., a small candy bar now) or a larger delayed reward (a large candy bar later). Even young children know that the larger reward would be preferable, but restraining oneself from taking the smaller, immediate reward poses a real problem. It is not until middle childhood or later that most children will defer the smaller, immediate reward for the larger reward when the delay is as short as a single day (without the benefit of interventions designed to facilitate the delay of gratification; Mischel, 1974; Mischel & Metzner, 1962).

Planning inherently involves delaying gratification, in the sense that while you are planning a procedure for solving a problem, you are not actually attaining the goal. Thus, the general difficulty, especially for young children, of delaying gratification may lead them to use planning less than would be optimal for solving the problem. They may either accept lesser rewards that are attainable without planning or may hope that more direct methods will produce a rapid solution.

Planning Requires Suppression of More Activated Procedures.
Even if children might abstractly prefer to wait for a larger, delayed reward, doing so often requires them to inhibit other, more dominant responses.

TABLE 8.1

10 Reasons Why People Don't Choose to Plan When They Could

1. Planning entails delays before launching into action, and the immediate attainment of goals is often assigned a higher value than delayed attainment.

2. Planning requires suppression of more activated procedures.

3. Planning may temporarily move the problem solver away from tangible goals.

4. Children are often overly optimistic about their likelihood of success without planning, which leads them either not to plan or to make only sketchy plans.

5. Planning takes time, and speed is often valued over accuracy.

6. Generating plans is no guarantee that plans will lead to successful outcomes.

7. Children may believe they have no control over outcomes, even if they do plan.

8. Planning is often subjectively unpleasant because it is difficult, tedious, or conflictual.

9. Children may assume a benign environment and avoid planning because they assume someone else will do it for them.

10. Unplanned action can be enjoyable and interesting in its own right.

The ability to inhibit action clearly develops over the course of childhood (Dempster, 1993).

This source of difficulty can be illustrated in the context of errand planning. In one such problem, children are presented with a model grocery store, a small plastic "shopper," and a list of items they need to retrieve from the shelves (Gauvain & Rogoff, 1989). Five-year-olds, who tend to be relatively unconcerned with the efficiency of their routes, usually solve this task by selecting a single item to be retrieved, browsing through the store to find it, and repeating this procedure for every item on the list. In contrast, 9-year-olds, who are more concerned with developing efficient routes, inhibit the tendency to pursue each individual goal directly in order to generate a more efficient overall procedure. They are more likely to employ both advance planning (i.e., scanning the store prior to moving the shopper) and planning-in-action (scanning for each item prior to making moves to retrieve it).

Planning May Appear to Move the Problem Solver Away From the Goal of Solving a Problem. Young children's planning tends to be aimed directly at meeting the main goal. Only later in development do children begin to form plans that incorporate hierarchically organized subgoals, especially ones that involve actions whose immediate impact is to take the problem solver further from the overall goal. The difficulty young children have with constructing plans that are not aimed directly at meeting the final goal can be observed in the Tower of Hanoi task.

The Tower of Hanoi problem begins with a series of disks stacked in a particular configuration on a set of pegs. The goal of the problem is to reposition the disks in a specified order in the fewest moves possible, moving only one disk at a time. Although there are a number of variants of the Tower of Hanoi puzzle (Klahr, 1978; Welsh, 1991), a typical Tower of Hanoi problem begins with three disks and three pegs. The disks are stacked on one peg with the largest disk on the bottom and the smallest disk on the top. The goal is to duplicate the original configuration (disks stacked in ascending size) on a new peg in the fewest moves possible, without violating either of two rules: Move only one disk at a time, and never place a larger disk on top of a smaller one. The property that makes the Tower of Hanoi task interesting for those who study planning is that making the correct first move is essential for successful problem solving. If it is not made, the only possible solution often involves undoing all subsequent moves and returning to the original configuration. Knowing which first move is correct, however, demands working through the problem from beginning to end. Thus, consistently solving such problems demands planning the entire sequence of moves before making any of them.

At times, solving Tower of Hanoi problems requires moving a disk already on the goal peg away from that peg, so that a larger disk can be put on the peg and the smaller one placed on top of it. Such moves away from the goal are very difficult for young children to make (Klahr & Robinson, 1981). Most 3-year-olds' plans are limited to direct attempts to reach the main goal. When they cannot move a disk to its goal because another disk is on top of it, they often simply plan to break the rules and put the disk there anyway. Most 5- and 6-year-olds react to such situations by establishing subgoals that move them in promising directions for fulfilling the original goals, though not always ones that work out. Even at age 6, it remains difficult to formulate plans that in the short run move further from the final goal so that it can be fully attained in the long run.

Children Are Often Overly Optimistic About Their Likelihood of Success Without Planning, Which Leads Them Either Not to Plan or to Make Only Sketchy Plans.   Preschoolers generally have unrealistically high expectations about their future performance. This optimistic bias has been observed in an impressive variety of domains, and it is present even after the children have received feedback about earlier performance (see Stipek, 1984, for a review). For example, when asked to predict the number of items they will be able to recall, preschoolers tend to predict they will recall more items than suggested by previous performance (Flavell, Friedrichs, & Hoyt, 1970; Yussen & Levy, 1975). One reason young children fail to adopt strategies that will improve their performance on memory or planning tasks is that they are confident they can do well without them.

Among the factors that underlie preschoolers' overoptimism is insufficient distinction between effort and outcome. Young children often evaluate task success in terms of the amount of effort expended, regardless of the effectiveness of the approach. They also tend to hold an incremental theory of their own intelligence, which implies that trying hard will make them smarter (Dweck, 1986). This is not entirely unrealistic; young children do "get smarter" through practice. However, such overoptimism may also cause to them not to plan when doing so would be beneficial.

Although attenuated, unrealistic expectations for success are observed among older children and adults as well. One domain in which children and adults often fail to plan is scientific reasoning. The failure to systematically vary critical variables in scientific experimentation has been attributed to a number of characteristics of human thought, including a tendency to seek evidence to confirm initial theories. It is also the case, however, that holding some variables constant while manipulating others is a complex task that cannot be achieved without forethought. The problems on which scientific reasoning is examined do not always appear so complex on the surface. For example, subjects may be told to find *the one* cause of a event (e.g., the single ingredient that makes a cake moist; Tschirgi, 1980). Children and adults are likely to underestimate the complexity of this problem and the demands it will place on their cognitive processes. As a result, they may think solving the problem is rather elementary and try to solve it directly, rather than planning an experimentation strategy or record-keeping system in advance. Development toward realizing the advantages of planful approaches continues well beyond early childhood. For example, 13-year-olds were found to be much more likely than 10-year-olds to adopt a planning system they had been taught for generating and keeping track of scientific experiments (Siegler & Liebert, 1975).

Planning Takes Time, and Speed Is Often Valued Over Accuracy.
Interest in solving problems quickly may lead people not to take the time to plan. This logic often backfires; taking the time to plan can save more time, through selection of more efficient strategies, avoidance of dead ends, and reduction of errors. Successful problem solvers, gifted students, and mature reasoners often differ from less successful individuals in expending more time on planning but taking less time overall to solve problems.

The advantages of spending greater time on a problem prior to applying other strategies are clearly evident in analogical problem solving. Sternberg and Rifkin (1979) found that 8-year-olds and adults use the same components to solve analogy problems of the form A:B : : C:? (with D_1 and D_2 provided as possible answers). However, the children and adults differed in the amount of cognitive resources they devoted to each component. Adults spent more time exhaustively encoding each term rather than trying to quickly identify a solution. The children's strategy of encoding only one or a few features of each term, and checking whether an answer could be found without additional thought, reduced the initial memory load, but ultimately lengthened the time needed to solve the problem.

Under sufficient time pressure, adults also forego planning in lieu of more direct problem-solving strategies. The cost of sacrificing planning to save time is clearly evident when groups solve problems. This is especially true on tasks where success depends on the coordination of individual information. Groups that jump directly into problem solving without first planning a means by which information will be shared or decisions made solve problems less efficiently than groups that plan how to coordinate efforts in advance. However, when pressured to solve problems quickly, groups often do not plan. This was illustrated by a study that examined information exchange among groups under three planning conditions (Shure, Rogers, Larsen, & Tassone, 1962). In the first condition, groups were allowed, but not required, to plan how they would exchange information. For these groups, time spent planning did not count toward total solution time. In the second condition, groups could plan, but the time spent planning did count toward final solution time. And, in the third condition, interaction between group members was limited to the actual exchange of information; group members were not allowed to communicate with each other about the processes of information exchange.

The groups where time spent planning contributed to total session length spent very little time planning, and took as long to solve the problems as the groups who were not allowed to plan. In addition, although all of the groups allowed the free planning period developed an efficient system for sharing information, only 20% of the groups where planning had upfront costs did so, despite the fact that members in most groups admitted that their performances would have improved had they planned.

Situational variations in emphasis on speed or accuracy also influences children's likelihood of planning. Gardner and Rogoff (1990) presented children with instructions that either emphasized accuracy or speed as the most important consideration in solving a maze puzzle. Emphasizing accuracy led to more than twice as much planning as emphasizing speed. Interestingly, on difficult mazes, children who planned routes in advance made fewer errors without adding to their overall solution times. It appears that the other children wished to save time by omitting the initial planning phase, but failed to anticipate the errors that would follow from this failure to plan.

Generating Plans Is No Guarantee That Plans Will Lead to Successful Outcomes.   Although planning can aid problem solving, it will fail to do so if other prerequisites are not present. This was evident in a study comparing the scientific reasoning skills of 15-year-olds, college students, and professors (Pitt, 1983). Subjects were asked to find which, if any, of four colored substances were present in a sample of an unidentified clear, colorless, odorless liquid. Instructing subjects to plan improved the performance of college students, but actually worsened the performance of 15-year-olds.

Even when potentially useful plans are generated, poor execution may lead to the plans not being beneficial. This was evidenced in a short-term longitudinal study in which 5th- and 6th-graders designed experiments to learn about design features and speed of race cars in a computerized microworld (Schauble, 1990). In this study, children constructed a large number of plans to assess how different features of the cars worked together, the individual effects of one or more features, and interactions between features. Although more than 80% of the plans would have yielded the desired information if executed correctly, only 30% were carried out in such a way that the tests actually yielded the information the plan was designed to provide.

Children May Believe They Have No Control Over Outcomes Even if They Do Plan.   Children may understand abstractly that planning could help them solve a problem, and even describe the structure of such a plan, but choose not to plan because they believe their efforts to solve the problem will be overshadowed by other factors that are beyond their control. Children (and adults) who believe they can control outcomes of problems are more likely to persist in the face of obstacles, apply problem-solving strategies appropriately, and remain highly engaged in learning activities (Bandura & Wood, 1989; Patrick, Skinner, & Connell, 1993; Schunk & Gunn, 1986). Those who do not believe they can effectively control outcomes may retreat from challenges and become disaffected, anxious, or depressed (Bandura, 1989; Seligman, 1975). The latter effects are sometimes so powerful that children are unable to solve problems identical to, or even simpler than, problems they had successfully solved in the past (Dweck & Leggett, 1988). This point may seem to contradict the previous point about overoptimism leading children not to plan, but both seem likely to be true. Children may not plan either because they are overoptimistic about their effectiveness without planning or overpessimistic about their effectiveness even if they do plan.

When the success of plans depends on the participation of other people, the view that the problem is largely out of the child's control may be accurate. For example, a child may fail to plan adequately for a weekend trip with his soccer team, not because he does not know he should return appropriate permission forms, pay fees, and pack his gear in advance, but because he cannot depend on the adults in his environment to sign the permission forms, provide the money, and launder his uniform.

Children understand that the effectiveness of different problem-solving strategies, including planning, will vary across settings. Presumably, one of the ways in which settings differ is the degree to which children can influence events in those settings. Children believe that planning and other strategic solutions are more likely to be successful on problems encountered outside of school, whereas academic problems are better solved by either changing one's perception of the problem or opting out of the environment (Berg, 1989). This finding suggests that many children feel they have little control over events that happen in school, and hence may help explain why children are less planful on academic tasks than would be optimal.

Planning Is Often Subjectively Unpleasant Because It Is Difficult, Tedious, or Conflictual.   When done with others and when done alone, planning can be subjectively unpleasant. Illustratively, planning for a trip can yield many desirable outcomes—having the right clothes along, not having to drag numerous carry-ons onto a plane, having appropriate distractions for children quickly available. Yet, thinking through the many contingencies that may arise on the trip is sufficiently unpleasant that many of us avoid planning and simply take whatever we think of at the last minute.

Although planning with other people sometimes encourages children to plan more, and to devise more complex plans than they might if solving a problem alone (Gauvain & Rogoff, 1989), planning with others requires a degree of coordination that can be challenging socially as well as cognitively. Observations of groups of 7- to 9-year-olds planning a play revealed that emotions often ran high, and sometimes interfered with progress on the task (Baker-Sennet, Matusov, & Rogoff, 1992). Some groups planned harmoniously and skillfully, yet others could not plan together and decided to act out individual plays; others required an adult to be present at all times to resolve disputes, guide the collaboration, and structure the task.

Children May Assume a Benign Environment and Avoid Planning Because They Assume Someone Else Will Do It for Them.   Much has been made of *scaffolding,* the tendency of older and more competent individuals to structure tasks so that younger and less competent individuals can participate and help solve problems (Rogoff, 1990). The flip side of these well-intentioned efforts can be an assumption among individuals who receive help that they do not need to engage in complex and demanding activities such as planning because other people will take care of it for them. As Pea (1982) commented after interviewing 8- to 12-year-olds on their views about planning, "you don't plan to do something if others plan it for you"(p. 19). Many children suffer little when they do not plan when they should. For example, parents often organize their children's time and resources and give many reminders to ensure that homework and school projects are completed in time (Ellis, Dowdy, Graham, & Jones, 1992).

Unplanned Action Can Be Enjoyable and Interesting in Its Own Right.   Many adults react to new household gadgets, electronic equipment, or software by gleefully jumping right in and trying to get things to work instead of planfully reading the instructions first. If asked, they might admit that reading the instructions would probably more quickly and consistently produce the goal of getting the new apparatus to work. However, it would prevent them from learning unexpected lessons on the way to the original goal, and would deny them the satisfaction of discovery by trial and error.

Analogously, seemingly unplanful behavior on the part of children may reflect a preference for obtaining information through exploration (Gibson, 1988; Wright & Vliestra, 1975). With development, children become more aware of the value of systematic and logical searching and increasingly understand that what adults, such as experimenters, consider optimal solutions are often distinguished by elegance and directness, rather than pleasantness of the solution process.

Vliestra (1982) documented developmental changes in preference for planful search over exploratory search in a series of studies on selective attention. In these studies, subjects were either instructed to search an array until all possible differences between items were found or to search until a single difference between items was found. In the find all condition, even 5-year-olds searched appropriately. However, in the find one condition, only 20% of 5-year-olds and 5% of 8-year-olds stopped upon finding a single difference. When 7-year-olds were exposed to a training session and reinforced for following instructions, their performance was as good as that of the older children and adults. This suggested that the tendency to engage in exhaustive searching reflects a preference for exploring rather than a lack of ability to stop at the desired point.

In many contexts, what seem like differences in planning ability may actually reflect different goals. For example, one difference between the errand planning of housewives and adolescents is that adolescents believe an afternoon in town running errands should include some time for "loafing", "hanging around, and "seeing what happens" (Lawrence, Dodds, & Volet, 1983, reported in Goodnow, 1987, p. 182). The seeming failure of the adolescents to plan actually reflects their pursuit of alternative objectives.

Complementarily, strict adherence to plans has a cost; it limits opportunities to explore the environment. Under some circumstances, even kindergartners can recognize and articulate this cost of planning. Illustratively, one kindergartner in a classroom in which children were required to plan in advance which of 11 activities (e.g., art, housekeeping, sandbox) they wished to pursue during a Free Choice period held each day complained, "I don't like it 'cause I want to go on everything and you can only go on things [in your plan]. If you make a mistake in your plan, you still have to go on it." (Gauvain, 1989, p. 113). Such costs need to be considered in any comprehensive account of when people do and do not plan.

PUSHING THE BALANCE IN FAVOR OF PLANNING

As the forgoings list illustrates, barriers to planning are often social in nature (Goodnow, 1987). For example, children may choose not to plan because they believe planning reflects badly on their abilities, especially in sociocultural contexts where quickness of thought is highly valued. They may also not encourage others to plan if they view planning as essentially wasted time.

This point is illustrated by studies that examine instructional interactions. For example, Ellis and Rogoff (1982) observed the teaching styles of urban, Euro-American third graders who had been asked to instruct a younger child in how to solve a problem. The third graders tended to adopt a highly directive teaching approach that promoted task completion but denied learners opportunities to plan independently (see Azmitia & Hesser, 1993; and Foot & Morgan, 1988, for similar observations). Several reasons for this approach seemed plausible: that these children did not possess the cognitive or social abilities to engage in effective instruction, that they lacked experience teaching younger children, that they were imitating the type of teaching that they most often had encountered, and/or that they were following the typical interactive style of their culture, which precludes many opportunities for novices to engage in planful problem solving.

Patterns of interaction such as those described by Ellis and Rogoff do not arise in a vacuum. Rather, they reflect cultural values and practices. Crosscultural comparisons allow us to disentangle the contributions of culture and developmental status to patterns of instructional exchange.

One way of viewing differences between cultures is in terms of their raising or lowering the supports needed to elicit certain types of cognitions. Clearly, children in all cultures are capable of planning. As Siegler's (1977) "20 Questions" study illustrated, however, the amount of support needed to get middle-class, Euro-American children to plan tends to be quite high. Other cultures may predispose children to plan under less supportive circumstances. Thus, it is interesting to compare the amount of planning generated by children from cultures that emphasize different cognitive values. The idea that people have cognitive values may at first seem strange, but cross-cultural work indicates clearly that different societies place differing emphases on accuracy, speed, tact, perseverance, grace of expression, and other qualities. Individuals within a culture also may differ in how much they value these qualities.

One culture that seems to embody quite different cognitive values than Euro-American culture is the Navajo culture of the Southwestern United States. Ethnographic studies of Navajo classrooms and communities reveal patterns of social interaction likely to impact on the kinds of cognitive opportunities experienced by Navajo children. Navajo children are reported to rely more on visual than verbal modes of communication (Cazden & John, 1971; Guilmet, 1978), to wait quietly rather than ask directly for assistance (Guilmet, 1978), and to wait for long periods before responding to questions. When they do speak, Navajo speakers take long turns and use a discursive style (Tharp & Gallimore, 1988), yet they are allowed to speak without interruption. This seeming contradiction between a style that emphasizes long waits and long speeches reflects the reverence with which words *and* silence are held by the Navajo.

Another aspect of Navajo culture that at first might seem contradictory involves attitudes toward cooperation and individual autonomy. Although Navajo social organization is widely portrayed as based on a cooperative orientation (Cazden & John, 1971; Lamphere, 1977; Shepardson & Hammond, 1970), it also strongly values individual autonomy. As Lamphere (1977) noted, the Navajo phrase *t'aa bee boholoniih* ("it's up to him to decide" or "it's his business"), which often can be heard in the context of group decision making, incorporates values of both cooperation and autonomy. It essentially means that one should not impose one's will on another, and that everyone is his own boss. Although there is a general obligation to be cooperative within Navajo culture, individuals reserve the right to decide on their own actions (Chisolm, 1983).

A study comparing collaborative problem solving of Navajo children with that of Euro-American children (Ellis & Schneiders, 1989) supported the view that cultural factors can shift the balance in favor of planning over more direct problem-solving strategies. In Ellis and Schneiders, the instructional and problem-solving strategies used by Navajo and Euro-American children were compared under conditions of collaborative and solitary instruction. Peer instructors worked either on their own or with a partner in instructing a younger child on a spatial problem-solving task involving both familiar and novel problems.

The problem-solving task was a maze resembling a rural scene: landmarks such as houses, a school, a clinic, and a trading post were connected by a number of roads (Fig. 8.2). Some of the roads were blocked by obstacles such as livestock, road construction, and overturned vehicles. To get from one target landmark to another, there was one short route and at least one long route. Several minor modifications, such as replacing the trading post with a convenience store, were made for use with the Euro-American sample. The goal of the task was to find the shortest path from one location to another without violating any of the task rules (it was forbidden to jump over obstacles, move off paths, or skip steps on the path). The maze was battery-operated; a stylus connected to one terminal of a battery completed a circuit to a buzzer when inserted through the holes. The maze paths linked the holes, and each hole on a legitimate path buzzed when the probe was inserted into it.

In the first phase of the study, the third graders mastered one segment of the maze (from home to grandmother's house). They subsequently taught a younger child that segment, as well as a segment of the maze with which they were not familiar (from grandmother's house to the store). In some cases, a single 3rd-grader taught the younger child; in other cases, two 3rd-graders did the teaching together. The interactions were videotaped and transcribed by native speakers who also noted each pause and possible instance of planning that occurred during the session. Each tape

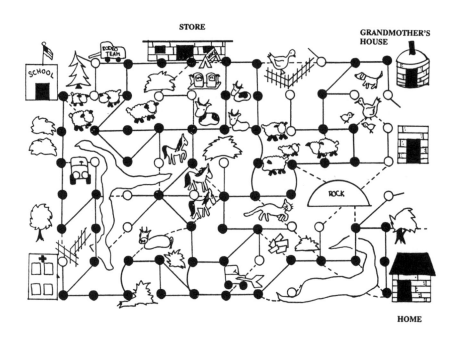

FIG. 8.2.   Schematic drawing of the maze used in Ellis and Schneiders, 1989. (From
Ellis and Gauvain, 1992. Copyright 1992 by Lawrence Erlbaum Associates.)

was then viewed by two coders who determined whether each pause
reflected planning. For a pause to be coded as planning, overt indices of
planning such as shifts in eye position, tracing solutions in the air with a
finger, or private speech had to be observed.

Given the general strategy choice model, where would planning be
expected to be used most often? The key principle is that strategies generally are used most often on problems where they are most effective relative
to available alternatives. Planning would be expected to be used most often
when more direct strategies would not yield effective performance. That is,
planning would be expected to be used most often in the most difficult
situations. Some evidence already supports this view. In Gardner and
Rogoff's (1990) maze puzzle study, children planned much more on difficult, than easy, mazes.

Which situations would be expected to be the most difficult, and therefore to yield the most planning, in the maze planning context? One key
variable would be the novelty of the maze segment. Both teachers and
learners would be expected to plan more on novel maze segments. Teachers
would be expected to plan most on the segment from grandmother's to the
store (Segment B), because they had not practiced this segment during the
training session. Learners would be expected to plan most on the segment

from their house to grandmother's (Segment A), as this segment was their first introduction to the task. Due to the same consideration of relative difficulty, we would expect more errors (as well as more planning) on the novel maze segments. One indication of whether the decision to plan on this task is, in fact, adaptive would be if children who planned made fewer errors on the novel maze segments.

Considerations of difficulty also suggested that both teachers and learners should plan more in the dyadic condition than in the triadic condition. Teaching alone should prove more challenging, if partners relied on each other to help teach and solve the maze. Less effective teaching would be expected to increase the difficulty of learning as well.

A further prediction was that Navajo children would plan more, because the culture does not value speeded performance as strongly as mainstream American culture. Further, Navajo children who engaged in joint problem solving would be expected to have more opportunities to plan, because Navajo values regarding independence and silence would discourage teachers from helping before the learner had an opportunity to plan or solve the problem.

The results supported all of these predictions (Table 8.2). On the novel segments, Navajo teachers planned more than Euro-American teachers under both solitary and collaborative teaching conditions. As expected, the differences were most striking in the amount of planning by solitary teachers: Navajo teachers planned an average of 49 seconds when working on the new maze segment, whereas Euro-American teachers planned less than 5 seconds on average when solving the same segment. Analysis of the errors made by teachers working alone showed that the Navajo teachers' greater planning was adaptive: Navajo teachers working alone made significantly fewer errors than Euro-American teachers working alone. Also in line with expectation, neither Navajo nor Euro-American teachers planned much on familiar segments; because these segments were well-learned, there was little need for planning on them.

One potential alternative explanation of the Navajo teachers' greater amount of planning on the novel segments was that the maze could have been more difficult to learn for the Navajo than for the Euro-American children, and that this greater difficulty elicited greater planning. Arguing against this possibility, however, was the fact that there were no differences in the number of errors made by the Navajo and Euro-American teachers when they initially learned the maze.

Navajo learners also engaged in more planning than did their Euro-American counterparts. The effect was present primarily when they worked with a single teacher— the condition under which they would be expected to receive the least instructional support (and which, therefore, was most difficult for them).

The most difficult condition was the one in which learners encountered the first novel segment with a single teacher. This was also the condition that

TABLE 8.2
Mean Amount of Planning Time on Familiar and Novel Segments (sec)

	TEACHER		LEARNER	
	Familiar (Segment A)	Novel (Segment B)	Novel (Segment A)	Novel (Segment B)
NAVAJO				
Dyads (N = 12) Total Planning	5	49	55	48
Triads (N = 11) Total Planning	1	22	15	12
EURO-AMERICAN				
Dyads (N = 13) Total Planning	3	4	5	3
Triads (N = 13) Total Planning	3	10	20	14

elicited the greatest differences in both the planning and the accuracy of the Navajo and Euro-American children. Navajo learners planned 11 times longer than Euro-American learners (55 versus 5 sec), and made only one quarter as many errors (a mean of 1 versus 4 per maze segment). The greater propensity of the Navajo children to plan thus yielded the greatest gains in accuracy under the high-difficulty conditions where the strategy choice model suggested planning would both be most prevalent and do the most good.

CONCLUSIONS

The theoretical framework and empirical research reviewed in this chapter point to three main conclusions regarding the study of planning and its development.

1. The proposal that planning can be profitably viewed within a strategy choice framework suggests significant changes in both conceptualizations of planning and tasks for study. Central to the model of strategy choice is the view that people know and use a variety of approaches for solving problems, and that they choose adaptively among those approaches. However, in many past studies of planning, the focus has been exclusively on the extent to which planning occurs; alternative approaches and their relative advantages have been ignored. This has limited potential understanding of why planning sometimes is and sometimes is not used. It has even more sharply curtailed understanding age-related changes in the use

of planning. Explaining developmental differences in planning will require documentation of the range of strategies children of different ages use to solve problems, and evaluation of the effectiveness of the different strategies, including planning, for children of each age.

2. Understanding planning requires considering its costs as well as its benefits. There are many reasons why children might not plan, even in situations where planning promotes effective problem solving. Most or all of them seem likely to change considerably with age, and thus to contribute to developmental changes in frequency of planning and circumstances under which children plan. Among the key factors are: degree of bias favoring immediate over delayed gratification; difficulty of suppressing direct problem-solving approaches; degree of bias against strategies that move away from tangible goals; overoptimism about the likelihood of success without planning; valuing of speed over accuracy; degree to which planning fails to lead to success; extent to which children do not believe they have control over outcomes; subjective unpleasantness of planning; assumptions that other people will take care of planning responsibilities; and enjoyment of strategies other than planning. This list suggests that understanding when people do and do not plan requires careful assessment of the beliefs, motivations, and goals of problem solvers, as well as the environmental and cognitive factors that influence planning. Although the focus of this chapter has been on planning in the context of achieving short-term goals, it is likely that the same factors will prove influential in decisions to engage in long-term planning. The relative weights of the factors may differ, however.

3. Because so many of the factors that influence planning reveal themselves most clearly in social settings, there should be more studies that examine planning in social contexts. As the research comparing planning among Navajo and Euro-American children illustrates, studies of planning in social context need not have as their primary goal documentation if how collaborative problem solving differs from that undertaken by individuals working alone. A useful alternative approach involves examining social contexts that vary on dimensions believed to influence planning and problem solving. Sometimes those contexts will involve different sociocultural groups, for example, when assessing how values concerning time, efficiency, accuracy, and social harmony impact on decisions to plan. Other times, varying the structure of social groups or problems to be solved will prove illuminating. Either way, the goals are: (a)to examine the range of available strategies, including planning, that can be used to solve problems; (b)to identify the costs and benefits that influence choices of whether to plan or to use an alternative approach; and (c)to determine how these costs and benefits vary in different sociocultural contexts.

ACKNOWLEDGMENTS

We are grateful for comments provided by Barbara Rogoff and the editors
of this volume on an earlier draft of the chapter. Preparation of this chapter
was supported in part by an NIMH postdoctoral training grant and by
NICHD Grant # HD-19011 and a grant from the Mellon Foundation.

REFERENCES

Azmitia, M., & Hesser, J. (1993). Why siblings are important agents of cognitive development:
    A comparison of siblings and peers. *Child Development, 64*, 430–444.
Baker-Sennett, J., Matusov, E., & Rogoff, B. (1992). Sociocultural processes of creative planning
    in children's playcrafting. In P. Light & G. Butterworth (Eds.), *Context and cognition: Ways
    of learning and knowing* (pp. 93–114). New York: Harvester Wheatsheaf.
Baker-Sennett, J., Matusov, E., & Rogoff, B. (1993). Planning as developmental process. In H.
    Reese (Ed.), *Advances in child development and behavior* (Vol. 24, pp. 253–281). New York:
    Academic Press.
Bandura, A. (1989). Regulation of cognitive processes through perceived self-efficacy. *Devel-
    opmental Psychology, 25*, 729–735.
Bandura, A., & Wood, R. E. (1989). Effects of perceived controllability and performance
    standards on self-regulation of complex decision-making. *Journal of Personality and Social
    Psychology, 56*, 805–814.
Berg, C. A. (1989). Knowledge of strategies for dealing with everyday problems from child-
    hood through adolescence. *Developmental Psychology, 25*, 607–618.
Case, R. (1985). *Intellectual development: A systematic reinterpretation.* New York: Academic Press.
Cazden, C. B., & John, V. P. (1971). Learning in American Indian children. In M. Wax, S.
    Diamond, & F. Goering (Eds.), *Anthropological perspectives on education* (pp. 252–271). New
    York: Basic Books.
Chisolm, J. S. (1983). *Navajo infancy: An ethological study of child development.* New York: Aldine.
DeLoache, J. L. (1984). Oh where, oh where: Memory-based searching by very young children.
    In C. Sophian (Ed.), *Origins of cognitive skills* (pp. 57–80). Hillsdale, NJ: Lawrence Erlbaum
    Associates.
Dempster, F. N. (1993). Resistance to interference: Developmental changes in a basic processing
    mechanism. In R. Pasnak & M. L. Howe (Eds.), *Emerging themes in cognitive development,*
    (Vol. 1, pp. 3–27) . New York: Springer.
Dweck, C. (1986). Motivational processes affecting learning. *American Psychologist, 41,*
    1040–1048.
Dweck, C., & Leggett, E. L. (1988). A socio-cognitive approach to motivation and personality.
    Psychological Review, 95, 256–273.
Ellis, S., Dowdy, B., Graham, P., & Jones, R. (1992, April). *Parental support of planning skills in
    the context of homework and family demands.* Paper presented at the meetings of the American
    Education Research Association, San Francisco, CA.
Ellis, S., & Gauvain, M. (1992). Social and cultural influences on children's collaborative
    interactions. In L. T. Winegar & J. Valsiner (Eds.), *Children's development within social context:
    Vol. 2. Research and methodology* (pp. 155–180). Hillsdale, NJ: Lawrence Erlbaum Associates.
Ellis, S., & Rogoff, B. (1982). The strategies and efficacy of child versus adult teachers. *Child
    Development, 53*, 730–735.
Ellis, S., & Schneiders, B. (1989, April). *Collaboration on children's instruction: A Navajo versus
    Anglo comparison.* Paper presented at the meetings of the Society for Research in Child
    Development, Kansas City, MO.
Flavell, J. H., Friedrichs, A. G., & Hoyt, J. D. (1970). Developmental changes in memorization
    processes. *Cognitive Psychology, 1*, 324–340.

Foot, H. C., & Morgan, M. J. (1988). *Process variables in peer tutoring: Children's understanding of misunderstanding.* (ESCR End of Award Report, C00232235). University of Wales, College of Cardiff.

Friedman, S. L. Scholnick, E. K., & Cocking, R. R. (1987). Reflections on reflection: What planning is and how it develops. In S. L. Friedman, E. K. Scholnick, & R. R. Cocking (Eds.), *Blueprints for thinking: The role of planning in cognitive development* (pp. 515–534). Cambridge, England: Cambridge University Press.

Friedman, S. L. Scholnick, S. K., & Cocking, R. R. (1987). *Blueprints for thinking: The role of planning in cognitive development.* Cambridge, England: Cambridge University Press.

Gardner, W. P., & Rogoff, B. (1990). Children's deliberateness of planning according to task circumstances. *Developmental Psychology, 26,* 480–487.

Gauvain, M. (1989). Children's planning in social contexts: An observational study of kindergarteners' planning in the classroom. In L. T. Winegar (Ed.), *Social interaction and the development of children's understanding* (pp. 95–117). Norwood, NJ: Ablex.

Gauvain, M., & Rogoff, B. (1989). Collaborative problem solving and children's planning skills. *Developmental Psychology, 25,* 139–151.

Gibson, E. J. (1988). Exploratory behavior in the development of perceiving, acting, and the acquiring of knowledge. *Annual Review of Psychology, 39,* 1–41.

Goldin-Meadow, S., Alibali, M. W., & Church, B. (1993). Transitions in concept acquisition: Using the hand to read the mind. *Psychological Review, 100,* 279–297

Goodnow, J. J. (1987). Social aspects of planning. In S. L. Friedman, E. K. Scholnick, & R. R. Cocking (Eds.), *Blueprints for thinking: The role of planning in cognitive development* (pp. 179–201). Cambridge, England: Cambridge University Press.

Guilmet, G. (1978). Navajo and Caucasian children's verbal and nonverbal–visual behavior in the urban classroom. *Anthropology and Education Quarterly, 9,* 196–215.

Klahr, D. (1978). Goal formation, planning, and learning by pre-school problem solvings or "My socks are in the dryer". In R. S. Siegler (Ed.), *Children's thinking: What develops?* (pp. 181–212). Hillsdale, NJ: Lawrence Erlbaum Associates.

Klahr, D., & Robinson, M. (1981). Formal assessment of problem solving and planning processes in children. *Cognitive Psychology, 13,* 113–148.

Lamphere, L. (1977). *To run after them.* Tucson: University of Arizona Press.

McGilly, K., & Siegler, R. S. (1989). How children choose among serial recall strategies. *Child Development, 60,* 172–182.

McGilly, K., & Siegler, R. S. (1990). The influence of encoding and strategic knowledge on children's choices among serial recall strategies. *Developmental Psychology, 26,* 931–941.

Mednick, S. A. (1962). The associative basis of the creative process. *Psychological Review, 69,* 220–232.

Mischel, W. (1974). Processes in delay of gratification. In L. Berkowitz (Ed.), *Advances in experimental social psychology* (Vol. 7, pp. 249–292). New York: Academic Press.

Mischel, W., & Metzner, R. (1962). Preference for delayed reward as a function of age, intelligence, and length of delay interval. Journal of Abnormal and Social Psychology, 64, 425–431.

Mischel, W., & Patterson, C. J. (1978). Effective plans for self-control in children. In W. A. Collins (Ed.), *Minnesota symposium on child psychology* (Vol. 11, pp. 199–230). Hillsdale, NJ: Lawrence Erlbaum Associates.

Patrick, B. C., Skinner, E. A., & Connell, J. P. (1993). What motivates children's behavior and emotion? Joint effects of perceived control and autonomy in the academic domain. *Journal of Personality and Social Psychology, 65,* 781–791.

Patterson, C. J., Massad, C. M., & Cosgrove, J. M. (1978). Children's referential communication: Components of plans for effective listening. *Developmental Psychology, 14,* 401–406.

Pea, R. D. (1982). What is planning development the development of? In D. Forbes & D. Lubin (Eds.), *New directions in child development: The development of planful behavior in children* (No. 18, pp. 5–27). San Francisco: Jossey-Bass.

Pitt, R. (1983). Development of a general problem-solving schema in adolescence and early adulthood. *Journal of Experimental Psychology: General, 112,* 547–584.

Rogoff, B. (1990). *Apprenticeship in thinking.* New York: Oxford University Press.

Schauble, L. (1990). Belief revision in children: The role of prior knowledge and strategies for generating evidence. *Journal of Experimental Child Psychology, 49,* 31–57.

Scholnick, E. K., & Friedman, S. L. (1993). Planning in context: Developmental and situational considerations. *International Journal of Behavioral Development, 16*, 145–167.

Schunk, D. H., & Gunn, T. P. (1986). Self-efficacy and skill development: Influence of task strategies and attributions. *Journal of Educational Research, 79*, 238–244.

Seligman, M. E. P. (1975). *Helplessness: On depression, development, and death.* San Francisco: Freeman.

Shepardson, M., & Hammond, B. (1970). *The Navajo Mountain community.* Berkeley: University of California Press.

Shure, G. H., Rogers, M. S., Larsen, I. M., & Tasone, J. (1962). Group planning and task effectiveness. *Sociometry, 25*, 263–282.

Siegler, R. S. (1977). The twenty questions game as a form of problem solving. *Child Development, 48*, 395–403.

Siegler, R. S. (1986). Unities across domains in children's strategy choices. In M. Perlmutter (Ed.), *Perspectives on intellectual development: The Minnesota symposia on child psychology* (Vol. 19, pp. 1–48). Hillsdale, NJ: Lawrence Erlbaum Associates.

Siegler, R. S. (1987). The perils of averaging data over strategies: An example from children's addition. *Journal of Experimental Psychology: General, 116*, 250–264.

Siegler, R. S. (1988). Strategy choice procedures and the development of multiplication skill. *Journal of Experimental Psychology: General, 117*, 258–275.

Siegler, R. S. (1996). *Emerging minds: The process of change in children's thinking.* New York: Oxford University Press.

Siegler, R. S., & Liebert, R. M. (1975). Acquisition of formal scientific reasoning by 10- and 13-year-olds: Designing a factorial experiment. *Developmental Psychology, 11*, 401–402.

Siegler, R. S., & McGilly, K. (1989). Strategy choices in children's time-telling. In I. Levin & D. Zackay (Eds.), *Psychological time: A life span perspective* (pp. 185–218). The Netherlands: Elsevier.

Siegler, R. S., & Robinson, M. (1982). The development of numerical understandings. In H. Reese & L. Lipsitt (Eds.), *Advances in child development and behavior* (Vol. 16, pp. 241–312). New York: Academic Press.

Siegler, R. S., & Shipley, C. (1995) Variation, selection, and cognitive change. In G. Halford & T. Simon (Eds.), *Developing cognitive competence: New approaches to process modeling* (pp. 31–76). Mahwah, NJ: Lawrence Erlbaum Associates.

Siegler, R. S., & Shrager, J. (1984). Strategy choices in addition and subtraction: How do children know what to do? In C. Sophian (Ed.), *Origins of cognitive skills* (pp. 229–293). Hillsdale, NJ: Lawrence Erlbaum Associates.

Sternberg, R. J., & Rifkin, B. (1979). The development of analogical reasoning processes. *Journal of Experimental Child Psychology, 27*, 195–232.

Stipek, D. J. (1984). Young children's performance expectations: Logical analysis or wishful thinking? In J. G. Nicholls & M. L. Maehr (Eds.), *Advances in motivation and achievement: The development of achievement motivation* (Vol. 3, pp. 33–56). Greenwich, CT: JAI Press.

Tharp, R. G., & Gallimore, R. (1988). *Rousing minds to life: Teaching, learning, and schooling in social context.* New York: Cambridge University Press.

Tschirgi, J. E. (1980). Sensible reasoning: A hypothesis about hypotheses. *Child Development, 51*, 1–10.

Vliestra, A. G. (1982). Children's responses to task instructions: Age changes and training effects. *Child Development, 53*, 534–542.

Welsh, M. C. (1991). Rule guided behavior and self-monitoring on the Tower of Hanoi disk-transfer task. *Cognitive Development, 6*, 59–76.

Willats, P. (1989). Development of problem solving in infancy. In A. Slater & J. G. Bremner (Eds.), *Infant development* (pp. 143–182). Hillsdale, NJ: Lawrence Erlbaum Associates.

Willats, P. (1990). Development of problem solving strategies in infancy. In D. Bjorklund (Ed.), *Children's strategies: Contemporary views of cognitive development* (pp. 23–66). Hillsdale, NJ: Lawrence Erlbaum Associates.

Wright, J. C., & Vliestra, A. G. (1975). The development of selective attention: From perceptual exploration to logical search. In H. W. Reese (Ed.), *Advances in child development and behavior* (Vol. 10, pp. 196–239). New York: Academic Press.

Yussen, S., & Levy, V. (1975). Developmental changes in predicting one's own span of short-term memory. *Journal of Experimental Child Psychology, 19*, 502–508.

9

Planning to Prevent Everyday Problems From Occurring

Cynthia A. Berg
JoNell Strough
Katerina Calderone
Sean P. Meegan
Carol Sansone
University of Utah

Planning has been defined as "the use of knowledge for a purpose, the construction of an effective way to meet some future goal" (Scholnick & Friedman, 1993, p. 145) and "goal-directed preparation for the future" (Lachman & Burack, 1993, p. 134). Much of the literature on the development of planning across the life span has focused on how individuals construct and execute plans in response to well-structured problems such as the Tower of Hanoi, mazes, and chess (see Friedman, Scholnick, & Cocking, 1987, for a review). More recently, investigators have become interested in the plans individuals construct in response to ill-structured everyday sorts of tasks such as errand running (Dreher & Oerter, 1987; Gauvain & Rogoff, 1989; B. Hayes-Roth & F. Hayes-Roth, 1979; Hudson & Fivush, 1991), party planning (e.g., Chalmers & Lawrence, 1993), and life planning (e.g., Smith & Baltes, 1990). What distinguishes many of these everyday problems from the well-structured problems often examined in planning is that the goal of the problem is unclear and there is no one correct means to achieve the goal (e.g., Meacham & Emont, 1989; Wood, 1983). With the inclusion of such everyday planning tasks, several researchers have noted that models of planning need to incorporate factors beyond those that are solely cognitive to include motivational, social, and environmental factors (Goodnow, 1987; Krietler & Krietler, 1987; Lachman & Burack, 1993; Rogoff, 1990).

Furthermore, recent models of planning behavior suggest that the components constituting the planning process may be somewhat different for ill-structured tasks than for well-structured tasks. Scholnick and Friedman

(1993) emphasized that numerous components of the planning process such as problem representation, goal setting, decisions to plan, plan formulation, and plan implementation may be influenced by the type of task involved. For instance, Scholnick and Friedman pointed out that on well-structured intellectual tasks such as the Tower of Hanoi, goals are typically highly constrained by the task demands and assumed to be similar for all problem solvers. However, on tasks reflective of more everyday demands, problem solvers are more likely to strive to set their own goals and resolve conflicting goals (Sinnott, 1989). Although variability in goals is often a defining feature of what constitutes ill-structured problems (see Sinnott, 1989; Wood, 1983), surprisingly little research has directly examined individual differences in goals within everyday problem-solving situations (cf. Sinnott, 1989; Strough, Berg, & Sansone, 1996). Our own work attempts to understand the development of planning and dealing with everyday problems in terms of how individuals represent and define everyday problems, which includes individuals' goals for the solution of their everyday problems.

The move toward understanding planning in everyday problem contexts may also involve broadening the type of planning that is examined. The literature on planning for both well-structured and ill-structured tasks has typically focused on planning behaviors that achieve some desired positive outcome in the future (e.g., completing errands, having a successful party). However, perhaps an equally important component of planning is whether and how individuals plan to prevent the occurrence of possible negative outcomes (e.g., preventing an interpersonal conflict between family members, avoiding disorganization in a collaborative group project). This type of planning may share many of the components included in typical formulations of planning, such as developing and implementing a plan. However, such planning may require other components not typically found in current models of planning, for example, anticipating the occurrence of a negative outcome.

Planning to prevent negative outcomes from occurring has not been examined in the everyday problem-solving literature. This literature focuses on the plans or strategies individuals utilize when they are in a problem-solving situation (e.g., Band & Weisz, 1988; Berg, 1989; Cornelius & Caspi, 1987; Denney, 1989). However, anticipating and preparing to prevent problems from occurring could be indicative of effective problem solving, particularly when such preparations actually prevent the problem's occurrence (Aspinwall & Taylor, 1995; Hammond, 1990). Work in the stress and coping literature examining anticipatory coping (i.e., anticipating the occurrence of a stressful event), found that such anticipation may hold some adaptive advantage. For instance, Ham and Larson (1990) found that across a diverse set of stressors, expected daily hassles were less upsetting than unexpected events for adolescents. Showers and Ruben (1990) found that optimists and defensive pessimists focused their resources before problems occurred, whereas depressed individuals expended energy in ruminating about events after they occurred. The ruminations of depressed individuals were associated with increased anxiety regarding the events.

There is some indication, however, that when stressful events are of a chronic nature, anticipation may actually exacerbate distress (e.g., Ham & Larson, 1990). This work suggests that although planning to prevent problems from occurring may often be advantageous, under some circumstances such planning may come at a cost to the planner. If the anticipation of the negative outcome motivates one to prepare to prevent its occurrence and those preparations are successful, clearly such planning is beneficial. However, in cases where anticipation does not lead one to prepare, or where those preparations are unsuccessful, planning may prolong negative emotional states, such as depression and anxiety.

This chapter presents research that examines planning to prevent everyday problems. This research was guided by our developmental model of how individuals adapt to their everyday environments. Our model emphasizes the importance of individuals' problem definitions of everyday situations for understanding planning and everyday problem solving across the life span. Problem definitions reflect numerous individual and contextual characteristics and, as such, broaden our understanding of planning beyond factors that are solely cognitive to include social and motivational features of everyday situations. First, our developmental model of everyday problem solving and our empirical work supportive of the model is presented. Second, the results of a life-span investigation of individuals' reports of their own everyday problems are discussed. The findings from this study illustrate developmental differences in individuals' reports of their abilities to predict and prepare for problems that actually occurred, and suggest that these differences may be related to problem definitions that differentially focus on interpersonal and competence concerns.

Third, we examine planning to prevent problems from occurring within a specific domain, a long-term collaborative group project in school. This is a domain in which interpersonal and competence concerns are particularly salient for preadolescents and adolescents. Students' reported abilities to anticipate and prevent problems that had occurred (postdiction) were compared with their abilities to anticipate and prevent the occurrence of problems that had not yet occurred (prediction). The results indicated both differences and similarities between problem anticipation and prevention, examined postdictively versus predictively. Finally, the multiple dimensions of problem definitions that may be important for understanding planning to prevent everyday problems are noted together with future directions for research.

MODEL OF EVERYDAY PROBLEM SOLVING

Our model of the everyday problem-solving process is situated within a contextual perspective to planning and problem solving[1] (e.g., Baltes, 1987; Dixon, 1992; Rogoff, 1982). Within this contextual view, everyday problem solving depends on how the individual, with his or her abilities and experiences, interacts with the physical and social demands and opportunities present in the context (see Berg & Calderone, 1994; Sansone & Berg, 1993). Although we will focus on the implications of this model for planning and problem solving, this model also applies to situations where a problem is not present or not perceived to be present in everyday activities. As such, we consider it more generally a model of how individuals adapt to their everyday environments (see Sansone & Berg, 1993, for details).

In our model (see Berg & Calderone, 1994; Sansone & Berg, 1993), contextual and individual characteristics affect an individual's planning and problem-solving performance through the individual's definition or interpretation of an activity. As can be seen in Fig. 9.1, an activity is defined out of a transaction of the individual with his or her context and may be updated and changed over time. This definition may be derived from all the possible contextual and individual features, or it may be based only on a subset of those features. Therefore, it is the person's own representation of the potential contextual and individual features that we view as critical for understanding how people adapt to their everyday environments, not the features that some outside observer might detail as present. For example, an individual's experience, social competence, perceptions of control, age, or gender all have the potential to affect activity definitions, but only a subset of these factors may affect a specific definition at a particular point in time. Similarly, the context of the activity might include other individuals and physical constraints, and yet only a subset of these factors may be reflected in an individual's activity definition at a particular point in time. In fact, such individual and contextual features may be differentially salient at various points in development, leading to systematic developmental differences in activity definitions.

Take, for example, the activity of a family reunion, which encompasses numerous subactivities (e.g., fixing an elaborate meal, playing cards, playing baseball, taking pictures, visiting, etc.). Individuals could define a family reunion in a variety of different ways: as an opportunity to catch up with one's relatives, as a duty to one's family, as an opportunity to display one's skills at cooking, cards, baseball, picture taking, and so forth. Such different definitions could result from a complex interplay of features of the context and characteristics of the individual that combine in systematic

---

[1]We propose this model of "problem solving" in the broad sense, defined as adapting to the environment and should be applicable to more traditional sorts of problem solving as well as to everyday problems.

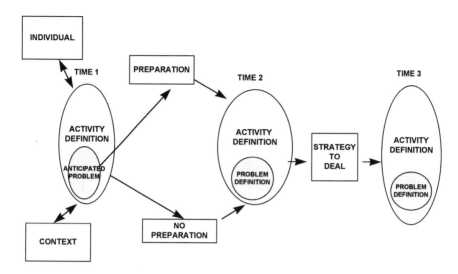

FIG 9.1.   Model of planning to prevent everyday problems from occurring.

ways across development. For instance, a school-aged child's concern with the display of competence (e.g., Erikson, 1963; Veroff & Veroff, 1980) could make competence features of the baseball game a central part of his or her activity definition. In contrast, an older adult's concern with generativity (e.g., Erikson, 1963; Nurmi, Pulliainen, & Salmela-Aro, 1992) could make the social features of the same event central to his or her activity definition.

We contend that individuals may define an *activity* in terms of a problem that has not yet occurred, but might. In our example, individuals could include in their activity definition of *family reunion*, the anticipation that a problem such as arguing with a particular family member or losing at cards would occur. Anticipated problems can vary in the extent of their anticipation, from being perceived as very likely to less likely. For problems that are anticipated, individuals can plan in advance to either prevent the problem's occurrence or mitigate the consequences of the problem. These plans can therefore include strategies such as direct action aimed at preventing the problem's occurrence (e.g., avoiding the family member one usually argues with) and cognitive strategies aimed at preparing the problem solver for the actual occurrence of the problem (e.g., resolving not to be upset by the impending argument).

Our work on planning to prevent everyday problems from occurring was guided by this model, examining whether individuals' anticipation of and preparation for everyday problems are related to individuals' problem definitions, as indexed by the goals they desire in that situation. We now trace the process that we posit individuals go through in planning to prevent everyday problems as well as in dealing with problems once they have occurred. As seen in Fig. 9.1, as individuals experience specific everyday activities, some individuals will anticipate that a problem may occur, thereby anticipating the possible occurrence of a future negative outcome (depicted as Time 1).

Some individuals who anticipate problems may plan and subsequently take some action to prevent the occurrence of the anticipated problem, which may in turn successfully prevent the problem. Other individuals may make no preparations for the anticipated problem. For both individuals, the anticipated problem may or may not occur, potentially due to the individual's own preparation or lack of preparation. That is, individuals who prepare to prevent the problem might not experience the anticipated problem, either due to their preparations or other factors. Similarly, individuals who do not make preparations may not experience the problem due to some factor unrelated to their inaction.

When individuals actually experience the problem, they do so with a particular problem definition present. For those individuals who anticipated that the problem would occur, this problem definition may involve a reappraisal of the problem at Time 2 that may be different than the problem definition at Time 1 (e.g., definition may be more differentiated). For individuals who did not anticipate that the problem would occur, Time 2 is their first definition or representation of the problem. Thus, compared to unanticipated problems, anticipated problems are ones with which the problem solver potentially has a longer history of problem definition and redefinition across time.

Once the problem does occur, our model suggests that individuals will utilize some strategy to deal with the experienced problem, as most other problem-solving models suggest (e.g., Newell & Simon, 1972; Rubin & Rose-Krasnor, 1992). Our previous work indicates that the strategies individuals employ to deal with a problem are related to the way in which the problem is defined (see Berg & Calderone, 1994; Berg, Strough, Calderone, Sansone, & Weir, in press). Subsequent to such strategy deployment, individuals may again reinterpret their problem, as is represented at Time 3. This reinterpretation may involve a change in the way the problem is defined or may involve defining the activity as no longer being a problem.

We emphasize that this model takes the position that for individuals who anticipate problems, one future goal to be met is the avoidance of the negative outcome or problem. Individuals may thus develop plans and subsequent strategies to avoid an outcome, in addition to achieving an outcome. The individual may view this goal to avoid the problem as a proximal subgoal toward a more distal goal (e.g., as one of the things that must be accomplished to successfully complete an activity; e.g., Bandura, 1986) or as an obstacle toward some higher level goal (e.g., Oppenheimer, 1987). Alternatively, the desire to avoid a particular outcome may be so strong as to become the definition of the activity. Whether the problem solver focuses on the negative outcome as a subgoal or the primary goal may, in large part, depend on how the problem solver him or herself identifies the potential negative outcome. Individuals may move between different levels of problem identification, depending on the goal to be accomplished at any particular point in time (Vallacher & Wegner, 1987).

This model establishes the possibility for numerous patterns of individual differences in problem anticipation and prevention. Our empirical work has been primarily focused on three such patterns: (a) individuals who do not anticipate the occurrence of an experienced problem, (b) individuals who anticipate the occurrence of an experienced problem and who are oriented toward taking steps to prevent the problem's occurrence, and (c) individuals who anticipate the occurrence of an experienced problem but report making no plans to prevent the problem's occurrence. In our example of individuals attending the family reunion described previously, these three types of patterns might occur with respect to an actual experienced problem of arguing with a particular family member. Some individuals may experience this problem, but not have anticipated it. Other individuals may anticipate such a problem and even utilize strategies such as trying to avoid the person, engaging in activities that this person is not involved in, or keeping the conversation away from particular topics to avoid the problem. Other individuals may anticipate the problem and yet not take any steps to avoid the problem, perhaps because they feel the problem is not something over which they have control.

We have examined whether these different patterns may be predicted from individuals' definitions of problem situations. Our notion of problem definition is similar to other notions of problem representation such as Sinnott's *essence* of the problem (1989), Forman and McPhail's idea of *task definition* (1993), Newell and Simon's (1972) idea of *problem space*, Lewin's (1936, 1951) activated portion of the *life space*, and Lazarus and Folkman's (1984) notion of *problem appraisal*. However, the dynamic nature of our problem definition distinguishes it from most of these previous concepts. Problem definitions could be captured in different ways including the level at which problems are interpreted (e.g., abstract vs. concrete, see Vallacher & Wegner, 1987), the category or type of problem (e.g., logical problem, pragmatic problem, see Sinnott, 1989), the extent of the problem space (e.g., confined within the constraints of the problem vs. encompassing experiential components of the person's life, see Laipple, 1991), and so on.

Our primary focus so far in examining problem definitions was whether individuals are oriented towards interpersonal or social components and/or task or competence components of problem situations, as such elements are so salient in individuals' descriptions of everyday situations (see Sansone & Berg, 1993; Sansone & Morgan, 1992). In fact, such components are differentially salient to individuals across the life span such that the salience of the interpersonal context increases from preadolescence to adolescence (e.g., Berg & Calderone, 1994) and is particularly salient during middle and later adulthood (e.g., Strough et al., 1996). In addition, several studies now support the idea that interpersonal and task/competence components of individuals' problem definitions are important for understanding developmental differences in everyday problem solving (Berg & Calderone, 1994; Berg, Klaczynski, Calderone, & Strough, 1994; Blanchard-Fields & Norris, 1994; Sinnott, 1989). For instance, Calderone and Berg (see Berg & Calderone, 1994; Calderone, 1993) found that preadolescents' and adolescents' interpersonal and task definitions of hypothetical everyday problems differed systematically as a function of age and gender. That is, females defined problems in terms of interpersonal components more often than did males, and definitions became more interpersonal with increasing age. In addition, these definitions had implications for how individuals judged potential strategies for dealing with the problem.

In this chapter we examine how developmental differences in the interpersonal nature of problem definitions relate to individual differences in anticipating and preventing everyday problems from occurring (see also Berg & Sansone, 1991; Sansone & Berg, 1993). Specifically, we examined two components of individuals' planning. First, we examined individuals' reports of anticipating that a problem would occur. Second, we examined individuals' reports of making some sort of plan to prevent that problem's occurrence. We explored whether the developmental differences uncovered in our data regarding the interpersonal nature of children's and adults' problem definitions (Berg & Calderone, 1994; Strough et al., 1996) would lead to differences in predicting and planning for future occurrences of everyday problems.

More specifically, we explored whether everyday problems defined primarily in terms of interpersonal components and/or in terms of task and competence components were differentially associated with reports of prediction of the problem's occurrence and attempts to prevent the problem's occurrence. In addition, we examined whether individuals with different problem definitions reported utilizing different strategies to prevent the problem's occurrence. Interpersonal definitions may reflect the salience of different features of the problem context (e.g., interpersonal constraints and contingencies) that, in fact, lead to different strategies for dealing with and preparing for problems (see Berg & Calderone, 1994; Dodge, Pettit, McClaskey, & Brown, 1986). For instance, an exclusive focus on the interpersonal components of the problem environment might lead individuals to try to influence other individuals to prevent the problem's occurrence rather than trying to change some aspect of the self (Goodnow, 1987).

The question of how problem definitions relate to anticipating and planning to prevent future problems from occurring was approached in two different studies. In the first study, preadolescents and adults of various ages were compared in their reports of prediction and preparation to prevent an everyday problem that actually did occur in these individuals' lives. Individuals were asked to relate a problem that had already occurred and to reflect on whether they had anticipated and done something to prevent the problem's occurrence. With respect to Fig. 9.1, individuals' problem definitions at Time 3 were assessed and individuals were asked to reflect on their anticipation and preparation attempts. In this study individuals' problem descriptions were elicited using a very open-ended method. In addition, this method allowed researchers to sense what was important to individuals, rather than imposing importance a priori, as is typically done in everyday problem-solving research. This study yielded rich information regarding the relation of individuals' problem definitions to their reports of anticipation and prevention of everyday problems. However, because the data were retrospective and focused on problems that did occur, the results gave a potentially biased view of problem prevention in that it focused on individuals' unsuccessful attempts at problem prevention.

In the second study, therefore, we examined problem anticipation and preparation prospectively in a sample of sixth and eighth graders who were working in collaborative groups on a school project. In this study we compared individuals' reports of anticipation and prevention for problems that actually occurred with their prediction and plans for preventing future problems that had not yet occurred. In terms of Fig. 9.1, their anticipation and preparation reports about problems after they occurred (Time 3) were compared with their initial predictions of what they expected they would do for problems that they anticipated (at Time 1).

PROBLEM DEFINITIONS AND PLANNING
TO PREVENT PROBLEMS ACROSS THE LIFE SPAN

Method

A subset of data from a study of everyday experiences and problems across the life span is discussed here (see Sansone & Berg, 1993, for more details about this sample). Subjects included 117 preadolescents (mean age = 10.9 years; 63 males, 54 females), 109 college students (mean age = 21.9 years; 56 males, 53 females), 139 middle-aged adults (mean age = 49.0 years; 48 males, 91 females), and 137 older adults (mean age = 71.0 years; 51 males, 86 females). Similar procedures were used across age groups, with one major exception: Data were collected in interview format for the preadolescents, and in questionnaire format for the three adult samples.

We asked adult participants to "Think about a recent problem (hassle, conflict, or challenge) and describe it from beginning to end to someone who has never had the problem." Similarly, we asked preadolescents to "describe something they had to work hard on, something that bugged them, or something that had to be fixed."

After relating a problem of their choice, participants were asked about their anticipation and prevention of this problem. To assess whether they had anticipated that the problem they described would occur, adults rated on a 7-point scale, "Before the problem happened, how likely did you think it was that the problem would have happened?" (1 corresponded to "not at all likely," 7 corresponded to "very likely"). Preadolescents were asked "Before the problem, did you see the problem coming, or was it a surprise?" To make the responses of adults comparable to those of preadolescents, adults who indicated that they saw the problem coming to any extent (i.e., rated 2 or above) were considered to have anticipated the problem's occurrence[2]. To examine their preparations to prevent the problem, individuals who reported that they saw the problem coming were asked "Did you do anything before the problem happened to stop it from happening?" If individuals indicated that they did prepare to prevent the problem, they were asked "What did you do?" If individuals indicated that they had not prepared, they were asked "Why not?"

To access individuals' problem definitions, we examined individuals' higher-order goals for dealing with their everyday problem. Goals were elicited by asking adults, "What was your goal in dealing with the problem?" Preadolescents were asked, "When you did [what they said they did to deal with the problem], what did you want to have happen?" Individuals' problem descriptions and problem-solving goals were examined in terms of whether individuals mentioned some competence or interpersonal component. *Competence goals* were operationalized as the express purpose of accomplishing, achieving, or getting better at something. An *interpersonal goal* was operationalized as the express purpose of bringing about some outcome involving others. Adopting a multiple-goals perspective (see also Dodge, Asher, & Parkhurst, 1989; Wentzel, 1991), a presence/absence judgement was made separately for the competence and interpersonal categories.

Thus, competence and interpersonal goals were not considered mutually exclusive. For example, some individuals mentioned both interpersonal and competence goals (e.g., getting my father to help with my homework), some mentioned interpersonal goals alone (e.g., spend more time with my father), some mentioned competence goals alone (e.g., getting a better grade on my homework) and some mentioned neither goal (e.g., to be happy). Two coders categorized a subset of all problem descriptions and goals into these categories, achieving excellent Kappas (see Berg et al., in press, for details). The remaining data were coded by only one of the coders.

The preparations that individuals reported using to prevent the problem's occurrence were coded into four distinct categories. These strate-

---

[2]Although the responses of adults did range across this 7-point scale, addition analyses using the more continuous range did not change the results reported here.

gies were drawn from other existing strategy coding schemes used to examine everyday problem-solving strategies (e.g., Berg, 1989; Cornelius & Caspi, 1987; Folkman, Lazarus, Pimley, & Novacek, 1987). *Cognitive self-regulation* involved thoughts of the problem solver directed at regulating how he or she thought about the problem (e.g., "should pay more attention, changed the way I thought about the problem"). *Behavioral self-regulation* involved self-initiated action by the problem solver to make his or her behavior conform to the demands of the problem (e.g., "study harder, exercise more"). *Regulation or inclusion of others* involved attempts by the problem solver to shape and change other people's behavior, beliefs, or feelings so that the problem situation fit better with the problem solver's needs and goals (e.g., "get Jane to see my point of view, ask her to fix the car"). *Regulation of the physical environment* involved shaping and changing physical aspects of the environment so that the problem environment fit better with the problem solver's needs and goals (e.g., "get the junk food out of the house, buy a lock for the front door"). Four coders were trained so that 80% agreement was achieved between all possible pairs of coders. Two coders at each age then categorized 25% of all strategies for reliability purposes, and the rest of the data at each age level was coded by one of the coders.

Results

Reported Problems. Before addressing questions related to individual differences in problem anticipation and prevention, we briefly describe the problems that individuals mentioned to give the reader a sense of the context of everyday problem solving as reflected in this study. Individuals' problem descriptions ranged widely in their content and scope. The problems that individuals mentioned ranged from major life events (e.g., death of parent, divorce) to more minor daily hassles (brother messing up their room, studying for exams, building models, arguments with coworkers, problems in dealing with parents, etc.). Previous analysis of these problems (see Sansone & Berg, 1993, for a more complete description) revealed that individuals mentioned problems from a wide assortment of domains, with the domains changing across age: preadolescents' problems largely dealt with problems at school, family, and their free time (50%, 17.3%, and 13.4%, respectively); college students' problems did not fall predominately in one domain; middle-aged adults' problems dealt most frequently with issues related to work and family (30.4% and 8.9% respectively); and older adults' problems dealt most frequently with family and health (19.4% and 12%, respectively).

Individual Differences in Problem Anticipation. We first examined whether the proportion of individuals who anticipated the problem's occurrence differed by age group, gender, or goal type. Recall that goal type served as an index of problem definition in these data. A logit analysis predicting problem anticipation with age group, gender, and goal type as predictor variables was developed. Logit modeling was used because it allowed for an examination of higher-order interactions between predictors, and localization of the source of such interactions. The logit analysis produced the following model: an effect for the predicted variable (Anticipation), 2 two-way associations (Age × Anticipation and Goal × Anticipation), and 1 three-way association (Age × Goal × Anticipation)[3]. The Anticipation term indicated that 65% of individuals reported that they anticipated their problem's occurrence.

The Age × Anticipation association indicated that problem anticipation varied by age, with preadolescents less likely to report anticipating their problem's occurrence than the other age groups (56.5% for preadolescents, 70.4%, 71.7%, and 63.6% for college, middle-aged, and older adults, respectively). The Goal × Anticipation association indicated that of those who anticipated their problem's occurrence, individuals were more likely to have goals containing a competence component only (30%), a competence component in combination with an interpersonal component (32.7%), or an interpersonal component only (24.4%), than neither an interpersonal nor a competence component (12.9%). The Anticipation × Age × Goal association, however, revealed that age differences in anticipation were most prominent whenever individuals had particular combinations of goal types (see Fig. 9.2). More specifically, the poorer anticipation of preadolescents was most prominent whenever individuals mentioned an interpersonal goal only, and to a lesser extent when they mentioned an interpersonal goal in conjunction with a competence goal. In fact, of the problems that each age group anticipated, preadolescents' anticipation was much higher when their problems contained competence components only.

Individual Differences in Problem Preparation.   For individuals who anticipated the problem's occurrence, we next examined differences in individuals' reports of preparing to prevent the problem from occurring. A logit model predicting problem preparation with age group, gender, and goal type as predictor variables was developed. The logit analysis produced the following model: a first-order effect for the predicted variable (preparation) and 1 two-way association (Goal × Preparation)[4]. The logit analysis did not reveal any significant associations among age, gender, and problem preparation. Although the individuals included in this analysis reported anticipating that the problem would occur, the Preparation term indicated that 60% of individuals reported that they did nothing in advance

---

[3]The selected logit model has adequate fit between observed and expected frequencies (see Tabachnick & Fidell, 1989), likelihood ratio G^2 (16) = 15.265, p = .479.

[4]Likelihood ratio G^2 (28) = 32.78, p = .244.

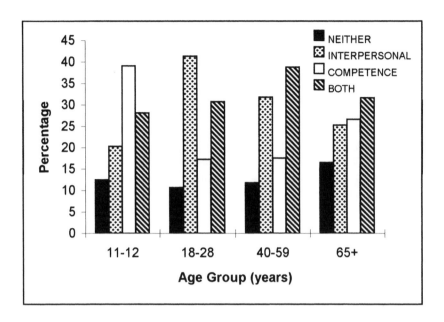

FIG. 9.2.   Percentage of reported anticipated problems by goal type within age group.

to prevent the problem's occurrence. However, as indicated by the Goal ×
Preparation association, preparation to prevent the problem did differ by
goal type.

Individuals who reported preparing to prevent the problem's occurrence
were much less likely to report goals with neither interpersonal nor competence components present (8.3%) than when other goal combinations were
present (29.5%, 28.0%, and 34.1% for interpersonal only, competence only, and
interpersonal in combination with competence components, respectively).
Additional coding of these data (see Strough et al., 1996) indicate that goals
that contained neither interpersonal nor competence components were more
often associated with the regulation of physical states than other goal types
(e.g., to get healthy, free from sickness), and situations where individuals
reported not being oriented toward achieving goals. Thus, preparation may
be more prevalent when individuals are oriented toward achieving specific
interpersonal or competence-based outcomes.

*Individual Differences in the Strategies Used to Prepare for the
Problem's Occurrence.*   We also examined age and gender differences
in the strategies individuals reported using to prevent the problem from
occurring. Age differences in strategies did occur (χ^2 (12) = 23.8, p < .05).
The most frequently used strategy for preadolescents and older adults was

behavioral self-regulation. For college students and middle-aged adults, the most frequent strategy was inclusion or regulation of others (see Fig. 9.3). This pattern of results is similar to the age differences found when individuals were asked what they did to deal with the problem when it did occur (see Berg et al., in press). We were also interested in understanding whether individuals who had different types of goals would report different strategies for attempting to prevent their problem's occurrence. However, the number of cases was not sufficient to provide a formal analysis of this question, as many individuals reported not preparing to prevent their problem's occurrence. There was, however, an indication that individuals who interpreted the problem in terms of interpersonal components (i.e., interpersonal goals only or interpersonal goals in combination with competence goals) were more likely to report utilizing the strategy of regulation or manipulation of others than individuals who focused on other components.[5]

Reasons for Not Preventing Problem. Because we were struck with the large percentage of individuals who reported doing nothing to prevent a problem that they anticipated, we examined the reasons participants gave as to why they did nothing to prevent the problem. The most frequently occurring reason for adults was that they didn't predict the severity of the consequences and/or their reaction to the consequences (e.g., "I never

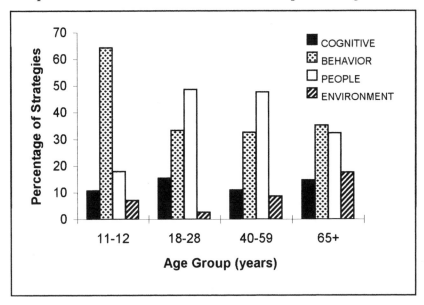

FIG 9.3.   Percentage of strategies for preventing problem occurrence by age group.

[5]This relation between goal type and strategies was similar for strategies that individuals reported using to deal with the problem (see Berg et al., in press; Sansone & Berg, 1993).

thought that the situation and the way I was being treated in the situation would get so extreme"). Other reasons individuals gave for not preparing to avoid problems included some personal characteristic or limitation (e.g., they were lazy, etc.), because the problem was out of their control, or because they actually wanted to be engaged in the problem at some level (e.g., "I kind of like being teased by the boys"). Thus, individuals' reasons for not preparing to prevent problems from occurring indicated that some individuals thought that such preparation could have occurred, whereas other individuals indicated that such preparation was either not desirable or would not have been effective.

In summary, the view of planning that emerges from this study is that planning to prevent problems from occurring is relatively infrequent. The age-related differences found in this study suggested that developmental differences in planning occur predominantly in anticipating that problems with interpersonal components will occur, and in the kinds of strategies employed to prevent the problems from occurring, not in the frequency with which preparations are made to prevent problems. Some of these age-related differences in problem prevention can be better understood in the context of individuals' problem definitions, as indexed by individuals' higher-order goals. For instance, preadolescents' poorer problem anticipation occurred only when their problems and goals were focused on the interpersonal components of the problem.

Additional results from this data set and other studies reveal relations with interpersonal definitions that may be useful in understanding planning to prevent everyday problems from occurring. First, interpersonal problem definitions were related to a person's lower level of internal control (see Morgan, 1993) and higher level of other control (see Klaczynski & Berg, 1992) over the problem environment. In addition, we found that adults who described their everyday problems with an interpersonal focus reported more difficult problems than did individuals who defined problems in a different fashion. These differences in perceived control and difficulty level may relate to preadolescents' lower anticipation of interpersonally defined problems, particularly given that they were often trying to accomplish something with others who had more influence over the situation than they did themselves.

The results from this study gave us a broad view of the frequency with which individuals report anticipating and preparing to prevent a problem's occurrence across a diverse set of problem-solving situations. The results suggest that although individuals largely report anticipating that their problem will occur, few individuals report actually preparing to prevent the problem's occurrence. The study, however, has some limitations that restrict our understanding of the process by which individuals anticipate and prepare to prevent their everyday problems from occurring. These limitations stem, in large part, from the retrospective nature with which problem definitions and reports of anticipation and preparation were assessed. First, the fact that so many individuals reported anticipating that their problem occurred may be due, in part, to the hindsight bias. The hindsight bias refers to the idea that people's estimation of the probability of an event is higher after that event has occurred (e.g., Fischhoff, 1977). In the present study, then, perhaps individuals' estimations of anticipating the problem's occurrence were inflated. This might explain why so many individuals reported doing nothing to prevent the problem's occurrence—as they really did not anticipate the problem's occurrence.

Second, because individuals in the study were asked to describe their anticipation and preparations for a "problem" that actually occurred, this study focused largely on the problems that individuals were unsuccessful in preventing, although individuals' attempts may have mitigated the problem to some extent. Thus, these data may not completely reflect the frequency with which planning to prevent everyday problems occurs nor the process by which individuals successfully prevent problems from occurring. Such successful attempts would be better addressed in a prospective study asking individuals to predict the occurrence of future problems and following their attempts at problem prevention.

To address these and other concerns, we conducted a second study in which we compared problem anticipation and planning in two conditions. We compared planning in which individuals were reflecting on their planning for problems that had already occurred (i.e, for postdiction) with the case in which individuals were reporting on the plans they would undertake in the future to prevent anticipated problems from occurring (i.e., for prediction). We chose to focus on this process in early and later adolescence because the previous study indicated that it is at this point in the life span that individuals show lower problem anticipation. Drawing on the results from the life-span study of individuals' open-ended problem descriptions, we chose to examine planning in the school environment, because this was the most salient problem context for preadolescents. Of the problems occurring in the school context, one of the most frequent problems that preadolescents described was working with group members on a collaborative project in which interpersonal components were present with task or competence concerns. Collaborative group projects provided an ideal context in which to examine how interpersonal and task-focused definitions impact aspects of the problem-anticipation and prevention process. Thus, the second study examined problem anticipation and prevention using the same problem environment (i.e., collaborative school projects) for all adolescents to better understand the process underlying planning.

PROBLEM PREVENTION:
PREDICTION VERSUS POSTDICTION
IN COLLABORATIVE GROUP PROJECTS

Method

Participants in this study were sixth-and eighth-grade students from Salt Lake City area public schools who had been assigned a group project as part of the requirements for their class. The sixth-grade students were involved in a group project on countries for their social studies class; eighth-grade students were involved in a translation project and play performance in their Spanish class. A total of 35 sixth graders (26 females and 9 males) and 41 eighth graders (27 females and 14 males) participated in the study; data for 28 sixth graders and 35 eighth graders were coded and are reported here.

The students were interviewed twice, once at the beginning of the group project and again, near the end of the project. Similar to the methods used in the life-span study, at the first and second interview we asked students to describe a problem they had encountered while working on their group project. In addition, students were asked to describe what they saw as the *main problem* in their overall problem description. That is, rather than trying to draw their definition of the problem from individuals' problem descriptions and goals, we asked participants in a more direct fashion to provide us with the problem definition. Individuals were also asked to describe what they did to deal with the problem.

After they had described this problem, students were asked to rate how well they were able to see the problem coming (1 = definitely didn't see it coming, 5 = definitely saw it coming), whether they did anything to stop the problem from happening, and if so, what. At the first interview, students were also asked to describe problems they thought might happen while working on their group project in the future. Students were prompted to describe as many possible future problems as they could. For the problem that students thought was most likely to occur they were asked to rate "how much do you think that this problem will occur?" (1 = definitely will not happen, 5 = definitely will happen). Students were then asked if they believed that there was anything they could do now before this problem occurred to keep it from happening, and if so, what. They were asked to rate "how likely do you think it would be for you to do the thing that could stop the problem?" (1 = definitely will not do it, 5 = definitely will do it). At the second interview, students were asked whether or not the problems they had predicted actually occurred. For the problem that students had rated as most likely to occur, they were asked whether they did what they predicted they would do to try and prevent the problem from happening.

Students' problem definitions were coded for their social and task content on a 3-point scale (0 = no mention, 2 = detailed mention). The social content involved the extent to which other people and the interactions among or with others was the source of the problem. The task content involved the extent to which the task and specific components of the task were described as the source of the problem.

Results

Reported Anticipation and Preparation for Problems That Had Occurred. At the first interview, most adolescents reported that they saw the problem coming (90%). Similar to the findings discussed for the life-span study, however, the vast majority of individuals reported doing nothing to prevent the problem from occurring. For sixth graders, of those who anticipated that the problem would occur, 61.2% reported that they did nothing, and for the eighth graders, 83.9% reported that they did nothing to prevent the problem from happening. Similar results were obtained when children were asked to describe a problem that had occurred at the second interview. Again, students reported that they largely saw the problem coming (74.6%). For those students who indicated that they saw the problem coming, 87% of the sixth graders reported doing nothing, and 66.7% of the eighth graders reported doing nothing to prevent the problem from happening. Thus, similar to the life-span study, although most individuals reported that they anticipated that their problem would occur, they also reported not preparing to prevent their problem's occurrence. However, a larger percentage of both early and late adolescents reported anticipating their problems than was true for individuals in the life-span study.

We have begun to examine the reasons that individuals gave for why they did not prepare to prevent a problem when they ostensibly anticipated its occurrence. Similar to the life-span study, individuals mentioned that they did not anticipate that the consequences of the problem would be so severe, that they did not think about the problem that much, that nothing could be done, and that they wanted to be involved in the problem. However, an additional class of reasons appears in these data. Individuals mentioned that they had mistakenly believed that other individuals in the group would do their share of the work, but that their prediction was incorrect ("I just gave the person the benefit of the doubt and thought well maybe they will do it," "I had faith in them that they'd memorize it"). This last type of reason suggests that the social context of planning may be a somewhat unpredictable and uncontrollable environment, or alternatively that the social context may provide a source of attributions for problems (i.e., other people) that the individual has failed to prevent (see Buehler, Griffin, & Ross, 1994).

As in the first study, we examined students' problem definitions and how they might be related to planning to prevent problems from occurring. More specifically we examined whether the task and/or social nature of students' problem definitions were related to greater anticipation of and preparation for their problems. Two separate Analyses of Variance (ANOVAs) for problems at Interviews 1 and 2 were performed, with how well students were able to see the problem coming as the dependent measure, and task, social definitions, and grade level as independent variables. The main effect of task definition was significant F (2, 40) = 4.956, $p < .05$ for problems elicited at the first interview, indicating that students reported greater anticipation of the problem if they defined the problem in terms of at least some task components (means of 2.87, 3.53, and 3.39 for levels of task definition of *none, some,* and *a lot*). No other effects were significant. The ANOVA for the problems elicited at the second interview yielded no significant effects, although the means for task definition were in the same direction as the first problem. The ANOVAs examining problem definition and reports of whether students prepared to prevent the anticipated problem from occurring did not yield any significant effects. Thus, the results are somewhat consistent with those from the life-span study in that adolescents were more likely to anticipate problems if they contained some task elements, which may have involved some of the competence-type goals examined in the life-span study.

Prediction of Future Problems.   A different picture of planning emerged when we examined students' predictions about future problems. Recall that students were asked at the first interview to predict as many problems as they could that might occur when working on the project. Students predicted that on average 2.25 problems would occur in the future. There were no grade and/or project differences in the number of problems predicted.[6] We did find grade and/or project differences in the number of predicted problems that students reported actually occurred at Time 2; $X = .61$ for sixth graders, $X = 1.3$ for eighth graders ($F(1, 59) = 6.89$, $p = .01$). It would appear that this difference is more of a grade difference than a project difference as there were no differences in the types of predicted problems across grade and project. Of these students 42% reported that the problem they predicted as most likely to occur at Time 1 actually did occur by the second interview.

At the first interview we found that students believed that they could do something to prevent the occurrence of their anticipated problems. For instance, when students were asked if there was anything they could do to prevent the problem that they thought was most likely to occur in the future, 86.2% of the sixth graders and 89.2% of the eighth graders said

---

[6]In the present study we cannot separate out grade effects from effects of project as they are confounded.

"yes." In addition, in the second interview, 85.7% of sixth graders and 84.6% of eighth graders reported that they executed the plan that they described at the first interview to prevent the problem. These findings are in contrast to the results for postdiction, which suggest that students are unlikely to do anything to prevent anticipated problems from happening. It is possible that our questioning students about strategies they could use to deal with problems set in motion a set of planning processes that students may not have used otherwise (Sherman, 1980). However, if true, this did not generalize to preparing to prevent other problems, as students were not more likely to report making preparations for their experienced problem at the second interview than for their experienced problem at the first interview.

We then explored reasons for the differential frequency with which individuals reported planning to prevent problems from occurring when these planning attempts were described postdictively (at Time 3 in Fig. 9.1) versus predictively (Time 1). These differences were not due to students mentioning different sorts of problems in these two instances (virtually no differences existed between problems reported at Interview 2 compared to those predicted at Interview 1) nor to students reporting to use different sorts of strategies in these two instances. We also looked closely at what distinguished individuals whose predicted problem occurred versus those whose predicted problem did not occur. Students who reported that their predicted problem occurred rated the problem at the first interview as more likely to occur than did those whose problem did not occur (means of 3.61 versus 3.19, respectively, $F(1, 53) = 5.6, p < .05$). However, these students did not differ from students whose problems did not occur in whether they thought there was anything they could do to stop the problem, how much perceived control they believed they had over stopping the problem at Interview 1, or whether they reported at Interview 2 doing what they said they were going to do to stop the problem from happening.

In summary, the results from this study indicate both differences and similarities between problem anticipation and prevention examined postdictively versus predictively. The differences between problem anticipation and prevention lie primarily in the reported frequency with which planning to prevent problems occurs. Although in both the cases of postdiction and prediction, individuals reported that they were able to anticipate that problems might occur, in postdiction they largely reported doing nothing to prevent the problem's occurrence. In prediction, however, the vast majority of individuals reported strategies to prevent the problem and actually reported using those strategies at a later time.

As mentioned earlier, the large number of individuals reporting that they anticipated that their problem would occur postdictively may be an illustration of the hindsight bias (e.g., Fischoff, 1977; Hawkins & Hastie, 1990). One finding from this study, however, would seem to argue against hindsight bias being completely responsible for these effects. That is, individuals who correctly predicted at Interview 1 a problem's occurrence by

Interview 2, rated these predicted problems as being more likely to occur at Interview 1 than individuals whose predicted problems did not occur. This higher perceived likelihood of occurrence before the problem occurred indicates some foresight about the probability of occurrence that is in line with the problem's occurrence. However, to fully address the role of the hindsight bias in these data, future research will need to assess individuals' subjective likelihoods of problem occurrence both before and after the problem occurs.

These differences in the frequency of planning for postdiction and prediction must be tempered by the fact that not all of the planning attempts were successful. Only slightly more than half of the students reported that the problem they predicted did not occur. Although we do not know if the problem's lack of occurrence was due to something the student directly did to prevent it or due to poor prediction of a problem, we do know that the majority of individuals reported that they did execute the strategy they thought would have been useful in preventing the problem. It is possible that the higher rate of planning when assessed predictively versus postdictively reflects students' optimism about their ability to prevent problems from occurring (see also Weinstein, 1980).

Recent work on the planning fallacy by Buehler, Griffin, and Ross (1994) provided an intriguing mechanism for the potentially optimistic views of our students when they were oriented toward the future. Their work suggested that when individuals make predictions they rarely consider their own experiences with such tasks. They argue that the forward nature of prediction makes it unlikely that individuals will look to the past for relevant experiences to inform their predictions. Even when individuals in their studies were focused on relevant past experiences, individuals made attributions for past failures that diminished the relevance of past experience to the prediction at hand. That is, individuals attributed past overestimation of events to external and unstable causes. In our study, then, when students anticipated the occurrence of a future event, they may have done so with a problem definition that was not informed by past experience and thus overestimated the likelihood of successful prevention attempts. Future research would benefit from the sort of "think aloud" procedures utilized by Buehler et al. to examine the thought processes underlying individuals' anticipation and plans to prevent problems from occurring.

SUMMARY AND CONCLUSIONS

In this chapter, we explored individual differences in planning to prevent everyday problems in a framework that emphasizes the role of individuals' definitions of their activities in understanding aspects of the problem-solving process. In our work we found evidence for a link between the nature of individuals' problem definitions and the planning attempts that individuals report using to prevent problems from occurring, as well as the strategies individuals report using to deal with problems once they do occur. In the first study, we found developmental differences largely in preadolescents' reported ability to anticipate a problem's occurrence and in the strategies utilized by different age groups to prevent the problem's occurrence.

Developmental differences were not found, however, in whether individuals prepared to prevent an anticipated problem. These age differences in planning were related to the interpersonal versus competence focus of individuals' problem definitions. For example, preadolescents were much less likely to anticipate problems that they defined as having an interpersonal focus than problems they defined as involving competence components only. In addition, for all age groups, problems that contained neither interpersonal nor competence components were much less likely to be associated with anticipation and preparation to prevent their occurrence.

In the second study we examined adolescents' planning by comparing their reports of prevention for a problem that did occur (postdiction) with their reports of prevention for a future anticipated problem that had not yet occurred (prediction). In general, similar to the results for preadolescents in the life-span study, individuals who defined the problem that actually occurred in terms of task components were more likely to report anticipating the problem's occurrence. In contrast to the life-span study, however, social definitions were not related to adolescents' lower level of anticipation of the problem's occurrence. The differences found in these two studies may be due to the different nature of adolescents' social definitions in these two contexts. In the life-span study the other individuals whom the adolescents were trying to influence were much more powerful than the preadolescents themselves (i.e., teachers, parents). In the study of collaborative problem solving, individuals were primarily trying to influence the behavior of their peers who were of more equal power. Individuals who perceive they are less powerful than those they are trying to influence may be less likely to anticipate their social problems (Cowan, Drinkard, & MacGavin, 1984)

In the study of collaborative problem solving, although the frequency of preparation varied depending on whether it was examined postdictively or predictively, numerous similarities were found in the types of problems reported and the strategies utilized to prevent the problems' occurrence. The differential frequency of planning and preparation attempts as examined predictively versus postdictively may be due to an additional source of problem definition not examined in the present studies. Based on the work of Buehler et al., we discussed how it may be important to examine whether individuals' problem definitions contain relevant information about similar problem experiences. We speculate that individuals' prediction attempts are less likely to be based on relevant past experiences, whereas their reflections on problems after they have occurred are so informed.

Our discussion thus far has described how problem definitions may lead individuals to anticipate and prevent everyday problems from occurring. However, an alternative direction of influence among these variables is also possible, and in fact quite probable given the present studies. As reflected in our model (see Fig. 9.1), problem definitions evolve and change throughout the problem-solving process and are most certainly updated over time. An important source of feedback for updating such problem definitions may be how successful the individual was in preparing for and dealing with the problem. For instance, an individual who predicts and prepares for future problems and who is unsuccessful at preventing such problems may attribute that failure to factors external to himself or herself, such as other people (see Buehler et al., 1994). Such attributions may be associated with perceptions that others are in control and may be reflected in an interpersonal definition of the problem situation. Future research should examine the relation between problem interpretations and planning both before and after problem prevention attempts are made to understand the potential direction of influence. In addressing this question, it will be important to utilize more experimental procedures to control for the impact of anticipation and preparation (e.g., Sherman, 1980).

These two studies illustrate the importance of the social context in understanding planning to prevent everyday problems from occurring. In the life-span study, a large percentage of individuals' reported preparations for dealing with problems involved shaping and changing other people's behaviors. Another social aspect of planning to prevent problems that has largely been unexamined in the present studies is the occurrence of what Goodnow (1987) referred to as using others as *co-planners*, where planners work collaboratively toward the completion of a plan. Our ongoing research with adolescents in group settings is beginning to examine how such collaborative planning may take place when students are actually engaged in working on their project in their groups.

Although the two studies reported here are an important step toward understanding individual differences in planning to prevent problems from occurring, numerous questions remain. First, the role that activity and problem definitions may play in individuals' planning attempts should be further explored. Aspects of individuals' representations in addition to their interpersonal and/or competence content should be explored for understanding problem prevention. For instance, the level of abstraction (e.g., Vallacher & Wegner, 1987) of anticipated problem definitions may be important because the more concrete level of problem definitions may lead to more concrete planning attempts. The degree of internal versus external control over problem situations would also be informative for understanding the frequency of problem prevention attempts. In addition, the extent to which prior experience is present in one's problem definition should be examined to better understand how such definitions influence the problem anticipation and prevention process. As Buehler et al. (1994) suggested, an individual's planning attempts may be improved when past experience is utilized to make predictions and plans for the future.

Second, in some sense these studies give us a better sense of why individuals do not plan, rather than why they do plan. Future research should explore why individuals do prepare to prevent their future anticipated problems from occurring, and whether such attempts provide some adaptive advantage. In this regard, it will be important to understand the process whereby individuals anticipate and plan to prevent their problems from occurring (Aspinwall & Taylor, in press). Computer simulation models of planning, such as Hammond's (1990) case-based planner, may be useful in mapping out this process and how the process may utilize memories of past experiences. In addition, individual difference factors that may lead individuals to plan for their everyday problems will need to be explored. Factors such as individuals' broader future time perspective (see Nurmi, 1991, for a review), familial influences on planning (see Benson, chapter 3, & Haith, chapter 2, this volume), personality profiles such as defensive pessimists (e.g., Norem & Illingworth, 1993; Showers, 1992) and broader self-conceptions (see Markus & Nurius, 1986, notion of feared selves) may be important to consider.

Third, the data reported here begin to address motivational reasons for individuals' failure to plan to prevent a problem, but further work is needed. Our work provides evidence that when individuals are not focused toward achieving goals in their everyday problem situations, they are much less likely to anticipate problems and to report preparing to prevent problems, even when those problems are anticipated. Furthermore, in planning to prevent a problem's occurrence one must acknowledge that a negative outcome is possible, and expend resources in dealing with that potential negative outcome. However, individuals appear reluctant to focus on potential negative outcomes (e.g., Buehler et al., 1994; Taylor & Brown, 1988). Our life-span study supports this reluctance of individuals to focus on negative outcomes; individuals most frequently mentioned that they did not prepare to prevent an anticipated problem because they did not realize the severity of the consequences. In addition, individuals focused on more positive experiences when they were not specifically directed to relate a problem (see Sansone & Berg, 1993; Sansone & Morgan, 1992). It is possible that individuals may have been relatively poor at predicting their problem's occurrence and preparing for its occurrence when it was predicted, because they found thinking of other more positive experiences more rewarding. Future work must thus include investigations of why individuals may choose to plan, in addition to whether and how they plan.

The view of planning to prevent everyday problems from occurring that emerges from our work is that planning can be understood within the context of individuals' definitions of everyday problem situations. Because these definitions reflect numerous individual and contextual characteristics, our work seeks to enlarge the view of successful planning from a view that focuses on cognitive abilities that underlie success to the social and motivational features that may also play a role in the successful prevention of everyday problems. Planning is not simply dependent on the individual's cognitive abilities and experience. Rather, planning is influenced by the larger context in which that planning takes place, and perhaps more importantly, the person's representation of that context. We believe that the importance of activity and problem definitions is not limited to planning to prevent everyday problems, but extends to nearly all planning attempts, particularly where the goal is somewhat ill-defined. Future research must examine the myriad ways in which planners define their problems in attempting to meet their goals.

ACKNOWLEDGMENTS

Study 1 was supported by grant HD 25728 from the National Institute of Child and Human Development and the National Institute of Aging awarded to Carol Sansone and Cynthia A. Berg, by a University of Research Committee Grant awarded to Cynthia A. Berg, and by grants from the Spencer Foundation and NIH Biomedical Research Support Program (BRSG S07 RR07092) awarded to Carol Sansone. Study 2 was supported by a Spencer Fellowship awarded from the National Academy of Education and a University of Research Committee Grant, both awarded to Cynthia A. Berg. The paper was prepared, in part, while Cynthia Berg was a visiting scientist at the Max Planck Institute for Human Development and Education, Berlin. Much appreciation is expressed to Paul Baltes, Ulman Lindenberger, Jacqui Smith, and Ursula Staudinger for comments on ideas presented in this chapter. JoNell Strough was supported by a Marriner S. Eccles Graduate Fellowship in Political Economy while writing this chapter. We would like to thank Sarah Friedman, Ellin Scholnick, Britt Abraham, and Carolyn Morgan for their comments on an earlier draft of this paper. We would also like to thank Carolyn Morgan and Charlene Weir for their assistance in the first study and numerous undergraduate assistants for their help in coding: Kristie Della-Piana, Alyson Fearnley, Kayleen Goodwin, Tami Ishimatsu, Rebecca Merrill, Tonya Myrup, Chad Allred, Greg Moll, Christy Callister, Mindy Russell, Mark Tresedor, Tanya Walters, and Janet Williams.

REFERENCES

Aspinwall, L. G. & Taylor, S. E. (in press). A stitch in time: Self-regulation and proactive coping. *Psychological Bulletin.*

234 Berg et al.

Baltes, P. B. (1987). Theoretical propositions of life-span developmental psychology: On the dynamics between growth and decline. *Developmental Psychology, 23,* 611–626.

Band, E., & Weisz, J. R. (1988). How to feel better when it feels bad: Children's perspectives on coping with everyday stress. *Developmental Psychology, 24,* 247–253.

Bandura, A. (1986). *Social foundations of thought and action: A social cognitive theory.* Englewood Cliffs, NJ: Prentice-Hall.

Berg, C. A. (1989). Knowledge of strategies for dealing with everyday problems from childhood through adolescence. *Developmental Psychology, 25,* 607–618.

Berg, C. A., & Calderone, K. S. (1994). The role of problem interpretations in understanding the development of everyday problem solving. In R. J. Sternberg & R. K. Wagner (Eds.), *Mind in context: Interactionist perspectives on human intelligence* (pp. 105–132). New York: Cambridge University Press.

Berg, C. A., Klaczynski, P. A., Calderone, K. S., & Strough, J. (1994). Adult age differences in cognitive strategies: Adaptive or deficient? In J. Sinnott (Ed.), *Handbook of adult lifespan learning* (pp. 371–388). Westport, CT: Greenwood.

Berg, C. A., & Sansone, C. (1991, April). To plan or not to plan?: Individual and contextual factors involved in planning to prevent everyday problems from recurring. In C. Berg & C. Sansone (Chairs), *New directions in the development of planning: Cognitive, social, and motivational components.* Symposium conducted at the Society for Research in Child Development, Seattle, WA.

Berg, C. A., Strough, J., Calderone, K. S., Sansone, C., & Weir, C. (in press). The role of problem definitions in understanding age and context effects on strategies for solving everyday problems. *Psychology and Aging.*

Blanchard-Fields, F., & Norris, L. (1994). Causal attributions from adolescence through adulthood: Age differences, ego level, and generalized response style. *Aging and Cognition, 1,* 67–86.

Buehler, R., Griffin, D., & Ross, M. (1994). Exploring the "planning fallacy": Why people underestimate their task completion times. *Journal of Personality and Social Psychology, 67,* 366–381.

Calderone, K. (1993). *The impact of children and adolescent's definitions of everyday problems on strategy effectiveness ratings.* Unpublished master's thesis, University of Utah, Salt Lake City.

Chalmers, D., & Lawrence, J. A. (1993). Investigating the effects of planning aids on adults' and adolescents' organization of a complex task. *International Journal of Behavioral Development, 16,* 191–214.

Cornelius, S. W., & Caspi, A. (1987). Everyday problem solving in adulthood and old age. *Psychology and Aging, 2,* 144–153.

Cowan, G., Drinkard, J., & MacGavin, L. (1984). The effects of target, age, and gender on use of power strategies. *Journal of Personality and Social Psychology, 47,* 1391–1398.

Denney, N. W. (1989). Everyday problem solving: Methodological issues, research findings, and a model. In L. W. Poon, D. C. Rubin, & B. A. Wilson (Eds.), *Everyday cognition in adulthood and late life* (pp. 330–351). Cambridge, England: Cambridge University Press.

Dixon, R. A. (1992). Contextual approaches to adult intellectual development. In R. J. Sternberg & C. A. Berg (Eds.), *Intellectual development* (pp. 350–380). Cambridge, MA: Cambridge University Press.

Dodge, K. A., Asher, S. R., & Parkhurst, J. T. (1989). Social life as a goal-coordination task. In C. Ames & R. Ames (Eds.), *Research on motivation and education: Vol. 3. Goals and cognitions* (pp. 107–135). New York: Academic Press.

Dodge, K. A., Pettit, G. S., McClaskey, C. L., & Brown, M. M. (1986). Social competence in children. *Monographs of the Society for Research in Child Development, 51,* 1–83.

Dreher, M., & Oerter, R. (1987). Action planning competencies during adolescence and early adulthood. In S. L. Friedman, E. K. Scholnick, & R. R. Cocking (Eds.), *Blueprints for thinking: The role of planning in cognitive development* (pp. 321–355). Cambridge, England: Cambridge University Press.

Erikson, E. (1963). *Childhood and society.* New York: Norton.

Fischhoff, B. (1977). Perceived informativeness of facts. *Journal of Experimental Psychology: Human Perception and Performance, 3,* 349–358.

Folkman, S., Lazarus, R. S., Pimley, S., & Novacek, J. (1987). Age differences in stress and coping processes. *Psychology and Aging, 2,* 171–184.

Forman, E. A., & McPhail, J. (1993). Vygotskian perspective on children's collaborative problem-solving activities. In E. A. Forman, N. Minick, & C. A. Stone (Eds.), *Contexts for learning: Sociocultural dynamics in children's development* (pp. 213–229). New York: Oxford University Press.

Friedman, S. L., Scholnick, E. K., & Cocking, R. R. (Eds.). (1987). *Blueprints for thinking: The role of planning in cognitive development.* Cambridge, England: Cambridge University Press.

Gauvain, M., & Rogoff, B. (1989). Collaborative problem solving and children's planning skills. *Developmental Psychology, 25,* 139–151.

Goodnow, J. J. (1987). Social aspects of planning. In S. L. Friedman, E. K. Scholnick, & R. R. Cocking (Eds.), *Blueprints for thinking: The role of planning in cognitive development* (pp. 179–201). Cambridge, England: Cambridge University Press.

Ham, M., & Larson, R. (1990). The cognitive moderation of daily stress in early adolescence. *American Journal of Community Psychology, 18,* 567–585.

Hammond, K. J. (1990). Case-based planning: A framework for planning from experience. *Cognitive Science, 14,* 385–443.

Hawkins, S. A., & Hastie, R. (1990). Hindsight: Biased judgments of past events after the outcomes are known. *Psychological Bulletin, 107,* 311–327.

Hayes-Roth, B., & Hayes-Roth, F. (1979). A cognitive model of planning. *Cognitive Science, 3,* 275–310.

Hudson, J. A., & Fivush, R. (1991). Planning in the preschool years: The emergence of plans from general event knowledge. *Cognitive Development, 6,* 393–415.

Klaczynski, P. A., & Berg, C. A. (1992, April). *What's the real problem: Age, perceived control and perceived difficulty as predictors of everyday problem definitions.* Paper presented at Cognitive Aging Conference, Atlanta, GA.

Kreitler, S., & Kreitler, H. (1987). Conceptions and processes of planning: The developmental perspective. In S. L. Friedman, E. K. Scholnick, & R. R. Cocking (Eds.), *Blueprints for thinking: The role of planning in cognitive developmnt* (pp. 110–178). Cambridge, England: Cambridge University Press.

Lachman, M. E., & Burack, O. R. (1993). Planning and control processes across the life span: An overview. *International Journal of Behavioral Development, 16,* 131–143.

Laipple, J. S. (1991). *Problem solving in young and old adulthood: The role of task interpretation.* Unpublished doctoral dissertation, West Virginia University.

Lazarus, R. S., & Folkman, S. (1984). *Stress, appraisal, and coping.* New York: Springer.

Lewin, K. (1936). *Principles of topological psychology.* New York: McGraw-Hill.

Lewin, K. (1951). *Field theory in social science: Selected theoretical papers* (D. Cartwright, Ed.). New York: Harper & Row.

Markus, H., & Nurius, P. (1986). Possible selves. *American Psychologist, 41,* 954–969.

Meacham, J. A., & Emont, N. C. (1989). The interpersonal basis of everyday problem solving. In J. D. Sinnott (Ed.), *Everyday problem solving* (pp. 7–23). New York: Praeger.

Morgan, C. (1993). *Gender differences in attributions: The effects of problem domain and goal type.* Unpublished master's thesis, University of Utah, Salt Lake City.

Newell, A., & Simon, H. A. (1972). *Human problem solving.* Englewood Cliffs, NJ: Prentice-Hall.

Norem, J. K., & Illingworth, K. S. S. (1993). Strategy-dependent effects of reflecting on self and tasks: Some implications of optimism and defensive pessimism. *Journal of Personality and Social Psychology, 65,* 822–835.

Nurmi, J. (1991). How do adolescents see their future? A review of the development of future orientation and planning. *Developmental Review, 11,* 1–59.

Nurmi, J. E., Pulliainen, H., & Salmela-Aro, K. (1992). Age differences in adults' control beliefs related to life goals and concerns. *Psychology and Aging, 7,* 194–196.

Oppenheimer, L. (1987). Cognitive and social variables in the plan of action. In S. L. Friedman, E. K. Scholnick, & R. R. Cocking (Eds.), *Blueprints for thinking: The role of planning in cognitive development* (pp. 356–394). Cambridge, England: Cambridge University Press.

Rogoff, B. (1982). Integrating context and development. In M. E. Lamb & A. L. Brown, (Eds.), *Advances in developmental psychology* (Vol. 2, pp. 125–170). Hillsdale, NJ: Lawrence Erlbaum Associates.

Rogoff, B. (1990). *Apprenticeship in thinking: Cognitive development in social context.* Cambridge, MA: Harvard University Press.

Rubin, K. H., & Rose-Krasnor, L. (1992). Interpersonal problem solving and social competence in children. In V. B. Van Hasselt & M. Hersen (Eds.), *Handbook of social development: A lifespan perspective* (pp. 283–323). New York: Plenum.

Sansone, C., & Berg, C. A. (1993). Adapting to the environment across the life span: Different process or different inputs? *International Journal of Behavioral Development, 16*, 215–241.

Sansone, C., & Morgan, C. (1992). Intrinsic motivation and education: Competence in context. *Motivation and Emotion, 16*, 249–270.

Scholnick, E. K., & Friedman, S. L. (1993). Planning in context: Developmental and situational considerations. *International Journal of Behavioral Development, 16*, 145–167.

Sherman, S. J. (1980). On the self-erasing nature of errors of prediction. *Journal of Personality and Social Psychology, 39*, 211–221.

Showers, C. (1992). The motivational and emotional consequences of considering positive or negative possibilities for an upcoming event. *Journal of Personality and Social Psychology, 63*, 474–484.

Showers, C., & Ruben, C. (1990). Distinguishing defensive pessimism from depression negative expectations and positive coping mechanism. *Cognitive Therapy and Research, 14*, 385–399.

Sinnott, J. D. (1989). A model for solution of ill-structured problems: Implications for everyday and abstract problem solving. In J. D. Sinnott (Ed.), *Everyday problem solving: Theory and applications* (pp. 72–99). New York: Praeger.

Smith, J., & Baltes, P. B. (1990). Wisdom-related knowledge: Age/cohort differences in response to life-planning problems. *Developmental Psychology, 26*, 494–505.

Strough, J., Berg, C. A., & Sansone, C. (1996). Goals for solving everyday problems across the life span: Age and gender differences in the salience of interpersonal concerns. *Developmental Psychology, 32*, 1106–1115.

Tabachnick, B. G., & Fidell, L. S. (1989). *Using multivariate statistics* (2nd ed.). New York: Harper & Row.

Taylor, S. E., & Brown, J. D. (1988). Illusion and well-being: A social psychological perspective on mental health. *Psychological Bulletin, 103*, 193–210.

Vallacher, R. R., & Wegner, D. M. (1987). What do people think they're doing: Action identification and human behavior. *Psychological Review, 94*, 3–15.

Veroff, J., & Veroff, J. B. (1980). *Social incentives: A life-span developmental approach*. New York: Academic Press.

Weinstein, N. D. (1980). Unrealistic optimism about future life events. *Journal of Personality and Social Psychology, 39*, 806–820.

Wentzel, K. R. (1991). Social and academic goals at school: Motivation and achievement in context. In M. L. Maehr & P. R. Pintrich (Eds.), *Advances in motivation and achievement* (pp. 185–212). Greenwich, CT: JAI Press.

Wood, P. K. (1983). Inquiring systems and problem structure: Implications for cognitive development. *Human Development, 26*, 249–265.

IV

Motivational and Personality Influences on Planning

10

Goal Setting, Planning, and Performance on Work Tasks for Individuals and Groups

Edwin A. Locke
Cathy C. Durham
University of Maryland

June M. L. Poon
Universiti Kebangsaan, Malaysia

Elizabeth Weldon
Indiana University

For the past 30 years, the first author and colleagues have studied the conscious, motivational determinants of performance on work tasks. Our approach involves three major concepts: goals, plans or task strategies, and performance. We define a *goal* as the object or aim of an action. (Our research is concerned only with conscious goals.) We define a *plan* as a procedure or means for attaining a goal. We use the terms *plan* and *task strategy* (a procedure for going about a task or achieving a goal on a task) more or less interchangeably. By *performance*, we mean how well one does on a task.

Our research focused primarily on the effects of different types of goals and strategies on performance of work tasks. For example, we examined whether research scientists are more productive if they try for specific, challenging goals or the goal of simply doing their best. We have also studied whether different types of goals, such as those just mentioned, lead to better or worse strategies for performing the task. Our work involved mainly adults working on laboratory or organizational tasks for periods ranging from minutes to years. Some studies assigned goals to subjects, whereas others let subjects set their own goals. More than 88 different tasks (ranging from brainstorming and reaction time to managerial work) were used, as well as numerous types of performance measures (quantity, quality, speed, etc.).

The result of this research program has been a theory of goal setting and task performance (Locke & Latham, 1990). The main tenets of the theory are that: (a) specific, difficult goals lead to higher levels of task performance than goals that are non-specific (e.g., "do your best") or easy; (b) goal-performance relationships are stronger when there is feedback showing progress in relation to the goal (as a corollary, goals mediate the effects of feedback on performance); (c) goals regulate performance more effectively when there is commitment to the goals, especially when goals are difficult; (d) commitment is highest when people believe that high performance or goal attainment is both possible and important; (e) participation in setting goals is no more effective in attaining commitment than assigning people goals as long as they are given a plausible rationale for the goal; (f) high self-efficacy (Bandura, 1986) promotes high performance independently of goals; and (g) self-efficacy also affects the level at which individuals set their own personal goals and their degree of commitment to hard, assigned goals. (Self-efficacy clearly has much in common with the concept of perceived control, which Schmitz and Skinner, 1993, and Skinner, 1992, have found to be an important factor in student motivation).

The majority of goal-setting studies have been carried out with individuals using fairly simple tasks. In recent years, however, there have been an increasing number of studies using group goals and/or somewhat complex tasks. As we will show, as tasks become more complex, the selection of appropriate plans or task strategies becomes increasingly important.

This chapter includes an integrated review of the findings of studies of goals and task strategies, including those that used groups as the unit of analysis. We also examine the group decision-making and problem-solving literatures insofar as they seem relevant to the issue of how groups develop effective plans for reaching goals.

INDIVIDUAL GOALS AND PLANNING

How do individual goals affect performance? Three mechanisms are brought into play habitually if not automatically once a person commits to a goal and decides to act on it (Locke & Latham, 1990). First, goals energize people to exert effort in proportion to the demands of the goal. Second, they motivate individuals to persist over time in pursuit of the goal. Third, they focus attention on what the person is attempting to accomplish. For example, consider a child playing a video game. Determined to "beat the game," the child is entranced (directed attention) in the world of video images. Hands perspiring and thumbs racing (effort), he ignores parents' calls for dinner, refusing to budge until the goal is accomplished (persistence).

Planning for Goal-Directed Tasks

In some situations, however, habitual mechanisms are insufficient for goal attainment, and the person must use his or her cognitive resources to develop strategies or action plans for performing the task (Locke & Latham, 1990). The child who easily manipulates a video game controller, for example, will have to discover new strategies for mastering another type of hardware such as a computer keyboard. Although there are no guarantees that the action plans selected will be appropriate (e.g., the child might decide that the "hunt and peck" approach is the most efficient way to learn the keyboard), planning generally increases one's likelihood of success. Because the discovery of new task strategies is not automatic, planning is considered an indirect mechanism for goal attainment. Klahr and Robinson (1981), Trabasso, Stein, Rodkin, Munger, and Baughn (1992), Trabasso and Stein (in press), and Welsh (1991) have found that children begin to grasp the idea of purposive planning around age 3 to 4.

Goals affect planning in at least three ways. First, goals stimulate the *execution* of known strategies. When confronted with a goal, people ask themselves how it might be achieved. If the task is simple or familiar, so that individuals have a repertoire of relevant knowledge and experience, developing a suitable plan is a straightforward matter. They simply put into effect a known plan based on past experience. The fourth-grader who is assigned the goal of learning the 50 state capitals may recall, for example, that flash cards worked well in the third grade when she was learning the multiplication tables and, therefore, may decide to use flash cards for her new learning task. It has been shown in numerous studies of nonsupervisory employees (Adam, 1975; Buller & Bell, 1986; Das, 1982; Kim, 1984; Latham & Baldes, 1975; Latham & Saari, 1982; McCuddy & Griggs, 1984), supervisory and management personnel (Bandura & Simon, 1977; Blau, Blank, & Katerberg, 1987; Campbell & Gingrich, 1986; Chesney & Locke, 1991; Lombardo, Hull, & Singer, 1983; Stedry & Kay, 1964), and other people (Earley & Perry, 1987; Klein, Whitener, & Ilgen, 1990; Locke & Bryan, 1966; Shaw, 1984; Terborg, 1976; Terborg & Miller, 1978) that when given a goal, individuals select and execute known task strategies spontaneously.

Similarly, goals enhance the utilization of strategies that have been explicitly taught, provided, or primed. In a study in which subjects were trained or "primed" with cognitive strategy information through either open or unobtrusive means, Earley and Perry (1987) found that specific, hard goals had the effect of enhancing the use of a primed strategy. This effect could either be beneficial or detrimental to the performance of subjects with goals, depending on whether the strategy matched the task. Moreover, when a task requires a broad search for strategy options or creative problem solving, focusing narrowly on a primed strategy may detract from strategy development for goal attainment (Janis & Mann, 1977). Several studies found that goals and strategies have interactive effects on performance. Shaw (1984) found subjects given both specific, difficult goals and effective task strategies performed better than subjects in other conditions. Earley, Lee, and Lituchy (1989) found that strategy training for a complex task had a significant effect for subjects with hard goals or learning goals, but not for subjects with do-your-best goals. Without strategy training, hard goals worked less well than do-your-best goals or learning goals because hard goal subjects picked poorer strategies than the subjects with the other two types of goals. Neale, Northcraft, and Earley (1987) found that hard goal subjects benefitted more from training than subjects with other goals.

Second, goals affect planning by influencing the *amount of planning* in which individuals engage. Studies have shown that specific, hard goals stimulate more planning than do-your-best goals (Earley & Perry, 1987; Earley, Wojnaroski, & Prest, 1987). A 15-year-old is likely to engage in more planning if her goal is to earn $3,000 to purchase her first car next summer than if her goal is more nebulous, less valued, or less immediate (e.g., saving for college). Earley (1986, 1988) found that goals plus specific performance feedback led to more reported planning than goals plus general feedback. This would suggest that teenagers saving money for a car will plan more if they receive regular reports about the growth of their savings accounts.

Third, goals can influence the *quality of planning*. Earley, Northcraft, Lee, and Lituchy (1990) found that specific, hard goals increased the probability that subjects would request useful information from a database and develop a high-quality investment strategy, compared to people working with do-your-best goals. These effects were enhanced if subjects were given outcome feedback and information as to the potential usefulness of the various items in the database. Chesney and Locke (1991) found that specific, challenging goals were associated with higher planning quality in a business strategy computer simulation. Finally, Siegler and Shrager (1984), in studies of children solving addition and subtraction problems, found that children changed their strategies as a function of the difficulty of the problems as well as experience. These data suggest that when goals are easy, individuals believe that success is certain no matter how they approach the task and, therefore, feel no need to plan carefully. But, as goal difficulty increases, the likelihood of planning increases.

Less planning might also be expected if goals were seen as impossible because failure would be certain regardless of attempts to plan. In line with this prediction, Earley, Shalley, and Northcraft (1992) found that goals that are challenging but attainable (i.e., moderate) are less likely to be immediately accepted or rejected by individuals than are easy or impossible goals, presumably because individuals need time to think about whether they want to commit to challenging goals. In addition, Earley et al. (1992) found that task strategy quality was partly a function of the amount of time spent deciding whether to accept or reject a goal and suggested that the additional cognitive processing that an individual engages in while deciding to accept a moderate goal may enhance insight concerning task strategies. Not surprisingly, moderate goals led to the best performance due to being associated with superior strategies.

Complex Tasks

Goal setting under conditions of task complexity has been the subject of considerable research in recent years (Earley, Connolly, & Ekegren, 1989; Earley, Hanson, & Lee, 1986; Gilliland & Landis, 1992; Huber, 1985; Wood, Bandura, & Bailey, 1990). In line with Wood (1986) we define task complexity as being a function of (a) a component complexity (number of acts and/or cues involved), (b) coordinative complexity (type and number of relationships among acts and cues), and (c) dynamic complexity (changes in acts and cues and the relationships among them).

A meta-analysis of 125 goal-setting studies from 1966 to 1985 (Wood, Mento, & Locke, 1987) revealed that task complexity acted as a moderator of goal-setting effectiveness; the magnitude of goal effects on performance decreased as the complexity of the task increased. On average, specific, difficult goals led to performance increases of 12.15% for simple tasks, 9.12% for moderately complex tasks, and 7.79% for highly complex tasks. Furthermore, in three studies employing complex tasks, individuals assigned specific goals actually performed worse than those with do-your-best goals (Earley, Connolly, & Ekegren, 1989; Huber, 1985; Kanfer & Ackerman, 1988). The meta-analysis effects might be attributed to the fact that action planning is more difficult and plays a more important role in regulating task performance as task complexity increases. This is not to suggest that performance on complex tasks is simply a matter of good planning. Different people can use or implement the same strategy with markedly differing degrees of effectiveness due to differences in skill and self-efficacy (Bandura, 1982). Task strategies, however, are crucial moderators of the effects of goals on the performance of complex tasks.

Wood and Locke (1990) developed a model to explain the differential effect of goals for simple versus complex tasks, which incorporates and summarizes much of the discussion of this paper thus far. They proposed that goals bring into awareness a repertoire of stored strategies or plans of two general forms: *stored universal plans* (i.e., the three direct motivating mechanisms noted previously, viz., effort, persistence, and directed attention) and *stored task specific plans* (i.e., plans that are developed through previous experience and are more cognitive in nature than stored universal plans). If the stored task-specific plans are judged not to be applicable to the task, then the individual attempts to develop new task-specific plans. According to the model, the use of specific task strategies is more important for performance on complex tasks than on simple tasks, whereas the use of universal strategies is important in both cases. Thus, goals for simple tasks can be met using stored universal plans, but task-specific strategies are also required when the task is complex. The difficulties associated with developing and implementing task-specific plans weaken the relationship between goal level and performance.

Moreover, studies mentioned previously show that specific, difficult goals may actually contribute to this problem. That is, under some conditions, specific, difficult goals are less functional than general goals for stimulating effective strategies for complex tasks. Three conditions are discussed here and summarized in Fig. 10.1.

First, challenging goals may be dysfunctional when subjects have *no prior experience or training* at the task, so that there are no proven strategies or problem-solving processes on which to fall back. Earley, Lee, and Hanson (1990) noted that individuals in entry-level positions (who typically have little work experience) are generally exposed to a variety of relevant and irrelevant stimuli from the work context and from the job itself. Their attention is focused on defining the new job situation and clarifying and establishing their roles and identity within the work context. In such a situation, Earley, Lee, and Hansen (1990) suggested that goals should have little or even negative impact on performance because goals merely increase the amount of novel information that the individual must process and thus may promote confusion. They stated that this may explain Weed and Mitchell's (1980) finding that goals are not beneficial to an individual's performance on novel tasks requiring a great deal of information processing. Earley, Lee, and Hansen (1990) predicted, therefore, that goals should enhance strategies on complex tasks only after individuals have gained sufficient experience to become familiar with their jobs. That is, for inexperienced people working on complex tasks, any positive effect of goals may be lagged in time.

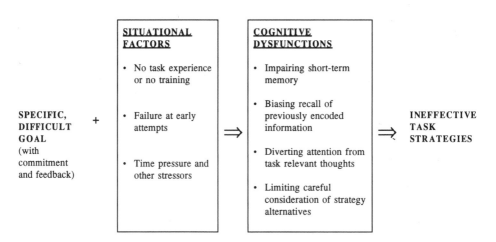

FIG 10.1. Effects of hard goals and situational factors on cognitive functions and strategy development for complex tasks.

Second, Cervone, Jiwani, and Wood (1991) suggested the possibility that hard goals lead to ineffective strategies because of the way individuals respond to *failure* with misdirected efforts to meet the goal. When there is a simple and direct relation between effort and performance (as is the case for simple tasks), dissatisfaction that enhances effort will positively affect goal attainment. On complex tasks, however, the effect of effort on performance is mediated by cognitive processes such as the testing and appraisal of alternatives or the development of novel, creative strategies. In this case, the negative effect of self-evaluation can undermine performance by impairing required short-term memory functions (Humphreys & Revelle, 1984), biasing recall of previously encoded information (Isen & Shalker, 1982; Isen, Shalker, Clark, & Karp, 1978), diverting attention from task-relevant thoughts (Sarason, Sarason, & Pierce, 1990), or limiting careful consideration of strategy alternatives (Bandura & Wood, 1989; Wood & Bandura, 1989; Wood et al., 1990).

Finally, the usual goal-setting findings are less likely to emerge when subjects have specific, difficult goals for a complex task and feel *pressure to perform well immediately.* Denied an opportunity to learn or experiment, subjects may develop tunnel vision, focusing more on the desire to get immediate results than on learning the best way of performing the task. Christensen-Szalanski (1980) found that time pressure led to less effective strategy choices. Earley, Lee, and Lituchy (1989) found that untrained subjects with a learning goal (as contrasted with a performance goal) performed better than those with a specific, hard goal. Minimizing anxiety producers such as performance pressure and rigid time constraints should facilitate goal planning and the learning of complex tasks and skills.

Gilliland and Landis (1992) in a stock-prediction task found that in the difficult task and easy quantity goal condition, difficult quality goals increased accuracy over easy quality goals. But in the difficult task and difficult quantity goal condition, difficult quality goals decreased accuracy over easy quality goals. Presumably, having difficult quantity and quality goals at the same time exerted too much pressure and even goal conflict. Subjects with easy quantity goals examined more information than subjects with difficult quantity goals. The main strategy promoting quantity was accessing fewer elements and searching rapidly, whereas a slower speed of search was associated with performance quality.

GROUP GOALS AND PLANNING

Although most of the empirical research on goal setting has been conducted at the individual level, a number of studies tested the effects of group goals on group performance (for reviews, see Locke & Latham, 1990; Weldon & Weingart, 1993). In these studies group goals (assigned or set by the group) defined the level of performance to be achieved by the group as a whole. At the group level at least two new issues potentially come into play as compared to the individual level, namely the effect of members on each other and the need for coordination of group activities. As in the case of individual goals, the group research showed that groups working toward specific, difficult goals outperform those working toward vague or easy goals (e.g. Becker, 1978; Buller & Bell, 1986; Weigart & weldon, 1991; Weldon, Jehn, & Pradhan, 1991). These studies also showed that group goals influence the direct motivational mechanisms known to mediate the individual goal effect. Group members focus more attention, work harder, and persist longer on a task when working toward a specific, difficult group goals (e.g. Weingart, 1992; Weingart & Weldon, 1991; Weldon et al. 1991). Thus stored universal strategies play a role in the group goal effect. In addition, these studies show that group goals produce better performance than individual goals for additive group tasks (e.g., Matsui, Kakuyama, & Onglatco, 1987) and those involving some interdependence among group members (e,g., Mitchell & Silver, 1990).

Planning in Groups

Four of these group studies also examined the role of planning and new task-specific plans. One study tested the effects of group goals on individual plans (Weingart & Weldon, 1991), two examined group plans (Smith, Locke, & Barry, 1990; Weingart, 1992), and one considered both (Weldon et al., 1991). Individual plans specify procedures for the performance of individual tasks assigned to group members, and the group plan specifies procedures to coordinate their actions. Together these four studies show that group goals can motivate group members to develop better individual and group strategies and that individual and group planning can contribute to improved group performance.

In the first study, Weingart and Weldon (1991) tested the effect of group goal difficulty on individual planning for a task with low coordination demands and limited interaction among group members (an additive task). In this study, groups of three to five students performed two trials of an idea-generation task in which group members worked alone to generate unusual uses for an object. Group performance was determined by summing the number of uses generated by each group member. After Trial 1, half the groups were assigned a specific, challenging group goal (total number of uses to be produced by summing the number produced by each group member), while the others continued working without a goal. The results showed that group members working toward the challenging goal were more likely to report that their individual performance strategy changed from Trial 1 to Trial 2, compared to group members who continued working without a goal. The results also showed a positive correlation between self-reports of strategy change and performance. Based on these results, we can conclude that (a) a group goal can motivate group members to engage in individual planning and strategy change, and (b) improvements to individual performance strategies can contribute to the group goal effect.

In the second study, Weldon et al. (1991) used an objective measure of individual strategy change (group members' actions captured on videotape) and found additional support for the importance of individual planning and strategy change. In this study, a production goal was assigned for a moderately complex task involving pooled and sequential interdependence (building Tinkertoy structures). After working on the task for 15 minutes, group members were told that their goal was to increase the number of structures produced by one or five during the next 15-minute session. Results showed that group members working toward the difficult group goal were more likely to improve their individual performance plans by rearranging their personal work space to create a more efficient layout, compared to group members working toward the easy goal, and these changes contributed to group performance. Group members in the difficult goal condition engaged in more group planning (measured by their discussion of who should do what, when, where, and how; what has been done; what needs to be done; and who is doing what to build the structure) and reported more change in group strategy compared to group members working toward an easy goal. Tests for mediation showed that group planning and reports of group strategy change also contributed to the group goal effect.

In a third study, Weingart (1992) tested the effects of goal difficulty and task component complexity (number of unique acts required to perform a task) on the quantity and quality of group planning. Weingart asked groups of three students to build Tinkertoy structures under one of four conditions in a 2 (goal difficulty) x 2 (task complexity) design. In the difficult goal condition, group members were told to produce nine structures. In the low goal condition, group members were told to produce three. In the low task complexity condition, the structure required three unique acts. In the high complexity condition, 11 unique acts were required. Results showed that task component complexity increased the quality of planning for supplies and reduced the quality of planning for coordination. The effect of task complexity on planning for supplies is consistent with the fact that increasing the number of unique acts also increased the number of unique supplies. Its effect on planning for coordination suggests that increased attention to supplies diverted attention from coordination. Contrary to earlier results, goal difficulty had no effect on quantity of planning. One possible explanation is that the task was new to group members in Weingart's experiment, whereas group members had previous experience with the task in earlier work. However, goal difficulty did increase the quality of planning for coordination. This last finding parallels somewhat the findings from the fourth study of group planning (Smith, Locke, & Barry, 1990). In that study, an organizational simulation game was used to examine the effect of assigned goals on planning quality. Results showed that specific, challenging goals enhanced the quality of planning (compared to vague goals), and planning quality was associated with increased performance. Weingart (1992), however, did not find a relationship between planning quality and performance. She attributed this result to the fact that coordination was possible through direct observation of other peoples' progress on their individual tasks, which reduced the importance of high quality planning.

Together these four studies show that increasing the quantity and quality of individual and group planning can contribute to the group goal effect. They also show that planning can be important when tasks require no interaction (Weingart & Weldon, 1991) and substantial interaction (Smith et al., 1990; Weingart, 1992; Weldon et al., 1991). However, there is still much to be learned about planning in goal-oriented groups.

First, potential moderators must be explored. Task complexity, work flow interdependence, experience with the task, availability of feedback (Weldon & Weingart, 1993), type of feedback, and barriers to interaction may all be important. The effects of task complexity, experience, and the presence or absence of feedback can be predicted from Locke and Latham's (1990) model of individual goals, whereas the effects of interdependence and interaction are peculiar to groups.

As explained by Locke and Latham, task complexity should moderate the effects of group goal level on planning because task complexity determines the complexity of the plan required for success and the extent to which alternative plans can be devised. Thus, little planning would be expected for a simple task, regardless of goal level. Planning, however, should increase with goal level when a complex task is involved. Task experience and feedback about progress toward the goal are expected to moderate the relationship between planning and performance because they both increase the likelihood of developing an effective plan. Task experience provides useful information, and feedback allows group members to assess the effectiveness of their current plan and their efforts to improve their plan. For feedback to be maximally effective, the type of feedback should be congruent with the type of goal (Saavedra, Earley, & Van Dyne, 1993). That is, group feedback should be given when group goals are involved.

Work flow interdependence among group members should influence planning because it determines the extent to which a plan for coordination (i.e., a group plan) is important to success. Group planning should increase with goal level when group members are interdependent, but remain low regardless of goal level when group members work independently. Barriers to interaction (actual or perceived) should moderate the impact of goals on planning because ease of communication should influence motivation to plan. Some indirect evidence for this hypothesis is provided by a study of how group goals and opportunity for group coordination influence motivation. In this study, Larson and Schaumann (1993) had groups of three people perform a task under varying levels of goal difficulty and coordination difficulty and found that a specific, difficult group goal had little effect on the motivation of individual group members when group members believed that barriers to coordination would impede goal attainment. Thus, it appears that perceived constraints can affect feelings of efficacy and, hence, motivation to plan.

Second, the nature of the planning process in goal-oriented groups should be researched. In her study, Weingart (1992) distinguished between *preplanning* and *inprocess planning* and found that the use of inprocess planning as a proportion of all planning increased with goal difficulty. The terms preplanning and inprocess planning are roughly equivalent to what B. Hayes-Roth and F. Hayes-Roth (1979) call top-down and bottom-up planning, respectively, in their cognitive model of planning. When group members use preplanning, they analyze the task and develop an action plan before they begin working on the task. When inprocess planning is used, group members determine the first few actions to be performed, perform those actions, and develop the remainder of the plan as they work. Weingart believes that difficult goals motivate inprocess planning because group members can plan as they learn more about the task. Future research might focus on conditions that motivate preplanning and inprocess planning and the conditions that influence their effectiveness (Weingart, 1992). The ad hoc and unintended aspects of strategy formation should also be assessed. Weldon (1994) suggested that group strategies often emerge inadvertently from ad hoc actions and decisions. That is, although group strategies may result from explicit attempts to analyze the task and develop a blueprint for future action as Weldon and Weingart (1993) and Weingart (1992) have suggested, in many cases group strategies emerge from the stream of ad hoc decisions made in response to unanticipated opportunities, sudden insights into work problems, and changing task demands. Mintzberg (1987; Mintzberg & McHugh, 1985) showed the importance of these emergent strategies in organizational strategy formation.

GROUP DECISION MAKING AND GROUP PLANNING

Knowing that group goals motivate group planning, it is worth asking, as a supplement to this work, whether implications exist for group planning in the group decision-making literature. It seems that many of the individual- and group-level factors known to influence group decision making (see, e.g., Hirokawa & Johnston's, 1989, model of group decision making) would have similar effects on group planning. Several important findings from studies of group decision making are considered here.

Individual Member Expertise

Considerable evidence suggests that the knowledge and expertise (ability) of individual group members are extremely important to the success of the group. In an extensive review of the literature, Hill (1982) concluded that group performance generally increases with the skills of its group members, and more recent studies support this finding. Using the Moon Survival task, Bottger and Yetton (1988) and Yetton and Bottger (1982) showed that group problem-solving effectiveness was a function of the degree to which task-relevant expertise was found among the group members, especially the two most knowledgeable members. In addition, Watson, Michaelsen, and Sharp's (1991) study of student groups showed that the competence of the best member, as well as average member competence, were highly correlated with group performance.

Of course, the relationship between member competence and group performance depends on the group's ability to recognize its most competent members and weight or utilize their suggestions more heavily than others. This is called a *best member* or *truth wins* strategy. Yetton and Bottger (1982) found that groups that followed a best member strategy (i.e., one in which the individual decision of a group's best member is adopted as the group's decision) were as effective as groups in which members made the decision together. Littlepage and Silbiger (1992) found that large groups were better able to recognize expertise than small ones.

Knowledge Seeking

When individual or group expertise is lacking, the seeking of additional knowledge would be expected, assuming that attaining more knowledge is possible. Knowledge seeking may be enhanced by the assignment of difficult goals, especially if existing knowledge resources are lacking within the group and additional information is attainable (Earley, Northcraft, Lee, & Lituchy, 1990).

Utilization of Distributed Expertise

Often expertise is not concentrated in one or two superior members but distributed across group members. That is, no single group member holds all the information needed to produce a good decision. In these situations, the most effective groups will (a) have large, heterogeneous (in knowledge) memberships, and (b) use group processes that elicit, identify, and integrate this distributed knowledge.

Regarding the first point, Yetton and Bottger (1983) found that group performance increased as a function of group size (up to about five members), although at a decreasing rate. Littlepage and Silbiger (1992) found increased size was beneficial up to 10 members. Based on their review of decision-making teams, Milliken and Vollrath (1991) recommended the use of groups that are heterogeneous in their knowledge make-up. They argue that groups "generally combine their efforts in an *additive* fashion" (p. 1234) and that a heterogeneous group "representing a broad cross-section of organizational functions is more likely to be effective" (p. 1238) in business than a homogeneous group.

Regarding the second point, it is important that group members employ processes that ensure that all relevant information and useful ideas are identified and used. Even when relevant knowledge is possessed by one or more group members, those members may not know they have correct information and other members may not successfully distinguish between who has and does not have correct information. Littlepage, Whisler, Schmidt, and Frost (1992), for example, found that members who did the most talking were perceived as possessing the most knowledge, even though amount of talking was unrelated to actual expertise. Littlepage and Mueller (1994) found that the knowledge of expert team members was only recognized and utilized by the group if the expert talked a lot.

When members do offer problem-relevant ideas, these ideas still must be evaluated, and accepted or rejected. Bottger and Yetton (1988) identified "positive" and "negative" group discussion behaviors among groups performing the Moon Survival exercise. Relevant positive actions included presenting logical arguments to support views, sharing information, encouraging a wide range of ideas, suggesting new alternatives, challenging underlying beliefs, and rejecting pressures to change ideas not supported by rational arguments. Negative behaviors included stating an opinion without any reason, using voting or coin tosses to resolve disagreements, suppressing differences, taking an "I win–you lose" approach, accepting early agreement without challenge, and changing opinions to appease others. Groups engaging in more positive and fewer negative behaviors devised better solutions than those who did the opposite because those using better discussion management skills were more likely to utilize the knowledge of the best members. In another study, Bottger and Yetton (1987) found that training group members in these skills improved group performance, although Ganster, Williams, and Poppler (1991) failed to replicate this finding.

Studies by Hirokawa and Pace (1983) and Hirokawa (1987) provide additional information about the importance of effective decision processes in groups. Hirokawa and Pace (1983) asked "blind" observers to view videotapes of student groups making recommendations concerning two student cases, one concerning plagiarism and the other malicious property damage. Each group had been judged either effective or ineffective based on the quality of its solution. The evaluations of the blind observers showed that effective and ineffective groups differed significantly on four attributes: (a) degree of rigor in evaluating opinions and assumptions; (b) degree of rigor in evaluating alternative courses of action; (c) accuracy of their premises and inferences; and (d) the quality of influence exerted by the most influential members, especially with respect to the first three attributes. In Hirokawa's next study (1987), students solved the Winter Survival problem (which was similar to the Moon Survival task.) Again, effective and ineffective groups (defined in terms of correctness of decisions) were studied and rated by "blind" observers, and the effective and ineffective groups differed on four attributes: (a) vigilant interaction, which was essentially the same as the behavior called rigorous evaluation in the earlier study; (b) second-guessing or retrospective questioning of previous evaluations and assumptions; (c) correct information processing (accepting valid information and rejecting faulty information); and (d) fantasy chaining (the use of extended but totally fanciful scenarios). The first three were associated with effective performance. The last was more common in ineffective groups. Integrating the eight attributes from these two studies suggests three basic principles for effective group decision making: (a) group members must engage in rigorous evaluation of every assumption and suggestion, (b) group members must possess correct information and make correct reality-based inferences from that data, and (c) the most knowledgeable members must have a strong impact on the group's decision.

These results are consistent with Larson and Christensen's (1993) proposal that group problem solving should be viewed as social information-processing. They describe several information processing activities, such as problem identification, problem conceptualization (framing), information acquisition, information storage, and information retrieval, that comprise group problem solving and suggest that the success with which group members perform each process has important implications for the quality of the group's decision.

Devil's Advocacy and Dialectical Inquiry.   Attempts to improve information processing in groups have produced two techniques that encourage effective decision making: devil's advocacy (DA) and dialectical inquiry (DI).[1] In the DA approach, one subgroup develops a plan and a second subgroup criticizes it. In the DI approach, one subgroup formulates a plan and another subgroup formulates an alternative plan based on opposite assumptions. With both approaches, the final step is to formulate an integrative solution. Typically, DA and DI approaches lead to better

---

[1]The term dialectical inquiry is an unfortunate legacy from Marx (who got it from Hegel). The erroneous philosophical principle involved is that knowledge is discovered through synthesizing opposites (thesis, antithesis, synthesis). This idea violates a fundamental principle of logic—the law of contradiction. Opposites cannot be integrated. In a group decision-making setting, the context is quite different. The purpose of encouraging conflict is to get members to thoroughly check their assumptions so that they end up with proposals that do *not* conflict with any known facts (i.e., that do *not* entail contradictions).

solutions than approaches that minimize conflict and emphasize consensus (C). For example, Schweiger and Sandberg (1989) asked MBA students to perform a strategic decision-making exercise and found that DA and DI groups both outperformed C groups with respect to the quality of their assumptions and final recommendations. Similarly, Schweiger, Sandberg, and Rechner (1989), using managers from a Fortune 500 company and two separate strategy cases, found that the DA and DI groups were superior to the C groups. A meta-analysis by Schwenk (1990) of studies comparing DA, DI, and C (which Schwenk called a non-conflict or expert-based approach) produced essentially the same result. Overall, there was no difference between the DA and DI approaches, and both tended to be superior to the C approach. The DA approach, however, produced more consistent results. In a recent study, Schwenk and Valacich (1994) found that individuals benefitted somewhat more using the DA approach than the DI approach, but groups were effective using either approach as compared to the C or expert approach (recommendations provided by members of a planning department or outside consultant).

Several other studies support the idea that structured conflict improves group decision making. In a correlational study, Tjosvold, Wedley, and Field (1986) found that managers' descriptions of the groups as engaging in "constructive controversy" were positively associated with outcome quality. In line with these results, Brown, Klastorin, and Valluzzi (1990) found that in a simulated project-management game, teams that were less harmonious at the outset performed better than those that were harmonious (i.e., cohesive, cooperative). Finally, a correlational study of employees in a freight transportation firm (Jehn, 1993) showed that conflict regarding the task (as compared to conflict over personality or administrative issues) was positively associated with group performance when the tasks were complex or non-routine, until very high levels of conflict were reached. Past a certain point, conflict had a negative effect. In contrast, conflict was negatively associated with performance when the tasks were simple or routine, although at very low levels an increase in conflict had a positive effect. However, Watson et al. (1991) found that the absence of constructive conflict was unrelated to group performance.

Stress

Another literature relevant to group decision making describes the effects of stress on information processing. It has long been known that stress, in which the core emotion is usually anxiety, impairs perception and information processing in individuals. Although early work focused on fairly simple laboratory tasks (e.g., Luchins, 1942; Postman & Bruner, 1948), recent studies (e.g., Bandura & Wood, 1989; Humphreys & Revelle, 1984; Isen & Shalker, 1982; Sarason et al., 1990) focused on more complex or naturally occurring events. As noted earlier, these studies show that failure on a task can impair short-term memory, bias recall of previously encoded information, divert attention from task-relevant thoughts, and limit careful consideration of strategy alternatives. Christianson's (1992) review of eye witness testimony showed that eyewitnesses retained the central details of a situation better than peripheral details when it was viewed under emotional stress. Conversely, peripheral details were remembered better than central when the witnesses were not aroused. Consistent with these findings, Keinan (1987) found that individuals under stress did less systematic scanning of relevant alternatives when making decisions, and as a result made poorer quality decisions. Barrett (1993) reports that military ground commanders working under pressure do not systematically generate alternatives to solve new problems; instead, they match the present situation to a past one, or pick one option generated based on previous experience.

Although fewer studies of stress and information processing in groups have been reported, existing data suggest that similar effects operate there. A review by Staw, Sandelands, and Dutton (1981) provides evidence that the quality of information processing in groups declines in times of stress. Group members consider fewer alternatives and engage in less thorough evaluation of their options. Gersick and Hackman (1990) cite evidence that groups who experience a failure rarely question existing task strategies or develop new ones because group decision-making processes close down. Consistent with these findings, Kelly and Karau (1993) found that fewer relevant facts were discussed by decision-making groups working under time pressure, compared to those working with loose time constraints. However, another study (Karau & Kelly, 1992) showed that time pressure can be beneficial because it creates a high level of task focus. Although in some cases task focus might compensate for impaired information processing, this would not always be true. For example, when inexperienced, untrained people work on complex tasks, time pressure may be harmful because careful strategy development is more important than focused attention.

Group decision making under stress could be improved by eliminating (if possible) the external stressors, training group members in stress management techniques (Locke & Taylor, 1990), or intensively training members to use task strategies known to be effective, leading to substantial automatization of the correct actions (Gersick & Hackman, 1990). Although the effectiveness of DA and DI techniques have not been tested under stressful conditions, these interventions might be particularly useful when group members work under stress because these techniques promote thorough information processing.

Summary and Integration

A summary and integration of the major findings of the group decision-making literature reviewed here is presented in Table 10.1. This model is very simple because our review focused on two major issues: (a) whether or not the group has relevant knowledge, and (b) whether or not that

TABLE 10.1
Factors Influencing Effective Group Decision Making

Requirements for Effective Decision Making	Procedure(s) for Implementing Requirement
1. Expertise of group members	• Select for knowledge and ability
	• Train members on task relevant skills
	• Include multiple members
	• Select for diversity in task-relevant knowledge and expertise
2. The use of group processes that maximize discovery and utilization of the members' knowledge and expertise	• Seek additional information
	• Learn to identify which members have correct information
	• Train in effective group discussion behavior
	• Evaluate with rigor all alternatives and proposed solutions through DA
3. Preventing disruption of thorough processing due to stressful emotions or excessive time pressure	• Eliminate stressors
	• Train members to manage stress
	• Automatize needed repertoire of actions
	• Allow more time

expertise is or can be used effectively. Based on this table, we can describe the important contingencies as follows: *If* the group has or gains and recognizes task-relevant expertise *and* uses positive discussion management skills *and* group processes are not disrupted by stress, *then* the knowledge of all group members may be brought out and integrated effectively toward a sound decision.

Because developing group strategies to attain group goals is similar in many ways to group decision making, we believe that these same contingencies might apply to group planning. Thus, group planning should be most effective under the following conditions:

1. Group members have or gain information, experience, and skill relevant to the group's task, and together group members hold all the information needed to develop a good plan and correctly identify who knows what. If knowledge is lacking, group members make attempts to acquire additional needed information (e.g., from external sources).

2. Group members utilize effective group decision-making skills. That is, the members are articulate, so that useful information is communicated effectively to other group members and the value of a good idea is clear; group members continually challenge assumptions and check the accuracy of information provided by other group members; and the members accept

this challenge as a legitimate and useful group process. Group members might also adopt the DA or DI technique, particularly when working under stress.

3. Stress due to time pressure and fear of failure are minimized. The effects of time pressure can be reduced by providing extra time for group members to plan, letting group members know that immediate results are not expected, and reducing the normal workload as group members plan. To help group members manage failure, they should be encouraged to review their group planning processes, diagnose their strengths and weaknesses as a planning group, and determine steps that group members can take to improve the quality of the planning process and the plans they produce.

The effects of these principles of group planning should be tested in laboratory and field research. Their effects on the quality of the group planning process, the quality of the plan produced, and subsequent group performance should be assessed.

The model in Fig. 10.2 integrates the content of Fig. 10.1 and Table 10.1 and summarizes our suggestions concerning the processes by which goals, individual factors, and situational factors affect strategy formulation and performance on complex tasks.

CHAPTER SUMMARY

This chapter reviews the extant literature on the relationships between goals, planning, and performance for both individuals and groups. We

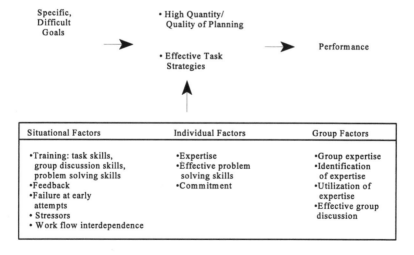

FIG. 10.2. Effects of goals and individual, group, and situational factors on planning, task strategies, and performance on complex tasks.

stress the important role of planning in complex tasks and distinguish between preplanning and inprocess planning. We also review relevant group-decision making literature and show its possible implications for the effectiveness of planning.

Individual goals affect planning by: (a) stimulating the execution of known strategies or enhancing the use of strategies that have been learned, provided, or primed; (b) influencing the amount of planning that takes place; and (c) influencing the quality of planning. In general, studies on individual goals and planning have found that specific, difficult goals enhance the use of a primed strategy, stimulate more planning, and lead to higher quality planning. The effect of goals on planning and performance is, however, moderated by the complexity of the task performed. As task complexity increases, the magnitude of the goal effect decreases. Challenging goals are even less likely to enhance planning on complex tasks when subjects have no prior experience or training at the task, are frustrated with failure at early efforts to meet the goals, or are under pressure to perform well immediately.

The research on group goals and planning has produced important results. Studies in this research area show that planning and strategy change are important mediators of the group goal effect, a finding that parallels results from studies of individual goals. This finding is important because we cannot assume that processes that mediate the individual goal effect will generalize to groups. The study of social psychology shows that people often behave differently when acting as part of a group. Planning is particularly interesting in this regard because studies show that the presence of others increases arousal (Geen & Bushman, 1987), and arousal can interfere with the cognitive processing required to develop plans (Janis & Mann, 1977). Based on these results, one might predict that planning will play a limited role in groups. However, these studies show that, in at least some situations, group members can and will plan when motivated to reach a goal. Future research might focus on variables that affect the quantity, quality, and process of planning in groups. Variables known to moderate the individual goal effect and those peculiar to groups should be assessed.

In examining the group decision-making literature and relating it to planning, we stress the importance of member knowledge and ability, knowledge seeking, vigilant processing, and stress management. In general, group planning should be most effective when the group (a) has or gains task-relevant information, experience, and skills; (b) uses effective group communication and decision-making skills; and (c) is not under excessive stress caused by time pressure or fear of failure. Because many important decisions are made in groups, there is a great practical need for additional research aimed toward improving our understanding of how to create conditions that facilitate the group planning process, improve the quality of the plans produced, and enhance group performance.

ACKNOWLEDGMENT

Preparation of this manuscript was facilitated by contract #MDA903-93-K-0016 from the Army Research Institute. The views, opinions, and/or findings contained in this paper are those of the authors and should not be construed as an official Department of the Army position, policy, or decision.

REFERENCES

Adam, E. E., Jr. (1975). Behavior modification in quality control. *Academy of Management Journal, 18,* 662–679.

Bandura, A. (1982). Self-efficacy mechanism in human agency. *American Psychologist, 37,* 122–147.

Bandura, A. (1986). *Social foundations of thought and action: A social cognitive theory.* Englewood Cliffs, NJ: Prentice-Hall.

Bandura, A., & Simon, K. M. (1977). The role of proximal intentions in self-regulation of refractory behavior. *Cognitive Therapy and Research, 1,* 177–193.

Bandura, A., & Wood, R. (1989). Effect of perceived controllability and performance standards of self-regulation of complex decision making. *Journal of Personality and Social Psychology, 56,* 805–814.

Barrett, L. E. (1993). *Decision making teams: Their study in the U.S. military* (Tech. Rep. No. 93–1). East Lansing: Michigan State University.

Becker, L. J. (1978). Joint effect of feedback and goal setting on performance: A field study of residential energy conservation. *Journal of Applied Psychology, 63,* 428–433.

Blau, G., Blank, W., & Katerberg, R. (1987). *Investigating the motivational determinants of job performance.* Unpublished manuscript.

Bottger, P. C., & Yetton, P. W. (1987). Improving group performance by training in individual problem solving. *Journal of Applied Psychology, 72,* 651–657.

Bottger, P. C., & Yetton, P. W. (1988). An integration of process and decision scheme explanations of group problem solving performance. *Organizational Behavior and Human Decision Processes, 42,* 234–249.

Brown, K., Klastorin, T., & Valluzzi, J. (1990). Project performance and the liability of group harmony. *IEEE Transactions on Engineering Management, 37*(2), 117–125.

Buller, P. F., & Bell, C. H., Jr. (1986). Effects of team building and goal setting on productivity: A field experiment. *Academy of Management Journal, 29,* 305–328.

Campbell, D. J., & Gingrich, K. F. (1986). The interactive effects of task complexity and participation on task performance: A field experiment. *Organizational Behavior and Human Decision Processes, 38,* 162–180.

Cervone, D., Jiwani, N., & Wood, R. (1991). Goal-setting and the differential influence of self-regulatory processes on complex decision-making performance. *Personality Processes and Individual Differences, 61,* 257–266.

Chesney, A. A., & Locke, E. A. (1991). Relationships among goal difficulty, business strategies, and performance on a complex management simulation task. *Academy of Management Journal, 34,* 400–424.

Christensen-Szalanski, J. J. J. (1980). A further examination of the selection of problem-solving strategies: The effects of deadlines and analytic aptitudes. *Organizational Behavior and Human Performance, 25,* 107–122.

Christianson, S. (1992). Emotional stress and eyewitness memory: A critical review. *Psychological Bulletin, 112,* 284–309.

Das, B. (1982). Effects of production feedback and standards on worker productivity in a repetitive production task. *AIIE Transactions,* March, 27–37.

Earley, P. C. (1986). An examination of the mechanisms underlying the relation of feedback to performance. *Academy of Management Proceedings*, 214–218.

Earley, P. C. (1988). Computer-generated performance feedback in the magazine-subscription industry. *Organizational Behavior and Human Decision Processes, 41,* 50–64.

Earley, P. C., Connolly, T., & Ekegren, G. (1989). Goals, strategy development and task performance: Some limits on the efficacy of goal setting. *Journal of Applied Psychology, 74,* 24–33.

Earley, P. C., Hanson, L. A., & Lee, C. (1986). Relation of task complexity, task strategies, individual differences and goals to performance. *Academy of Management Best Papers Proceedings*, 184–188.

Earley, P. C., Lee, C., & Hanson, L. A. (1990). Joint moderating effects of job experience and task component complexity: Relations among goal setting, task strategies, and performance. *Journal of Organizational Behavior, 11,* 3–15.

Earley, P. C., Lee, C., & Lituchy, T. R. (1989). *Task strategy and judgments in goal setting: Learning goals and training sequencing on performance.* Unpublished manuscript, University of Arizona, Department of Management and Policy.

Earley, P. C., Northcraft, G. B., Lee, C., & Lituchy, T. R. (1990). Impact of process and outcome feedback on the relation of goal setting to task performance. *Academy of Management Journal, 33,* 87–105.

Earley, P. C., & Perry, B. C. (1987). Work plan availability and performance: An assessment of task strategy priming on subsequent task completion. *Organizational Behavior and Human Decision Processes, 39,* 279–302.

Earley, P. C., Shalley, C. E., & Northcraft, G. B. (1992). I think I can, I think I can ... Processing time and strategy effects of goal acceptance/rejection decisions. *Organizational Behavior and Human Decision Processes, 53,* 1–13.

Earley, P. C., Wojnaroski, P., & Prest, W. (1987). Task planning and energy expended: Exploration of how goals influence performance. *Journal of Applied Psychology, 72,* 107–114.

Ganster, D. C., Williams, S., & Poppler, P. (1991). Does training in problem solving improve the quality of group decisions? *Journal of Applied Psychology, 76,* 479–483.

Geen, R. G., & Bushman, B. J. (1987). Drive theory: Effects of socially engendered arousal. In B. Mullen & G. Goethals (Eds.), *Theories of group behavior* (pp. 89–110). New York: Springer-Verlag.

Gersick, C. J. G., & Hackman, J. R. (1990). Habitual routines in task–performing groups. *Organizational Behavior and Human Decision Processes, 47,* 65–97.

Gilliland, S. W., & Landis, R. S. (1992). Quality and quantity goals in a complex decision task: Strategies and outcomes. *Journal of Applied Psychology, 77,* 672–681.

Hayes-Roth, B., & Hayes-Roth, F. (1979). A cognitive model of planning. *Cognitive Science, 3,* 275–310.

Hill, G. W. (1982). Group versus individual performance: Are N + 1 heads better than one? *Psychological Bulletin, 91,* 517–539.

Hirokawa, R. Y. (1987). Why informed groups make faulty decisions: An investigation of possible interaction-based explanations. *Small Group Behavior, 18,* 3–29.

Hirokawa, R. Y., & Johnston, D. D. (1989). Toward a general theory of group decision making: Development of an integrated model. *Small Group Behavior, 20,* 500–523.

Hirokawa, R. Y., & Pace, R. (1983). A descriptive investigation of the possible communication-based reasons for effective and ineffective group decision making. *Communication Monographs, 50,* 363–379.

Huber, V. L. (1985). Effects of task difficulty, goal setting, and strategy on performance of a heuristic task. *Journal of Applied Psychology, 70,* 492–504.

Humphreys, M. S., & Revelle, W. (1984). Personality, motivation, and performance: A theory of the relationship between individual differences and information processing. *Psychological Review, 91,* 153–184.

Isen, A. M., & Shalker, T. E. (1982). The effect of feeling state on evaluation of positive, neutral, and negative stimuli: When you "accentuate the positive" do you "eliminate the negative?" *Social Psychology Quarterly, 45,* 58–63.

Isen, A. M., Shalker, T. E., Clark, M., & Karp, L. (1978). Affect, accessibility of material in memory, and behavior: A cognitive loop? *Journal of Personality and Social Psychology, 36,* 1–12.

Janis, I. L., & Mann, L. (1977). *Decision making: A psychological analysis of conflict, choice, and commitment*. New York: Free Press.

Jehn, K. A. (1993). *The impact of intragroup conflict on effectiveness*. Paper presented at the 53rd Annual Meeting of the Academy of Management, Atlanta, GA.

Kanfer, R., & Ackerman, P. L. (1988). *Motivation and cognitive_abilities: An integrative/aptitude–treatment interaction approach to skill acquisition*. Unpublished manuscript.

Karau, S. J., & Kelly, J. R. (1992). The effects of time scarcity and time abundance on group performance quality and interaction process. *Journal of Experimental Social Psychology, 28,* 542–571.

Keinan, G. (1987). Decision making under stress: Scanning of alternatives under controllable and uncontrollable threats. *Journal of Personality and Social Psychology, 52,* 639–644.

Kelly, J. R., & Karau, S. J. (1993). *Group decision making: The effects of time pressure and initial preferences*. Unpublished manuscript.

Kim, J. S. (1984). Effect of behavior plus outcome goal setting feedback on employee satisfaction and performance. *Academy of Management Journal, 27,* 139–49.

Klahr, D., & Robinson, M. (1981). Formal assessment of problem-solving and planning processes in preschool children. *Cognitive Psychology, 13,* 113–148.

Klein, H. J., Whitener, E. M., & Ilgen, D. R. (1990). The role of goal specificity in the goal setting process. *Motivation and Emotion, 14,* 179–193.

Larson, J. R., Jr., & Christensen, C. (1993). Groups as problem-solving units: Toward a new meaning of social cognition. *British Journal of Social Psychology, 32,* 5–30.

Larson, J. R., Jr., & Schaumann, L. J. (1993). Group goals, group coordination, and group member motivation. *Human_Performance, 6,* 49–69.

Latham, G. P., & Baldes, J. J. (1975). The practical significance of Locke's theory of goal setting. *Journal of Applied Psychology, 60,* 122–124.

Latham, G. P., & Saari, L. M. (1982). The importance of union acceptance for productivity improvement through goal setting. *Personnel Psychology, 35,* 781–787.

Littlepage, G. E., & Mueller, A. L. (1994, April). *Recognition of expertise in groups: Expert characteristics and behavior*. Paper presented at the Ninth Annual Conference of the Society for Industrial & Organizational Psychology, Nashville, TN.

Littlepage, G. E., & Silbiger, H. (1992). Recognition of expertise in decision-making groups: Effects of group size and participation patterns. *Small Group Research, 23,* 344–355.

Littlepage, G., Whisler, E., Schmidt, G., & Frost, A. (1992, March). *Member characteristics and group processes related to influence and performance in problem solving groups*. Paper presented at the meeting of the Southeastern Psychological Association, Knoxville, TN.

Locke, E. A., & Bryan, J. F. (1966). The effects of goal-setting, rule-learning, and knowledge of score on performance. *American Journal of Psychology, 79,* 451–457.

Locke, E. A., & Latham, G. P. (1990). *A theory of goal setting and task performance*. Englewood Cliffs, NJ: Prentice Hall.

Locke, E. A., & Taylor, M. S. (1990). Stress, coping, and the meaning of work. In W. Nord & A. Brief (Eds.), *The meaning of work* (pp. 135–170). New York: Heath.

Lombardo, T., Hull, D. B., Singer, D. C. (1983). Variables affecting achievement of direct service goals of mental health center outpatient services. *Administration in Mental Health, 11,* 64–66.

Luchins, A. S. (1942). Mechanization in problem solving. *Psychological Monographs, 54,* 1–95.

Matsui, T., Kakuyama, T., & Onglatco, M. L. U. (1987). Effects of goal and feedback on performance in groups. *Journal of Applied Psychology, 72,* 407–415.

McCuddy, M. K., & Griggs, M. H. (1984). Goal setting and feedback in the management of a professional department: A case study. *Journal of Organizational Behavior Management, 6,* 53–64.

Milliken, F. J., & Vollrath, D. A. (1991). Strategic decision-making tasks and group effectiveness: Insights from theory and research on small group performance. *Human Relations, 44,* 1229–1253.

Mintzberg, H. (1987). Crafting strategy. *Harvard Business Review, 65,* 66–75.

Mintzberg, H., & McHugh, A. (1985). Strategy formation in an adhocracy. *Administrative Science Quarterly, 30,* 160–197.

Mitchell, T. R., & Silver, W. S. (1990). Individual and group goals when workers are interdependent: Effects on task strategies and performance. *Journal of Applied Psychology, 75,* 185–193.

Neale, M. A., Northcraft, G. B., & Earley, P. C. (1987). *Working hard vs. working smart: A comparison of anchoring and strategy–development effects of goal setting.* Unpublished manuscript, Northwestern University, Kellogg School of Management.

Postman, L., & Bruner, J. S. (1948). Perception under stress. *Psychological Review, 55,* 314–323.

Saavedra, R., Earley, P. C., & Van Dyne, L. (1993). Complex interdependence in task-performing groups. *Journal of Applied Psychology, 78,* 61–72.

Sarason, I. G., Sarason, B. R., & Pierce, G. R. (1990). Anxiety, cognitive interference, and performance. *Journal of Social Behavior and Personality, 5,* 1–18.

Schmitz, B., & Skinner, E. (1993). Perceived control, effort, and academic performance: Interindividual, intraindividual, and multivariate time-series analyses. *Journal of Personality and Social Psychology, 64,* 1010–1028.

Schweiger, D. M., & Sandberg, W. R. (1989). The utilization of individual capabilities in group approaches to strategic decision making. *Strategic Management Journal, 10,* 31–43.

Schweiger, D. M., Sandberg, W. R., & Rechner, P. (1989). Experiential effects of dialectical inquiry, devil's advocacy and consensus approaches to strategic decision making. *Academy of Management Journal, 32,* 745–772.

Schwenk, C. R. (1990). Effects of devil's advocacy and dialectical inquiry on decision making: A meta-analysis. *Organizational Behavior and Human Decision Processes, 47,* 161–176.

Schwenk, C., & Valacich, J. S. (1994). Effects of devil's advocacy and dialectical inquiry on individuals versus groups. *Organizational Behavior and Human Decision Processes, 59,* 210–222.

Shaw, K. N. (1984). *A laboratory investigation of the relationship among goals, strategies, and task performance.* Unpublished doctoral dissertation, University of Maryland, College Park.

Siegler, R. S., & Shrager, J. (1984). Strategy choices in addition and subtraction: How do children know what to do? In C. Sophian (Ed.), *Origins of cognitive skills* (pp. 229–293). Hillsdale, NJ: Lawrence Erlbaum Associates.

Skinner, E. A. (1992). Perceived control: Motivation, coping, and development. In R. Schwarzer (Ed.), *Self-efficacy: Thought control of action* (pp. 91–106). Washington: Hemisphere Publishing.

Smith, K. G., Locke, E. A., & Barry, D. (1990). Goal setting, planning, and organizational performance: An experimental simulation. *Organizational Behavior and Human Decision Processes, 46,* 118–134.

Staw, B. M., Sandelands, L., & Dutton, J. (1981). Threat-rigidity effects in organizational behavior: A multilevel analysis. *Administrative Science Quarterly, 26,* 501–524.

Stedry, A. C., & Kay, E. (1964). The effects of goal difficulty on performance: A field experiment. *Behavioral Science, 11,* 459–470.

Terborg, J. R. (1976). The motivational components of goal setting. *Journal of Applied Psychology, 61,* 613–621.

Terborg, J. R., & Miller, H. E. (1978). Motivation, behavior, and performance: A closer examination of goal setting and monetary incentives. *Journal of Applied Psychology, 63,* 29–39.

Tjosvold, D., Wedley, W. C., & Field, R. H. G. (1986). Constructive controversy, the Vroom-Yetton model, and managerial decision-making. *Journal of Occupational Behaviour, 7,* 125–138.

Trabasso, T., & Stein, N. (in press). Using goal/plan knowledge to merge the past with the present and the future in narrating events on-line. In M. Haith (Ed.), *The development of future oriented processes.*

Trabasso, T., Stein, N., Rodkin, P., Munger, M., & Baughn, C. (1992). Knowledge of goals and plans in the on-line narration of events. *Cognitive Development, 7,* 133–170.

Watson, W., Michaelsen, L. K., & Sharp, W. (1991). Member competence, group interaction, and group decision making: A longitudinal study. *Journal of Applied Psychology, 76,* 803–809.

Weed, S. E., & Mitchell, T. R. (1980). The role of environmental and behavioral uncertainty as a mediator of situation–performance relationships. *Academy of Management Journal, 23,* 38–60.

Weingart, L. R. (1992). Impact of group goals, task component complexity, effort, and planning on group performance. *Journal of Applied Psychology, 77,* 682–693.

Weingart, L. R., & Weldon, E. (1991). Processes that mediate the relationship between a group goal and group member performance. *Human Performance, 4,* 33–54.

Weldon, E. (1994). *Strategy formation in empowered work teams: A research proposal.* Working paper, School of Business, Indiana University.

Weldon, E., Jehn, K. A., & Pradhan, P. (1991). Processes that mediate the relationship between a group goal and improved group performance. *Journal of Personality and Social Psychology, 61,* 555–569.

Weldon, E., & Weingart, L. R. (1993). Group goals and group performance. *British Journal of Social Psychology, 32,* 307–334.

Welsh, M. C. (1991). Rule-guided behavior and self-monitoring on the Tower of Hanoi disk-transfer task. *Cognitive Development, 6,* 59–76.

Wood, R. E. (1986). Task complexity: Definition of the construct. *Organizational Behavior and Human Decision Processes, 37,* 60–82.

Wood, R. E., & Bandura, A. (1989). Impact of conceptions of ability on self-regulatory mechanisms and complex decision making. *Journal of Personality and Social Psychology, 56,* 407–415.

Wood, R. E., Bandura, A., & Bailey, T. (1990). Mechanisms governing organizational productivity in complex decision-making environments. *Organizational Behavior and Human Decision Processes, 46,* 181–201.

Wood, R. E., & Locke, E. A. (1990). Goal setting and strategy effects on complex tasks. In B. Staw & L. Cummings (Eds.), *Research in organizational behavior* (Vol. 12, pp. 73–110). Greenwich, CT: JAI Press.

Wood, R. E., Mento, A. J., & Locke, E. A. (1987). Task complexity as a moderator of goal effects: A meta-analysis. *Journal of Applied Psychology, 72,* 416–25.

Yetton, P. W., & Bottger, P. C. (1982). Individual versus group problem solving: An empirical test of a best-member strategy. *Organizational Behavior and Human Performance, 29,* 307–321.

Yetton, P. W., & Bottger, P. C. (1983). The relationships among group size, member ability, social decision schemes, and performance. *Organizational Behavior and Human Performance, 32,* 145–159.

11

Planning and Perceived Control

Ellen A. Skinner
Portland State University

Planning can be a challenging cognitive task, involving complex problem solving, the prioritizing and sequencing of multiple activities, and the coordination of anticipated actions with constraints imposed by context, time, and resources. Analyses of planning and its development have tended to focus on cognitive abilities and corresponding changes in skills, strategies, and knowledge with age. This research has been useful in identifying the cognitive prerequisites for effective planning. Accordingly, it placed relatively less emphasis on the factors that influence when an individual will actually employ the planning skills in his or her cognitive repertoire. Recent analyses of the expression of planning behavior, however, suggest that the search for factors that influence, for example, the decision to plan or the revision of a plan in the face of obstacles, extends beyond cognition, to include other aspects of the individual, such as emotion, motivation, and personality, as well as features of the task and social context (Scholnick & Friedman, 1993).

The goal of this chapter is to discuss the role of motivation in the expression of planning, and, specifically, to consider the effects of an important motivational factor: perceived control. The central notion is that individuals who possess the cognitive skills needed to generate and organize effective plans will not do so if they believe that the desired outcome is not amenable to personal control. Across the life span, people's sense of how much they can influence important events in their lives, captured in constructs like locus of control, learned helplessness, self-efficacy, causal attributions, and perceived competence, has been found to exert a strong influence on goal-directed action. From a simplistic control perspective, planning can be seen as one more aspect of behavior that would be undercut by a sense of uncontrollability. However, a careful analysis of recent conceptualizations of both planning and perceived control reveal that they may have additional complex and interesting interrelationships, and ones that change with development.

Given the seemingly obvious links between planning and control, it may seem surprising to discover how rarely they have been considered in the same conceptual or empirical analyses. In fact, a recent special issue explicitly devoted to planning and control processes across the life span (Lachman, 1993) emphasized both the importance of this connection and pointed out the paucity of research on the topic. The editor and her co-author began the issue with the statement "There has been much interest in the topics of planning and control, but little examination of how these constructs are related" (Lachman & Burack, 1993, p. 131). In fact, even in the special issue, each article had as its primary focus *either* control or planning processes; few articles concentrated on their relationships.

Hence, this chapter includes both a brief examination of the reasons why research on these seemingly related constructs continues independently, as well as a more detailed argument for the potential benefits from a meaningful integration of the two. In so doing, both constructs are briefly defined, as are the perspectives from which they are typically discussed. Then, new conceptualizations of both planning and perceived control are mentioned, which make more explicit their common ground. This integration is used as a basis for suggesting a research agenda that should not only broaden understanding of planning, but also ground analyses of perceived control. The chapter concludes with a general discussion of the role of motivation in planning and how it may change with development.

THE GULF BETWEEN PLANNING AND PERCEIVED CONTROL

The simplest explanation for the conceptual and empirical distance between planning and control can be found in their traditional definitions. As mentioned previously, planning was usually considered a cognitive task, showing normative developmental changes as children's, adolescents', and elderly adults' cognitive capacities grow and decline. Planning was typically examined in very specific kinds of tasks, such as the Tower of Hanoi, story comprehension tasks, or planning parties or errands. Factors such as motivation were either ignored or treated as factors to be controlled for in the construction of tasks and instructions.

In contrast, perceived control was widely viewed as an individual difference variable, that, although continuing to exert an influence on motivation and performance across the life span, remained relatively stable for individuals. It was largely viewed as a relatively general, almost personality-like factor. Its influence was assumed to be largely motivational, that is, mediated primarily by its effects on effort exertion and persistence. Although multiple specific effects were documented in the lab, the most interesting consequences of perceived control are relatively general ones, such as mental and physical health and reactions to difficult and stressful situations.

Hence, the traditional view of planning as a cognitive activity undergoing normative developmental changes studied in specific task-contexts can be contrasted with a view of perceived control as a relatively stable individual difference variable with motivational implications, generally studied in stressful life contexts. However, recent conceptualizations of both planning and perceived control may provide a bridge between these two constructs.

NEW PERSPECTIVES ON PLANNING
AND PERCEIVED CONTROL

Recent discussions of these two constructs emphasize their relations to goal-directed action, point out their embeddedness in action contexts, and examine the interplay between cognition and motivation in their formation and expression. These innovations provided common ground for the integration of planning and perceived control. For this discussion, I rely on the conceptualization of planning provided by Scholnick and Friedman (1993) and on our own and related work on perceived control (Chapman & Skinner, 1985; Skinner, 1991, 1995, 1996; Skinner, Chapman, & Baltes, 1988; Skinner & Connell, 1986; Skinner, Wellborn, & Connell, 1990).

Planning as Goal-Directed Action

Although recognizing the heterogeneity inherent in the construct, Scholnick and Friedman (1993) defined planning as "the use of knowledge for a purpose, the construction of an effective way to meet some future goal" (p. 145). They also stated "plans are the designs we construct to guide our attempts to reach a goal in a given environment" (p. 146). In their idealized description of the prototypic planning process, they identified components that resemble a sequence of action steps: building a representation of the environment for action, selecting a goal, deciding to plan, formulating or adapting a plan, and implementing and monitoring the plan.

Considering the components of planning not only draws attention to their differential centrality in the performance of different kinds of planning tasks, but also allows for a developmental analysis of each. For the purposes of the present chapter, the most important aspect of this conceptualization is its focus on planning as goal-directed action. This conception differs from cognitive conceptions that focus on the *ability* to plan; it highlights aspects of the planning process that determine the use of planning, that is, whether current abilities will be deployed. The focus here is on the motivational and volitional determinants of the use of planning.

Perceived Control in an Action Theoretical Perspective

Innovations in the study of perceived control have placed it closer to the study of planning in both general and specific ways. At a general level, perceived control is no longer considered a stable personality factor, but rather a set of beliefs that children and adults hold about how the causal world works and about their own individual role in producing desired (and preventing undesired) events in their own lives. Control beliefs are considered to be actively constructed by individuals based on their interactions with the social and physical context in different life domains, and shaped by their participation in and interpretation of those experiences.

At a more specific level, an action theoretical perspective was used to both differentiate and integrate a profile of control-related beliefs. Action theory, which considers not behavior but action (intentional goal-directed behavior) as the central unit of analysis, emphasizes the distinctions among agents, means, and ends. Correspondingly, our conceptualization includes control-related beliefs about the connections between each of these action components. Specifically, we distinguish: (a) *strategy (or means–ends) beliefs* that refer to generalized expectations about the extent to which certain categories of means are effective in producing desired or preventing undesired outcomes; (b) *capacity (or agency) beliefs* that refer to generalized expectations about the extent to which the self has access to certain categories of potential means; and (c) *control beliefs* that refer to generalized expectations about the extent to which an agent can produce desired or prevent undesired outcomes, without specific mention of the means involved (Skinner et al., 1988). This chapter focuses on how these different beliefs influence the deployment of planning skills.

Connections Between Planning and Control

Conceptualizing planning as goal-directed action, potentially consisting of sequential components, provides multiple entry points for considering the effects of perceived control. Similarly, the conceptualization of perceived control as naive accounts of action, consisting of beliefs not only about the self's capacities and competencies, but also about the effectiveness of multiple means in producing desired and preventing undesired events, also provides several entry points for considering its impact on the processes of planning.

What does research on perceived control have to offer the study of planning? In this chapter, I will argue that it can be helpful in addressing the key issues of this volume, namely, the "how, when, and why" issues of planning. Research on perceived control can be used to make general points about the contexts of planning, as well as contribute to an analysis of the mechanisms that influence the expression of different components in the planning process. Recent work integrating individual differences and developmental perspectives on control can be helpful in pointing out questions about developmental changes in the links between planning and control.

THE CONTEXTS OF PLANNING
AND PERCEIVED CONTROL

Planning and Resistance

Perceived control should not always have an effect on planning. In conducting routine everyday tasks that are familiar and predictable, such as preparing a list before going grocery shopping, it is likely that the best predictor of planning is the extent to which the task is one in which scripts call for planning (e.g., list preparation). Perceived control begins to play a role in regulating action only when individuals encounter resistance from the environment (or anticipate resistance) in accomplishing their goals (Bandura & Schunk, 1981; Heckhausen, 1991; Weiner, 1985b).

In research on perceived control, the use of talk-aloud protocols has demonstrated a variety of task conditions that are typically experienced as resistance. They include repeated failure, unexpected success, novel tasks, and changing contingencies and competencies. In these situations, individuals are more likely to ruminate about their perceived control and to regulate their own actions and action steps. Hence, it seems that perceived control will have its greatest impact on planning in situations that tax the individual's resources.

The consideration of planning in relation to the concept of resistance can be used to clarify questions about whether planning is generally adaptive. Lachman and Burack (1993) pointed out that although both planning and control have been associated with adaptive outcomes, "too much control or planning may be maladaptive" (p. 137). On the one hand, planning can be a reaction to anticipated resistance, with more planning suggesting more vulnerability to the challenges posed by a task. On the other hand, given a certain level of resistance, planning can be seen as an effective strategy for reducing task demands and increasing the probability of success. In this case, more planning suggests a more effective response to challenge.

Planning and Domain Specificity

The effects of perceived control on planning would not be expected to be uniform across planning in all kinds of contexts, nor in service of goals in all areas of life. In research on perceived control, it is clear that people hold both generalized beliefs and relatively specific beliefs about their competencies and their potential to influence outcomes in particular domains, such as academics, work, close relationships, sports, health, and politics. Hence, it is expected that the particular effects of control on planning would depend on the profile of beliefs held in that domain.

Specifically, individuals would be expected to formulate plans more frequently in domains in which they anticipate more resistance. Further, they would be likely to use their domain-specific beliefs to regulate and interpret their actions in that domain. As is typical in research on perceived control, domain-specific beliefs would be expected to show higher relations with planning in the corresponding domains, but little relationship to behavior outside the respective domain. More generalized perceived control beliefs, in contrast, would be expected to play a role in planning in two ways. First, generalized control beliefs would be expected to have less impact on domain-specific planning, but more connections to planning across a range of different domains. Second, generalized control would also be expected to have a bigger impact on planning in domains that are novel or unfamiliar.

THE MECHANISMS OF PLANNING
AND PERCEIVED CONTROL

Perceived control and planning intersect on the issue of action. Planning is considered to involve goal-directed action (Scholnick & Friedman, 1993), and action is the proximal outcome of perceived control and the mediational link through which perceived control affects performance and level of success and failure (Skinner, 1995). A great deal of research has been directed toward understanding how perceived control affects action, its organization, and regulation; this can be applied to planning processes as well. Two major psychological mechanisms have been identified: motivation and volition.

Motivational Mechanisms

Motivational mechanisms are quite simply the pathways thorough which perceived control affects an individual's engagement in an activity. When people believe they have no control, they become disaffected. They initiate less behavior, are more passive, exert themselves less, and give up more easily. They also are more pessimistic about the future and less willing to act in ways designed to affect desired future outcomes.

Equally apparent are the positive effects of a sense of control. People with high efficacy and high response–outcome expectations are more likely to show enthusiastic, interested involvement, to be active, to initiate activities, to exert themselves and persist even in the face of challenges and failures. They are optimistic about the future and actively participate in shaping it toward their desired goals. The beneficial effects of a sense of control and the detrimental consequences of helplessness have been found across the life span. (For reviews, see Abramsen, Seligman, & Teasdale, 1978; Baltes & Baltes, 1986; Bandura, 1977, 1981, 1986, 1989; Brim, 1974; Dweck & Elliott, 1983; Dweck & Leggett, 1988; Harter, 1978,1983; Heckhausen, 1991; Lefcourt, 1981, 1982, 1983, 1992; Peterson & Seligman 1984; Seligman, 1975; Strickland, 1989; Weiner, 1985a, 1986).

Functional Mechanisms

Although for several decades it has been assumed that the primary (or even the exclusive) mechanism through which control affects action is motivational (Heckhausen, 1991), recent research on volition (Heck-hausen & Gollwitzer, 1987), action versus state orientation (Kuhl, 1984), self-regulation (Bandura, 1989), and goals (Dweck, 1991) has suggested that another important pathway may be through the effects of control on the implementation of action, or through volition. These effects impair performance directly by restricting access to existing cognitive resources needed for effective task implementation. Hence, deficits caused by these mechanisms are not considered motivational, but functional (Kuhl, 1981).

Volitional mechanisms are ways that perceived control interferes with or promotes the enactment of intentions. According to volitional theories (Heckhausen, 1991; Kuhl, 1984) people can better implement intentions when they are guided by "fully elaborated intentions" or show an "action orientation". A fully elaborated intention includes a personal commitment to the intention, a belief in the self as agent, a representation of the context for action, and a visualization of the intended action steps.

People with high control tend to show an action orientation. During action, this allows them to concentrate completely on the task at hand (selective attention and encoding), to have full access to their working memory capacity (information processing), and to boost their intentions in the face of obstacles (determining emotions) (Kuhl, 1984). As a result, they show a pattern of more effective strategy selection, hypothesis testing, problem solving, and general analytic thinking (Bandura, 1989; Dweck, 1991). In contrast, people with low control show a "state orientation" (Kuhl, 1981). Degenerated intentions take up working memory capacity, they interfere with holistic information processing, and distract attention from task involvement.

COMPONENTS OF PLANNING
AND PERCEIVED CONTROL

Motivation and volitional effects of perceived control would be expected to be apparent in different aspects of the planning process. This section considers how perceived control might affect each of the components of planning.

Representation of the Action Space

In planning, representation refers to "using past knowledge to build a representation of the environment that will provide the information relevant for action" (Scholnick & Friedman, 1993, pp. 146–147). Important aspects of these representations include the current versus desired end state of the environment, and the action steps needed to transform one into the other.

Although not studied explicitly from this perspective, the work on perceived control suggests that, almost by definition, people with high control view the world in general as a more structured system than do people with low perceived control. They perceive efforts as closely connected to outcomes and experience the environment as more predictable, responsive, contingent, and (of course) controllable. They expect to find many alternative strategies for reaching goals. Even in situations of lower contingency, they see themselves as capable of actions effective in maximizing desired and minimizing undesired outcomes. In contrast, people with low control see the world as a relatively more chaotic place. They experience the world as less predictable, containing few response–outcome contingencies, and fewer opportunities to influence outcomes; the self is seen as commanding fewer resources and as less able to operate existing contingencies.

If this general difference is applied to the representation of the environment for planning, it would be expected that people with high control would have more elaborated, organized, and causally structured representations of the action space. They would code more means–ends relations and more opportunities for action. People with low control would form representations that are more truncated, less organized, and more chaotic. They would not expect or search for many pathways to the desired outcome. The differences between structured versus chaotic representations would be expected to have cumulative effects on the other steps in the planning process.

Goal Setting

"The term 'goal' refers both to the end state of a task and the reason for undertaking it" (Scholnick & Friedman, 1993, p. 150). During the planning process, individuals must "decide whether it is realistic and worthwhile to achieve their goals in the current circumstances" (p. 147). There is no evidence that perceived control has any direct impact on the values or priorities people place on desired and undesired outcomes. However, once a set of desired outcomes or goals has been identified, an individual's estimates of the likelihood that these can be achieved through effort has been shown to make a difference to the selection of a goal, and most especially to the level of the goal set.

Not surprisingly, people with high control set higher goals, and the setting of higher goals facilitates better performance (e.g., Schunk, 1989). Less obviously, people with high control also set more concrete and specific goals, a process that has also been shown experimentally to improve performance (Bandura, 1989). In general, these people seem to have more positive, higher, and better-defined goals; it is less clear why these kinds of goals should facilitate effective performance. Perhaps its because they make planning and strategizing easier.

The "Decision" to Plan

The third step involves "a decision about whether it is realistic and worthwhile to formulate a plan in advance" (Scholnick & Friedman, 1993, p. 147). It is in this step that the complexity of the relationship between control and planning can be seen. There are multiple reasons for planning and not planning, and each of these may show a differential relation to control (see Scholnick & Friedman, 1993, pp. 159–160).

Two reasons why individuals do not plan stem from the previous phases of the action process. First, individuals may not plan because their initial representation of the problem space has already made clear the sequence of action steps necessary to reach the goal. In this case, on easy tasks, people with high perceived control would be more likely to do well without stopping to plan (relative to people with low perceived control).

Second, people may not plan when they actually should because they underestimate the complexity of the task and, hence, do not recognize the need for planning. People with low control, who presumably have less elaborated representations of the action space, might be expected to fail to plan on difficult tasks and as a result to perform more poorly on these tasks. In contrast, people with high control are more likely to plan appropriately for difficult tasks, because they recognize the challenge in coordinating resources with constraints.

A second set of reasons is motivational. People with low control do not plan because there is no point; it is not expected that the goal can be achieved by the efforts of the individual. Although this belief is obviously analogous to a control belief, it can be spurred by two complementary evaluations of the source of the uncontrollability. The individual can believe that the desired outcome is not contingent on action, a set of beliefs referred to as strategy beliefs (or universal helplessness, low response–outcome expectations, low contingency judgments, or external locus of control.) Alternatively the individual can believe that the source of the problem lies not in the connections between means and ends, but in his or her own ability to execute the effective strategies, referred to a capacity beliefs (or personal helplessness, low self-efficacy, or low perceived competence; see Skinner, 1996, for a review of these concepts). Research that has examined these two aspects of beliefs separately consistently finds that children's and adults' beliefs about their capacities are better predictors of their motivation and performance than strategy beliefs alone. However, the two belief sets also seem to interact, such that the most maladaptive profile is to believe that one does not have access (low capacity) to those means that are most effective (high strategy) (e.g., Skinner et al., 1990).

In general, people with high control are more likely to plan appropriately, deciding to plan when tasks are challenging, and dispensing with specific plans when the task is less complex. People with high control should plan more appropriately because they have a better representation of the structure of the problem space and are motivated by the general belief that their efforts can make a difference in the specific domain. People with low control are more likely to be inappropriate in their planning. They may feel overwhelmed by relatively simple tasks and feel the need to plan because they cannot spontaneously imagine a sequence of effective action steps. They may fail to plan enough (or at all) on complex tasks because their impoverished representations of the action space lead them to underestimate task difficulty. In general, people with low control should plan less because they lack the motivation provided by the conviction that their efforts can make a difference.

Different aspects of the profile of control beliefs may have different kinds of effects on the decision to plan. As pointed out by Scholnick and Friedman (1993), belief in the efficacy of one's own efforts may have a linear relationship to planning efforts, whereas ability estimates may have a curvilinear relationship. If work on the other consequences of control are an indication, it is also possible that perceived control will have an impact on planning only in complex, difficult, or stressful situations. In these circumstances, all aspects of control would be expected to promote engagement in the planning process.

In this context, it may be important to point out that the "decision" not to plan may not actually be an active intentional process, that is, the individual may not reflect on the advantages and disadvantages of planning and then conclude that planning is not necessary to reach the goal. Especially for children, it may not even occur to them to plan. Even for adults, stressful and novel situations may prevent them from ever really considering the possibility of planning.

Plan Construction

Formulating a plan involves the "choice of a strategy to reach a goal" (Scholnick & Friedman, 1993, p. 147); plans can be designed, selected, or adapted. The general conception of perceived control suggests that strategies will be selected not only on the basis of their perceived effectiveness in reaching the goal, but also on the basis of the individuals' perceptions of their capacity for successfully executing the strategy (Bandura, 1977). As a result, the most straightforward relation between perceived control and plan formation will be found in the belief that effort is an effective means to reach the outcome and that the self can exert the needed effort; these are referred to as *strategy* and *capacity beliefs* for effort (or efficacy and response–outcome expectations (Bandura, 1977); competence and contingency estimates (Weisz, 1983); action–outcome and outcome–consequence expectations (Heckhausen, 1991).

However, even when people perceive that their efforts are not likely to be effective, they may not become helpless. If their generalized control beliefs are high, they may make plans to improve the situation. They may plan to improve means–ends relations by locating, moving to, or changing circumstances in a way that increases the contingencies between actions and outcomes. Alternatively, they may plan to improve capacities by increasing their resources or competencies so as to make better use of existing contingencies and circumstances.

The specifics of the conception of perceived control also suggest that individuals may organize their plans around means other than their own efforts. In a consideration of the core categories of means to which people usually ascribe success and failure, causal attribution theorists suggest the causal categories of effort or action, attributes (such as ability, personality, genes, attractiveness), other people (powerful others like teachers, parents, doctors, or God, as well as peers like friends or spouses), luck (chance or fate), macropolitical conditions (such as economic or social climate), and unknown causes.

The theory of perceived control suggests that if people perceive means outside of their own efforts to be more effective than their own and if they believe that they can obtain access to those means, that they will make attempts to do so. In simple terms, people may make plans to get other people to obtain their goals for them. As a simple example, Chalmers and Lawrence (1993) reported the response of an elderly participant in a study on planning who was requested to plan a difficult party "'I wouldn't do that ... I would just call up my daughter to have the party. I would help her with the cooking'" (p. 212). In a more serious vein, children may plan to get help from their teachers or parents on difficult academic tasks; spouses may make plans to convince a spouse to do more childcare; a patient may make a plan to find a more competent specialist; an elderly person may plan to recruit more help with the yard or housework.

Plan Implementation and Revision

The next step in planning involves monitoring the plan, or deciding "when it needs to be revised, how much effort should be expended, and when the goal has been satisfied" (Scholnick & Friedman, 1993, p. 147). Perceived control should have an impact on two different aspects of this phase of planning. First, it should influence plan execution if supervision of the plan taxes limits of processing capacity. Here, volitional mechanisms should determine if all existing capacities are available for use in plan implementation. Second, motivational and volitional mechanisms should play a big part when plans do not unfold as expected. When the execution of a plan runs into obstacles, perceived control is a key factor in determining how the individual will respond. Children with low control should tend to abandon goals and planning attempts when strategies do not lead to desired results.

In contrast, children with high control are more likely to persist with implementation efforts, adapt them flexibly to changing circumstances, strategically revise a plan midstream, or, if needed, go back to the drawing board to begin plan construction again. Throughout this process, the child's conviction that a pathway to the desired outcome must exist supports more positive emotional tone, less anxiety, and more interest and enthusiasm. In addition, for children with high control, access to reserves of processing capacity ensure that they will formulate the optimal plan of which they are capable and that revisions will also reflect their peak performance capabilities.

Learning from Planning

Although not explicitly discussed as a component of planning, there is also a "post-implementation" phase of the process during which people "step back to evaluate what they have learned about their goals, strategies, plans, and environmental implementation" (Scholnick & Friedman, 1993, p. 147). People who interpret performances as a function of their own efforts would be likely to use this phase to consolidate knowledge about the effectiveness of particular strategies in reaching goals, and about the self's capacity to execute effective strategies. In addition, details about strategy implementation and adaptation would likely be noted.

In contrast, people who view the outcomes of an action sequence as largely due to influences outside their control would be less likely to derive concrete knowledge that would benefit future planning. They do not hone any specific skills or infer any general meta-planning strategies. For people who do not plan or who plan badly, these experiences may simply serve to cement beliefs that planning is usually a waste of time.

Summary

Perceived control should have an impact on the processes of planning that is most evident in novel, taxing, and stressful situations. Perceived control should influence the components of planning not only through its impact on motivation, which influences the extent of effort and persistence exerted in service of a goal, but also through volitional mechanisms, which facilitate or interfere with the implementation of intentions.

Furthermore, control should influence representations of the planning environment, such that people with high control construct more organized, elaborated, and structured representations of means–ends relations, compared to the more chaotic and truncated representations formed by people with low control. People with a sense of control should also have higher, more concrete goals and be better able to visualize the action steps leading to an outcome. This allows them to dispense with formal planning when appropriate, but also to recognize when the complexity of the situation makes planning essential. People with low control may feel overwhelmed by even simple tasks and so plan unnecessarily, or they may fail to appreciate the advantages of planning in difficult circumstances. In general, people with high control are more likely to plan because they believe that their efforts can make a difference to successful goal attainment.

In the formulation of plans, people who believe in the effectiveness of effort and their capacity to deploy it, will select plans organized around actions. If effort–outcome contingencies are perceived to be low, people with high efficacy may nevertheless formulate plans to improve environmental conditions or to increase their own capacities. If the efforts of others are seen as efficacious, people may plan to involve those others in the process of obtaining desired outcomes. Perceived control influences plan execution and monitoring by supporting or undermining effort exertion and persistence, especially when obstacles require plans to be adapted, revised, or abandoned. The volitional effects of perceived control should be apparent in these processes when plan supervision or revision taxes cognitive resources.

PERCEIVED CONTROL, ACTION, AND THE STUDY OF PLANNING

Taken together, the motivational and volitional effects of a sense of control increase the likelihood that, at each phase of planning, a child or adult will show the optimal performance of which he or she is capable. This analysis has implications for the kinds of planning tasks on which perceived control is most likely to make a difference, for the aspects of planning that must be differentiated in order to observe the effects of perceived control, and for an analysis of the reciprocal effects of planning on control.

Perceived Control in Different Planning Tasks

Different kinds of planning tasks emphasize different elements in the planning process (Scholnick & Friedman, 1993). Hence, they also differ in the extent to which they should be influenced by perceived control. For example, in tasks of comprehension of plans depicted in stories, a child's ability to understand goal-directed action is tapped. However, children are not required to decide whether to plan, or to generate, implement, or monitor a plan. Hence, the impact of motivational factors, such as perceived control, would be minimized.

This kind of planning can be contrasted with the planning required to solve intellectual puzzles, such as the Tower of Hanoi. The successful completion of these tasks requires heavy computational work with "a premium on the representation of the problem space that determines the shape of the plan that must be assembled from relatively unfamiliar elements or from very general problem-solving strategies" (Scholnick & Friedman, 1993, p. 154). In addition, these tasks are likely to be at the upper boundary of difficulty and so will require the maximum processing capacity reserves of the child. They also require persistent strategic re-engagement when action steps do not work out as expected.

As a result, planning in these problem-solving tasks is likely to be influenced greatly by motivation. Perceived control should have an impact on the amount of structure in the representation, the accuracy of the assessment of task difficulty, the recognition of the need to plan, the decision that is it realistic to attempt the task, the amount of working memory available for plan construction and implementation, the persistence of strategy use and hypothesis testing in the face of breakdowns, and the quality of plan revision. At the same time that, from a planning perspective, perceived control may be most interesting in the study of problem-solving plans, from a motivational perspective, problem solving is one of the less interesting kinds of planning. This is because, in motivational terms, it is relatively indistinguishable from other cognitive problem-solving tasks that are typically used to analyze the effects of perceived control.

However, as a middle ground between comprehending plans in story form and plans as solutions to specific cognitive puzzles, falls *everyday planning*. Of course, *everyday planning* runs the range from planning errands to planning how to deal with a parent's failing health. A motivational analysis specifies the conditions under which perceived control would and would not be expected to play a role in these processes. Motivation is highlighted when goals are personally important, and yet their attainment is uncertain. Planning in conditions that are novel, ambiguous, challenging, stressful, and demanding should elicit the effects of perceived control. In addition, situations in which a new plan must be formulated and implemented, especially one which requires maximum processing capacity, are likely to be affected by both the motivational and functional effects of control. Finally, plans that run into obstacles and need to be debugged, revised, or abandoned should highlight the role of perceived control in supporting effort exertion, persistence, and continued strategic re-engagement.

Differentiation of the Components of Planning

For the effects of perceived control to be observed in any kind of planning task, however, it would be important to empirically separate the different phases of planning. For example, in order to test predictions about the structured versus chaotic representations of the environment constructed by children who differ in their control beliefs, a valid measure of the child's representation of the action space would be needed, independent of the assessment of the plan itself. Likewise, in order to study the mechanisms through which perceived control influences the decision to plan, tasks are needed in which participants can decide *not* to plan; in addition, assessments should distinguish among objective levels of complexity of the activity (in order to decide whether plans are actually needed), organization of representations (to see whether clear representations lead to lack of planning on easy tasks whereas incomplete representations lead to underplanning on difficult tasks), quality of planning, and effectiveness of action (with and without plans).

To establish the differences among different types of planning decisions, it might also be useful to assess participants' reasons for planning or not planning. In addition, tasks might be structured to allow for strategies other than effort, or for plans that aim to improve response–outcome contingencies. Especially interesting would be the analysis of plans in low control circumstances. To fully examine the effects of control, planning tasks would need to include the execution of the plan, and assess both the quality of its supervision and individuals' reactions to obstacles and setbacks in implementation.

Planning as an Organizational Construct

When planning is not considered solely as a cognitive task, then a richer array of contexts in which to study its processes is suggested (Scholnick & Friedman, 1993). These include an analysis of planning in the study of coping (Compas, 1987; Folkman, 1984; Lazarus & Folkman, 1984; Garmezy & Rutter, 1983), life planning (Brim, 1992; Baltes, Staudinger, Maercker, & Smith, 1995), self-regulation (Eisenberg, Fabes, & Guthrie, in press; Kopp, 1982; Skinner & Wellborn, 1994), and the regulation of development (Baltes & Baltes, 1990; Brandtstaedter, 1989; Brandtstaedter, Wentura, & Greve, 1993; Schulz, Heckhausen, & Locher, 1991). These are contexts in which the effects of motivation are marked. For that reason, the planning that takes place in them may be less interesting to psychologists interested in the "pure cognitive mechanics" of planning, but they are more interesting to researchers trying to study the interplay of cognition, emotion, and motivation in planning processes.

The impact of perceived control, or motivational factors in general, is maximized in these contexts because planning takes place when people are confronted with complex, ambiguous problems in important life areas. People are more likely to make plans under these circumstances as well, because spontaneous planning is less likely than planning in response to blocked goals, setbacks, or difficulties. Especially for very young children, planning may not be initiated at all until obstacles are encountered. The study of planning in stressful circumstances is interesting because, on the one hand, these are probably situations in which effective planning can make a material difference to successful outcomes. On the other hand, the very stressfulness of the circumstances makes planning a more cognitive and motivationally challenging acitivity.

The general perspectives taken in these research areas suggest a few implications for the study of planning. First, it points out an important set of planning goals exist that has been overlooked in the planning literature: planning in order to prevent the occurrence of an undesired outcome. For adults, prevention of the (re)occurrence of traumatic events is a theme in the coping literatures on victimization, health, life-planning, and aging. Even children make plans about how to avoid certain outcomes, such as how to avoid being bullied, getting into fights, or failing tests (Skinner, Altman, & Sherwood, 1993).

Research on coping also suggests that the concept of planning can be considered as a continuum. In the planning literature, the opposite of planning is typically considered to be not planning. However, when reactions to a stressful situation are described, the negative pole might also include confusion, disorganization, denial, and procrastination (Lachman & Burack, 1993; Skinner & Wellborn, 1994). This research also points out the pivotal nature of the decision whether to engage in planning, given the importance and complexity attached to stressful situations. In some high risk situations, the decision to plan becomes a turning point for the better in children's and adolescents' developmental trajectories (Rutter, 1989).

At the other end of the continuum, planning itself would range from simple reflection about the next action step, to action sequences, to a full-blown, multi-step, future-oriented plan coordinating the actions of multiple people. Planning can be aimed at reaching a goal, or at setting up an environment for action that increases the likelihood for success, or at changing the self to be better suited to carrying out action strategies (Rothbaum, Weisz, & Snyder, 1982). In keeping with this general perspective, planning would be considered a process that unfolds over time—sometimes weeks, months, or even years.

Finally, although the quality of the plan will determine whether it leads to the desired outcome, another critical determinant of a plan's success in stressful situations is whether the individual can make him or herself adhere to the plan, that is, whether they can successfully regulate their own behavior in carrying out the plan. As plans unfold over time in uncertain contexts, they will call for flexible adaptation and revision. The ability to review and update plans, including reassessment and possible abandonment of goals is critical to long-term success (Brandtstaedter & Renner, 1990; Heckhausen & Schulz, 1995).

DEVELOPMENT OF THE RELATIONSHIP
BETWEEN PLANNING AND CONTROL

This final section considers two ways in which development interacts with the connections between planning and control. The first is a suggestion of how the reciprocal relationship between planning and control may influence the development of differential trajectories of both constructs in specific domains. The second suggestion points out the constraints placed on the connections between perceived control and the deployment of planning by development.

The Effects of Planning on Perceived Control

For a complete understanding of the links between control and planning, it is necessary to expand upon the one-sided view of the relationship considered in this chapter, by examining the effects of the planning process on beliefs about control. In reflecting upon the reverse relationship, it becomes clear that many aspects of the planning process should have an effect on a person's sense of control as well.

As a starting point, it is interesting to note that the representation of the planning space may itself impose structure on what can initially seem like a chaotic situation. In addition, the decision to plan, even before any plans have been formulated, implies quite strongly that structure exists in the problem space, that strategies can be found that will be effective in meeting goals, and that the self will be capable of executing them. A parent's simple statement to a child, "Well, then, let's make a plan," communicates a wealth of control-relevant information.

The formulation of a plan is also a phase in which structure is discovered or created. Even before any action is taken, the consideration of a variety of alternative strategies makes the outcome seem more contingent, and may make the needed action steps seem more accessible. Again, simple parent questions, like "What should we do first?", send very clear messages about control: it is available and we can discover how it is to be achieved. Especially in chaotic and challenging situations, simply making a plan imposes some structure and order on the threatening situation and leads people to feel more optimistic and hopeful.

The actual implementation phase, with its sequential strategies, adaptations, revisions, and re-engagement, is probably the central location of the experience of control. If the plan succeeds, especially in the face of obstacles and setbacks, a belief in control is heightened. Success encourages a person to view the self as more competent and the environment as more contingent. Even if the outcome is not reached, the experience can still be used to learn a great deal about means–ends relations in the environment and about constraints and opportunities for action. In action analyses of perceived control, the post-action phase of performance evaluation and interpretation is an important determinant of how interactions will (or will not) shape subsequent control beliefs (Heckhausen, 1991; Skinner, 1991).

The planning process should not only affect an individual's general sense of control, but should also lead adults and children to view the environment as a more structured context, and be more attuned to response–outcome contingencies. The planning process should suggest to them that effort and action are important causes of outcomes and should also lead them to view themselves as capable of implementing effective responses. Finally, it should augment their estimation of their own self-efficacy in coping with obstacles and difficulties in the execution of action plans. In short, the planning process should have an effect on the entire profile of beliefs about control. In times of stress, planning may be an important tool for discovering and creating structure and for concentrating the power of the individual to make a difference.

Cycles of Control and Planning

If perceived control influences the different elements of the planning process, and, in turn, is affected by the processes and outcomes of planning, then control and planning together may be one example of the "beliefs–action–beliefs" cycles described in the perceived control literature (Seligman, 1975; Skinner, 1991). In the current context, it would be expected that children who have more control are more likely to plan appropriately and effectively implement and adapt their plans, leading to more success, and the experience of more structure and competence. In contrast, children with initially low control would shy away from difficult tasks that require planning, or if they do plan, would underplan or fail to implement or adapt plans, especially in the face of obstacles; this in turn leads to more failures and experiences of the world as chaotic and the self as incompetent. These general patterns have been found to lead to developmental trajectories of relatively stable inter-individual differences in which the "rich get richer" and the "poor get poorer" (Skinner, Zimmer-Gembeck, & Connell, 1995).

Cumulatively, these cycles lead children who may not have differed initially on actual planning competencies to begin to diverge over time. Differential engagement in planning tasks not only influences short-term success and failure on the specific tasks, but also contributes to the development of planning skills, knowledge, and meta-planning strategies. Over time, initially helpless children would develop the kind of low-grade planning skills that would render veridical their views that planning (at least the kind of which they are capable) does not make a very big difference to the successful attainment of goals.

Other Sources of Motivation

Finally, the consideration of a broad definition of planning, although it makes clear the potential role played by perceived control, should not obscure the importance of other sources of motivation and other self-system processes in addition to control (Connell & Wellborn, 1991). In fact, the need for competence or control may be considered as the motivational complement of planning. All the processes of planning are completely consistent with the desire for competence and effectance; they allow people to be more effective in their interactions with the environment (Harter, 1978; White, 1959).

In contrast, other motivational needs may be at cross-purposes with planning. The need for autonomy and self-determination (DeCharms, 1968; Deci & Ryan, 1985) is a likely candidate in this regard, especially if people are coerced into planning or if plans prevent people from engaging in the behaviors they choose. Plans that restrict spontaneity, flexibility, and fun may undermine the need for autonomy. In a similar vein, plans that add too much structure to interpersonal interactions may interfere with the need for relatedness, or connections to other people (Bowlby, 1969). Hence, even if people have the cognitive capabilities to plan and even if they believe that their plans will be effective and they can make them work, they may nevertheless not engage in planning behavior if it interferes with the need for relationships or for spontaneity and freedom of action. Analyses of planning will be richer to the extent that they consider other sources of motivation in addition to perceived control.

ACKNOWLEDGMENTS

Support from research grant no. HD19914 from the National Institute of Child Health and Human Development, from Training Grant No. 527594 from the National Institute Mental Health, and from a Faculty Scholar's Award from The William T. Grant Foundation are gratefully acknowledged.

REFERENCES

Abramson, L. Y., Seligman, M. E. P., & Teasdale, J. D. (1978). Learned helplessness in humans. *Journal of Abnormal Psychology, 87*, 49–74.

Baltes, M. M., & Baltes, P. B. (1986). *The psychology of control and aging*. Hillsdale, NJ: Lawrence Erlbaum Associates.

Baltes, P. B., & Baltes, M. M. (1990). Psychological perspectives on successful aging: The model of selective optimization with compensation. In P. B. Baltes & M. M. Baltes (Eds.), *Successful aging: Perspectives from the behavioral sciences* (pp. 1–34). Cambridge, England: Cambridge University Press.

Baltes, P. B., Staudinger, U. M., Maercker, A., & Smith, J. (1995). People nominated as wise: A comparative study of wisdom-related knowledge. *Psychology and Aging, 10*, 155–166.

Bandura, A. (1977). Self-efficacy: Toward a unified theory of behavioral change. *Psychological Review, 84*, 191–215.

Bandura, A. (1981). Self-referent thought: A developmental analysis of self-efficacy. In J. H. Flavell & L. Ross (Eds.), *Social cognitive development: Frontiers and possible futures* (pp. 200–239). Cambridge, England: Cambridge University Press.

Bandura, A. (1986). *The social foundations of thought and action: A social cognitive theory*. Englewood Cliffs, NJ: Prentice Hall.

Bandura, A. (1989). Human agency in social cognitive theory. *American Psychologist, 44*(9), 1175–1184.

Bandura, A., & Schunk, D. H. (1981). Cultivating competence, self-efficacy, and intrinsic interest through proximal self-motivation. *Journal of Personality and Social Psychology, 41*, 586–598.

Bowlby, J. (1969). *Attachment and loss: Vol. 1. Attachment*. New York: Basic Books.

Brandtstaedter, J. (1984). Personal and social control over development: Some implications of an action perspective in life-span developmental psychology. In P. B. Baltes & O. G. Brim (Eds.), *Life-span development and behavior* (pp. 1–32). New York: Academic Press.

Brandtstaedter, J. (1989). Personal self-regulation of development: Cross-sequential analyses of development-related control beliefs and emotions. *Developmental Psychology, 25*, 96–108.

Brandtstaedter, J., & Renner, G. (1990). Tenacious goal pursuit and flexible goal adjustment: Explication and age-related analysis of assimilative and accommodative strategies of coping. *Psychology and Aging, 5*(1), 58–67.

Brandtstaedter, J., Wentura, D., & Greve, W. (1993). Adaptive resources of the aging self: Outlines of an emergent perspective. *International Journal of Behavioral Development, 16*(2), 323–349.

Brim, O. G. (1974 August). *The sense of personal control over one's life*. Invited address at the 82nd Annual Convention of the American Psychological Association, New Orleans.

Brim, O. G. (1992). *Ambition: How we manage success and failure throughout our lives*. New York: Basic Books.

Chalmers, D., & Lawrence, J. A. (1993). Investigating the effects of planning aids on adults' and adolescents' organization of a complex task. *International Journal of Behavioral Development, 16*(2), 191–214.

Chapman, M., & Skinner, E. A. (1985). Action in development/Development in action. In M. Frese & J. Sabini (Eds.), *Goal directed behavior: The concept of action in psychology* (pp. 199–213). Hillsdale, NJ: Lawrence Erlbaum Associates.

Compas, B. E. (1987). Coping with stress during childhood and adolescence. *Psychological Bulletin, 101*, 393–403.

Connell, J. P., & Wellborn, J. G. (1991). Competence, autonomy and relatedness: A motivational analysis of self-system processes. In M. Gunnar & A. Sroufe (Eds.), *Minnesota symposium on child psychology* (pp. 43–77). Chicago: University of Chicago Press.

DeCharms, R. (1968). *Personal causation*. New York: Academic Press.

Deci, E. L., & Ryan, R. M. (1985). *Intrinsic motivation and self-determination in human behavior*. New York: Plenum.

Dweck, C. S. (1991). Self-theories and goals: Their role in motivation, personality, and development. In R. A. Dientsbier (Ed.), *Nebraska Symposium on Motivation, 1990*. Lincoln: University of Nebraska Press.

Dweck, C. S., & Elliott, E. S. (1983). Achievement motivation. In E. M. Hetherington (Ed.), *Handbook of child psychology: Vol. IV. Social and personality development* (pp. 643–691). New York: Wiley.

Dweck, C. S., & Leggett, E. L. (1988). A social–cognitive approach to motivation and personality. *Psychological Review, 95,* 256–273.

Eisenberg, N., Fabes, R. A., & Guthrie, I. (in press). Coping with stress: The roles of regulation and development. In I. N. Sandler & S. A. Wolchik (Eds.), *Handbook of children's coping with common stressors: Linking theory, research, and intervention.* New York: Plenum.

Folkman, S. (1984). Personal control and stress and coping processes: A theoretical analysis. *Journal of Personality and Social Psychology, 46*(4), 839–852.

Garmezy, N., & Rutter, M. (Eds.). (1983). *Stress, coping and development in children.* New York: McGraw-Hill.

Harter, S. (1978). Effective motivation reconsidered: Toward a developmental model. *Human Development, 21* 36–64.

Harter, S. (1983). Developmental perspectives on the self system. In E. M. Hetherington (Ed.), *Handbook of child psychology: Socialization, personality, and social development.* New York: Wiley.

Heckhausen, H. (1991). *Motivation and action* (P. K. Leppmann, Trans.). Berlin: Springer-Verlag.

Heckhausen, H., & Gollwitzer, P. M. (1987). Thought contents and cognitive functioning in motivational versus volitional states of mind. *Motivation and Emotion, 11*(2), 101–120.

Heckhausen, J. & Schulz, R. (1995). A life-span theory of control. *Psychological Review, 102,* 284–304.

Kopp, C. (1982). Antecedents of self-regulation: A developmental perspective. *Developmental Psychology, 18*(2), 199–214.

Kuhl, J. (1981). Motivational and functional helplessness: The moderating effect of state versus action orientation. *Journal of Personality and Social Psychology, 40*(1), 155–170.

Kuhl, J. (1984). Volitional aspects of achievement motivation and learned helplessness: Toward a comprehensive theory of action control. In B. A. Maber (Ed.), *Progress in experimental personalities research* (pp. 99–171). New York: Academic Press.

Lachman, M. (Ed.). (1993). Planning and control processes across the life span. *International Journal of Behavioral Development, 16*(2).

Lachman, M. E., & Burack, O. R. (1993). Planning and control processes across the life span: An overview. *International Journal of Behavioral Development, 16*(2), 131–143.

Lazarus, R. S., & Folkman, S. (1984). *Stress, appraisal, and coping.* New York: Springer.

Lefcourt, H. M. (1981). *Research with the locus of control construct: Vol. 1. Assessment methods.* New York: Academic Press.

Lefcourt, H. M. (1982). *Locus of control: Current trends in theory and research.* New York: Wiley.

Lefcourt, H. M. (1983). *Research with the locus of control construct: Vol. 2. Developments and social problems.* New York: Academic Press.

Lefcourt, H. M. (1992). Durability and impact of the locus of control construct. *Psychological Bulletin, 112*(3), 411–414.

Peterson, C., & Seligman, M. E. P. (1984). Causal explanations as a risk factor for depression: Theory and evidence. *Psychological Review, 91,* 347–374.

Rothbaum, F., Weisz, J. R., & Snyder, S. S. (1982). Changing the world and changing the self: A two-process model of perceived control. *Journal of Personality and Social Psychology, 42*(1), 5–37.

Rutter, M. (1989). Pathways from childhood to adult life. *Journal of Child Psychology, 30*(1), 23–51.

Scholnick, E. K., & Friedman, S. L. (1993). Planning in context: Developmental and situational considerations. *International Journal of Behavioral Development, 16*(2), 145–167.

Schulz, R., Heckhausen, J., & Locher, J. L. (1991). Adult development, control, and adaptive functioning. *Journal of Social Issues, 47*(4), 177–196.

Schunk, D. (1989). Self-efficacy and achievement behaviors. *Educational Psychology Review, 1,* 173–208.

Seligman, M. E. P. (1975). *Helplessness: On depression, development, and death.* San Francisco: Freeman.

Skinner, E. A. (1991). Development and perceived control: A dynamic model of action in context. In M. Gunnar & L. A. Sroufe (Eds.), *Minnesota symposium on child psychology* (pp. 167–216). Hillsdale, NJ: Lawrence Erlbaum Associates.

Skinner, E. A. (1995). *Perceived control, motivation, and coping.* Beverly Hills, CA: Sage.

Skinner, E. A. (1996). A guide to constructs of control. *Journal of Personality and Social Psychology, 71,* 549–570.

Skinner, E. A., Altman, J., & Sherwood, H. (1993). *An analysis of open-ended interviews of children's coping in the domains of academics and friendship.* Manual, University of Rochester.

Skinner, E. A., Chapman, M., & Baltes, P. B. (1988). Control, means–ends, and agency beliefs: A new conceptualization and its measurement during childhood. *Journal of Personality and Social Psychology, 54,* 117–133.

Skinner, E. A., & Connell, J. P. (1986). Control understanding: Suggestions for a developmental framework. In M. M. Baltes & P. B. Baltes (Eds.), *The psychology of control and aging* (pp. 35–69). Hillsdale, NJ: Lawrence Erlbaum Associates.

Skinner, E. A., & Wellborn, J. G. (1994). Coping during childhood and adolescence: A motivational perspective. In D. Featherman, R. Lerner, & M. Perlmutter (Eds.), *Life-span development and behavior* (pp. 91–133). Hillsdale, NJ: Lawrence Erlbaum Associates.

Skinner, E. A., Wellborn, J. G., & Connell, J. P. (1990). What it takes to do well in school and whether I've got it: The role of perceived control in children's engagement and school achievement. *Journal of Educational Psychology, 82,* 22–32.

Skinner, E. A., Zimmer-Gembeck, M., & Connell, J. P. (1995, April). *Individual trajectories of perceived control across three years: Relations to context, action, and outcomes.* Paper presented at the meetings of the Society for Research in Child Development, Indianapolis, IN.

Strickland, B. R. (1989). Internal-external control expectancies: From contingency to creativity. *American Psychologist, 44*(1), 1–12.

Weiner, B. (1985a). An attributional theory of achievement motivation and emotion. *Psychological Review, 92,* 548–573.

Weiner, B. (1985b). "Spontaneous" causal thinking. *Psychological Bulletin, 97,* 74–84.

Weiner, B. (1986). *An attributional theory of motivation and emotion.* New York: Springer-Verlag.

Weisz, J. R. (1983). Can I control it? The pursuit of veridical answers across the life span. In P. B. Baltes & O. G. Brim, Jr. (Eds.), *Life-span development and behavior* (pp. 233–300). New York: Academic Press.

White, R. W. (1959). Motivation reconsidered: The concept of competence. *Psychological Review, 66,* 297–333.

12

Where Planning Meets Coping: Proactive Coping and the Detection and Management of Potential Stressors

Lisa G. Aspinwall
University of Maryland, College Park

In many areas of life, people experience good outcomes or avoid bad ones because of their proactive efforts. *Proactive coping* consists of efforts undertaken to prevent a stressful event or to offset its effects. Captured by colorful expressions such as "reading the writing on the wall" and "heading it off at the pass," such efforts clearly reflect the idea that people cope in advance; that is, they perceive cues suggesting trouble is imminent and act to forestall or to minimize an adverse event.

Although a voluminous body of research has focused on people's efforts to cope with stressful events once they occur (see Taylor & Aspinwall, 1996, for a review), proactive coping is all but unstudied (McGrath & Beehr, 1990; Sansone & Berg, 1993). One reason for the lack of empirical attention is that proactive coping may be difficult to detect. Specifically, when we act successfully to avert or minimize a potential stressor, relatively little happens (cf. McGrath & Beehr, 1990). Nonevents are rarely selected for scientific study, and therefore a great deal of proactive coping may go unrecognized. For example, an administrator who shuffles funds to avert a financial shortfall that would jeopardize the payroll and discredit her company may receive little notice for her work, because the net result, as seen by outside observers, was that nothing happened. Instead, our attention is drawn to business people who lose such gambles.

Consider a worker who anticipates an economic downturn in her field and begins to acquire new job skills. If and when layoffs begin, she is more likely to be reemployed. For this reason, she is also less likely to be represented in a study of long-term unemployment. Even if she is included in an outcome study of some kind, the critical actions she took to offset the stressfulness of the focal event (e.g., the layoff) were undertaken in advance of the stressor and so would not be assessed in a study of coping with job loss in which the majority of assessments focused on reactions to the event.

As in the case of the administrator, proactive coping may involve simple and specific actions that are executed at one point in time to address short-term concrete problems. Or as in the case of the worker, they may involve complex action sequences directed to major life decisions or tasks that extend indefinitely into the future. It is important to note that not all of life's stressors can be anticipated and managed in this way, but rather that certain kinds of occupational, interpersonal, academic, and health stressors may be proactively managed.

OVERVIEW

A major goal of this chapter is to highlight the various activities undertaken to avoid or to reduce stress and to prevent the development of problems early in their course. We review individual differences and self-regulatory processes examined in the stress and coping literature that have not yet been applied to the study of planning, and suggest that these factors may go a long way in understanding such activities. Our analysis also considers how such factors may explain both failures to anticipate potential stressors and failures to make and execute successful offsetting plans. Our review begins by examining the relation of proactive coping to related activities, such as planning, problem solving, and anticipatory coping. Next, we present a model of proactive coping developed jointly from the stress and coping and self-regulation literatures. At each stage in the model, the role of cognitive and noncognitive factors in the process of detecting and managing potential stressors is discussed. The complete model is then illustrated with reference to a program of research on the role of optimistic beliefs in the detection and management of potential stressors. We conclude with a consideration of what the study of planning and proactive coping have to offer each other and some suggestions for future research at the intersection of these two research areas. It is hoped that integrating the study of stress and coping with the study of self-regulation, planning, and other future-oriented, goal-directed behaviors will elucidate the processes underlying both cognitive and behavioral efforts to avoid future harm or to reach future goals.

PROACTIVE COPING, SELF-REGULATION, AND PLANNING

The activities of detecting and managing potential stressors bear a great deal of similarity to the activities of planning, but are also different in many important ways. To elucidate the relation of proactive coping to planning and other self-regulatory efforts, we discuss (a)the relation of proactive coping to goal-directed behavior, (b) the nature of the problem faced by the proactive coper and the corresponding challenges inherent in detection and management of such problems, and (c) additional influences on the proactive coping process that are not typically incorporated in models of planning.

Proactive Coping and Goal-Directed Behavior

Understanding how people anticipate and manage potential stressors involves two critical elements: self-regulation and coping. Self-regulation is defined as the ways in which people control and direct their own actions, usually in the service of some goal or goals (Fiske & Taylor, 1991). Models of self-regulation have the monitoring of one's progress and one's rate of progress toward a goal with respect to some reference value as a central feature (Carver & Scheier, 1981, 1990). Coping is defined as the process of managing internal or external demands that are appraised as taxing or exceeding the resources of a person (Lazarus & Folkman, 1984). Importantly, coping efforts may be directed toward two different aspects of managing stressors: efforts directed toward addressing the problem itself (problem-focused coping) and efforts directed toward managing emotions that arise from experiencing the stressor (emotion-focused coping). Research suggests that people use both problem-focused and emotion-focused coping to manage most stressful events (Folkman & Lazarus, 1980).

Proactive coping combines elements of self-regulation and coping by addressing the processes through which people try to detect and anticipate future threats to specific goals or to general physical and psychological well-being. If a *stressor* is an environmental or intrapsychic demand that is perceived as representing threat or harm and exceeding one's resources to manage it (cf. Lazarus & Folkman, 1984), a *potential stressor* is something that may ultimately do so, if left unchecked. The activities of detecting and managing potential stressors may occur either before the stressor actually occurs, when the potential stressor is just a possibility, or relatively early in its development, after some warning signs have been detected. That is, people may respond proactively to potential stressors that are detected through internal processes, such as reflection, or to those signaled by warning signs in the environment.

As people identify potential stressors that might threaten their goals, both coping and self-regulatory processes are invoked. That is, people engaged in proactive coping are simultaneously trying to anticipate and solve problems, to manage their emotions, and to assess their progress toward important goals. Thus, proactive coping and planning share the idea that problems arise from unmet goals (or, in the case of proactive coping, threatened or potentially threatened goals) and share a concern with the strategies undertaken to work toward these goals.

The Nature of the Problem

There are several important differences between the ways in which the proactive coping and planning frameworks conceptualize the nature of problems and represent the skills needed to address them. The first such differences concern the development of the problem and the potential for the problem to be avoided or offset. The prototypical "problem" considered in proactive coping is one that develops gradually and that may be anticipated and offset. This conceptualization of a problem as a *potential* stressor differs from the conceptualization used in the stress and coping literature, which usually takes as a point of departure some fully developed stressor that is already adversely affecting the person, such as chronic illness, financial strain, interpersonal discord, or academic failure. The coping concept most closely related to proactive coping, *anticipatory coping*, is also fundamentally different. Anticipatory coping involves preparation for the stressful consequences of an upcoming event whose occurrence is a certainty, such as major surgery or academic examinations (Breznitz, 1983a; Folkman & Lazarus, 1985), whereas proactive coping involves preventive activities that might be undertaken to avert stressful events altogether or change their form.

Second, a potential problem, by definition, is at least somewhat *ambiguous*, because little or nothing has happened yet. Potential stressors may provide ambiguous cues and warning signs that must be appraised, interpreted, and monitored over time to determine whether one is, in fact, facing a problem. In this sense, whether one is experiencing a problem or not depends heavily on whether and how one attends to and appraises these warning signals. That is, the same warning signs may be interpreted as problematic by one person and benign by another, or they may be ignored. Even if a potential stressor is appraised as such, people must decide whether they will take steps to address it and evaluate the costs of doing so (cf. Hobfoll, 1989; Schonpflug, 1986).

In contrast, in much of the problem-solving literature, the problem has already arisen and is known to be problematic. It is also clearly defined. Finally, people are given the task of solving it. The protoypical problem in such research is the Tower of Hanoi, in which the sequencing of strategies and cognitive abilities required to plan one's movements of the rings from one tower to another by means of a third tower may be systematically assessed (see Scholnick, 1994, and Scholnick & Friedman, 1993, for discussions of the effects of studying constrained problem spaces on our understanding of planning). Recently, many authors have called for an extension of problem solving research to more complex and involving everyday planning tasks (Dreher & Oerter, 1987; Goodnow, 1987; Kreitler & Kreitler, 1987; Rogoff, Gauvain, & Gardner, 1987; Scholnick & Friedman, 1993). In many of these more naturalistic and interesting problems, however, the problem is relatively clear-cut, has been defined as a problem, exists already, and is usually solvable.

What are the implications of the nature of potential stressors for the challenges posed by efforts to offset them? First, because it is unclear whether the potential stressor will ultimately develop into a problem, it must be *monitored* over time. The importance of monitoring in planning and problem solving has been recognized by many planning researchers (see Scholnick & Friedman, 1987, for a review). Proactive coping presents some unusual challenges in monitoring in that the potential stressor can turn out to be benign, or it may change form to pose a greater threat to well-being. Additionally, one's efforts either to solve it or to obtain additional information about it may *aggravate* the problem (Schonpflug, 1986). For example, a person who is concerned that a valuable interpersonal relationship may be weakening must try to obtain information about the current status of that relationship; however, efforts to do so may be seen as intrusive and aggravate the problem if it did indeed exist, or even create the seeds of a new problem (cf. Schonpflug, 1986).

The proactive coping and planning frameworks also differ in how they conceptualize the costs of engaging in planning efforts in the first place and in the costs of failing to solve the problem. Because of the evolving nature of potential stressors, it is important to understand the factors involved in addressing problems early in their course when they require fewer resources to manage and when they pose less harm to the person. The relatively static, well-defined problems and brain teasers employed in studies of problem solving rarely have these properties. Specifically, such problems pose little direct harm to the person if they are not addressed quickly, and the problems themselves do not evolve over time. Additionally, because research participants are not generally trying to solve other concurrent tasks in the laboratory, devoting attention to the solution of these problems has little potential to compromise other ongoing self-regulatory activities. Finally, because these problems are typically solvable, there is little motivational cost to pursuing them, whereas many naturalistic coping situations present intractable stressors, for which persistence drains resources and creates motivational deficits. Even if the situation is not intractable, would-be proactive copers must weigh the costs of proaction against the costs of the failure to engage in offsetting activities (cf. Hobfoll, 1989; Schonpflug, 1986).

Returning to our earlier examples, if the administrator is wrong about the payroll shortfall, she has diverted resources from other activities for nothing. If the worker is wrong about the anticipated layoffs, she has acquired those extra skills in vain. If she is correct about the layoffs, but incorrect about the field in which to acquire those extra skills, she may be worse off for her proactive efforts. It is important, therefore, to understand the factors that influence the quality and accuracy of appraisals of potential stressors and how people respond to information that might qualify these initial assessments. Additionally, as we will describe, a central concern of the proactive coping framework is how people are able to distinguish solvable problems from unsolvable ones and allocate their resources accordingly.

Additional Influences on Proactive Coping

In addition to differences in the nature of the problem when it is first encountered and the challenged posed by monitoring its development and devoting resources to its solution, the proactive coping framework examines two influences on the process of anticipating and managing potential stressors that have not typically been considered in planning models. These two factors are individual differences and the regulation of negative emotional arousal[1] engendered by considering potential sources of stress.

Our review focuses on noncognitive individual differences in proactive coping for several reasons. First, proactive coping presents an ideal setting in which individual differences may operate. Specifically, because the stressor has yet to occur, the would-be proactive coper must attend to and respond to early, ambiguous suggestions of impending difficulty. At this point, appraisals of potential stressors are less likely to be uniquely driven or constrained by the stimulus configuration of a problem or situation (cf. Folkman, 1984). Therefore, individual differences may be especially likely to influence appraisals of potential stressors. Second, at the proactive coping stage, it may also be unclear how a potential stressor should be addressed. As we will illustrate, other individual differences, such as tendencies to use certain kinds of coping strategies, are likely to play a more pronounced role in proactive coping than in coping with stressors that are fully realized. There is simply more room for such differences to operate when the situation is not clearly defined. An important qualification to these statements, however, is that the nature of the stressful event itself may be an important determinant of proactive coping efforts (cf. Paterson & Neufeld, 1987). Some kinds of stressful events announce themselves in advance or can be anticipated, thus potentiating any individual differences in proactive coping skills, whereas other kinds of stressful events, such as those that are sudden-onset, uncontrollable events, are likely to minimize the degree to which individual differences in proactive coping skills can emerge.

A second set of influences, related to the first, concerns the regulation of negative emotional arousal. Considering potential sources of stress may

---

[1]Recent research has identified two distinct patterns of physiological arousal, one corresponding to a positive state of energy mobilization to meet the demands of a task and the other representing a negative state of perceived threat or stress (cf. Blascovich & Tomaka, 1996; Dienstbier, 1989; Manuck, Kamarck, Kasprowicz, & Waldstein, 1993). We use the term *negative emotional arousal* to denote this latter state.

evoke negative affects, such as fear and anxiety. These affects—and the person's attempt to regulate them—may have a variety of influences on subsequent processing of information about the potential stressor. We reviewed research suggesting that cognitive and behavioral efforts to manage negative affect may influence subsequent attention to and appraisals of potential stressors, with corresponding effects on the development and enactment of offsetting plans. Such influences have yet to be examined in the planning literature. Specifically, planning usually concerns the allocation of cognitive and other resources to meet goals and events that are anticipated and not expected to be problematic (Scholnick, 1994). As we will show, because the anticipation of a stressful event involves apprehension or a sense of impending danger, the need to regulate negative emotional arousal (i.e., emotion-focused coping) plays an important role in proactive coping.

THE PROACTIVE COPING MODEL

To illustrate some of these influences and their role in proactive coping, we first discuss the proactive coping model, a conceptual and temporal framework derived jointly from the coping and self-regulation literatures (Aspinwall & Taylor, in press). As shown in Fig. 12.1, the model divides proactive coping into five stages: accumulation of resources, recognition of potential stressors, initial appraisals, preliminary coping efforts, and the elicitation and use of feedback. Figure 12.1 also shows the critical tasks undertaken at each stage and the feedback loops among the stages. We first discuss each stage of the model, highlighting research that examines the specific cognitive skills and individual difference variables that may be implicated at a particular stage. Our review, which is selective, rather than exhaustive, suggests that cognitive processes such as attention, mental simulation, and monitoring of the stressor and efforts to offset it, and noncognitive variables may play critical and interrelated roles in the process of anticipating and remediating potential threats to well-being.

Resource Accumulation

The first step in proactive coping is the accumulation of resources. As suggested earlier, devoting attention and effort to potential stressors and their management is costly. Moreover, proactive activity, that is, spending small amounts of resources now to prevent greater losses later, is somewhat of a luxury, in that one must have an excess of resources with respect to current demands to undertake proactive efforts (Hobfoll, 1989). Time, money, social support, and freedom from chronic stress may be important resources that influence the likelihood that potential problems will be

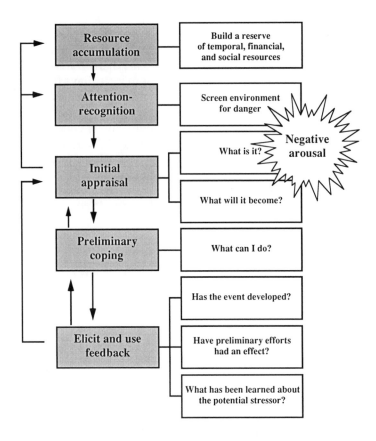

FIG. 12.1. The five stages of proactive coping, and the potential feedback loops among them. Proactive coping requires a reserve of temporal, social, and/or financial resources. These resources facilitate the detection of potential problems, either from warning signs in the environment or from internal processes such as reflection. Once a potential stressor has been detected, it must be appraised. Initial appraisals of potential stressors give rise to preliminary coping efforts. These efforts, in turn, may elicit information about the nature of the problem and the appropriateness of one's preliminary efforts to address it. This information may, in turn, qualify one's appraisals and lead to the modification of coping efforts . Additionally, the need to regulate negative emotional arousal related to the potential stressor may compromise proactive coping efforts at each stage of the model. From Aspinwall and Taylor (in press). Copyright 1997 by the American Psychological Association. Reprinted with permission.

detected, that such problems will be appraised accurately, and that offsetting plans and strategies can be enacted (see Aspinwall & Taylor, in press, for a discussion of how these particular resources may function). As an example, consider the worker who anticipates downsizing and wishes to acquire other job skills. If that person is working 70 hours per week or is a single parent, that person may not have the time or energy to read about trends in her industry to assess the likelihood of downsizing or to evaluate hints from management and other workers about what is likely to happen. Even if the person is able to detect the possibility of downsizing and decides that it would be desirable to be retrained, she may not have the time, money, or energy to attend evening classes to acquire new skills. Finally, she may not have other people to assist in appraising her situation, developing and executing alternative plans, and dealing with the distress engendered by potential job loss.

Recognition of Potential Stressors

Recognition refers to the ability to see a potential stressful event coming. It depends on the ability to screen the environment for danger and to be sensitive to potential signs of threat. It also may depend on a future temporal orientation (Jones, 1994; Zimbardo & Gonzalez, 1984) and the degree to which people think about their futures or use information about future outcomes in judging current outcomes (e.g., Strathman, Gleicher, Boninger, & Edwards, 1994). Such distinctions are obviously important in the study of proactive processes, because one must be able to anticipate the future to behave proactively, expending current resources to offset potentially greater subsequent costs.

Because successful proactive coping requires attention to potentially threatening information, the ability to maintain attention to negative information and process it accurately may be a critical element of proactive coping. Several individual difference variables are linked to either heightened or dampened attention to threatening information. Intrapsychic processes, such as repression (Hansen, Hansen & Schantz, 1992; Weinberger, 1990) and blunting (Miller, 1987), compromise processing of threatening information (either at attention or at encoding), whereas other individual differences, such as vigilance, sensitization, and monitoring, are linked to heightened attention to potentially threatening information in the environment (Davidson & Bobey, 1970; Goldstein, Jones, Clemens, Flagg, & Alexander, 1965; Miller, 1987; Neufeld & Davidson, 1971). Additionally, other constructs, such as trait anxiety (Davey, Hampton, Farrell, & Davidson, 1992; Jerusalem, 1990; Steptoe & Vogele, 1992) and neuroticism (Bolger & Schilling, 1991), have been linked to increased reactivity to threatening or negative information.

In the early stages of proactive coping, factors that blunt or reduce attention to threatening information or interfere with its encoding may compromise proactive coping by compromising the quality of initial appraisals; that is, if information about potential stressors is processed in a way that removes threatening aspects of the information, people may be unlikely to conclude that proactive coping is necessary. For factors that increase attention to negative information, a different sequence of events may occur. Although such factors may facilitate proactive coping by helping people identify potential stressors, they may also compromise proactive coping by heightening emotional and physiological arousal. As we describe, efforts to manage such arousal may divert resources from subsequent stages of the model, such as initial appraisals, preliminary coping efforts, and the modification of such efforts.

The detection process has received relatively little attention in the problem-solving literature, because the problem of interest is usually presented to subjects, is clearly defined, and already exists. Therefore, little is known about how people decide whether something is a problem. In the special case of proactive coping, people must also determine whether some ambiguous warning sign or imagined possibility has the potential to become a problem, an assessment that occurs in the next stage, the initial appraisal stage.

Initial Appraisals of Potential Stressors

Once a potential stressor has been detected, it must be appraised. *Initial Appraisals* consist of preliminary assessments of such questions as "What is it?", "Should I be worried about this?", and "Is this something on which I should take action now?" This step is quite different from how appraisals are conceptualized in the planning literature. In the planning literature, appraisals are driven by the decision to plan (cf. Scholnick & Friedman, 1993); that is, once one has detected a difference between one's current situation and some desired end state and has decided to plan to make up the difference, one appraises the situation with respect to the desired goal and available strategies. A proactive coping analysis reverses the order of events, in that one detects and appraises potential stressors to assess the need for offsetting plans. Therefore, the starting point of the two processes is different. As shown in Fig. 12.1, the proactive coping framework considers three interrelated elements that are essential to understanding the initial appraisal stage: how potential warning signs are interpreted, the effects of needs to regulate emotional arousal on appraisal processes, and the need to engage in mental simulation to anticipate how the potential stressor is likely to unfold.

Interpreting Potential Warning Signs. Research from social cognition on schemas, and especially on matching data to schemas or scenarios in long-term memory, is helpful in understanding the processes people may go through when they are attempting to make sense of an incipient or ambiguous cue that may suggest a stressful event to come. Variables, such as salience, strength, accessibility, and representativeness, constitute some criteria by which people interpret potential danger signals (cf. Fiske & Taylor, 1991). The following examples illustrate how these variables may operate as people interpret warning signs about their job security (Aspinwall & Taylor, in press). If one's next-door neighbor is laid off, this event is more likely to elicit the scenario of potential job loss than a less proximal, but perhaps more relevant, layoff (salient cues). Hearing about multiple layoffs is more likely to trigger a job loss scenario than hearing about a single job loss (strong cues). If a relative is laid off and his family's consequent struggle with loss of income is fresh in one's mind, then a job loss scenario may loom especially large (accessible cues, e.g., Bargh, Bond, Lombardi, & Tota, 1986). If one's company has a history of closing plants in response to an economic downturn, then plant closure is the representative scenario likely to come to mind when the danger signal of an impending recession is detected. In contrast, if one's company has a history of cutting back evenly at all plants, and especially in certain departments, then the scenario of selective layoffs is most likely to be cued (representative cues, Tversky & Kahneman, 1982). Differences in the scenarios evoked—depending on these different factors—will lead to differences in the estimation of whether one's job is at risk.

Regulation of Arousal.   An important part of the model is that the task of initial appraisal may really be two simultaneous interrelated tasks: definition of the problem and regulation of arousal (Aspinwall & Taylor, in press). Specifically, in addition to trying to figure out what the potential stressor is, the would-be proactive coper must also simultaneously manage the negative emotional arousal engendered from thinking about the stressor and its likely development. Success in regulating negative emotional arousal may, in turn, be critical in maintaining attention to the potential stressor, thereby increasing the likelihood that the resulting appraisal corresponds reasonably well to the potential stressor. The quality of these initial appraisals is crucial, because they influence the decision to plan and give rise to the specific offsetting strategies undertaken. The costs of inaccurate initial appraisals may be high: a poor understanding of the potential stressor may lead people to expend a great deal of energy trying to offset the wrong thing or to make initial appraisals that lead them to believe that further offsetting efforts are unnecessary. Additionally, the need to regulate negative emotional arousal may interfere not only with efforts to monitor the problem, but also with efforts to monitor the success of one's efforts to address it, a process that occurs in the final stage of the model.

A promising new line of experimental research in social psychophysiology offers a direct window into the interplay among initial appraisals, arousal, and task performance under stressful conditions. These studies yielded evidence consistent with the idea that some individual differences help people manage negative emotional arousal during motivated performance tasks, such as rapid serial subtraction. In one recent study, Tomaka and Blascovich (1994) found that participants with high levels of just world beliefs (exaggerated control beliefs that one's behavior determines one's outcomes in life, such that people are seen as responsible for their successes and misfortunes; Lerner, 1980; Rubin & Peplau, 1975) appraised a demanding mental subtraction task as less stressful and more challenging prior to performing it, showed lower levels of stress-related physiological arousal during the task, and dramatically outperformed subjects with low just world beliefs (see also Tomaka, Blascovich, & Kelsey, 1992). Similar results were obtained for constructive thinking, a multifaceted construct of which optimistic beliefs are a part (Epstein & Meier, 1989; Katz & Epstein, 1991).

These studies suggest that beliefs that foster low threat appraisals have the seemingly paradoxical consequence of making people more equal to the threatening task at hand. In contrast, there is some evidence that high-threat appraisals—and the individual differences that give rise to them—may produce insufficient processing of relevant information (cf. Aspinwall & Taylor, in press; Hansen et al., 1992). For example, Baumeister and Cairns (1992) found that subjects high in repression paid considerable attention to negative information about themselves under some conditions, but showed low subsequent recall for this negative information. These findings suggest that, although people may successfully orient toward negative information, early increases in arousal in response to such information may derail the process of gathering information about potential stressors (cf. Lyon & Bugental, 1997, for an application to sexual decision making).

High threat appraisals may also preclude instrumental action and prompt disengagement from the stressor or task (Carver & Scheier, 1990, 1994; Folkman, 1984). At an extreme, people may simply deny the threatening information outright or distort it in others ways, resulting in less serious initial appraisals than may be warranted by the potential stressor (cf. Croyle, 1992; Jemmott, Ditto, & Croyle, 1986).[2] In summary, recent examinations of the role of individual differences in the appraisal and management of stressful situations suggest that chronically favorable appraisals of potential stressors may allow people to make use of threatening information, whereas individual differences that foster chronically unfavorable appraisals may lead to avoidance or other deficits in the processing of threat-relevant information.

Mental Simulation. As noted previously, proactive coping presents some unusual challenges, in that the incipient problem must be monitored over time. One consequence of this property of potential stressors is that it is usually insufficient to make a single, static appraisal of the current status of a potential stressor. One must also engage in mental simulation in order to anticipate how the incipient stressor is likely to develop over time. *Mental*

---

[2]See Lazarus, 1983, and Breznitz, 1983b, for more extended discussions of different kinds of denial.

simulation is the imitative representation of real or hypothetical events, including rehearsals of likely future events and fantasies about the future (Taylor & Schneider, 1989). Although it is beyond the scope of this chapter to provide a full review of the effects of mental simulation of problem solving and performance, there is clear research evidence that mental simulations have a variety of effects that may affect planning, such as making simulated events seem more subjectively likely or true (see Taylor & Pham, 1996; Taylor & Schneider, 1989 for reviews). What one initially simulates, then, is likely to be an important determinant of one's interpretation of the meaning of a danger cue and how it is likely to unfold. Expert knowledge and past experience with similar stressors may also be implicated in the quality of these initial appraisals and subsequent simulations (cf. Hammond, 1990; Scholnick, 1994).

An important property of mental simulations is that they may suggest action plans that give rise to preliminary coping efforts. Imagining how events are going to take place provides information about those events, such as their sequence or relation to each other. Consequently, simulation provides information rudimentary to a plan of action (Hayes-Roth & Hayes-Roth, 1977; Miller, Galanter, & Pribram, 1960). Mental simulation, then, may not only help an individual to define what a danger signal means, but may also bridge the gap between initial appraisals and preliminary coping efforts by providing information relevant to action (Johnson & Sherman, 1990; Oettingen, 1996; Taylor & Schneider, 1989).

Individual Differences in Appraisals.   Studies of appraisals of naturalistic stressors are difficult to interpret, because it is impossible to disentangle appraisals from objective differences in the stressors faced by respondents (cf. Dohrenwend, Dohrenwend, Dodson, & Shrout, 1984; see Taylor & Aspinwall, 1996, for a discussion of this issue). Given these limitations, there is some evidence that individual differences are linked to primary appraisals of threat, harm, or challenge. Specifically, high levels of optimism, self-efficacy, and hardiness have been linked to lower perceived threat or negativity of events (Jerusalem, 1993; Wiebe, 1991), whereas anxiety has been linked to amplified threat appraisals (Davey et al., 1992; Matthews, 1990; Steptoe & Vogele, 1992). Such links between individual differences and favorable or unfavorable appraisals are important determinants of proactive coping, because of the interrelations among appraisal processes, the regulation of negative emotional arousal, and subsequent attention to the stressor illustrated by the model.

Preliminary Coping Efforts

Once a potential stressor has been appraised, it must next be managed. Despite their different starting points, planning and proactive coping share some striking similarities after a decision to plan or an appraisal suggesting the presence of a potential stressor has been made. Specifically, both frameworks suggest a process through which people develop plans to address problems and monitor the success of their efforts (cf. Aspinwall & Taylor, in press; Hammond, 1990; Scholnick, 1994; Scholnick & Friedman, 1993). Importantly, both frameworks incorporate feedback loops in which the success of one's strategies is used to inform subsequent efforts.

Preliminary Coping Efforts.   Activities undertaken to prevent or minimize a stressor are identified as preliminary coping efforts. Many coping researchers distinguish between active and avoidant forms of coping[3]. Active coping typically consists of efforts to solve the problem, including learning more about it and seeking social support. Avoidant coping, in contrast, involves reducing contact with the problem situation, abusing drugs or alcohol, and other efforts to avoid thinking about the problem, strategies that are unlikely to facilitate the anticipation and management of subsequent problems (Suls & Fletcher, 1985; Taylor & Clark, 1986). We suggest that proactive coping at this stage is virtually always active, involving either cognitive activities, such as planning, or behavioral activities, such as taking preliminary action.

A large literature has examined individual differences that predict active versus avoidant forms of coping. Variables such as optimism, control beliefs (and related constructs, such as hardiness, or more domain-specific beliefs in personal agency, such as self-efficacy), and self-esteem, are consistently related to more active than avoidant forms of coping (see Taylor & Aspinwall, 1996, for a review). In contrast, other variables, such as neuroticism, are reliably linked to avoidant coping (Bolger, 1990). Many longitudinal studies of stress support the view that the beneficial psychosocial outcomes reported by people high in optimism, control beliefs, and self-esteem are mediated by respondents' greater levels of active coping and lower levels of avoidant coping (Carver et al., 1993; see Taylor & Aspinwall, 1996, for a review).

---

[3]Although the dichotomy between active and avoidant coping has been useful in studying the correlates of coping behavior, it is surely an oversimplification. Other researchers have argued for much greater differentiation of strategies within these two broad categories, taking into account such conceptually distinct coping strategies as problem solving, planning, suppression of competing activities, seeking instrumental social support, seeking emotional social support, positive reinterpretation, acceptance, denial, use of religion, venting feelings, use of humor, and other strategies (Carver, Scheier, & Weintraub, 1989; Carver et al., 1993). Taylor and Aspinwall (1996) have suggested that the diversity of strategies within a given class of coping efforts (problem-focused versus emotion-focused coping, or active versus avoidant coping) may depend on the nature of the problem or stressor. Studies of stressors that are amenable to problem solving tend to yield more differentiated ways of problem-focused coping, whereas studies of stressors that are not amenable to direct action tend to yield more differentiated ways of emotion-focused coping.

Eliciting and Using Feedback

Eliciting and using feedback is posited to be the final step in the proactive coping process. It centers around obtaining and making use of feedback about the development of the stressful event itself ("Has it advanced, changed form, or improved?"), whether the event will change in response to one's coping efforts ("Can I do something now or should I wait to see if it's a problem?"), and the effects one's preliminary efforts have had so far on the stressful event ("Was I successful in staving it off?"). This final step is similar to the monitoring and debugging steps in planning models (cf. Hammond, 1990; Scholnick, 1994; see Scholnick & Friedman, 1987, for a review).

Debugging one's coping efforts and additional monitoring of the potential stressor are especially important in proactive coping for two reasons. First, it is likely that additional information about the stressor will become available over time and that people may need to revise their appraisals and moderate their coping efforts accordingly. Second, it is also possible that the stressor in question may prove to be uncontrollable or intractable. In this case, it is important to understand the factors involved in whether (and at what point in their efforts) people can successfully recognize that active coping efforts may not be useful in addressing particular kinds of stressors or whether they will continue to devote attention and effort toward such lost causes.

Individual Differences in the Elicitation and Use of Feedback.
Researchers are sharply divided on the question of whether noncognitive individual differences—such as optimism, control beliefs, and self-esteem—facilitate or impede responsiveness to feedback about the success of one's coping efforts. Baumeister (1989) hypothesized a curvilinear relation between such factors and adaptational outcomes, and argued that people with excessive self-esteem will fail to recognize their limits and, ultimately, fail (cf. Baumeister, Heatherton, & Tice, 1993). Consistent with this point, several experimental studies have linked self-esteem (Janoff-Bulman & Brickman, 1982; McFarlin, Baumeister, & Blascovich, 1984) and perceived control (Sieber et al., 1992) to increased persistence on insoluble tasks. These studies suggest that the same individual differences that foster and sustain active engagement in attempts to cope with stressors may make people somewhat resistant to the new information yielded by the attempts. If this is the case, people with high levels of such individual differences would fail to adjust their proactive efforts in response to new information and engage in efforts that do not correspond well to the demands of the potential stressor.

A competing view is that the effects of such individual differences are moderated by the contingencies of the situation (Taylor & Aspinwall, 1996).

Studies examining the relation of optimistic beliefs to adaptation to uncontrollable stressors support this idea. For example, optimists reported working actively to fix problems appraised as controllable, but reported using strategies to manage their emotions in the face of problems appraised as uncontrollable (Scheier, Weintraub, & Carver, 1986). Consistent with these findings, research on adjustment to serious chronic illness suggests that optimism and other beliefs that foster active coping are associated with changing goals and coping strategies to adapt to the illness (cf. Collins, Taylor, & Skokan, 1990; Taylor, 1989). For example, these studies suggest that people abandon their original goal of controlling the illness itself and shift their effort to more manageable tasks, such as the management of symptoms and the establishment of personal priorities. These findings suggest that people with optimistic beliefs, though they are predisposed toward active coping, seem to be able to recognize situations where continued effort is unwarranted and to moderate their efforts accordingly. Research on control-related beliefs, such hardiness (Wiebe & Williams, 1992) and internal locus of control (Vitaliano, Russo, & Maiuro, 1987), also supports that idea that people with favorable beliefs seem to be able to moderate their appraisals and coping efforts to match the characteristics of the stressor.

These findings highlight the importance of the model's feedback loop between preliminary coping and the elicitation and use of feedback. Different kinds of preliminary coping efforts are differentially successful not only in addressing problems, but in eliciting information about them. The reciprocal relation between these two stages of the model raises the possibility that even when preliminary efforts are unsuccessful, their failure is likely to be informative about the nature of the problem and the strategies that may be successful in offsetting it. One implication of this process is that variables such as optimism, control beliefs, and self-esteem that lead people to behave in more active ways should also be linked to greater elicitation of information about the stressor and its contingencies.

What evidence is there that active engagement with stressors yields more information about them? A study by Knudson, Sommers, and Golding (1980) provided a fascinating illustration of the spiraling effects of engagement versus avoidance on couples' shared understanding of a disagreement. Married couples were asked to discuss topics that had been previously identified as sources of conflict for them. The partners' discussions were then coded as to whether they had addressed the issues or avoided them. Individual members of the couple were then shown a videotape of the interaction and asked to complete questionnaires concerning their beliefs about their partner's motives and how they believed their partner perceived their own behavior at several different points in the interaction. The results were striking: over the course of the interaction, couples who addressed the conflictual issue moved in the direction of greater shared agreement about each other's perspectives and motives, whereas couples who avoided the issue grew further apart in their assessments of the same interaction.

Of course, generating information and using it are not always the same thing. Being able to process additional information about the potential stressor and to modify one's appraisals and coping efforts are vital to the success of this final step of the model. Several factors may affect people's ability to respond to feedback. As we suggested in our discussion of attention and appraisal, individual differences such as anxiety and repression that lead to heightened attention to negative information and/or to amplified threat appraisals may divert resources away from the stressor to the management of negative emotional arousal. If this is the case, one's ability to track the success of one's efforts against the development of the stressor should be impaired. Additionally, because potential stressors develop over time and require monitoring both of one's offsetting efforts and of the stressor itself, factors that influence people's interest in and responsiveness to new information, once they have made initial appraisals, should play a large role in the successful moderation of proactive coping.

Individual differences such as need for closure (Kruglanski & Webster, 1996) and tolerance for ambiguity (Andersen & Schwartz, 1992) have strong influences on people's ability and willingness to suspend judgment until additional information has been obtained or to modify their judgments in response to new information. Finally, in the case where one's preliminary coping efforts are unsuccessful, one must maintain the motivational and cognitive resources to persist in the face of failure or noncontingency; that is, one must avoid learned helplessness (Maier & Seligman, 1976; Seligman, 1975) and cognitive exhaustion (Sedek, Kofta, & Tyszka, 1993). Researchers are just beginning to identify individual differences, such as anxiety (Jerusalem, 1990), that may exacerbate the effects of initial failure on subsequent problem-solving efforts.

ILLUSTRATION OF THE MODEL: THE ROLE OF OPTIMISTIC BELIEFS IN PROACTIVE COPING

To illustrate the potential heuristic value of the proactive coping model (and by extension, the potential value of considering concepts from coping and self-regulation in the study of planing), we examine how one noncognitive individual difference, namely dispositional optimism, may be related to the stages of proactive coping. Dispositional optimism is defined as generalized positive expectancies about future outcomes (Scheier & Carver, 1985). We appointed optimism to serve as an ambassador from the study of coping and self-regulation to the study of planning for three reasons: (a) research on the role of expectations in human behavior has a long and distinguished history in psychology, (b) optimistic beliefs are widely studied in stress and coping research and prospectively predict superior adjustment to a wide range of stressors (see Scheier & Carver, 1987, 1992, and Taylor & Aspinwall, 1996, for reviews), and (c) optimism has a strong conceptual link to self-regulatory processes (cf. Carver & Scheier, 1990). To illustrate the role of optimistic beliefs in proactive coping, we first examine the conceptual background of optimism and then describe a program of research that examines how optimistic beliefs may be implicated in attention to potential stressors, appraisals of same, preliminary coping efforts, and the elicitation and use of feedback.

The Conceptual Background and Measurement of Optimism

Carver and Scheier's control theory (1981, 1990) states that as people encounter difficulty or declines in progress in their movement toward goals, they often reevaluate their expectations about meeting specific goals. If expectations are sufficiently favorable, people will continue working toward their goals, even in the face of difficulty. In contrast, if expectations are sufficiently unfavorable, people will disengage, either behaviorally (by leaving the situation) or mentally (by giving up the goal, even if leaving the situation is impossible).

Favorable expectations that exist at the dispositional level are termed *dispositional optimism*. Dispositional optimism is measured by Scheier and Carver's (1985) Life Orientation Test (LOT).[4] Sample items from the LOT are, "In uncertain times, I usually expect the best" and "If something can go wrong for me, it will." Optimistic beliefs have also been assessed in

---

[4]For the purposes of this discussion, it is important to distinguish the generalized positive expectancies that define dispositional optimism from control-related constructs, such as self-efficacy and control beliefs. Self-efficacy refers to beliefs that one is able to enact specific behaviors (Bandura, 1977), and control beliefs refer to general beliefs that any agent can bring about the outcome, regardless of the specific agent (cf. Skinner, chapter 11, this volume). In contrast, dispositional optimism refers to the belief that a good outcome will occur, regardless of who or what brings it about or how it occurs (cf. Carver & Scheier, 1990; Scheier & Carver, 1987). Although dispositional optimism is significantly correlated with a variety of widely studied control beliefs, the LOT has differential and independent relations to coping and psychosocial outcomes (Aspinwall & Taylor, 1992; Scheier, Carver & Bridges, 1994; see Cozzarelli, 1993, for an exception). Specifically, the prospective effects of optimism on coping and psychological well-being persist when control-related beliefs, such as locus of control, desire for control, and self-mastery, are statistically controlled (Aspinwall & Taylor, 1992; Scheier et al., 1994).

Additionally, it is also important to note that dispositional optimism refers to favorable expectancies about future outcomes in general and not to favorable appraisals of related beliefs, such as coping ability, outcome efficacy, or personal risk. It is, however, consistent with the proactive coping model that optimistic beliefs will lead people to attend to threatening information in certain ways, to make favorable appraisals much of the time, and to cope in ways that give rise to favorable subsequent appraisals. For this reason, optimistic beliefs should be correlated with such appraisals, but are not synonymous with them.

specific domains, such as general health (Aspinwall & Brunhart, 1996) and specific illnesses, such as AIDS (Taylor et al., 1992), or as perceptions of risk relative to others (cf. Weinstein, 1980, 1987). Although there are some conceptual differences among these measures, it is likely that these domain-specific measures may provide a more stringent test of the benefits and liabilities of optimistic beliefs, because they are more closely related to criterion appraisals and behaviors (cf. Taylor et al., 1992). For this reason, some of the studies we review use domain-specific measures of optimistic beliefs in addition to generalized dispositional optimism.

Optimism and the Detection of Potential Stressors

We first focus on potentially threatening information. One controversial aspect of optimistic beliefs has been the suggestion that favorable beliefs, particularly unrealistically optimistic beliefs about one's vulnerability to illness or other kinds of adversity, reduce people's interest in information about a particular threat (Weinstein, 1980). Our primary interest was testing whether optimists, when presented with threatening health information, would shield themselves from it, a phenomenon akin to denial, or whether optimists would pay more attention to information about self-relevant threats, perhaps in order to manage them.

In one recent study (Aspinwall & Brunhart, 1996), healthy college students ($N = 57$) were presented with computerized menus of risk, benefit, and neutral information about two health behaviors (tanning and vitamin use). For example, risk topics for vitamin use were "Vitamin supplements can have harmful interactions" and "Vitamins can hide serious illnesses." Subjects were asked to read any topics they were interested in and were free to bypass any or all of the passages.

To test the relation of health-specific optimistic beliefs to attention to health risk information, we developed a measure that assessed favorable beliefs about one's ability to prevent and to withstand illness, such as "Positive thinking can prevent illness from occurring" and "If I had a serious illness, my treatment would be successful." A regression analysis of reading time for the passages yielded a significant interaction between optimistic beliefs and information valence. In contrast to the idea that people who hold favorable expectations maintain them by ignoring negative information, subjects who were optimistic about their health spent more time reading risk information than either benefit or neutral information. An identical, but slightly weaker, pattern of results was obtained for dispositional optimism. Additionally, the results of a surprise recall test indicated that participants who were optimistic about their health remembered more information overall and showed especially superior recall for risk information. Finally, additional analyses demonstrated that attention to risk information about vitamin use increased as a function of lifetime practice of the behavior, a finding that suggests that optimists differentially attend to self-relevant risk information. It is interesting to note that the positive beliefs assessed by the health-specific optimism measure appear to facilitate attention to and recall of risk information even though some of the beliefs, such as the belief that one can cure oneself through positive thinking, are likely to be overly sanguine, given current medical knowledge.

Optimism and the Interrelations Among Appraisal, Arousal, and Attention

These results provide the first evidence that optimistic beliefs are associated with greater, not lesser, attention to self-relevant risk information (see Trope & Neter, 1994, for conceptually similar findings concerning positive experiences). As such, they raise questions concerning the mechanism underlying this seemingly paradoxical finding. One possibility, suggested by the feedback loops among attention, appraisal, and the regulation of negative emotional arousal in the proactive coping model, is that any factor that leads people to make more favorable appraisals of potential stressors may allow them to maintain attention to negative or threatening information. The results of a second study provide some insight into this process.

In a study designed to assess the interrelations among perceptions of personal vulnerability to skin cancer, worry about getting skin cancer, and attention to computerized information about skin cancer (Aspinwall & Brunhart, 1997), young adult women (ages 18 to 23, $N = 72$) were randomly assigned to one of two experimental conditions. Specifically, participants were told that the average melanoma patient was either a 25-year-old woman (proximal threat condition) or a 55-year-old woman (distal threat condition). An analysis of reading time yielded a strong interaction between optimistic risk perceptions and threat proximity: In the proximal threat condition, women who were optimistic about their chances of developing skin cancer (that is, those who believed they were at lower risk than their peers) paid nearly twice as much attention to information about UV exposure than women who were less relatively optimistic about their chances. Interestingly, for women who were relatively pessimistic about their vulnerability, the threat proximity manipulation failed to increase reading time for information about UV exposure.

To test the role of negative emotional arousal in this process, subsequent analyses examined self-reported worry about getting skin cancer. Not surprisingly, women low in optimism reported higher levels of worry about getting skin cancer; however, greater levels of worry predicted lower reading times. Mediational analyses supported the idea that increased worry about getting skin cancer accounted for the lower reading times among women low in optimism. These results raise the possibility that people with favorable beliefs about their vulnerability to health threats may be able to tolerate threatening information, because they are less worried about their personal vulnerability.

One important implication of these findings with respect to proactive coping is that the ability to tolerate threatening information may confer some advantages in terms of the quality of both initial and subsequent appraisals of emerging stressors. Specifically, being able to tolerate threatening information may prevent premature disengagement from efforts to appraise the stressor and may therefore facilitate revisions of one's appraisals over time as new information becomes available. Consistent with this possibility, a recent follow-up study in which participants completed stimulated recall interviews after the experimental session indicated that dispositionally optimistic subjects in the proximal threat condition were more likely than subjects low in optimism to discuss and elaborate risk-relevant information from the passages (Aspinwall & Brunhart, 1997).

Optimism and Preliminary Coping Efforts

Once a potential stressor has been appraised, some initial steps may be taken to offset it. As noted earlier, optimistic beliefs are consistently associated with self-reports of higher levels of active coping and lower levels of avoidant coping across a wide range of stressors. It is important to note that most of these studies have assessed the role of optimism in coping with major illnesses and stressors, such as breast cancer surgery (Carver et al., 1993), heart surgery (Scheier et al., 1989), HIV seropositivity (Taylor et al., 1992), and emigration (Jerusalem, 1993). Proactive coping, however, rarely involves such extreme stressors. Instead, successful proactive coping usually requires that people attend to and cope with relatively mild incipient problems before they become major ones. We wondered whether favorable expectations would lead people to downplay or ignore small problems, or whether optimism would facilitate efforts to address small problems early in their development.

In a preliminary test of this question, we examined the relation of dispositional optimism to responses to both large and small problems in dating relationships (Aspinwall, Hartman, & Brunhart, 1997). We conducted two studies in which we asked college students (Ns = 49, 74) to identify two problems (one mild and one severe) in their current dating relationship and to complete a brief inventory of their responses to each problem. The inventory assessed four factorially derived responses to interpersonal problems: active problem solving (discussed issue with partner, tried to solve problem), avoiding the partner (stopped talking to partner, spent more time with family and friends), downplaying the problem (decided the problem was not important, let it "slide"), and conflict (criticized partner, argued with partner). Respondents seemed to have no difficulty generating both mild and severe problems. The most frequently cited mild problem was one partner's unilateral desire to spend more time with the other, and the most frequently cited severe problems involved jealousy and infidelity. Importantly, there were no significant differences in the severity of problems reported by respondents as a function of optimism.

The results of both studies were consistent with the idea that optimism predicts more active forms of coping for both mild and severe problems. Regardless of problem severity, dispositionally optimistic respondents were less likely to report downplaying the problem or avoiding their partners in response to the problem and were more likely to report active problem-solving efforts. Additionally, in Study 2, an interaction between optimism and problem severity indicated that respondents high in dispositional optimism were significantly more likely than respondents low in optimism to report undertaking active efforts to address mild problems. This pattern of results bears directly on one important task of proactive coping, which is to detect and remediate small problems before they become large ones. Although there is no direct evidence concerning the timing of optimists' efforts to fix incipient problems in their romantic relationships, these studies suggest that optimists—because of their greater levels of active coping and lower levels of avoiding their partners and downplaying their problems—may be more successful in addressing problems before they threaten the relationship. Support for this assertion comes from studies of close relationships that have identified greater levels of active responses to mild problems and/or lower levels of negative responding overall as robust predictors of relationship satisfaction (Huston & Vangelisti, 1991; Rusbult, Johnson, & Morrow, 1986; Rusbult, Verette, Whitney, Slovik, & Lipkus, 1991).

Optimism and the Moderation of Preliminary Coping Efforts

Although we have not conducted an explicit test of the relation of optimism to the use of feedback, the findings of the three studies presented are consistent with the idea that optimists will be more successful in monitoring and moderating their efforts. Specifically, the studies we presented suggest two important features of optimists' approaches to problems: (a) optimists show heightened attention to risk information, especially when the information is self-relevant and/or proximal, and (b) optimists report more active attempts to cope with their problems. How are these two aspects linked to the moderation of coping efforts? We suggest that the feedback loop between the initial coping and elicitation-and-use-of-feedback stages of the proactive coping model provides some insight.

Specifically, the key to understanding how people moderate their coping efforts to correspond more closely to the contingencies of a task or stressor may lie in the temporal patterning of initial coping efforts and the degree to which such efforts yield information about the stressor. The feedback loops in the model allow for the revision of coping efforts on the basis of whether they have been successful in advancing the problem. An essential part of this process is that optimists' greater levels of active coping may be successful in eliciting information about the problem, even in cases where their inital coping efforts are unsuccessful. That is, any factor such as optimism, that leads people to engage more actively in attempts to remediate a potential stressor should be more successful in eliciting information about the stressor than factors linked to passive responses, such as avoidance, denial, or disengagement. Unless the same factor that prompts active coping also interferes with processing of the information yielded by such attempts (and the two studies of attention to threatening health information suggest that optimism does not), the person who copes actively should ultimately learn more about the particular problem.

This analysis also has several implications for the development of procedural knowledge about proactive coping. People with chronically favorable expectancies may engage in more frequent and more pronounced efforts to anticipate and solve problems than people with chronically unfavorable expectancies. As people experiment with ways to address problems, they gain information about the kinds of situations that are amenable to change and those that are not, as well as knowledge about how and when to exert effort in different situations (Skinner, chapter 11, this volume; Taylor, 1989). If this is the case, optimists and other people predisposed toward active coping should acquire superior knowledge about how to manage different kinds of situations. This analysis suggests that even if preliminary coping efforts are unsuccessful for a particular problem, such efforts may contribute to one's overall understanding of the contingencies of different kinds of stressors. Although we have applied this analysis to optimism, the successful moderation of coping efforts would be facilitated by any individual difference variable that predisposed people to cope actively and did not interfere with their use of the resulting information to modify their efforts and appraisals.

SUMMARY AND IMPLICATIONS

Throughout this chapter, we have suggested that people may engage in quite a bit of planful activity in the service of anticipating, detecting, and managing potential stressors. To date, the large literatures on coping and self-regulation have evolved independently from the study of planning and problem solving. By integrating the study of self-regulation and coping with the study of planning, we hope to call attention to the processes through which people identify potential stressors and make, execute, and revise specific plans for avoiding or offsetting them. We focused on three questions: (a)What is the relation of proactive coping to activities such as planning and problem solving? (b)What are the mechanisms through which successful proactive coping is achieved? and (c)how do cognitive and noncognitive factors foster or compromise proactive coping at each stage? In this final section, we summarize some of the issues raised by the proactive coping framework, highlight influences on proactive coping that may be relevant to the study of planning, and identify some directions for future research that may integrate research on these kindred processes.

We reviewed five tasks of proactive coping, namely the accumulation of resources, the recognition of potential stressors, initial appraisals, preliminary coping efforts, and the use of feedback to discern whether the stressor has changed and whether one's efforts to modify it have been successful. At all stages, the successful regulation of negative emotional arousal is important in determining the degree to which people are able to maintain attention to potential problems, devote effort to their solution, and track the success of their efforts against the development of the stressor.

Our analysis also considered the role of individual differences at all stages of the model. Our review suggests that individual differences play a larger and more antecedent role in the stress process than has been previously discussed (cf. Taylor & Aspinwall, 1996). Specifically, three large classes of individual difference variables may be critical factors in the success or failure of proactive coping. First, individual differences that amplify threatening information (e.g., neuroticism, repression, trait anxiety), as well as those that dampen threatening information (e.g., repression, denial, blunting) may influence the detection and appraisal of potential stressors, as well as the use of feedback about the success of one's coping efforts. Second, individual differences, such as optimism and control beliefs, may influence people's tendencies to respond actively, as opposed to avoidantly, to incipient stressors in the preliminary coping stage. We suggested that such beliefs affect not only specific actions undertaken to avoid or offset the potential stressor, but may also play a critical role in whether preliminary coping efforts elicit information about the stressor. Finally, we suggested that several cognitive and motivational factors, such as need for closure, tolerance for ambiguity, and learned helplessness, may affect people's willingness and ability to use new information to modify their appraisals and efforts.

To illustrate how noncognitive factors may influence proactive coping, we provided a more detailed review of the role of optimistic beliefs in detecting and managing potential and actual stressors. We suggested that an individual may be well-served by optimistic beliefs at several stages of the model. Specifically, optimistic beliefs may allow people to attend to negative information without being overwhelmed by it and to maintain attention to the potential stressor during the appraisal process. Optimistic beliefs may also foster more active coping efforts, thus generating information that may elucidate the nature of the potential stressor. To the extent that optimists attend to and process such feedback, their subsequent efforts should be more successful. Over time, greater active and proactive coping efforts may ultimately lead people with optimistic beliefs to develop a more sophisticated understanding of the contingencies surrounding different kinds of stressful situations. This knowledge may then inform one's decision to cope proactively or to plan in the future.

An important implication of this analysis for understanding some of the potential costs of proactive coping is that favorable beliefs, such as optimism, may not necessarily lead people to persist in efforts to remediate stressors that are not amenable to their efforts. Instead, people holding such beliefs may be more able to recognize the contingencies that influence which coping strategies will be effective than individuals who do not use active coping strategies. Such considerations are important in understanding how people maintain motivational and other resources to devote to planning and other forward-looking behavior (cf. Hobfoll, 1989).

In terms of the planning literature, our review suggests that optimism and other individual differences are implicated in attention to information that suggests the presence of potential problems, appraisals of problems, choice of strategies, and monitoring and debugging of plans. A question that necessarily arises is, are factors such as optimism sufficient to prompt planning, or do they come into play only when a potential stressor has been detected? With respect to optimism, it would seem that beliefs about what the future holds are likely to be critical determinants of why people make plans to meet goals or to offset threats to goal attainment in the first place. To be optimistic is, by definition, to hold favorable expectations about future outcomes. Holding such beliefs may make people more likely to strive toward good outcomes (cf. Carver & Scheier, 1990), and there is emerging evidence that optimistic expectancies are related to the development of action plans (Oettingen, 1996). In summary, although it has yet to be empirically determined whether beliefs that the future will be good in and of themselves are sufficient to prompt preparatory or preventive behaviors, it seems clear from the present review that optimism may assist people in managing incoming negative information and that optimistic beliefs may influence the nature of preliminary efforts undertaken to offset such potential stressors. For these reasons, optimists may handle threats to valued goals differently and, perhaps, more successfully once they arise.

Other beliefs about the future may also be implicated in both planning and proactive coping. Individual differences, such as depressive predictive certainty (a factor leading to automatic judgments that the future holds bad outcomes; Andersen, 1990; Andersen, Spielman, & Bargh, 1992) and defensive pessimism (a belief held by competent people that they are certain to fail, such that the resulting arousal spurs preparatory activities like studying; Cantor & Norem, 1989; Norem & Cantor, 1986; Showers, 1988, 1992; Showers & Ruben, 1990), are likely to influence the decision to plan, either by making planning seem useless in the face of low odds of success or by making planning seem essential because of the high likelihood of failure if no offsetting plans are undertaken.

Additional Implications of the Proactive Coping Framework for Research on Planning

In addition to noncognitive influences in planning, our review suggests two additional aspects of coping and self-regulatory processes that may prove fruitful for the study of planning. The first concerns the regulation of negative emotional arousal and its impact on problem solving, and the second concerns the process of identifying and disengaging from intractable problems.

The Influence of Negative Emotional Arousal and Its Regulation on Problem Solving. As noted at the outset, the problems addressed in the planning literature are relatively dispassionate. They may evoke frustration or fear of failure (which may have their own effects on subsequent cognitive processing and behavior), but they do not pose direct harm to the person who fails to anticipate or solve them. Our review suggests that the need to regulate emotional arousal may compromise the quality of initial appraisals by short-circuiting attention to, and controlled processing of, negative information, and may also interfere with the enactment of offsetting plans. In particular, recent research in social psychophysiology has provided fine-grained information about the relations among negative emotional arousal, appraisals of tasks as threatening or challenging, and subsequent performance on demanding tasks. Extending the study of planning to situations and goals that might evoke negative affects, such as fear, anxiety, a sense of impending doom, and the like, might add to our understanding of the effects of such affective states on the nature and quality of offsetting plans.

To date, examinations of the role of emotional management in coping have focused mostly on the possibility that the need to regulate negative emotions draws resources away from problem-focused coping; however, it is likely that negative affect and its regulation exert much more pervasive influences on the processes through which relevant information is obtained, appraised, and used. Specifically, negative affect may influence the cognitive processes involved in planning through such mechanisms as mood-congruent processing (see Blaney, 1986, and Bower, 1981, for reviews), the use of affect as information (Schwarz, 1990), and the use of systematic versus heuristic processing strategies (see Forgas, 1995, for a review). Such approaches have yet to be integrated either in the study of stress and coping or self-regulation, but have the potential to elucidate the role of affect in the component processes of planning.

The Process of Identifying and Disengaging From Intractable Problems. A second critical concern of the proactive coping framework is how people identify and disengage from insoluble problems. Such questions are important to understanding: (a) how people preserve resources, such as energy, motivation, time, and money, and (b) how people reduce the costs of proactivity. We suggested that active copers are more likely to develop procedural knowledge about different kinds of stressors and their contingencies. This analysis leads to the prediction that people who are predisposed toward active coping should be more, rather than less, likely to disengage from insoluble stressors. The key to this process is using feedback about the success of one's efforts. Current planning research may be unlikely to capture how people identify and disengage from insoluble problems. When people are given clearly defined and soluble problems, the main task of monitoring involves fine-tuning one's strategies to solve the problem. In contrast, situations involving proactive coping invoke several additional monitoring goals. People must be vigilant to the possibility that they have adopted goals that cannot be accomplished (ever, or with available resources) or that can be accomplished, but are too costly. In such cases, failures to plan successfully may rest not with the choice of inefficient strategies, but rather with initially inappropriate choices of planning goals and a failure in the monitoring and debugging stages to respond to information that the strategies are not working or are not worth the effort. Making such decisions early (e.g., quitting while one is ahead) is clearly an important self-regulatory activity, yet little is known about it. Planning research to date has focused on factors that make people fail to plan when they should (cf. Ellis & Siegler, chapter 8, this volume; Sansone & Berg, 1993), but has yet to examine factors that make people plan or persist in planning when they should not. Extending planning research to consider unsolvable problems may contribute to knowledge about the monitoring and debugging stages, as well as highlight the necessity of managing resources and costs in planning.

One avenue of research that may be fruitful in understanding goal selection and disengagement concerns social factors in proactive coping and planning. Although the present review considered the case of a solitary proactive coper engaged in the process of detecting and remediating potential threats to well-being, there is an enormous literature that suggests that such activities are often informed by other people, for better or for worse. Although a detailed review is beyond the scope of this chapter (see Aspinwall & Taylor, in press; Goodnow, 1987, chapter 14, this volume), there are documented social influences on appraisals of negative information (cf. Croyle, 1992), in the provision of coping assistance (Taylor, Buunk, & Aspinwall, 1990; Thoits, 1986), and on the provision of feedback about one's actions (Ashford & Cummings, 1983). The less constrained the problem space and the less experience the problem solver has with the particular problem, the greater the corresponding need for social information to inform one's appraisals and offsetting efforts. Social information may also be critical to adaptive early disengagement from unsolvable stressors (e.g., "I can't believe you're still trying to do that ... "). Greater attention to the social context in which forward-looking behavior takes place and is modified may provide a more complete account of social influences on proactive coping.

Importing Concepts from Planning to the Stress and Coping Literature

Throughout the chapter, we highlighted ways in which research on proactive coping may be fruitfully applied to the study of planning and suggested that variables such as optimism might serve as ambassadors to the planning literature. An equally important question is: What should the ambassadors bring back in their suitcases? The study of planning and problem solving has much to offer the study of stress and coping. As a starting point for such cross-fertilization, we identify two conceptual and methodological approaches from planning research that have the potential to inform coping research.

Understanding the Component Skills of Proactive Coping.   The planning and problem-solving literatures might aid coping researchers in understanding the component skills involved in successful proactive and active coping. Prior coping research has tended to obscure the different component skills that comprise active coping (see Carver et al., 1989, for an exception). The predominant measurement strategy in coping research is to obtain retrospective self-reports of the frequency with which different coping strategies were brought to bear on a particular stressful event over a certain period of time (6 months, for example). Responses to these items are then subjected to a factor analysis and the resulting set of items indicating active ways of coping are then typically summed to form an overall measure of active coping.

This global approach to active coping may be the only practical way of assessing coping in certain settings (for example, where respondents are seriously ill or highly fatigued), but fails to take into account the possibility that active coping is not a single entity, but rather a set of social cognitive skills, involving such activities as the regulation of attention and arousal, mental simulation, avoiding early closure in one's consideration of potential stressors, and the suppression of competing activities (Aspinwall & Taylor, in press; Carver et al., 1989). Even though Folkman and Lazarus' (1980) Ways of Coping Instrument, the most widely used coping measure, has items that appear to measure such skills, the global measurement approach makes it impossible to know which skills were implicated at what point in time with what specific coping or regulatory task. Identifying other component skills, such as goal setting, anticipatory skills, representational skills, parsing problems into their components, and planning, has the potential to provide a more fine-grained account of how coping is accomplished and where it may fail.

Temporal Aspects of Coping and Feedback Loops.   A second aspect of coping that may benefit from the methods employed in the study of planning concerns the temporal sequencing of coping efforts and the role of feedback in coping. Lazarus and Folkman's seminal work on the transactional model of stress has always characterized appraisals and coping efforts as recursive processes, but these aspects of stress and coping are rarely studied in ways that would detect such reciprocal relations (cf. Lazarus, 1990). Such considerations may be especially important in understanding proactive coping. As a stressor unfolds, people may try a variety of coping strategies, each of which may affect the stressor, the person's understanding of same, and available resources. The additional wrinkle offered by proactive coping situations is that such efforts are more likely to change the nature, course, and rate of progress of the stressor itself, because it is an emerging stressor and not a bounded, well-defined problem. The challenge of tracking the success of one's efforts is also greater, because the problem may continue to develop, even if its effects are reduced or offset.

As is the case with the component skills of active coping, the predominantly global approach to the assessment of active coping is insensitive to the sequencing of strategies and the use of feedback elicited by them. Summing coping strategies across time is likely to obscure valuable information about the temporal development of the stressor and people's attempts to understand and manage it as it unfolds. Similarly, laboratory investigations of coping rarely offer enough task or problem trials to assess such patterns. Attention to the temporal sequencing of coping efforts is just beginning to be explored in the coping literature (cf. Carver & Scheier, 1994; Ptacek, Smith, & Zanas, 1992). To advance these efforts, it will be important to develop methodologies that can track the ways in which initial coping efforts elicit information that may inform subsequent coping efforts. There is, therefore, great potential for research on the processes, component skills, and resource requirements of monitoring and debugging to inform the study of coping over time.

Addressing the Intersection of Coping and Planning: Revisiting Anticipatory Coping

As this brief review has suggested, there is great potential for reciprocal influences between the coping and planning literatures. We close by suggesting that research on proactive and anticipatory processes may provide a worthwhile starting point for researchers wishing to examine the intersection of these two literatures. We suggest that anticipatory coping may represent the middle ground between proactive coping and problem solving. In proactive coping, it is unknown whether a potential stressor will evolve into a stressor. In problem solving, the problem is present and clearly defined. In anticipatory coping, the problem is relatively clearly defined and known to be imminent, but not yet present or fully experienced. Anticipatory coping usually requires offsetting plans, but may also evoke negative emotional arousal. In this case, the distinctions between coping and planning may blur—planning may be one form of coping (albeit, usually an adaptive one), but other anticipatory coping responses may be undertaken, including active avoidance of all thoughts and actions related to the incipient stressor (cf. Breznitz, 1983a) or the adoption of a wait-and-see approach.

One way to examine the decision to plan in such circumstances would be to conduct longitudinal studies of people who are facing known threats. For example, prospective studies of people who are likely to face stressors, such as layoffs, scheduled surgery, relocation due to highway construction, and so on, might elucidate the potential for anticipatory coping efforts and plans to reduce the impact of unavoidable stressful events and highlight some of the cognitive and motivational skills that are required. Experimental studies, too, have the promise of elucidating people's efforts to manage stressful situations before they occur. For example, Ptacek, Smith, and Dodge (1994) designed a speech anticipation paradigm in which research participants are scheduled to deliver a speech in two days and the temporal patterning of their coping behavior in the interim is assessed as the stressful situation approaches. Although such studies do not address the attention and detection stages of proactive coping, they could provide some insight into appraisals and coping efforts directed toward both problem-focused coping and emotion-focused coping that are undertaken once an imminent stressful circumstance becomes known.

CONCLUSION

Examining how people detect, appraise, manage, and monitor potential stressors may provide a window into forward-looking and purposeful behaviors, such as planning and proactive coping. The bulk of our review focused on noncognitive factors that may influence such processes. These factors may be especially important in the less-constrained problem spaces offered by naturalistic stressors and, in the special case of proactive coping, stressors and problems that have not yet materialized and about which relatively little may be known. Our review suggested that individual differences may play an important role in determining what is seen as a potential stressor, determining the amount of attention that may be successfully allocated to negative information, how threatening information is processed, specific strategies undertaken to avoid the stressor or reduce its impact, and the process of monitoring and modifying one's proactive efforts. These differences may affect whether proactive coping is undertaken at all, and whether the specific cognitive and behavioral measures undertaken are successful in avoiding or offsetting potential stressors. Continued examination of the individual differences, motivational factors, cognitive skills, and problem features that help people to avoid stress, as well as to manage it when it occurs, offers intriguing potential for future study.

ACKNOWLEDGMENTS

Portions of this chapter are based on a more complete explication of the proactive coping model developed in collaboration with Shelley Taylor (Aspinwall & Taylor, in press). Lisa Aspinwall was supported in this work by the University of Maryland Department of Psychology.

REFERENCES

Andersen, S. M. (1990). The inevitability of future suffering: The role of depressive predictive certainty in depression. *Social Cognition, 8,* 203–228.

Andersen, S. M., & Schwartz, A. H. (1992). Intolerance of ambiguity and depression: A cognitive vulnerability factor linked to hopelessness. *Social Cognition, 10,* 271–298.

Andersen, S. M., Spielman, L. A., & Bargh, J. A. (1992). Future-event schemas and certainty about the future: Automaticity in depressives' future-event predictions. *Journal of Personality and Social Psychology, 63,* 711–723.

Ashford, S. J., & Cummings, L. L. (1983). Feedback as an individual resource: Personal strategies of creating information. *Organizational Behavior and Human Performance, 32,* 379–398.

Aspinwall, L. G., & Brunhart, S. M. (1996). Distinguishing optimism from denial: Optimistic beliefs predict attention to health threats. *Personality and Social Psychology Bulletin, 22.* 993–1003.

Aspinwall, L. G., & Brunhart, S. M. (1997). *Optimism and attention to proximal threats to health.* Manuscript in preparation.

Aspinwall, L. G., Hartman, H. M., & Brunhart, S. M. (1997). *Optimism and responses to problems in close relationships.* Manuscript in preparation.

Aspinwall, L. G., & Taylor, S. E. (1992). Modeling cognitive adaptation: A longitudinal investigation of the impact of individual differences and coping on college adjustment and performance. *Journal of Personality and Social Psychology, 63,* 989–1003.

Aspinwall, L. G., & Taylor, S. E. (in press). A stitch in time: Self-regulation and proactive coping. *Psychological Bulletin.*

Bandura, A. (1977). Self-efficacy: Toward a unifying theory of behavior change. *Psychological Review, 84,* 191–215.

Bargh, J. A., Bond, R. N., Lombardi, W. J., & Tota, M. E. (1986). The additive nature of chronic and temporary sources of construct accessibility. *Journal of Personality and Social Psychology, 50,* 869–878.

Baumeister, R. F. (1989). The optimal margin of illusion. *Journal of Social and Clinical Psychology, 8*, 176–189.

Baumeister, R. F., & Cairns, K. J. (1992). Repression and self-presentation: When audiences interfere with self-deceptive strategies. *Journal of Personality and Social Psychology, 62*, 851–862.

Baumeister, R. F., Heatherton, T. F., & Tice, D. M. (1993). When ego threats lead to self-regulation failure: Negative consequences of high self-esteem. *Journal of Personality and Social Psychology, 64*, 141–156.

Blaney, P. H. (1986). Affect and memory: A review. *Psychological Bulletin, 99*, 229–246.

Blascovich, J., & Tomaka, J. (1996). The biopsychosocial model of arousal regulation. In M. Zanna (Ed.) *Advances in experimental social psychology* (Vol. 28, pp. 1–51). New York: Academic Press.

Bower, G. H. (1981). Mood and memory. *American Psychologist, 36*, 129–148.

Bolger, N. (1990). Coping as a personality process: A prospective study. *Journal of Personality and Social Psychology, 59*, 525–537.

Bolger, N., & Schilling, E. A. (1991). Personality and the problems of everyday life: The role of neuroticism in exposure and reactivity to daily stressors. *Journal of Personality. 59*, 355–386.

Breznitz, S. (1983a). Anticipatory stress and denial. In S. Breznitz (Ed.), *The denial of stress* (pp. 225–255). New York: International Universities Press.

Breznitz, S. (1983b). The seven kinds of denial. In S. Breznitz (Ed.), *The denial of stress* (pp. 257–280). New York: International Universities Press.

Cantor, N., & Norem, J. K. (1989). Defensive pessimism and stress and coping. *Social Cognition, 7*, 92–112.

Carver, C. V., Pozo, C., Harris, S. D., Noriega, V., Scheier, M. F., Robinson, D. S., Ketcham, A. S., Moffat, F. L., Jr., & Clark, K. C. (1993). How coping mediates the effect of optimism on distress: A study of women with early stage breast cancer. *Journal of Personality and Social Psychology, 65*, 375–390.

Carver, C. S., & Scheier, M. F. (1981). *Attention and self-regulation: A control-theory approach to human behavior.* New York: Springer-Verlag.

Carver, C. S., & Scheier, M. F. (1990). Principles of self-regulation: Action and emotion. In E. T. Higgins & R. M. Sorrentino (Eds.), *Handbook of motivation and cognition* (Vol. 2, pp. 3–52). New York: Guilford.

Carver, C. S., & Scheier, M. F. (1994). Situational coping and coping dispositions in a stressful transaction. *Journal of Personality and Social Psychology, 66*, 184–195.

Carver, C. S., Scheier, M. F., & Weintraub, J. K. (1989). Assessing coping strategies: A theoretically based approach. *Journal of Personality and Social Psychology, 56*, 267–283.

Collins, R. L., Taylor, S. E., & Skokan, L. A. (1990). A better world or a shattered vision? Changes in perspective following victimization. *Social Cognition, 8*, 263–285.

Cozzarelli, C. (1993). Personality and self-efficacy as predictors of coping with abortion. *Journal of Personality and Social Psychology, 65*, 1224–1236.

Croyle, R. T. (1992). Appraisal of health threats: Cognition, motivation, and social comparison. *Cognitive Theory and Research, 16*, 165–182.

Davey, G. C. L., Hampton, J., Farrell, J., & Davidson, S. (1992). Some characteristics of worrying: Evidence for worrying and anxiety as separate constructs. *Personality and Individual Differences, 13*, 133–147.

Davidson, P. P., & Bobey, M. J. (1970). Repressor–sensitizer differences on repeated exposures to pain. *Perceptual and Motor Skills, 31*, 711–714.

Dohrenwend, B. S., Dohrenwend, B. P., Dodson, M., & Shrout, P. E. (1984). Symptoms, hassles, social supports, and life events: Problems of confounded measures. *Journal of Abnormal Psychology, 93*, 222–230.

Dreher, M., & Oerter, R. (1987). Action planning competencies during adolescence and early adulthood. In S. L. Friedman, E. K. Scholnick, & R. R. Cocking (Eds.), *Blueprints for thinking: The role of planning in cognitive development* (pp. 321–355). Cambridge, England: Cambridge University Press.

Epstein, S., & Meier, P. (1989). Constructive thinking: A broad coping variable with specific components. *Journal of Personality and Social Psychology, 57*, 332–350.

Fiske, S. T., & Taylor, S. E. (1991). *Social cognition* (2nd ed.). New York: McGraw-Hill.

Folkman, S. (1984). Personal control and stress and coping processes: A theoretical analysis. *Journal of Personality and Social Psychology, 46*, 839–852.

Folkman, S., & Lazarus, R. S. (1980). An analysis of coping in a middle-aged community sample. *Journal of Health and Social Behavior, 21*, 219–239.

Folkman, S., & Lazarus, R. S. (1985). If it changes, it must be a process: Study of emotion and coping during three stages of a college examination. *Journal of Personality and Social Psychology, 48*, 150–170.

Forgas, J. P. (1995). Mood and judgment: The Affect Infusion Model. *Psychological Bulletin, 117*, 39–66.

Goldstein, M. J., Jones, R. B., Clemens, T. L., Flagg, G. W., & Alexander, F. G. (1965). Coping style as a factor in psychophysiological response to a tension-arousing film. *Journal of Personality and Social Psychology, 1*, 290–302.

Goodnow, J. J. (1987). Social aspects of planning. In S. L. Friedman, E. K. Scholnick, & R. R. Cocking (Eds.), *Blueprints for thinking: The role of planning in cognitive development* (pp. 179–201). Cambridge, England: Cambridge University Press.

Hammond, K. J. (1990). Case-based planning: A framework for planning from experience. *Cognitive Science, 14*, 385–444.

Hansen, C. H., Hansen, R. D., & Shantz, D. W. (1992). Repression at encoding: Discrete appraisals of emotional stimuli. *Journal of Personality and Social Psychology, 63*, 1026–1035.

Hayes-Roth, B., & Hayes-Roth, F. (1979). A cognitive model of planning. *Cognitive Science, 3*, 275–310.

Hobfoll, S. E. (1989). Conservation of resources: A new attempt at conceptualizing stress. *American Psychologist, 44*, 513–524.

Huston, T. L, & Vangelisti, A. L. (1991). Socioemotional behavior and satisfaction in marital relationships: A longitudinal study. *Journal of Personality and Social Psychology, 61*, 721–733.

Janoff-Bulman, R., & Brickman, P. (1982). Expectations and what people learn from failure. In N. T. Feather (Ed.), *Expectations and actions: Expectancy-value models in psychology* (pp. 207–237). Hillsdale, NJ: Lawrence Erlbaum Associates.

Jemmott, J. B., III, Ditto, P. H., & Croyle, R. T. (1986). Judging health status: Effects of perceived prevalence and personal relevance. *Journal of Personality and Social Psychology, 50*, 899–905.

Jerusalem, M. (1990). Temporal patterns of stress appraisals for high- and low-anxious individuals. *Anxiety Research, 3*, 113–129.

Jerusalem, M. (1993). Personal resources, environmental constraints, and adaptational processes: The predictive power of a theoretical stress model. *Personality and Individual Differences, 14*, 15–24.

Johnson, M. K., & Sherman, S. J. (1990). Constructing and reconstructing the past and the future in the present. In E. T. Higgins & R. M. Sorrentino (Eds.), *Handbook of motivation and social cognition: Foundations of social behavior* (pp. 482–526). New York: Guilford.

Jones, J. M. (1994). An exploration of temporality in human behavior. In R. C. Schank & E. Langer (Eds.), *Beliefs, reasoning, and decision-making: Psycho-logic in honor of Bob Abelson* (pp. 389–411). Hillsdale, NJ: Lawrence Erlbaum Associates.

Katz, L., & Epstein, S. (1991). Constructive thinking and coping with laboratory-induced stress. *Journal of Personality and Social Psychology, 61*, 789–800.

Knudson, R. M., Sommers, A. A., & Golding, S. L. (1980). Interpersonal perception and mode of resolution in marital conflict. *Journal of Personality and Social Psychology, 38*, 751–763.

Kreitler, S., & Kreitler, H. (1987). Plans and planning: Their motivational and cognitive antecedents. In S.L. Friedman, E. K. Scholnick, & R. R. Cocking (Eds.), *Blueprints for thinking: The role of planning in cognitive development* (pp. 110–178). Cambridge, England: Cambridge University Press.

Kruglanski, A. W., & Webster, D. M. (1996). Motivated closing of the mind: "Seizing" and "freezing." *Psychological Review, 103*, 263–283.

Lazarus, R. S. (1983). The costs and benefits of denial. In S. Breznitz (Ed.), *The denial of stress* (pp. 1–30). New York: International Universities Press.

Lazarus, R. S. (1990). Theory-based stress measurement. *Psychological Inquiry, 1*, 3–13.

Lazarus, R. S., & Folkman, S. (1984). *Stress, appraisal, and coping.* New York: Springer.

Lerner, M. J. (1980). *The belief in a just world: A fundamental delusion.* New York: Plenum.

Lyon, J. E., & Bugental, D. (1997). *Relationship power and risk for sexually-transmitted diseases: The role of attentional "capture" during sexual encounters.* Manuscript submitted for publication.

Maier, S. F., & Seligman, M. E. P. (1976). Learned helplessness: Theory and evidence. *Journal of Experimental Psychology: General, 195,* 3–46.

Manuck, S. B., Kamarck, T. W., Kasprowicz, A. S., & Waldstein, S. R. (1993). Stability and patterning of behaviorally evoked cardiovascular reactivity. In J. Blascovich & E. S. Katkin (Eds.), *Cardiovascular reactivity to psychological stress and disease: An examination of the evidence* (pp. 83–108). Washington, DC: American Psychological Association.

Matthews, A. (1990). Why worry? The cognitive function of anxiety. *Behavior Research and Therapy, 28,* 455–468.

McFarlin, D. B., Baumeister, R. F., & Blascovich, J. (1984). On knowing when to quit: Task failure, self-esteem, advice, and nonproductive persistence. *Journal of Personality, 52,* 139–155.

McGrath, J. E., & Beehr, T. A. (1990). Time and the stress process: Some temporal issues in the conceptualization and measurement of stress. *Stress Medicine, 6,* 93–104.

Miller, G. A., Galanter, E., & Pribram, K. H. (1960). *Plans and the structure of behavior.* New York: Holt, Rinehart & Winston.

Miller, S. M. (1987). Monitoring and blunting: Validation of a questionnaire to assess styles of information-seeking under threat. *Journal of Personality and Social Psychology, 52,* 345–353.

Neufeld, R. W. J., & Davidson, P. O. (1971). The effects of vicarious and cognitive rehearsal on pain tolerance. *Journal of Psychosomatic Research, 15,* 329–335.

Norem, J. K., & Cantor, N. (1986). Defensive pessimism: "Harnessing" anxiety as motivation. *Journal of Personality and Social Psychology, 51,* 1208–1217.

Oettingen, G. (1996). Positive fantasy and motivation. In P. M. Gollwitzer & J. A. Bargh (Eds.), *The psychology of action: Linking cognition and motivation to behavior* (pp. 236–259). New York: Guilford.

Paterson, R. J., & Neufeld, R. W. J. (1987). Clear danger: Situational determinants of the appraisal of threat. *Psychological Bulletin, 101,* 404–416.

Ptacek, J. T., Smith, R. E., & Dodge, K. L. (1994). Gender differences in coping with stress: When stressors and appraisals do not differ. *Personality and Social Psychology Bulletin, 20,* 421–430.

Ptacek, J. T., Smith, R. E., & Zanas, J. (1992). Gender, appraisal, and coping: A longitudinal analysis. *Journal of Personality, 60,* 747–770.

Rogoff, B., Gauvain, M., & Gardner, W. (1987). Children's adjustment of plans to circumstances. In S. L. Friedman, E. K. Scholnick, & R. R. Cocking (Eds.), *Blueprints for thinking: The role of planning in cognitive development* (pp. 303–320). Cambridge, England: Cambridge University Press.

Rubin, Z., & Peplau, L. A. (1975). Who believes in a just world? *Journal of Social Issues, 31*(3), 65–89.

Rusbult, C. E., Johnson, D. J., & Morrow, G. D. (1986). Impact of couple patterns of problem solving on distress and nondistress in dating relationships. *Journal of Personality and Social Psychology, 50,* 744–753.

Rusbult, C. E., Verette, J., Whitney, G. A., Slovik, L. F., & Lipkus, I. (1991). Accommodation processes in close relationships: Theory and preliminary empirical evidence. *Journal of Personality and Social Psychology, 60,* 53–78.

Sansone, C., & Berg, C. A. (1993). Adapting to the environment across the life span: Different process or different inputs? *International Journal of Behavioral Development, 16,* 215–241.

Scheier, M. F., & Carver, C. S. (1985). Optimism, coping and health: Assessment and implications of generalized outcome expectancies. *Health Psychology, 4,* 219–247.

Scheier, M. F., & Carver, C. S. (1987). Dispositional optimism and physical well-being: The influence of generalized outcome expectancies on health. *Journal of Personality, 55,* 169–210.

Scheier, M. F., & Carver, C. S. (1992). Effects of optimism on psychological and physical well-being: Theoretical overview and empirical update. *Cognitive Therapy and Research, 16,* 201–228.

Scheier, M. F., Carver, C. S., & Bridges, M. W. (1994). Distinguishing optimism from neuroticism (and trait anxiety, self-mastery, and self-esteem): A re-evaluation of the Life Orientation Test. *Journal of Personality and Social Psychology, 67,* 1063–1078.

Scheier, M. F., Matthews, K. A., Owens, J., Magovern, G. J., Sr., Lefebvre, R. C., Abbott, R. A., & Carver, C. S. (1989). Dispositional optimism and recovery from coronary artery bypass surgery: The beneficial effects on physical and psychological well-being. *Journal of Personality and Social Psychology, 57,* 1024–1040.

Scheier, M. F., Weintraub, J. K., & Carver, C. S. (1986). Coping with stress: Divergent strategies of optimists and pessimists. *Journal of Personality and Social Psychology, 51*, 1257–1264.

Scholnick, E. K. (1994). Planning. *Encyclopedia of human behavior* (Vol. 3, pp. 525–534). New York: Academic Press.

Scholnick, E. K., & Friedman, S. L. (1987). The planning construct in the psychological literature. In S. L. Friedman, E. K. Scholnick, & R.R. Cocking (Eds.), *Blueprints for thinking: The role of planning in cognitive development* (pp. 3–38). Cambridge, England: Cambridge University Press.

Scholnick, E. K., & Friedman, S. A. (1993). Planning in context: Developmental and situational considerations. *International Journal of Behavioral Development, 16*, 145–167.

Schonpflug, W. (1986). Behavior economics as an approach to stress theory. In M. H. Appley & R. Trumbull (Eds.), *Dynamics of stress: Physiological, psychological, and social perspectives* (pp. 81–98). New York: Plenum.

Schwarz, N. (1990). Feelings as information: Informational and motivational functions of affective states. In E. T. Higgins & R. M. Sorrentino (Eds.), *Handbook of motivation and cognition* (Vol. 2, pp. 527–561). New York: Guilford.

Sedek, G., Kofta, M., & Tyszka, T. (1993). Effects of uncontrollability on subsequent decision making: Testing the cognitive exhaustion hypothesis. *Journal of Personality and Social Psychology, 65*, 1270–1281.

Seligman, M. E. P. (1975). *Helplessness: On depression, development and death.* San Francisco: Freeman.

Showers, C. (1988). The effects of how and why thinking on perceptions of future negative events. *Cognitive Therapy and Research, 12*, 225–240.

Showers, C. (1992). The motivational and emotional consequences of considering positive or negative possibilities for an upcoming event. *Journal of Personality and Social Psychology, 63*, 474–484.

Showers, C., & Ruben, C. (1990). Distinguishing defensive pessimism from depression: Negative expectations and positive coping mechanisms. *Cognitive Therapy and Research, 14*, 385–399.

Sieber, W. J., Rodin, J., Larson, L., Ortega, S., Cummings, N., Levy, S., Whiteside, T., & Herberman, R. (1992). Modulation of human natural killer cell activity by exposure to uncontrollable stress. *Brain, Behavior, and Immunity, 6*, 141–156.

Steptoe, A., & Vogele, C. (1992). Individual differences in the perception of bodily sensations: The role of trait anxiety and coping style. *Behavior Research Therapy, 30*, 597–607.

Strathman, A., Gleicher, F., Boninger, D. S., & Edwards, C. S. (1994). The consideration of future consequences: Weighing immediate and distant outcomes of behavior. *Journal of Personality and Social Psychology, 66*, 742–752.

Suls, J., & Fletcher, B. (1985). The relative efficacy of avoidant and nonavoidant coping strategies: A meta-analysis. *Health Psychology, 4*, 249–288.

Taylor, S. E. (1989). *Positive illusions: Creative self-deception and the healthy mind.* New York: Basic Books.

Taylor, S. E., & Aspinwall, L. G. (1996). Mediating and moderating processes in psychosocial stress: Appraisal, coping, resistance and vulnerability. In H. B. Kaplan (Ed.), *Psychosocial stress: Perspectives on structure, theory, life course, and methods* (pp. 71–110). San Diego: Academic Press.

Taylor, S. E., Buunk, B. P., & Aspinwall, L. G. (1990). Social comparison, stress and coping. *Personality and Social Psychology Bulletin, 16*, 74–89.

Taylor, S. E., & Clark, L. F. (1986). Does information improve adjustment to noxious events? In M. J. Saks & L. Saxe (Eds.), *Advances in applied social psychology* (Vol. 3, pp. 1–28). Hillsdale, NJ: Lawrence Erlbaum Associates.

Taylor, S. E., Kemeny, M. E., Aspinwall, L. G., Schneider, S. C., Rodriguez, R., & Herbert, M. (1992). Optimism, coping, psychological distress, and high-risk sexual behavior among men at risk for AIDS. *Journal of Personality and Social Psychology, 63*, 460–473.

Taylor, S. E., & Pham, L. B. (1996). Mental simulation, motivation, and action. In P. M. Gollwitzer & J. A. Bargh (Eds.), *The psychology of action: Linking cognition and motivation to behavior* (pp. 219–235). New York: Guilford.

Taylor, S. E., & Schneider, S. K. (1989). Coping and the simulation of events. *Social Cognition, 7*, 176–196.

Thoits, P. A. (1986). Social support as coping assistance. *Journal of Consulting and Clinical Psychology, 54,* 416–423.

Tomaka, J., & Blascovich, J. (1994). Effects of justice beliefs on cognitive appraisal of and subjective, physiological, and behavioral responses to potential stress. *Journal of Personality and Social Psychology, 67,* 732–740.

Tomaka, J., Blascovich, J., & Kelsey, R. M. (1992). Effects of self-deception, social desirability, and repressive coping on psychophysiological reactivity to stress. *Personality and Social Psychology Bulletin, 18,* 616–624.

Trope, Y., & Neter, E. (1994). Reconciling competing motives in self-evaluation: The role of self-control in feedback seeking. *Journal of Personality and Social Psychology, 66,* 646–657.

Tversky, A., & Kahneman, D. (1982). Judgments of and by representativeness. In D. Kahneman, P. Slovic, & A. Tversky (Eds.), *Judgment under uncertainty: Heuristics and biases* (pp. 84–100). New York: Cambridge University Press.

Vitaliano, P. O., Russo, J., & Maiuro, R. D. (1987). Locus of control, type of stressor, and appraisal within a cognitive-phenomenological model of stress. *Journal of Research in Personality, 21,* 224–237.

Weinberger, D. A. (1990). The construct validity of the repressive coping style. In J. L. Singer (Ed.), *Repression and disassociation* (pp. 337–386). Chicago: University of Chicago Press.

Weinstein, N. D. (1980). Unrealistic optimism about future life events. *Journal of Personality and Social Psychology, 39,* 806–820.

Weinstein, N. D. (1987). Unrealistic optimism about susceptibility to health problems: Conclusions from a community-wide sample. *Journal of Behavioral Medicine, 10,* 481–500.

Wiebe, D. J. (1991). Hardiness and stress moderation: A test of proposed mechanisms. *Journal of Personality and Social Psychology, 60,* 89–99.

Wiebe, D. J., & Williams, P. G. (1992). Hardiness and health: A social psychophysiological perspective on stress and adaptation. *Journal of Social and Clinical Psychology, 11,* 238–262.

Zimbardo, P. G., & Gonzalez, A. (1984, February). The times of your life. *Psychology Today, 18,* 54.

13

Planning Skills in Adolescence: The Case of Contraceptive Use and Non-Use

Nancy E. Adler
Philip J. Moore
Jeanne M. Tschann
University of California, San Francisco

A major issue addressed in this volume is the failure of individuals to plan, even when the capacity to plan exists. In everyday life, the failure to plan can have serious adverse consequences. Among the more obvious examples is the failure of sexually active adolescents to plan for protecting themselves against the risks of pregnancy and sexually transmitted diseases. Approximately one fifth of sexually active females age 15 to 19 become pregnant in any given year, resulting in 1 million teenage pregnancies annually. The vast majority of these pregnancies were not planned (Haynes, 1987). Additionally, rates of many sexually transmitted diseases are higher among adolescents than in other age groups. For example, approximately one out of seven teenagers in the United States may now have a sexually transmitted disease (Sunenblick, 1988), about twice the rate for adults in their 20s (Hein, 1989). This chapter presents some of the reasons for the widespread failure of adolescents to plan adequately for sexual activity. As most of the research has examined these issues in relation to adolescent females, the discussion is be limited to their experiences. For the remainder of the chapter, we use the term *adolescent* to refer to the adolescent female.

Although *planning* may be conceptualized in many different ways, most definitions in the literature involve individuals applying information and other (typically intellectual) resources toward the completion of a specific objective. Hayes-Roth and Hayes-Roth (1979) defined planning as "the predetermination of action aimed at achieving some goal" (pp. 275–276). Most models of planning include both a preparatory component as well as an executive or action phase. The preparatory stage involves defining the problem or issue, choosing a set of goals, and working out the specifics of the plan itself. The execution of the plan includes putting it into action, as well as monitoring and adjusting to its success or failure. In this way, knowledge, consideration, and use of contraception can be seen as predetermined action (i.e., plan) directed toward the goal of avoiding pregnancy and/or sexually transmitted diseases (STDs).

Given that the vast majority of adolescents who become pregnant report that they had not used birth control at the time of conception (Shah, Zelnik, & Kantner, 1975), the high rates of teenage pregnancy and sexually transmitted diseases can be seen as a failure on the part of adolescents to plan for sexual activity or to execute their plan. This failure may reflect inadequate knowledge that prevents adolescents from formulating or executing an effective plan, or may also reflect inadequate capacity to plan. Surprisingly, there is very little research on the extent to which adolescents have the capacity to plan. Although there has been a great deal of research on the topic of planning skills, there is a dearth of information regarding the planning skills of adolescents. A computerized literature search on planning skills identified 1,239 citations concerning planning skills. Remarkably, only 79 of these even mentioned adolescents. Moreover, only 26 citations discussed the planning skills of adolescents in the general population, and the majority focused on adolescents with either mental or physical handicaps, or behavioral problems.

In the absence of direct evidence of the capacity of adolescents to plan for sexual activity, inferences are made on the basis of outcomes. The failure of adolescents to use adequate contraception is taken as evidence of lack of planning. However, as discussed later, there are a number of forces that may deflect adolescents who have the requisite knowledge and skills from engaging in adequate planning in this area. Some of those forces are reviewed and the implications for making inferences about adolescents' planning skills are considered.

ADOLESCENTS' CONTRACEPTIVE KNOWLEDGE

Because planning involves continuous processing of information, we first consider the possibility that young women become pregnant because they lack sufficient information about sexuality and methods of contraception. This has long been a centerpiece of federal government policy to reduce teenage pregnancy (Franklin, 1987), and has led to a significant increase in the number of sex education programs offered to adolescents.

Information is important, and there is evidence that lack of information as well as having misinformation is associated with higher risk of pregnancy. Sex education courses typically have not been very effective, however, in improving contraceptive behavior (Kirby & Waszak, 1992). One reason for this may be that these classes often present information in a relatively abstract way, focusing on biology and reproductive functions and providing little specific information on how to plan contraceptive use. Although information may be necessary, it is not sufficient to enable teenagers to avoid pregnancy, particularly if the information is about general aspects of reproduction and contraception (Smith, Nenney, Weinman, & Mumford, 1982). Concrete information about how to obtain and use various contraceptive methods is also important and may not be easily accessible. In a survey of adolescents, Herz and Reis (1987) reported that although respondents were aware of various contraceptive methods, they lacked practical information about how to obtain these methods and use them effectively.

Even when contraceptives are available, however, many sexually active teenagers who say they do not want to get pregnant nonetheless fail to use them (Adler, 1974; Rosen & Martindale, 1978; Zelnik & Kantner, 1980). Thus, although lack of access and of procedural knowledge about contraceptives may reduce contraceptive use, there are additional factors that also contribute to non-use of contraception.

ADOLESCENTS' ABILITY TO PLAN

One of the questions about planning among adolescents involves the extent to which they possess the cognitive ability to plan adequately. Some assert that adolescents lack the cognitive skills needed to formulate an effective plan. Drawing on the work of Piaget (1952), they argue that adolescents who have not achieved formal operational thought cannot represent hypothetical or probabilistic outcomes. Because the occurrence of pregnancy or a sexually transmitted disease is a probabilistic event, adolescents who are at the level of concrete operations presumably would not be able to conceptualize the degree and nature of the risks involved in unprotected sexual activity. It is only after attaining formal operational thought that one is said to have developed an appreciation for the consequences of one's behavior and the ability to move cognitively beyond the "here and now." More recent work, however, has questioned the extent to which children and adolescents pass through developmental stages with the rigidity and order posited by Piaget (e.g., Brown & Desforges, 1977; Schuberth, 1983).

Processes other than lack of formal operational thought have also been asserted to account for adolescents' lack of planning. For example, rather than seeing risky behaviors as resulting from a failure to understand consequences, Elkind (1967) suggested that adolescents develop an unrealistic sense of their own vulnerability. This sense of invulnerability is thought to emerge out of their increasing ability to assume other people's perspectives. Elkind posits that two processes take place as adolescents begin to think about the views of others. One is that adolescent presume others are as aware of them as they are of themselves: This is referred to as the *imaginary audience*. The second is that adolescents believe they are unique in their thoughts and attributes: the *personal fable*. Although the imaginary audience contributes to the heightened self-consciousness of adolescents, the sense of uniqueness associated with the personal fable is hypothesized to lead adolescents to believe that they are uniquely invulnerable to adverse outcomes of risky behavior. Thus, to the extent that one feels invulnerable to adverse consequences, one would have little motivation to engage in planning to avoid these potential consequences. However, Dolcini, et al. (1989) found that adolescent females who scored higher on a scale assessing feelings of personal uniqueness actually showed *higher* levels of perceived risk.

There is no direct evidence regarding the extent to which cognitive ability / skill affects adolescents' ability to plan. Although lack of knowledge and stage of cognitive development may make it more difficult for adolescents to plan adequately, there is reason to believe that many adolescents do have the knowledge base and cognitive abilities to engage in planning with regard to contraceptive use. Instead, their failure to plan may be more closely linked to social factors that deter planning activities than to lack of planning skills.

Evidence that the social environment has a major impact on behaviors needed to avert pregnancy and STDs comes from cross-national data. With comparable rates of sexual activity, adolescents in the United States have dramatically higher rates of pregnancy and of STDs than in other developed countries—almost double the rates in Canada and triple the rates in some of the Scandinavian countries (Jones et al., 1986). It is unlikely that adolescents in those countries are more cognitively developed or have better planning skills than do adolescents in the United States. What is more likely is that the social environments of those countries encourage easier information acquisition and provide a better environment for planning.

The context in which planning occurs will have a substantial impact on planning behavior. Neither planning nor implementation of behavior, especially behaviors as intensely interactive as sexual and reproductive behaviors, occurs in a vacuum. For most adolescents in the United States, the context in which contraceptive behavior occurs is one that makes planful behavior difficult. Scholnick and Friedman (1993) identified characteristics of the ideal planning environment. In the following section, we consider how these characteristics map onto the environment in which an adolescent typically makes decisions about contraception, particularly for coitus-dependent contraceptive methods such as the condom. In essence, what appears to be poor teenage planning may, in large part, reflect the conflicting pressures of the environment in which this planning must take place.

THE CONTRACEPTIVE PLANNING ENVIRONMENT

Predictability and Control Over Environment

According to Scholnick and Friedman (1993) the ideal environment for planning to occur is one that "is predictable and contains accessible resources and movable pieces individuals believe they can control" (p. 151). These factors are unlikely to characterize the typical environment of adolescents who are potential users of contraception. First, the environment in which sexual activity occurs is often not predictable for teenagers, particularly when they are just becoming sexually active or initiating sexual relations with a new partner (Chilman, 1973; Hatcher, 1976; Miller, 1976). Many women cite the unexpectedness of sex as the primary reason for contraceptive non-use (Zelnik & Kantner, 1979). Findings of Foreit and Foreit (1981) suggest that non-use of effective contraception is mediated by the unpredictability of sexual intercourse. Given the normative sanctions against teenage sexual activity (see the following section), young people may have difficulty acknowledging that they are planning to initiate sexual activity. In addition, parental disapproval may limit the settings in which young people can have the privacy to have sex and thus make its occurrence subject to chance opportunities.

Control over "movable pieces" in the ideal planning environment requires control not only over the resources to obtain effective contraception, but also over one's partner, whose cooperation may be needed to use contraceptives effectively. Young women may not perceive their partners as easily controlled, and indeed they may not be. Furstenberg (1976) and Nadelson, Notman, & Gillon, (1980) reported that males frequently hold power in determining birth control usage in adolescent relationships. In addition, D'Augelli and Cross (1975) found that men's levels of moral reasoning were better predictors of couples' sexual behavior than were female levels. This suggests that the personalities of the men were more influential than those of the women in setting sexual and contraceptive standards for couples.

Insofar as coitus-dependent methods require the participation of the partner, concerns about the partner's willingness to use a contraceptive method may be especially likely to inhibit planning. These forces are likely to be operative in adults as well. For example, Miller (1986) found that among married couples, if the husband was not pleased with a given method, contraceptive use by the couple was less effective. Finally, although it may be true that males often exert a disproportionately large influence on couples' contraceptive practices, it is interesting to note that Thompson and Spanier (1978) found the persuasion of one's partner to be the most powerful influence on the use of contraception by both men *and* women. These results illustrate the impact that a sexual partner can have on another's contraceptive decision making and, hence, the importance of considering this influence when evaluating contraceptive planning.

Acceptability of Planning

A second element of the ideal planning environment is that the "task should be one where planning is expected and acceptable" (Scholnick & Friedman, 1993, p. 151). To plan to use contraception means that the young woman must anticipate having sex. Such acknowledgment of one's intention to have sex may be difficult for adolescents who are subjected to conflicting pressures about their sexual activity. Specifically, prevailing adult and parental norms oppose adolescent sexual activity, whereas peer norms may favor it. As Rodgers and Rowe (1990) wrote, "Although sexual activity becomes more normative with increasing age, for young adolescents it falls within the set of behaviors that most parents would not condone" (p. 278).

Conflicting pressures are especially strong for adolescent females. Despite change in some social norms in our culture, there is still a widespread view that "good girls" do not have sex, and planning to have sex is associated with being promiscuous. Such beliefs are reinforced within some religious communities in which premarital sex is considered to be a sin and, thus, planning makes it a premeditated sin. This view has led to pressure to prohibit the discussion of pregnancy prevention in high school sex education classes in some communities (Kenney, Guardado, & Brown, 1989). This may be one of the key differences between the United States and the Scandinavian countries, where the topics of sex and birth control are both openly discussed and contraceptives are available to adolescents.

Normative disapproval of adolescent sexual behavior can cause a variety of negative emotional responses to sex among adolescents such as anxiety, guilt, and fear. Each of these responses may inhibit sexual behavior. However, when these responses are not sufficiently strong to preclude sexual intercourse, they can interfere with the ability to plan for and cope with the consequences of sexual activity (Gerrard, Gibbons, & McCoy, 1993). For example, guilt associated with sexual activity was found to be associated with lower contraceptive use among sexually active women (Geis & Gerrard, 1984; Mosher & Vonderheide, 1985; Upchurch, 1978).

Similarly, Studer and Thornton (1987) found that young women who attended religious services more frequently were less likely to have initiated sexual activity than were those who seldom or never attended services. However, among adolescents who were sexually active, those who seldom or never attended services were more likely to use effective birth control than those who attended more frequently. In addition to causing feelings of guilt, adult disapproval of adolescent sexual activity may also create embarrassment, which may, in turn, become a barrier to obtaining a method of contraception. Herold (1981) found this to be the case with samples of sexually active high school and university females, among whom those who were more embarrassed were less likely to obtain contraceptives from a physician or pharmacist.

It may be particularly difficult during the early phases of sexual activity for a young woman to admit that she is a sexually active person, and that she plans to have sex. Lindemann (1974, 1977) described this period of sexual activity as the *natural* stage in a woman's contraceptive career, during which sexual intercourse is relatively rare and unplanned, and the woman does not yet see herself as a sexual being. Thus, it is not surprising to find that the time of greatest risk of unwanted pregnancy is during the first 6 months after initiating sexual activity (Zabin, Kantner, & Zelnik, 1979).

Pressures against planning for sex because of social norms or religious beliefs may be magnified by pressures for romantic, passionate love. Young women sometimes describe their sexual encounters as ones in which they are "swept away" by the passion of the moment (Chilman, 1973; Hatcher, 1976; Miller, 1976; Shah et al., 1975; Sorensen, 1973). This may provide justification for engaging in a proscribed behavior, and although some adolescents may be "swept away" every Saturday night, they may find it difficult to admit to themselves or others that they are planning for this to happen.

Costs and Benefits

A third element of the ideal planning environment is that the "consequences of failing to plan should outweigh the effort that must be devoted to planning" (Scholnick & Friedman, 1993, p. 151). In the case of contraceptive use, there are substantial costs involved in planning to avoid unwanted pregnancy. Not only must one admit to anticipating and planning one's sexual activity, but it may be difficult to obtain the needed information and plan adequately for contraceptive protection. In addition, the actual financial cost of obtaining contraceptives and, in some instances, the need for a doctor's prescription may also inhibit action, as may the side effects associated with the use of some methods.

Many adolescents lack access to the services needed to obtain effective contraception. Contraceptive non-use has been associated with both problems of access to family planning services (e.g., Evans, Selstad, & Weicher, 1976; Zabin & Clark, 1983) and a lack of counseling (Berger et al., 1987). As for the contraceptive methods themselves, each has substantial barriers to its use; currently available methods all have potentially unpleasant or harmful side effects or behavioral demands that place a burden on the user. As Miller (1986) noted, individuals must balance the unpleasantness of use of contraceptives against the anxiety of non-use. The balance that is struck between anxiety and unpleasantness may be biased toward greater saliency of unpleasantness. The problems associated with the use of any given method (e.g., expense, physical discomfort, side effects) are generally immediate and concrete. In contrast, the consequences of non-use are uncertain, in the future, and may seem abstract (Thornburg, 1981). In terms of absolute risk, there is a small probability of getting a sexually transmitted disease or of becoming pregnant from any given act of intercourse. The concept of cumulative risk may not be compelling for any given moment, whereas the burden of contraceptive use is clear.

Personal Efficacy

Another element of the ideal planning environment identified by Scholnick and Friedman (1993) is that individuals have positive beliefs about their own capacity to engage in planning. Even if an adolescent has the knowledge base and cognitive ability to plan, if her confidence in her ability to plan for and use contraception is low, she may not actually engage in planning or persist in the behavior if obstacles are encountered. Although there is no research examining the effects of beliefs about one's capacity to plan, a number of studies have examined the role of contraceptive self-efficacy in contraceptive use.

The notion of contraceptive self-efficacy (CSE) is adapted from Bandura's Self-Efficacy Theory (Bandura, 1977) that has been used to address a variety of dysfunctional behaviors that persist despite people's desire to change them (Bandura, 1989; Bandura, Adams, Hardy, & Howels, 1980). According to the theory, self-efficacy reflects an individual's expectations that they have the capacity to execute a particular behavior. These expectations influence the initiative and persistence used to achieve broader, end-goal behavior. Contraceptive self-efficacy represents the strength of an individual's conviction that she can exercise control within various sexual and contraceptive situations to achieve contraceptive protection.

Contraceptive use involves complex and often challenging behaviors. For example, condom use may require a young woman to convince her partner to use a condom, something she may assume he will not want to do and that he may, in fact, resist. Young women with low self-efficacy may feel less able to be assertive with their partners and less confident that they can perform the other behaviors necessary to use effective contraception. This lack of confidence may reduce the chances that they will either initiate or follow through in performing the behaviors needed for contraception protection.

Studies that have assessed contraceptive self-efficacy have shown that women who have greater self-efficacy are more effective contraceptors (e.g., Heinrich, 1993; Levinson, 1984, 1986). Contraceptive self-efficacy involves beliefs specific to contraceptive use. In addition, an adolescent's more general beliefs about her efficacy and associated feelings of self-esteem may also play a role in contraceptive planning. Diminished self-esteem and low general efficacy may contribute to diminished contraceptive self-efficacy. These factors may also affect contraceptive use indirectly through influencing the adolescents' evaluation of how negative it would be to become pregnant. Young women with low self-esteem may view motherhood as a pathway to achieving status and esteem; this will reduce their motivation to avoid pregnancy, as is discussed later in this chapter. Evidence for the impact of self-esteem and motivation for contraceptive use comes from our recently completed study of sexually active female adolescents. This study showed that the lower a young woman's self-esteem, the more value she placed on becoming pregnant in the next year, and the less vigilant was her subsequent contraceptive behavior (Adler & Tschann, 1994).

Executing a Plan

Finally, Scholnick and Friedman (1993) identified several factors that facilitate the execution of a plan. They noted that young children learn to execute plans by apprenticeship and learning, and that individuals make use of social support to try out and repair strategies. In the area of contraceptive use, these facilitating conditions generally are not available. Planning for contraceptive use is typically a private matter—it is not something that children usually observe and learn from their parents.

Sex and contraception are rarely discussed openly; in fact, many children and adolescents find it difficult to believe that their parents are sexual beings, or that they had intercourse any more often than it took to produce the number of children in the family. Nor do the media, which can be a major source of both information and societal norms, generally provide useful information. Although acts of sexual intercourse are often shown on television and in the movies, they are rarely accompanied by contraceptive planning or use. Thus, what is modeled is a lack of planning and protection. More importantly, this lack of planning typically does not result in adverse consequences. The numerous acts of intercourse without contraception shown on television and in movies are rarely followed by an unintended pregnancy or STD. The message from such portrayals is that contraceptive use is not only atypical, but unnecessary.

Lacking explicit information from elsewhere, adolescents frequently use their peers for information and support (Thornburg, 1981). Unfortunately, their peers are usually no more informed than are they, and it may be difficult to obtain accurate information to repair faulty strategies. Moreover, what information they do receive is often limited to characteristics of the contraceptives themselves, rather than information about reducing barriers to their use. As Morrison (1989) concluded in a discussion of unwanted pregnancies among adolescents: "they [adolescents] may be less in need of technical information about contraceptives and more in need of information about how to overcome the situational constraints that block contraceptive use" (p. 1449).

OTHER BARRIERS TO PLANNING

In addition to the environmental barriers outlined by Scholnick and Friedman (1993), other factors may also deter adolescents from engaging in planning to avoid pregnancy and/or STDs. Key among those are optimistic bias, feedback loops, and the extent of an adolescent's motivation to avoid pregnancy.

Optimistic Bias

Optimistic bias refers to the tendency for people to underestimate their risk relative to other people of experiencing adverse outcomes. When asked, people typically rate themselves as less likely than others to experience negative or unpleasant events: The average person rates himself as being at less than average risk. In samples of adults, for example, Weinstein (1982, 1987) found that subjects exhibited an optimistic bias when estimating their risk for various health problems, including unintended pregnancy. Having an optimistic bias about one's susceptibility to adverse outcomes may reduce one's motivation to engage in planning to avoid those outcomes.

By reducing the perceived risk of the consequences of failing to use contraception, optimistic bias may decrease motivation to use contraception and, in turn, reduce contraceptive planning and use. To test this hypothesis, Burger and Burns (1988) studied a group of female college students and found that women who were sexually active exhibited optimistic bias, tending to see themselves as less likely than other women students, other women their age, and other women of child-bearing age to become pregnant. Moreover, the level of optimistic bias was negatively related to contraception: The young women who were more optimistically biased about their chances of getting pregnant were less likely to be using effective contraception. On the other hand, Whitley and Hern (1991) found a *positive* association between optimistic bias and contraceptive use in another sample of female college students. In this sample, those who were better contraceptors were accurate in perceiving that they were at a reduced risk for pregnancy relative to less effective contraceptors.

There have been no studies of optimistic bias and contraceptive use among adolescents. Some might expect that adolescents would show greater optimistic bias than do adults. However, research that has directly compared adults and adolescents showed found them to be equally inclined to exhibit optimistic bias (Quadrel, Fischoff, & Davis, 1994). Research conducted outside the framework of optimistic bias on the perception of risk for pregnancy suggests that adolescents may underestimate their risk of pregnancy and that this underestimation may reduce motivation for contraceptive planning and use. Kantner and Zelnik (1973) found that over twice as many teens who thought they could easily conceive versus those who felt they could not easily get pregnant reported using a contraceptive method the first time they had intercourse.

Feedback Loop

Adolescents may underestimate their chances of pregnancy because they believe themselves to be too young to conceive (Morrison, 1985). This is the reason often given by pregnant adolescents for why they did not use contraception. As this is obviously not true, what can account for the misperception that they were unable to become pregnant?

One contributing factor may be the message adolescents receive from well-intentioned sex education classes and other sources about the chances of pregnancy. Being told emphatically that "it only takes once," adolescents may initially expect that any act of unprotected intercourse will lead to pregnancy. Several studies have indicated that adolescents overestimate the likelihood of conceiving from a single instance of unprotected intercourse (Cvetkovich & Grote, 1981; Foreit & Foreit, 1981; Smith, Nenney, Weinman, & Mumford, 1982). Almost 50% of teenagers report not using any contraceptive method at first intercourse; due to the probabilistic nature of conception, the majority of these adolescents do not become pregnant as a result of this initial exposure. The feedback from this experience may then dramatically change their estimates. Specifically, these adolescents may attribute their failure to get pregnant to their being too young to become pregnant or to there being something wrong with their bodies. In either case, their subjective estimates of the chances of pregnancy may go from close to 100% to near 0%, and essentially eliminate the perceived need for contraception.

It may also be hard for adolescents to develop a subjective sense of the likelihood of pregnancy. As Cvetkovich and Grote (1981) noted, adolescents may interpret probabilities lower than 100% certainty to be low. Because pregnancy is probable but not certain, this may be subjectively experienced as a low probability. We know relatively little about how adolescents—or for that matter, adults—translate objective statistical probabilities into subjective likelihood estimates. Such subjective estimates are important to understand, for they are likely to influence subsequent behavior.

Motivation to Avoid Pregnancy

The previous discussion of barriers to contraceptive planning and behavior assumed that the adolescents were motivated to plan to avoid pregnancy and STDs. Although adolescents will undoubtedly wish to avoid contracting an STD, it is not clear that all adolescents wish to avoid pregnancy (Weisman et al., 1991). There has been a good deal of speculation about the extent to which adolescents are motivated—consciously or unconsciously—to become pregnant. Individuals may vary in the extent to which they are motivated to avoid pregnancy, and thus in their motivation to use any contraceptive method.

Relatively few unmarried adolescents explicitly plan to conceive. Rather, it appears that for some young women, pregnancy is not anticipated to be highly negative. Depending on their situation, adolescents may expect that positive outcomes will result from pregnancy. These include, for example, achieving adult status, gaining independence from family, strengthening their relationship with their boyfriend, having someone to love and to receive love, and gaining respect from peers (Adler & Tschann, 1993). These factors may be particularly relevant to inner-city youth who may not see other pathways to achieving identity and esteem (Burton, 1990; Geronimus, 1987). If young women anticipate positive consequences of pregnancy, which may balance some of the adverse consequences, they may not be strongly motivated to avoid conception.

Before one can attribute non-use of contraception to lack of planning or failure to apply planning skills, it is important to assess the strength of their motivation to avoid pregnancy. One must first establish that the adolescent actually holds the goal of avoiding pregnancy. If this goal is not strong and salient, it is unlikely that an adolescent will be able to overcome the obstacles to engaging in effective planning that have been discussed in this chapter.

SUMMARY

This chapter examined the impact of informational, environmental, and motivational factors on adolescent contraceptive planning and use and, in doing so, many of the inherent challenges to effective planning in the context of sexual behavior were discussed. First, although both descriptive and procedural information about contraception is necessary, it may not be sufficient to ensure that adolescents effectively plan for sexual activity and protect themselves against the risks of STDs and pregnancy. Second, the problems identified are not due simply to the inability of adolescents to plan, but are also the result of difficulties inherent in the environmental context in which contraceptive planning must occur. These difficulties are particularly salient during the initial stages of sexual activity when social approval for planning, open discussion, and concrete information are especially limited. Finally, an adequate understanding of adolescent contraceptive use and non-use must include an evaluation of the motivational context in which contraceptive behavior occurs.

The ability of adolescents to plan is an important theoretical and applied question. There is very little research that bears directly on this question. In the absence of direct information, there has been a tendency to point to behaviors that have adverse consequences—in particular the high rates of teenage pregnancy in the United States—as an indication that adolescents lack the capacity to plan. In this chapter the problems in making this leap of judgment were identified. Environmental elements that facilitate planning were shown to be lacking in the environments of most sexually active adolescents. Although we have focused on the planning difficulties for adolescents, one could apply many elements of this discussion to adults as well.

Considering the planning environment, rather than planning skills alone, provides a valuable check on our inferences about individuals and it provides possibilities for interventions to reduce the incidence of teenage pregnancy. Research is clearly needed on the development and implementation of planning skills. There is a surprising lack of empirical data on this subject, particularly regarding research on the extent to which adolescents engage in planning and addressing problems in their own lives. Research on planning skills in the real world will be much more useful if it explicitly takes into account the context in which planning must occur. What is needed is research that examines the application of planning skills in the context of environmental constraints and facilitators of effective planning. Careful elucidation of the situational and personal forces that may deflect individuals from making the best choices will help us to intervene more effectively to encourage behaviors that should, in the long term, be more adaptive.

This approach is particularly important in relation to contraceptive use among sexually active adolescents. Their failure to use contraceptives effectively—and the resulting exposure to STDs and unintended pregnancy—carry high personal and social costs. There are a variety of significant social, emotional, and behavioral barriers to effective contraceptive use for adolescents. As described in this chapter, few of the elements of the ideal planning environment are present for the majority of adolescents who become sexually active. Interventions to address the crucial problem of teenage pregnancy will be more successful if they include consideration both of planning skills and motivations of adolescents, as well as the environmental context in which these plans are made and carried out.

REFERENCES

Adler, N. (1974, August). *Factors affecting contraceptive use.* Paper presented at the meeting of the American Psychological Association, New Orleans, LA.

Adler, N. E., & Tschann, J. M. (1994). Conscious and preconscious motivations for pregnancy among female adolescents. In A. Lawson and D. Rhode (Eds.), The politics of pregnancy: Adolescent sexuality and public policy. New Haven: Yale University, 144–158.

Bandura, A., (1977). Self-efficacy: Toward a unifying theory of behavioral change. *Psychological Review, 84,* 191–215.

Bandura, A. (1989). Self regulation of motivation and action through interval standards and goal systems. In L. Pervin (Eds.), *Goal concepts in personality and social psychology* (pp. 19–85).

Bandura, A., Adams, N. E., Hardy, A. B., & Howells, G. M. (1980). Tests of the generality of self-efficacy theory. *Cognitive Therapy and Research, 4,* 39–66.

Berger, D. K., Perez, G., Kyman, W., Perez, L., Garson, J., Mendez, M., Bistritz, J., Blanchard, H., & Dombrowski, C. (1987). Influence of family planning counseling in an adolescent clinic on sexual activity and contraceptive use. *Journal of Adolescent Health Care, 8,* 436–440.

Brown, G., & Desforges, C. (1977). Piagetian psychology and education: Time for revision. *British Journal of Educational Psychology, 47,* 7–17.

Burger, J. M., & Burns, L. (1988). The illusion of unique invulnerability and the use of effective contraception. *Personality and Social Psychology Bulletin, 14,* 264–270.

Burton, L. M. (1990). Teenage childbearing as an alternative life-course strategy in multigeneration Black families. Human Nature, 1, (2), 123–143.

Chilman, C. (1973). Why do unmarried women fail to use contraception? *Medical Aspects of Human Sexuality, 7,* 167–168.

Cvetkovich, G., & Grote, B. (1981). Psychosocial maturity and teenage contraceptive use: An investigation of decision-making and communication skills. *Population and Environment, 4,* 211–226.

D'Augelli, J. F., & Cross, H. J. (1975). Relationships of sex guilt and moral reasoning to premarital sex in college women and in couples. *Journal of Consulting & Clinical Psychology, 43,* 40–47

Dolcini, M. M., Cohn, L. D., Adler, N. E., Millstein, S. G., Irwin, C. E., Jr., Kegeles, S. M., & Stone, G. C. (1989). Adult egocentrism and feelings of invulnerability: Are they related? *Journal of Early Adolescence, 9*(4), 409–418.

Elkind, D. (1967). Egocentrism in adolescence. *Child Development, 38,* 1025–1034.

Evans, J., Selstad, G., & Welcher, W. (1976). Teenagers: Fertility control behavior and attitudes before and after abortion, childbearing, or negative pregnancy test. *Family Planning Perspectives, 8,* 192–200.

Foreit, J. R., & Foreit, K. G. (1981). Risk-taking and contraceptive behavior among unmarried college students. *Population and Environment, 4,* 174–188.

Franklin, D. L. (1987). Black adolescent pregnancy: A literature review. Special Issue: The Black adolescent parent. *Child & Youth Services, 9,* 15–39.

Furstenberg, F. F. (1976). *Unplanned parenthood.* New York: Free Press.

Geis, B. D., & Gerrard, M. (1984). Predicting male and female contraceptive behavior: A discriminant analysis of groups high, moderate, and low in contraceptive effectiveness. *Journal of Personality & Social Psychology, 46,* 669–680.

Geronimus, A. T. (1987). On teenage childbearing and neonatal mortality in the United States. *Population and Development Review, 13,* 245–279.

Gerrard, M., Gibbons, F. X., & McCoy, S. B. (1993). Emotional inhibition of effective contraception. *Anxiety, Stress & Coping, 6,* 73–88.

Hatcher, S. (1976). Understanding adolescent pregnancy and abortion. *Primary Care, 3,* 407–425.

Hayes, C. D. (Ed.). (1987). *Risking the future: Adolescent sexuality, pregnancy, and childbearing.* Washington, DC: National Academy Press.

Hayes-Roth, B., & Hayes-Roth, F. (1979). A cognitive model of planning. *Cognitive Science, 3,* 275–310.

Hein, K. (1989). AIDS in adolescence. *Journal of Adolescent Health Care, 10,* 10S–35S.

Heinrich, L. B. (1993). Contraceptive self-efficacy in college women. Journal of Adolescent Health, 14, (2), 269–276.

Herold, E. S. (1981). Contraceptive embarrassment and contraceptive behavior among young single women. Journal of Youth and Adolescence, 10, 233–242.

Herz, E. J., & Reis, J. S. (1987). Family life education for young inner-city teens: Identifying needs. Journal of Youth and Adolescence, 16, 361–377.

Jones, E. F., Forrest, J., Goldman, N., Henshaw, S., Lincoln, R., Rossoff, J., Westoff, C., & Wulf, D. (1986). Teenage pregnancy in industrialized countries. New Haven: Yale University Press.

Kantner, J., & Zelnik, M. (1973). Contraception and pregnancy: Experience of young unmarried women in the United States. Family Planning Perspectives, 5, 21–35.

Kenney, A. M., Guardado, S., & Brown, L. (1989). Sex education and AIDS education in the schools: What states and large school districts are doing. Family Planning Perspectives, 21, 56–64.

Kirby, D., & Waszak, C. (1992). School-based clinics. In B.C. Miller, J. J. Card, R. L. Paikoff, J. L. Peterson (Eds.), Preventing adolescent pregnancy: Model programs and evaluations (Sage focus editions, pp. 185–219). Newbury Park, CA: Sage.

Levinson, R. A. (1984). Contraceptive self-efficacy: A primary prevention strategy. Journal of Social Work and Human Sexuality, 3, 1–15.

Levinson, R. A. (1986). Contraceptive self-efficacy: A perspective on teenage girls' contraceptive behavior. The Journal of Sex Research, 22, 347–369.

Lindemann, C. (1974). Birth control and unmarried young women. New York: Springer.

Lindemann, C. (1977). Factors affecting the use of contraception in the nonmarital context. In R. Gemme & C. C. Wheeler (Eds.), Progress in sexology (pp. 397–408). New York: Plenum.

Miller, W. (1976). Sexual and contraceptive behavior in young unmarried women. Primary Care, 3, 427–453.

Miller, W. B. (1986). Why some people women fail to use their contraceptive method: A psychological investigation. Family Planning Perspectives, 18, 27–32.

Morrison, D. M. (1985). Adolescent contraceptive behavior: A review. Psychological Bulletin, 98 (3), 538–568.

Morrison, D. M. (1989). Predicting contraceptive efficacy: A discriminant analysis of three groups of adolescent women. Journal of Applied Social Psychology, 19, 1431–1452.

Mosher, D. L., & Vonderheide, S. G. (1985). Contribution of sex guilt and masturbation guilt to women's contraceptive attitudes and use. Journal of Sex Research, 21, 24–39.

Nadelson, D., Notman, M. T., and Gillon, J. W. (1980). Sexual knowledge and attitudes of adolescents: Relationship to contraceptive use. Obstetrics & Gynecology, 55, 340–345.

Piaget, J. (1952). The origins of intelligence in children. (M. Cook, Trans.). New York: International Universities Press.

Quadrel, M. J., Fischoff, B. & Davis, W. (1993). Adolescent (in)vulnerability. American Psychologist, 48, 102–116.

Rodgers, J. L., & Rowe, D. C. (1990). Adolescent sexual activity and mildly deviant behavior: Sibling and friendship effects. Journal of Family Issues, 11, 274–293.

Rosen, R. H., & Martindale, L. (1978). Sex role perceptions and the abortion decision. The Journal of Sex Research, 14, 231–245.

Scholnick, E. K., & Friedman, S. L. (1993). Planning in context: Developmental and situational considerations. International Journal of Behavioral Development, 16(2), 145–167.

Schuberth, R. E. (1983). The infant's search for objects: Alternatives to Piaget's theory of object concept development. Advances in Infancy Research, 2, 137–182.

Shah, F., Zelnik, M., & Kantner, J. F. (1975). Unprotected intercourse among unwed teenage mothers. Family Planning Perspectives, 1, 39–44.

Smith, P. B., Nenney, S. W., Weinman, M. L., & Mumford, D. M. (1982). Factors affecting perception of pregnancy risk in the adolescent. Journal of Youth and Adolescence, 11, 207–215.

Sorensen, R. C. (1973). Adolescent sexuality in America: Personal values and sexual behavior ages 13-19. New York: Abrams.

Studer, M., & Thornton, A. (1987). Adolescents religiosity and contraceptive usage. Journal of Marriage & the Family 49. 117–128.

Sunenblick, M. B. (1988). The AIDS epidemic: Sexual behavior of adolescents. Smith College Studies in Social Work, 59(1), 21–37.

Thompson, L. & Spanier, G. B. (1978). Influence of parents, peers, and partners on the contraceptive use of college men and women. *Journal of Marriage and the Family, 40*, 481–492.

Thornburg, H. D. (1981). The amount of sex information learning obtained during early adolescence. *Journal of Early Adolescence, 1*, 171–183.

Upchurch, M. L. (1978). Sex guilt and contraceptive use. *Journal of Sex Education and Therapy, 4*, 27–31.

Weinstein, N. D. (1982). Unrealistic optimism about susceptibility to health problems. *Journal of Behavioral Medicine, 5*, 441–460.

Weinstein, N. D. (1987). Unrealistic optimism about susceptibility to health problems: Conclusions from a community-wide sample. *Journal of Behavioral Medicine, 10*, 481–500.

Weisman, C. S., Plichta, S., Nathanson, C. A., Chase, G. A., Ensminger, M. E., & Robinson, J. C. (1991). Adolescent women's contraceptive decision making. *Perspectives, 12*, 230–237.

Whitley, B., & Hern, A. L. (1991). Perceptions of vulnerability to pregnancy and the use of effective contraception. *Personality and Social Psychology Bulletin, 17*, 104–110.

Zabin, L. S., and Clark, S. D. (1983). Institutional factors affecting teenager's choice and reasons for delay in attending a family planning clinic. *Family Planning Perspectives, 15*, 25–29.

Zabin, L. S., Kantner, J. F., & Zelnik, M. (1979). Risk of adolescent pregnancy in the first months of intercourse. *Family Planning Perspectives, 11*, 355–357.

Zelnik, M., & Kantner, J. (1979). Reasons for nonuse of contraception by sexually active women aged 15 to 19. *Family Planning Perspectives, 11*, 289–296.

Zelnik, M., & Kantner, J. F. (1980). Sexual activity, contraceptive use and pregnancy among metropolitan-area teenagers: 1971–1979. *Family Planning Perspectives, 12*, 230–237.

V

Social Influences on Planning

14

The Interpersonal and Social Aspects of Planning

Jacqueline J. Goodnow
Macquarie University, Australia

When psychologists study planning, they typically bring to the task two kinds of theoretical perspectives (Friedman & Scholnick, 1991; Scholnick & Friedman, 1987). One of these emphasizes cognitive aspects: the individual's ability to construct a top-down sequence, perceive a difficulty, work out alternative steps, estimate relative costs and benefits, monitor progress, or work out repair strategies. The main goal is to account for differences in the nature and the effectiveness of plans. The sources of individual differences are seen as based on experience (this is regarded as providing a useful knowledge of the content area) and age (providing shifts in general ability).

The other perspective emphasizes motivations and beliefs, beliefs about fate or chance, about one's capacity to control events, about the value of planning or the "norms ... the rules or standards" (Kreitler & Kreitler, 1987, pp. 1–13) that should govern the actions one takes. There is, again, an interest in accounting for the nature of plans, but the main goal is to account for the decision to plan and the extent to which persistent effort is put into making and executing a plan. The sources of individual differences are seen as based on individual experience (these are now experiences of demands for planning and of success in planning) and in the social or cultural value placed on planning.

The material to be discussed is closer to the second perspective than to the first. I shall depart from it, however, in two ways. The first departure consists of the proposal that both perspectives may benefit from analyzing situations that are not of the solitary-planner type. With this in mind, the first two sections of this chapter look toward situations that involve more than one person. These may be situations where the plans of two or more people are involved, raising questions about coordination and conflict. They may also be situations where the planning is done by one person, but other people are part of the plan. They are, for instance, the pieces to be moved, to be cleared from one's path or persuaded into accepting responsibility for part of the action. Interpersonal situations of this kind raise questions about the expected roles of others, the perceived legitimacy of delegation, and the extent to which plans are expected to cover contingencies after delegation.

A second approach different from most "motivational" or "belief structure" perspectives is the emphasis on a social or cultural background rather than upon individual experience. The nature of the general social environment influences not only the individual's beliefs about control or efficacy, but also the actual costs of recovery from error and the perceptions of recovery or repair as possible. The nature of the general social environment gives rise also to variations in the extent to which planning meets with approval or disapproval and in the content areas for which planning is seen as appropriate. Planning may not always regarded in positive terms. Instead, the value given to planning in particular content areas— planning for one's death as the main example—may vary from one social group to another and, within a group, from one historical time to another.

The majority of examples in this chapter are drawn from planning for events outside the laboratory: events that range from planning a party to the operation of a household or the charting of a career path. A view of planning is presented as the movement of a number of pieces in order to reach a goal, with freedom of movement constrained by limits set by the experimenters or by the individual's perception of what represents "moveable bits and squeezable pieces" (Goodnow, 1987, p. 181).

INTERPERSONAL ASPECTS: PLANNING IN COMPANY

The analysis of cognition in general has shown an increasing concern with what happens when people work together on a problem, either spontaneously or on request. The labels under which the research appears may vary: guided participation, peer tutoring, reciprocal teaching, sociocognitive conflict, interpersonal goal conflict, and so on. The common concern, however, is with the need to ask what happens in situations that involve two or more people working on a task.

Studies of planning display some of the same trend. The most consistent set of studies comes from Rogoff and her colleagues (e.g., Rogoff, 1990, Rogoff, Gauvain, & Gardner, 1987). These studies focus on the extent to which working with others improves children's plans (e.g., their plans in grocery shopping: Gauvain & Rogoff, 1989) and on the conditions under which advice from adults is helpful (e.g., improves children's performance in planning a route through a maze, see Rogoff, 1990). Related studies have been reported by Glachan and Light (1982, e.g., children working together on a Tower of Hanoi problem) and by several researchers in Geneva (e.g., Doise & Mugny, 1981), who found children jointly manipulate levers in order to move a marker along a particular path).

The usual assumptions in such studies are:(a) that two heads will be better than one; (b) that the major issue will be the child's ability, at various ages, to make use of the input provided by others or to take the perspective of the other into account; and (c) that people will share the same goals and the same ideas about what should regulate each person's contribution (areas of sharing that leave the field clear for cognitive ability to be the decisive factor). In practice, none of these assumptions may hold.

Take, for instance, the assumption that two heads will be better than one. As Rogoff et al. (1987) pointed out, this does not always happen, in large part because collaboration does not actually occur. Children may, for instance, solve the request to work together by taking turns at decision-making, a phenomenon noted both by Gauvain and Rogoff (1989) and by Mugny, de Paolis, and Carugati (1984). Adults who take turns at chairing committees or—in the case of Israel—heading a government employ a similar strategy. Children may also allow one member of a dyad to take control. In Mugny et al.'s (1984) terms, these are solutions based on *social regulation* rather than on *cognitive resolution*. The individuals involved have the cognitive ability to coordinate their plans, but they choose not to do so.

The assumption that people will share the same goals, and the same ideas about what each should contribute, deserves a longer inspection. Even in laboratory studies, the assumption may not hold. Children who solve a joint task "relationally" rather than "cognitively," for instance, are essentially adopting a goal that is different from the experimenter's goal.

Two examples from the world of paid work will make the point more strongly. Both come from situations where there is a conflict between members of the bureaucracy and practitioners who are providing a front-line service: in one case teachers, in the other, physicians.

The example related to teachers comes from analyses of industrial action in several "Western" countries (Australia, Canada, the United States, see Corwin, 1974; Kerchner & Mitchell, 1988; Warton, Goodnow, & Bowes, 1992). In each of these cases, one recurring cause of teachers' dissatisfaction was the wish of administrative boards to take control over areas that the teachers felt that they (the teachers) should plan for themselves. In some cases, the area was curriculum planning, with the central administration arguing for statewide or national plans and the teachers arguing for more local initiatives. In others, the area was the use of teachers' time: the setting of mandatory versus discretionary time at schools over and beyond the time when pupils are present. The conflict in each case was not about whether planning should occur, but over whose plan should prevail.

The example related to physicians comes from Engestrom's (1988) analysis of a national health center in Finland. The preference of the center's administrator was for a schedule that made all visits of a standard length and that allotted patients to whatever physician was available at the time. There would then be no unfilled slots of time and each physician would see a set number of patients within a regular office day. The preference of the physicians was for a plan in which they were treated less as moveable pieces in someone else's plan. They wished to see patients for varying lengths of time, depending on need. They also wished to work towards continuity: in effect, to have a number of clients become "their" patients. The clash between the personalized and the commodified plans was a cause of continuing tension.

In these examples from paid work, the conflict in plans is explicit. It is also related particularly to differences in goals. A difference in goals, however, is not the only source of difficulty when two or more people are involved in planning. Expert–novice studies provide the example. In theory, one person practices under the guidance of a person more expert at the task. The expectation is that the expert will gradually hand over responsibility for the autonomous performance of larger and larger sections of the task and that the competence of the novice will be the deciding factor. In effect, the expert plans to fall back as the novice progresses, and the novice expects to move up the ladder of control as soon as competence is demonstrated.

In practice, however, the two parties may not share the same amicable expectation that one party will yield to the other as soon as competence is demonstrated. Take, for instance, the case of parents and children. They do not always agree on the point at which the child's competence warrants the child's taking over or acting independently. Nor do they always agree on how much or what parts of a plan should be controlled by each of them. Parents may hope, for example, to see children display increasing self-regulation in such areas as the planning of homework or of contributions to the work of the household.

Children, however, may see self-regulation as meaning that they will execute a parent's plan, rather than establish one of their own. What they may wish for is the right to set the plan or at the least, to decide when various parts of it will be put into play. "I wish," says a 10-year-old child when asked about wished-for changes at home, "they set the jobs, but we decided when they get done" (Goodnow & Burns, 1985, p. 50). What is particularly objectionable, say a number of adolescents, are reminders (reminders that a job needs to be done) that take no account of their own time schedules, of their being willing but also "having other things to do first" (Goodnow & Warton, 1992, p. 101).

One last point needs to be made with regard to situations in which planning involves more than one person. It has to do with the degree of coordination needed, the degree of need for interweaving or cross-checking at various points, a point by M. Gauvain (personal communication, 1988). Some dyadic situations, she commented, call for the close coordination of plans and of actions at each step of the way. It would be difficult, for instance, to play a four-hand piano piece without tight interweaving. Other situations call for agreement on a goal but allow for divergent paths. We agree, for instance, to meet at point X in an hour, but how we each get there is left to our own decisions. Environments and tasks, Gauvain pointed out, vary in the extent to which they require tight or loose coordination. The cognitive and social demands of combining on a plan must be expected to vary accordingly.

INTERPERSONAL ASPECTS: OTHERS AS PART OF ONE PERSON'S PLAN

The preceding section was concerned with situations where two people are overtly involved, or expected to be involved, in planning toward a common goal. Interpersonal factors also come into play, however, when one person is the planner and the plan calls for the involvement of others. My plan, for example, calls for you to change what you are doing, to step aside, or to take over part of the work. On such occasions, my plan for you may well be incompatible with your own. My plan for you may also be out of line with our expected roles (how much of this is usually my job or yours?) and with the norms that specify the social legitimacy of particular moves. Under what circumstances, for instance, is it regarded as appropriate for me to ask for help or to delegate a task? At what point does a plan that involves others come to be regarded as unreasonable, exploitative, or insulting?

Issues of reasonableness and legitimacy do not surface as readily in most laboratory tasks as they do in everyday life. The reason, I suggest, lies in the way tasks are designed and presented.

In theory, it is possible to construct a task in which all pieces can be moved with complete freedom. In practice, some constraints are built-in. Explicit constraints on time are common. In a task such as the planning of errands, for instance, the hospital is described as having restricted visiting hours, and the bookstore closes at a certain hour (the implication is that all these hours are fixed, with no room for flexibility or persuasion). A further constraint comes from the implication that one must perform all these actions oneself. There may be no explicit warning against delegating tasks or enlisting help. This kind of move, however, is not presented as a possibility and, despite the extent to which it occurs in everyday life, it is seldom mentioned by participants as a solution to their laboratory problems.

What happens, then, when the involvement of others becomes an explicit part of the planning task? First, consider a design that brings up issues related to past roles and then one that brings up issues of social legitimacy.

Expected Roles.   Chalmers and Lawrence (1993) varied an errand-type of task so that the involvement of others becomes an explicit part of the planning task. They asked adolescents, adults in midlife, and retired adults (60 plus, living in a retirement center) to plan—for a teenager—an unexpected party (24 hours' lead time). Along with the usual list of specific jobs to be done (for the party and for other demands, such as having to take the cat to the vet on the day of the party), Chalmers and Lawrence supplied stickers that represented three people who could be asked to help. For the adolescents, these were their parents and a same-aged friend. For the adults, they were their spouse and two teenagers.

This kind of task brings out the presence of ideas about the expected roles of others. Here, for instance, is one woman's comment on involving others.[1]

> I would rather clean the room myself because otherwise … it doesn't get done. They mess around. Because I've got teenage daughters. I know what they're like so if you've got something going, I mean it's better—you know—to do it yourself. They could always help get the food ready. Dad could always, well … it's his job say to wash the car, get him out of the way (laughs) …. He can, you know, run and pick up the food. Doesn't hurt him to do that.

The adult men in this sample are particularly explicit about expected roles. They are the ones who more often comment, at both age levels, that they would involve the teenagers in the planning, not simply in the execution of the adult's plan. If this were a real rather than a hypothetical party, a 43-year-old male comments:

> I'd get them to plan it. And then they could come to me, for advice if you like. Let them do more work and tell … let them tell me what's required. It's for them (the party), not for me.

The men in this sample are more likely to refer responsibility to a spouse (this seems particularly pronounced among the retired males):

> Well, I leave it all to the rest of them. Well, the wife looks after the food, and the teenagers really should look after most of that and I'd just be a looker-on (male, aged 73).

> The only way to run a party, for a start, first ask the teenagers … what is their thoughts about what they would like as a party …. And then call a meeting of your son and your wife. She's got to be in charge of it—it's her home—and discuss every aspect … We'd have a committee (age 74).

Within this data set, the movement of tasks to other people is mainly constrained by what they have done in the past (e.g., "I left all that to my wife; I just did as I was told"). It is in a further group of studies, focused specifically on what can be asked of others and how this should be done,

---

[1]These and other quotations from this study are from transcripts of interviews, supplied by Chalmers and Lawrence.

that there arise issues more clearly related to what is morally right or just. These issues concern: (a) the legitimacy of some ways of involving others, and (b) the extent to which a plan that involves delegation should also contain some provision for follow-through (in effect, some strategies for ensuring that the task does get done).

Issues of Social Legitimacy.   Issues of legitimacy were part of the tension in Engestrom's (1988) case study of physicians and administrators, with physicians objecting to being regarded as chess pieces on an administrator's board. The issues are particularly salient, however, in any situation that involves delegating or leaving tasks to others. Secretaries may object to being expected to serve coffee, wash cups, or do personal shopping for their employer. Any member of a group may feel poorly treated if he or she is expected to finish what others have started and abandoned, or to solve problems that others have created.

The legitimacy of moving tasks to others—and of a major principle related to it—is an explicit issue in a study asking Anglo-Australian[2] mothers of 9-to-11-year-olds what they would do if a child's job was not done (Goodnow & Delaney, 1989). Ignoring special circumstances or "special favors," would the mother: (a) leave the job in the child's hands (e.g., insist that it be done or let it wait until the child needed whatever was involved), (b) do it herself, or (c) ask a sibling to take over the job? The answers depended markedly on whether the job was of a "family-care" type (e.g., setting or clearing the table, taking out the trash) or a "self-care" type (e.g. putting away one's schoolbag or toys one has used, making one's own bed).

For family-care tasks, mothers seldom did the job themselves (2% of mothers). They would either insist that the original owner do the job (41%) or ask a sibling (57%). For self-care tasks, mothers often did the job themselves (41%) or insisted that the original owner did the job (59%). What the mothers would not do was to move the job to another sibling. The reasons were two-fold. First, the request would not be right or just. Second, the sibling would object strenuously, using arguments of the kind, "I didn't take that stuff out."

The constraint to free movement on these occasions comes from a principle that may be called, colloquially, "your mess, your job, your stuff, your job." More formally, "if you created this problem, you should fix it or at least help fix it." This principle of causation as determining ownership of a task and limiting its movability, we have found, applies well beyond mothers commenting on jobs being shifted from one sibling to another.

---

[2]Anglo-Australian refers to people who are Australian-born, whose home language is English, and whose parents' home language was English. We do not yet know how far the same sensitivity to particular forms of legitimacy occurs in other ethnic groups.

Adults in a couple relationship, for instance, apply the same principle to the movement of jobs from one partner to the other. To be more specific, when adults share household tasks, two tasks stand out as often shared on the basis of "to each our own": ironing, and washing and cleaning one's car (Goodnow & Bowes, 1994). The rationale in the case of ironing is often put in terms of "my whim, my job" e.g., "I'm the one that likes to wear all-cotton clothes, why should anyone else pay the cost of my fancy?" The rationale in the case of cleaning a car is frequently put in terms of idiosyncratic standards, either very high (e.g., "I'm fussy, so I do it") or very low (e.g., "I don't see why I should clean out all the McDonald's® cartons that he has stashed in his car."[3] In both cases, the issue of cause—of who creates the need for a job to be done—restricted the perception of a job as moveable from one person to another.

Cause, however, is not likely to be the only condition that influences people's judgments about whether a piece of work can be moved from one person to another. Parents, when asked why they would feel easy or reluctant about asking each other or a teenager to take on a household job, describe themselves as considering—in addition to who gave rise to the need for work to be done—factors such as efficiency, degrees of competence, and the extent to which the other person liked or disliked a job (Goodnow, Bowes, Warton, Dawes, & Taylor, 1991). Gender was not explicitly mentioned as a consideration.

When children, however, are asked whether they could ask their mother, father, sister, or brother to take on a job for them, gender does emerge as a consideration. It remains true that the task least likely to be asked of any other member of the family is a self-care task: making your bed. To the extent that anyone can be asked to do this job for you, however, the people to be asked are mothers and sisters, not fathers or brothers. Cleaning a bathtub or basin is more moveable than making one's bed, but its movement is also almost entirely to females in the family. In contrast, the job of washing the car is reported, by the same 8-, 11-, and 14-year-olds, as moveable to fathers or brothers but seldom to mothers or sisters. In contrast also, the job of setting the table moves along age lines but not along gender lines. Children say they could ask a brother or sister, but not a mother or father (Goodnow et al., 1991). In short, part of learning what to do when a change is needed from the usual work script involves learning about the particular pieces that can be moved to particular people.

Delegation and Follow-Through. Up to this point, what has been considered is only whether children and adults perceive it as feasible or legitimate to move a job (normally theirs) to someone else. That is not, however, the only contingency that planning involves. How far, one needs to ask, is the perception of a job as moveable accompanied by the perception

---

[3]Comments are from interview transcripts.

that follow-through is also required? Suppose, for instance, that I ask you to do for me a job that I usually do. You agree. Is that the end of the matter? Or, should I also regard it as part of my job to go over any difficult parts of the job, to give a reminder, and to check that the job is done? The majority of children from 8 to 14 years (with no age changes) agree that the asker should do all these things, although the manner in which these things are done needs to take into account the sensitivity of the other party to any suggestion that he or she is less than completely competent or trustworthy (Goodnow & Warton, 1992).

The point of surprise in our studies of delegation came with the question: "If the job is not done, is it fair that you get into trouble?" The percentage of "no" answers to this question were 90%, 87%, and 71 % for the 8-, 11-, and 14-year-olds, respectively (Warton & Goodnow, 1991). There is apparently a limit to the extent to which the asker—the original owner—continues to carry responsibility when a job moves from one person to the other. At ages 8 to 21 years, in fact, the preferred solution is to assign equal blame to both parties, with the amount of blame assigned to the person who agreed to do the task increasing with each effort that the asker makes to ensure that the task is done. If, for example, I review with you any problems that might arise, or if I leave a reminder, then the larger share of the blame goes to you. "You do that much," comments one 14-year old, "you've practically done the job yourself" (Goodnow & Warton, 1996, p. 177). In short, there are limits to the extent to which anticipating is seen as the responsibility of one person only.

Beyond Family Shifts.   Most of the data on "moveable pieces" comes from asking about the possible movement of jobs from one member of the family to the other. This is not, however, the only type of situation in which perceptions of movability matter. Jennifer Bowes and I, for instance, asked adults about moving work to paid help, outside the family. That question again raised ideas, not only about the cost of such a move, but also about its legitimacy, about the importance of "being able to do it yourself," for instance, and the propriety of asking others to do what you are yourself reluctant to do (Goodnow & Bowes, 1994).

In addition, we would by no means expect issues of causation or delegation to be relevant only to families. Responsibility when one is an indirect cause (e.g., when others act as one's agent) is a critical issue in law, and people are expected to plan with that type of responsibility in mind (Hart & Honoré, 1985). The point to be underlined—in families or in marketplaces—is that plans often involve assigning part of the action to others, and the normative beliefs held regarding appropriate assignments need to be considered as part of our understanding of planning.

Two last points need to be made about perceptions of movability. First, we cannot assume that what is regarded as right is always translated into action. The vast majority of children (from 8-years-old and on) agree that it is "fair" to be expected to remember one's jobs. Other people should not need to remind them. The same vast majority, however, also reports that in practice they often need to be reminded (Warton & Goodnow, 1991). The complaint—"why didn't you remind me?"—is not unfamiliar to parents.

Second, it is possible to combine these points with some other accounts of planning. Social legitimacy, for instance, may be regarded as part of Kreitler and Kreitler's (1987) interest in a particular set of beliefs: "beliefs about norms, expressing moral, social, aesthetic, practical, or arbitrary rules and standards concerning states, events, or acts (e.g., one should drive on ice carefully; a person should not boast)" (p. 113). Social legitimacy may also be seen as part of Von Wright's concept of internalized "role-holder duties," as one determinant of action (cited by Oppenheimer, 1987, p. 370). Here are selected norms or duties related to the movement of tasks from one person to another: norms that have a particular relevance to the forms that a plan may take.

SOCIAL ASPECTS: THE COSTS OF RECOVERY FROM ERROR

In this section and the next, the goal is to step away from the impact of face-to-face or proximal social interactions and to ask how some general features of the social or cultural environment may influence either whether planning occurs or the type of plan that people make.

Asking about such effects is by no means unknown in analyses of planning. The argument has been made, for instance, that environments (e.g., occupations, schools) vary in the extent to which they call for planning and in the extent to which the causal structure of the environment is likely to encourage an individual's belief in the possibility of control (e.g., Skinner, 1985).

To that argument, it can be added that the causal structure of an environment—the contingencies that exist—also affect other components of planning. One can single out the extent to which errors are likely to occur and the extent to which recovery from error is possible (or perceived as possible).

As an example, consider progression through an education system. For many people, deliberate planning is not an issue for many of the years spent in schooling. There is a routine program available, and the opportunities for departing from the set route—along with the need to anticipate consequences—are small. There are, nonetheless, branching paths that arise along the way. In some countries, for instance, competitive exams around the age of 11 to 12 years determine the type of high school attended, and that determines the accessibility of university education. In some countries also, the choice of school subjects in the early years of high school can determine access to particular universities or particular faculties.

The nature of these contingency structures is relevant, first of all, to the knowledge base that people bring to planning. It is not only that the more arcane or byzantine the route, the greater demand for knowledge—what happens also is that one's position in society may alter the likelihood of having the information needed. The working class parents in Jackson and Marsden's (1966) study provide an example. Their children were in the type of high school ("grammar school") needed to gain access to universities. Both the children and their parents, in many cases, also had university education as a goal, often to the point of having a particular university in mind. What they did not know, however, was that these universities required some particular subjects (Latin was the main stumbling block) as a prerequisite for entry. For some, the lack of information stemmed from not suspecting that this was an area of information they should explore. For others, the problem was that parents were reluctant to appear ambitious but ignorant in the eyes of the teachers (the people they might have asked), and yet the teachers assumed that parents did not need to be given the critical information.

Errors of the type made by the parents in Jackson and Marsden's (1966) study, along with other departures from routine sequences (departures such as dropping out before high school is finished), are less serious when recovery is easy. The ease of recovery, however, may depend not only on the individual's resilience but also on the actual contingencies in one's social context. In some societies, recovery within the school system is relatively easy. In others the failure to take (and to succeed in) a particular step at a particular time means that some particular goals may have to be abandoned and a new plan developed. There are no second chances and no alternative routes.

The impact of such contingencies is especially clear at times when they change within a culture. Over the last 20 years, for example, Australia has seen the emergence of a number of possible routes for entry at the university level. In many university faculties, places are set aside for "mature-age" students, most of whom did not complete high school but have now taken "make-up" exams by way of courses taught at Technical Colleges established for adults. In some faculties, "mature age" students with relevant experience may even be given preference over students who have followed the usual path and have higher prerequisite scores. Because admission to various faculties (medicine, dentistry, arts, science) is, in Australia, most often a direct step from high school status (there is, for instance, no "pre-med" period), and is usually determined only by the scores obtained in a state-wide examination at the end of high school, the provision of these recovery routes has meant a major change in many career plans. For some, the expected plan has simply become relaxed. They can plan for a certain degree of time-out and return. For others, a life plan that originally did not include university education has come to be rewritten.[4]

SOCIAL ASPECTS: PLANNING IS A VIRTUE?

In an earlier chapter on the social aspects of planning (Goodnow, 1987) two arguments were offered, both related to the extent of approval or disapproval given to planning as a way of solving particular problems. The first argument was to the effect that in some cultures, a positive value is placed on proceeding by one step at a time or even without a plan ("giving it a go," "barging ahead," "crashing through," "improvising"). The second was to the effect that, within any culture, certain content areas come to be tagged as inappropriate for detailed planning.

A first addition to those arguments is a reminder of the extent to which many cognitive tasks are built on value judgments. Planning tasks are not unique in this respect. A second is that there are occasional advantages to a form of planning that is often described in negative terms—one-step planning. A third is the argument that changes can occur in the degree of approval given to various forms and degrees of planning, with these changes providing some insights into the conditions that can give rise to variations in approval or disapproval. Planning for the manner of one's dying is the main example used.

The Presence of Cognitive Values.   It is easy to regard cognition as the study of rational processes, regarding all departures from a computer-style approach as error, bias, lack of motivation, or the intrusion of affect upon judgment. In fact, value judgments are rife, even in supposedly neutral cognitive science. We distinguish significant from trivial problems. We regard some cognitive performances as better, more elegant, more stylish than others (Goodnow, 1990). Even the judgment that a particular way of proceeding is better because it is more efficient—involving least effort, least waste, least error—is a value judgment. One might well regard as better a performance that plays with error, that involves some bravura, or that is maximalist rather than minimalist in style.

It would not be fair to say that psychologists are completely unaware of the value judgments inherent in their approaches. The study of heuristics provides an example. The short-cuts that people use were once regarded as strange lapses from logic. They have now come to be seen as reasonable ways to proceed and as interesting in their own right. It may even be that

---

[4]The size of the change can be seen from the fact that, at one point—a time when mature-age entry coincided with the temporary abolition of university fees (Australian universities, with one exception, are federally funded), 35% of Macquarie University's undergraduate body consisted of mature-age students, predominantly women.

systematic processing is best regarded as a default process, turned to only when a heuristic does not work. The study of planning, it is suggested, might benefit from a similar second look, with a kinder interpretation made of one-step planning (some forms of it at least) than seems to occur at present.

The Possible Virtues of One-Step Planning.   There are times when it may be more effective to act with minimal planning, to "just get started" rather than be paralyzed into inaction (Goodnow, 1987). Now, consider a more extended defense of some forms of one-step planning. The defense is prompted by negative comments about one-step planning. One example comes from Kreitler and Kreitler (1987, p. 119). They described a one-step plan—"those people should employ a better gardener"—as reflecting a "weaker preplanning CO (cognitive orientation) cluster" than is implied by the combined responses, "A garden should be designed nicely," "this garden is ugly," and perhaps "I would like to design this garden" (p. 119).

A second example refers to delegation. This form of one-step planning is often an effective way to act and should be appealing to the young as well as to the old. It is then surprising to read that delegation is likely to be used only by older subjects because "the subject has to attribute responsibility to another person and has to generate more complex strategies" (Dreher & Oerter, 1987, p. 331). Under some circumstances, that may be true. In Dreher and Oerter's (1987) task, for instance, one essential part of a plan consists of changing money. The advice is given that "a friend could change it for you" but the advice is followed by complications: "but you have to call him beforehand, and you would have to be home from 5:00 p.m. until 5:15 p.m. to receive the money and give him back the money he advanced" (p. 324). Under these circumstances, delegation is indeed not the easiest of strategies.

As a contrast, one might well consider the ease with which young children in everyday life delegate planning to others (e.g., "my mother will remember") and the extent to which people in cultures with strong obligation systems encourage the development of one-step planning in the form of turning to a contact. The ideal, it is implied, is not to try to do or to know everything yourself but to know someone who is in a better position to know or to influence the system than you are.

As "Westerners," we may be surprised by the extent of such reliance on mentors or inside contacts, especially when they are sought in situations where the information needed is actually public and readily accessible. Given certain assumptions about the way the world works, however, this way of planning makes good sense. It is not even unique to "Eastern" cultures, although one can offer only anecdotes from newspaper stories on that score. The Kennedy children, it has been written, were often given in the morning—by their mother—a topic to be talked about at the evening meal, and the children developed great skill in locating an expert who could quickly brief them. Nelson Rockefeller, in a departure from the idea of "do it yourself" that strikes one as even stronger, is said to have placed on his desk a card with the question "Could someone else do this?" If the answer was "yes," then the task was immediately delegated, leaving Rockefeller time to concentrate on tasks that he himself needed to handle. That managerial perspective could be an effective moderator, or antidote, to the emphasis certainly present in my own background—on doing things "yourself," with the implication that "if you can, you should."

In what content area is planning appropriate? The examples used previously (Goodnow, 1987) were mainly from the area of close relationships. In countries with a romantic tradition, for instance, one should not explicitly plan to fall in love or to marry in a particular year. The appropriate procedure is to "fall in love," to "be swept off one's feet," "to be carried away" by passion or romance. The concept that marriage is too important an area to be left to such procedures—and should be planned by others—is not present. The arrangement of a marriage is in fact often regarded as "strange" when it is encountered in other cultural groups.

Intimacy still remains a useful content area, providing ready examples both for cultural differences and changes over time in the extent to which planning —overt planning especially— is regarded as appropriate. In the last 10 to 20 years, for instance, there has been a shift in the extent to which the rush of passion is expected to be suspended by planning, not only for the avoidance of pregnancy, but also for "safe sex." The shift is certainly not total. For many women, it is said, taking a condom or a diaphragm to a party still remains embarrassing because it implies that they plan to engage in sex, rather than be overwhelmed by the feelings of the moment. Producing a condom with the goal of safe sex may be felt to be even more inappropriate, because it implies a lack of trust in one's partner, at a time when love should incline one to perceiving the other as without blemish.

The attitudes that many people take toward planning for leisure or for household time supply a further set of examples. In Lawrence, Dodds, and Volet's (1983) study of errand-planning, for instance, adolescents did not perform as well as adult housewives. They were, however, the equal of adults when the task was one of planning a party (Chalmers & Lawrence, 1993). The difference on the errand task is clearly not based on intellectual capacity. It stems instead from the adolescents' perception that fitting the maximum number of errands into an afternoon is no way to spend a free afternoon.

In similar fashion, some adults regard the tight planning of time as inappropriate for the management of a household. These are adults for whom paid work takes up the larger share of their day, and for whom a relatively haphazard approach to shopping and cleaning is a welcome contrast to the precision and planning of their office time (Goodnow & Bowes, 1994). Planning by way of rosters, it turns out, is especially likely to be rejected. This style of organization not only fails to provide a contrast to one's own paid work, it is also felt to be inappropriate to the relationship (too "managerial"), a perception that in our Australian sample leads adults to use explicit rosters only at the start of a new division of labor (Goodnow & Bowes, 1994).

The most provocative examples of appropriate versus inappropriate areas for planning and of change in recent times, however, come not from discussions of love or leisure but instead from public discussions about the management of death and dying. I would not have thought of this content area as a source of examples when preparing the 1987 chapter on planning. Since then, however, the management of death and dying has become an area in which planning has acquired a degree of social appropriateness that it did not have in earlier times. The discussions are predominantly about the end of adult life, although there appears to be also more open discussion about the management of life and death in the case of children in comas, or anencephalic children.

At the adult level, the following phenomena are worth noting (they do not occur in all countries but these examples come from Australia and the United States):

- The provision on drivers' licenses for a statement about whether one is willing to donate organs to others. The understanding is that this permission will apply in case of sudden accidental death, as in traffic accidents (Australia). In practice, hospitals may ask for this expression of willingness to be ratified by a close relative. The fact remains that a statement of willingness has already become bureaucratized, and that there are open statements in the media from people who argue that the donation of one's organs immediately after death helps to make death less of a negative event.
- The availability of "living wills," specifying that no extraordinary measures are to be taken in the event of a close-to-terminal state and—in the U.S.—giving one's partner the power of attorney to make the decision as to what is extraordinary in case one is not in a position to make that decision. The legal power of these wills is still to be determined, but again the fact remains that there are standard forms available that will express an individual's plan.
- The success of the book "Exit," a "how-to" book for the management of one's death. A bestseller in the United States, sold in every airport bookshop, this book was at first banned from being imported into Australia, indicating that the two cultures are not identical in their discussions of death and dying. In late 1992, it became available in bookshops, but it was enclosed in a hard plastic wrapper and could not be sold to anyone under the age of 18.
- The open existence of a Hemlock Society (U.S.).
- The public discussion of death with dignity, and the acceptance in hospices of the right to starve and not be force-fed (Australia and the U.S.).

It is certainly true that some level of planning for one's death has always met with approval. One should make a will, for instance, although some people with sizeable assets still die without doing so. People are also expected to budget for the expenses of a funeral, although planning the details "too far" can seem strange. In one of Robertson Davies' novels, for instance, a woman who plans the service, the music, and the coffin is clearly felt to have gone "a little too far."

The notion, however, that one might think seriously about the timing of one's death, and consider planning for the nature and the timing of one's "exit," has an acceptability, and is the topic of explicit discussion, to a degree that seems in strong contrast to even 10 years earlier. The current discussion is certainly a far cry from the hope for a short spell before dying in which to make peace with one's family or one's God, one definition of good death in the Middle Ages.

What has happened to bring about this change in the openness with which the possibility of planning is discussed, with the beginnings of approval "under some circumstances"? The following conditions seem relevant:

- A changed recognition of the length of time for which life may be preserved (or, as some put it, dying may be prolonged).
- The financial cost of preservation.
- The degree to which some quick terminators of life are no longer present (e.g., pneumonia, once known as "the old person's friend").
- A changed view of the ownership of bodies. Within limits, one has a right to spend one's own money as one wishes. One's own body seems to be moving into a similar category, viewed as one's own rather than as a vehicle of God's grace, as an expression of cosmic forces, or as the disposable property of others.
- An apparently declining belief in the wisdom of medical practitioners. They now seem to be perceived as paralyzed by the fear of malpractice suits.
- The publicity given to cases of choice and of disagreement on principles. The debate on issues of choice in this contract has not moderated since the initial wide publicity given to the assisted suicide of a woman with early Alzheimer's and to a denial by the state of parents' wishes; in one case, to end the 7-year coma of their daughter, and, in another, to donate the organs of an anencephalic infant, in the face of a life expected to be short in any case and of an inevitable death, once life ceased to be maintained by artificial means.

This list of possible conditions is speculative. The fact of the matter is that there is as yet no clear data on what gives rise to changes in the degree of approval or disapproval given to various forms or degrees of planning in particular content areas. The most likely source of data may be a comparison of both historical periods and of cultures. Germany, for instance, is one country where there currently does not occur the open discussion of planning for one's death, especially with the implication of assistance, that is occurring in neighboring countries such as the Netherlands.

Perhaps the most effective way to proceed is to turn the question on its head, to ask not why planning is sometimes disapproved of, but what gives rise to its being seen in a positive light in the first place. Approval for planning would appear to stem partly from considerations of the costs that not planning could give rise to, costs both to the person who should do the planning and to those who may be left with the task of "picking up the pieces."

It seems equally the case, as Habermas (1971) and Berger, Berger, and Kellner (1974) argued, that the approval of planning in a number of areas in modern life stems from an unquestioned extension of values that have their primary base in other areas. "Science," in this view, has "colonized" areas of living where decisions were once made by reference to religion, custom, or aesthetics, and are now expected to be made on the basis of numbers, evidence, and efficiency. From this point of view, the assumption that planning is "a good thing"—or the decline in approval of the attitude that "God will provide" (*La divina providenza providera,* in an Italian phrase)—is the phenomenon to be accounted for, rather than the absence of planning.

A FINAL COMMENT

Two conceptual perspectives were outlined that have been brought to analyses of planning: one emphasizing ability and the sequence of steps; the other emphasizing motivations and beliefs. A preference has been to add to both perspectives a concern with the contexts in which planning occurs (the interpersonal contexts especially) and with the values that are an essential part of any attention to motivations or beliefs. Those values, it is suggested, are often not the result of an individual's experiences with past plans but reflect instead cultural norms that are shared with most of the members of one's group.

The final comment is an endorsement of the need to place planning within general theoretical frameworks. My preference is to place it within frameworks that emphasize the social context of action or of thought, and that bring with them questions about the expected involvement of others, about tranfers of responsibility, and about the ways in which some modes of thought come to be "privileged" (Wertsch, 1990). Planning might also be regarded as a form of self-regulation or as subsumable under a theory of scripts. The precise conceptual placement may vary, along with the questions that each placement may provoke. Whatever the placement, however, future research on planning calls for a continuation of the push toward the conceptual framing and questioning that were such strong features of the provocative earlier volume on this topic (Friedman, Scholnick, & Cocking, 1987).

ACKNOWLEDGMENTS

For a number of discussions of planning, I am in debt to several friends and colleagues who share an interest in the way thinking proceeds, and is expected to proceed, in everyday life. Alphabetically, they are Denise Chalmers, Mary Gauvain, Jeannette Lawrence, Barbara Rogoff, and Jacqui Smith. Particular thanks are due to Jeannette Lawrence and Denise Chalmers, who generously supplied me with interview transcripts from a study of planning that was unpublished at the time this chapter was written.

REFERENCES

Berger, P. L., Berger, R., & Kellner, H. (1974). *The homeless mind*. Hammondsworth: Penguin.

Chalmers, D., & Lawrence, J. A.(1993). Planning an unexpected party: Adults' and adolescents' facilitated organization of an unexpected task. *International Journal of Behavioral Development, 16*, 191–214.

Corwin, R. G. (1974). *Education in crisis: A sociological analysis of schools and universities in transition*. New York: Wiley.

Doise, W., & Mugny, G. (1981). *La construction sociale de l'intelligence [The social construction of intelligence]*. Paris: Intereditions.

Dreher, M., & Oerter, R. (1987). Action planning competencies during adolescence and early adulthood, In S. L. Friedman, E. K. Scholnick, & R. R. Cocking (Eds.), *Blueprints for thinking: The role of planning in cognitive development* (pp. 321–355). Cambridge, England: Cambridge University Press.

Engestrom, Y. (1988). Reconstructing work as object of research. *Quarterly Newsletter of the Laboratory of Comparative Human Cognition, 10*, 21–28.

Friedman, S. L., & Scholnick, E. K. (1991, April). *The* development of planning skills: A discussion of new directions. Paper presented at Biennial meeting of the Society for Research in Child Development, Seattle, WA.

Friedman, S. L., Scholnick, E. K., & Cocking, R. R. (1987). *Blueprints for thinking: The role of planning in cognitive development*. Cambridge, England: Cambridge University Press.

Gauvain, M., & Rogoff, B. (1989). Collaborative problem solving and children's planning skills. *Developmental Psychology, 25*, 139–151.

Glachan, M., & Light, P. (1982). Peer interaction and learning: Can two wrongs make a right? In G. Butterworth & P. Light (Eds.), *Social cognition: Studies of the development of understanding* (pp. 238–282). Chicago: University of Chicago Press.

Goodnow, J. J. (1987). Social aspects of planning. In S. L. Friedman, E. K. Scholnick, & R. R. Cocking (Eds.), *Blueprints for thinking: The role of planning in cognitive development* (pp. 179–204). Cambridge, England: Cambridge University Press.

Goodnow, J. J. (1990). The socialization of cognition: Acquiring cognitive values. In J. Stigler, R. Schweder & G. Herdt (Eds.), *Culture and human development* (pp. 259–286). Chicago: University of Chicago Press.

Goodnow J. J., & Bowes, J.(1994). *Men, women, and household work*: Melbourne/New York: Oxford University Press.

Goodnow, J. J, Bowes, J., Warton, P.M., Dawes, L. J., & Taylor, A. (1991). Would you ask someone else to do this task? Parents' and children's ideas about household task requests. *Developmental Psychology, 27*, 817–828.

Goodnow, J. J. & Burns, A. M. (1985). *Home and school: Child's eye view.* Sydney: Allen & Unwin.

Goodnow, J. J., & Delaney, S. (1989). Children's household work: Task differences, styles of assignment, and links to family relationships. *Journal of Applied Developmental Psychology, 10*, 209–226.

Goodnow, J. J., & Warton, P. M. (1992). Understanding responsibility: Adolescents' views of delegation and follow-through within the family. *Social Development, 1*, 89–106.

Goodnow, J. J., & Warton, P. M. (1996). Direct and indirect responsibility: Distributing blame. *Journal of Moral Education, 25*, 173–184.

Habermas, J. (1971). *Towards a rational society.* Frankfurt : Schrkemp Verlag.

Hart, H. L. A., & Honoré, A. M. (1985). *Causation in the law.* Oxford, England: Clarendon Press.

Jackson, B., & Marsden, D. (1966). *Education and the working class.* Hammondsworth: Penguin.

Kerchner, C. T., & Mitchell, D. E. (1988). *The changing idea of a teachers' union.* New York: Falmer Press.

Kreitler, S., & Kreitler, H. (1987). Plans and planning: Their motivational and cognitive antecedents. In S. L. Friedman, E. K. Scholnick, & R. R. Cocking (Eds.), *Blueprints for thinking: The role of planning in cognitive development* (pp. 110–178). Cambridge, England: Cambridge University Press.

Lawrence, J. A., Dodds, A., & Volet, S. (1983). An afternoon off: A comparative study of adults' and adolescents' planning activities. *Proceedings of the Australian Association for Research in Education.* Canberra: Australian Association for Research in Education.

Mugny, G., de Paolis, P., & Carugati, F. (1984). Social regulations in cognitive development. In W. Doise & A. Palmonari (Eds.), *Social interaction in individual development* (pp. 125–146). Cambridge, England: Cambridge University Press.

Oppenheimer, L. (1987). Cognitive and social variables in the plan of action. In S. L. Friedman, E. K. Scholnick, & R. R. Cocking (Eds.), *Blueprints for thinking: The role of planning in cognitive development* (pp. 356–394). Cambridge, England: Cambridge University Press.

Rogoff, B. (1990). *Apprenticeship in thinking.* New York: Oxford University Press.

Rogoff, B., Gauvain, M., & Gardner, W. (1987). Children's adjustment of plans to circumstances. In S. L. Friedman, E. K. Scholnick, & R. R. Cocking (Eds.), *Blueprints for thinking: The role of planning in cognitive development* (pp. 303–320). Cambridge, England: Cambridge University Press.

Scholnick, E. K., & Friedman, S. L. (1987). The planning construct in the psychological literature. In S. L. Friedman, E. K. Scholnick, & R. R. Cocking (Eds.), *Blueprints for thinking: The role of planning in cognitive development* (pp.3–38). Cambridge, England: Cambridge University Press.

Skinner, E. A. (1985). Action, control judgements, and the structure of control experience. *Psychological Review, 92*, 39–58.

Warton, P. M., & Goodnow, J. J. (1991). The nature of responsibility: Children's understanding of "your job." *Child Development, 62*, 156–615.

Warton, P. M., Goodnow, J. J., & Bowes, J. (1992). Teaching as a form of work: Effects of teachers' roles and role definition on working-to-rule. *Australian Journal of Research in Education.*

Wertsch, J. (1990). *Voices of the mind, 36*, 170–180. Cambridge, MA: Harvard University Press.

Author Index

Subject Index

A

Ability to plan, 3, 9, 265
  adolescent contraceptive planning,
    322–324, 332–333
  and formal operations, 5–6
  infants, 184–185
Action alternatives
  event knowledge/planning, 78, 80
  and goals, 25–28, 78, 80
  infants, 27
Action suppression, 193
Action theory, 266
Active coping, 298–300, 307, 312–313
Adolescents, *see also* Contraceptive planning
  and alcohol, 4, 8, 12
  cultural influences, 9, 13, 324–327, 329,
    331, 352
  domain knowledge, 7–8
  and driving, 4, 8, 12
  family influence, 13
  and formal operations, 5
  and imaginary audience, 323
  peer groups, 9, 332
  and personal fable, 324
  planning competency, 4
  planning limitation, 4
  prevention of everyday problems,
    215–216, 224, 230–231
  risk-taking behavior, 4, 12
  and smoking, 9
Adults, *see also* Family influences; Parents
  control-based expectations, 36
  and formal operations, 5
  future thinking, 25, 31, 33–34, 36
  prevention of everyday problems, 213,
    215–224
Advance plans, 82–86, 94–100, 162, *see also*
  Future thinking

Age differences, *see also* Adolescents; Children; Children, preschool
  in event knowledge/planning, 82–89,
    96–100
  in expectations, 11
  in planning skills, 4–5, 7–8, 12, 44
AIDS development, 31
Alcohol, 4, 8, 12
Amnesia, 29
Anger, 115–116, 118–119
Animacy, 37–38, 111
Anticipation, 5–6, *see also* Expectations; Future thinking
  prevention of everyday problems,
    210–211, 213–218, 220,
    223–224, 226–232
Anticipatory coping, 285–288, 290–293,
  313–314
Appropriateness of planning
  for contraception, 326–327, 352
  for death, 353–354
  social influences, 340, 350–355
Attention, 7, 12
Avoidant coping, 298, 300–301
Awareness
  in emotion management, 106, 109, 112
  and memory, 28

B

Behavior, *see also* Control; Self-regulation
  biobehavioral rhythms, 46–47
  in cognitive complexity theory, 158, 161
  content of, 158
  in emotion management, 103–115
  goal-directed, 241–243, 265, 270–271, 287
  imitated by children, 33–34, 48–53
  imitated by infants, 34, 49–50

E

Education, 11, 341–342, 348–350
Emergency planning, 163, 168–169
Emotional influences, 9–10
Emotion-focused coping, 287, 314
Emotion management, *see also* Control; Perceived control; Prevention of everyday problems; Proactive coping; Self-regulation
  anger, 115–116, 118–119
  and children's pretend play, 111
  and children's security objects, 117
  and cognitive functioning, 116–117, 119–120
  controlling distressful events, 107–108, 110, 114–115
controlling distressful events/planning link, 106, 108–109, 114–115
  coping, 104
  fear, 115–117
  frustration, 117–118
  individual temperaments, 118–119
  infants, 103, 105–109, 116, 119
  infants' use of hands in, 108
  instrumental use of knowledge in, 109
  knowledge acquisition in, 109
  and language, 112–113
  mature planning behavior, 103–104, 109t, 114
  multiple behaviors for, 110–111
  nature of distressful events, 104, 106–107, 110
  of negative emotions, 115–119
  optimism in, 297, 304–305
  parental support for, 106, 108, 116–117, 119
  and planning behavior development, 103–106, 108–109
  and planning behavior functions, 106–115
  and planning development/context link, 104, 115–120
  preschool children, 103–106, 109–120
  proactive coping, 287, 290–291, 295–297, 301, 304–305, 310
  procedural knowledge in, 107–108
  protoplan for, 110, 113–114
  psychological control, 104
  scripts for, 110–111
  self-awareness in, 106, 109, 112
  special purpose responses, 107
  toddlers, 103, 105–106, 109–115, 119
Environmental influences, *see also* Cultural influences; Social influences

  in cognitive complexity theory, 161, 163–165, 181
  on contraceptive planning, 325–330, 332–333
  on event knowledge/planning, 78–80
  on grocery shopping planning, 10
  and historical planning perspectives, 10, 12
  on prevention of everyday problems, 211–212, 219, 222
  resources for proactive coping, 289–293, 311–312
Errand planning, 7, 127–128, 209, 352, *see also* Grocery shopping planning; Task comparisons
Essence of problem, 215
Event knowledge/planning, *see also* Future thinking; Goals; Temporal sequence knowledge
  action alternatives, 78, 80
  advance plans, 82–86, 94–100, 162
  age differences, 82–89, 96–100
  case-based planning model, 79, 232
  clustered display, 87–89
  collaborative influences, 79–80
  coordinated, 80, 86, 342–343
  dynamic memory model, 79
  effects of indirect instruction on, 94–98
  effects of temporal–causal structure on events, 79, 86, 90–100
  effects of temporal–causal structure on sequencing, 92–100
  environmental influences, 78–80
  external aids, 78–80, 87–89, 92–100
  failure, 79, 82, 85, 91–94, 97–100
  generalized event representation (GER), 77–78, 80–82, 94, 98–100
  grocery shopping planning, 4, 7, 77–78, 83–89
  interleaved display, 87–89
  internal aids, 78–80, 92–94, 98–100
  memory in, 78–79, 87, 90, 93–94, 100
  multiple event goal planning, 80, 86–89
  novel event, 80–81, 90–98
  open slots, 78, 80, 98
  plan construction/execution relation, 87–88
  plans equal GER, 80–81
  prevention plans, 82, 85–86
  relationship between, 78–81
  remedy plans, 82, 85–86
  scripts/plans/execution comparison, 91–94
  scripts vs. event planning, 77–79, 81–86, 98–100
  simultaneous planning condition, 87–89